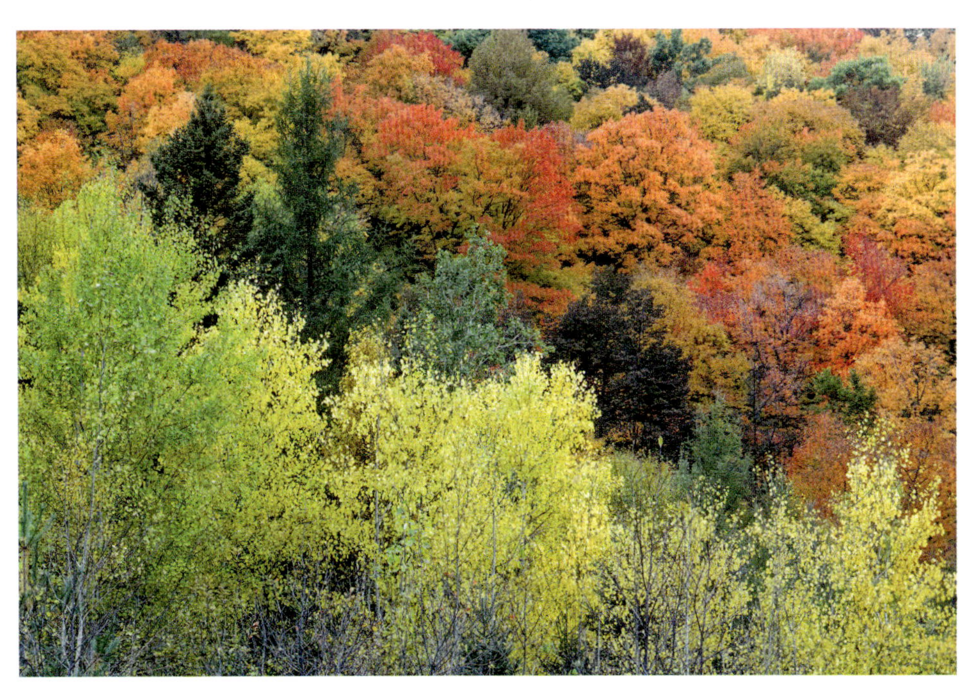

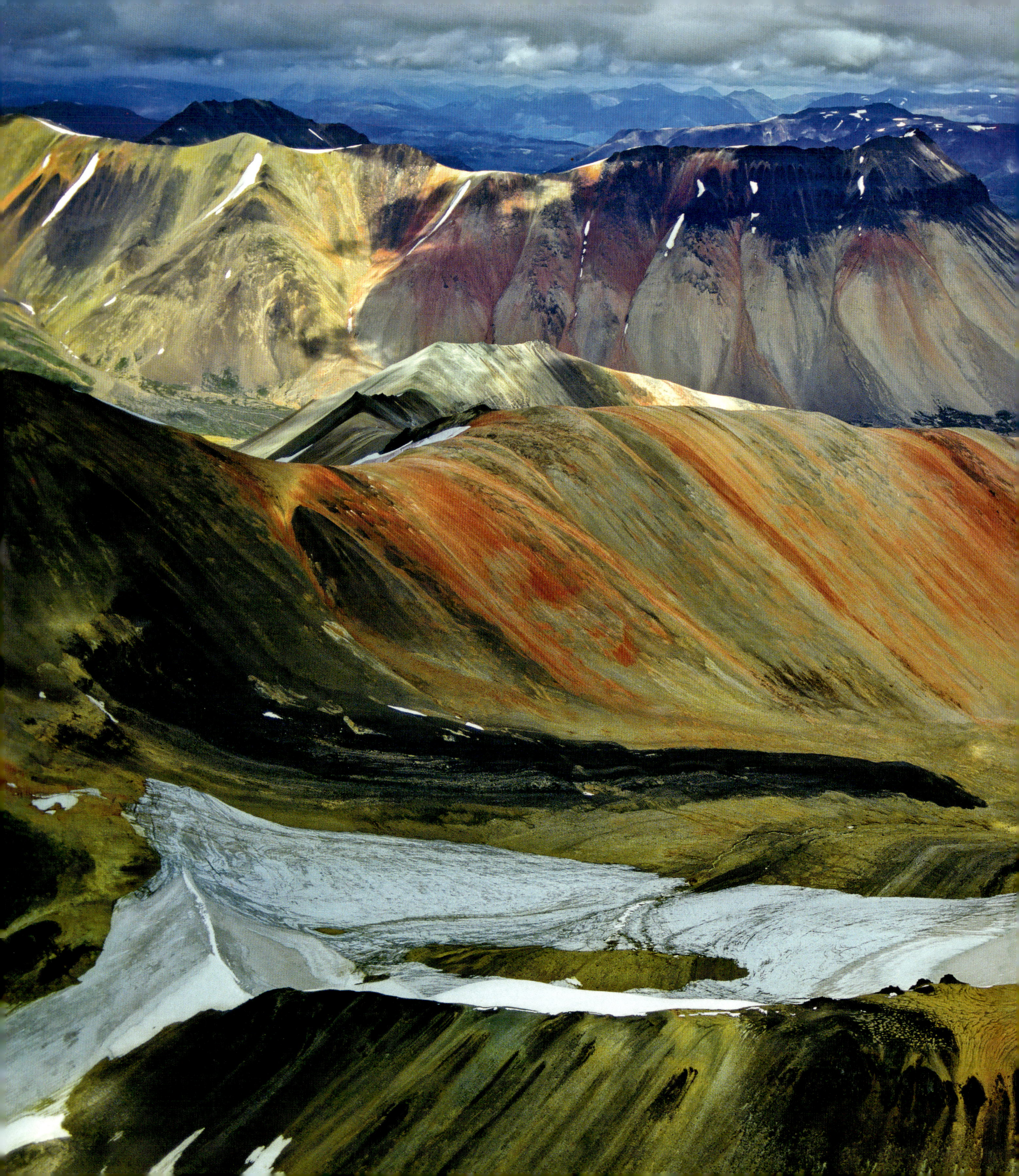

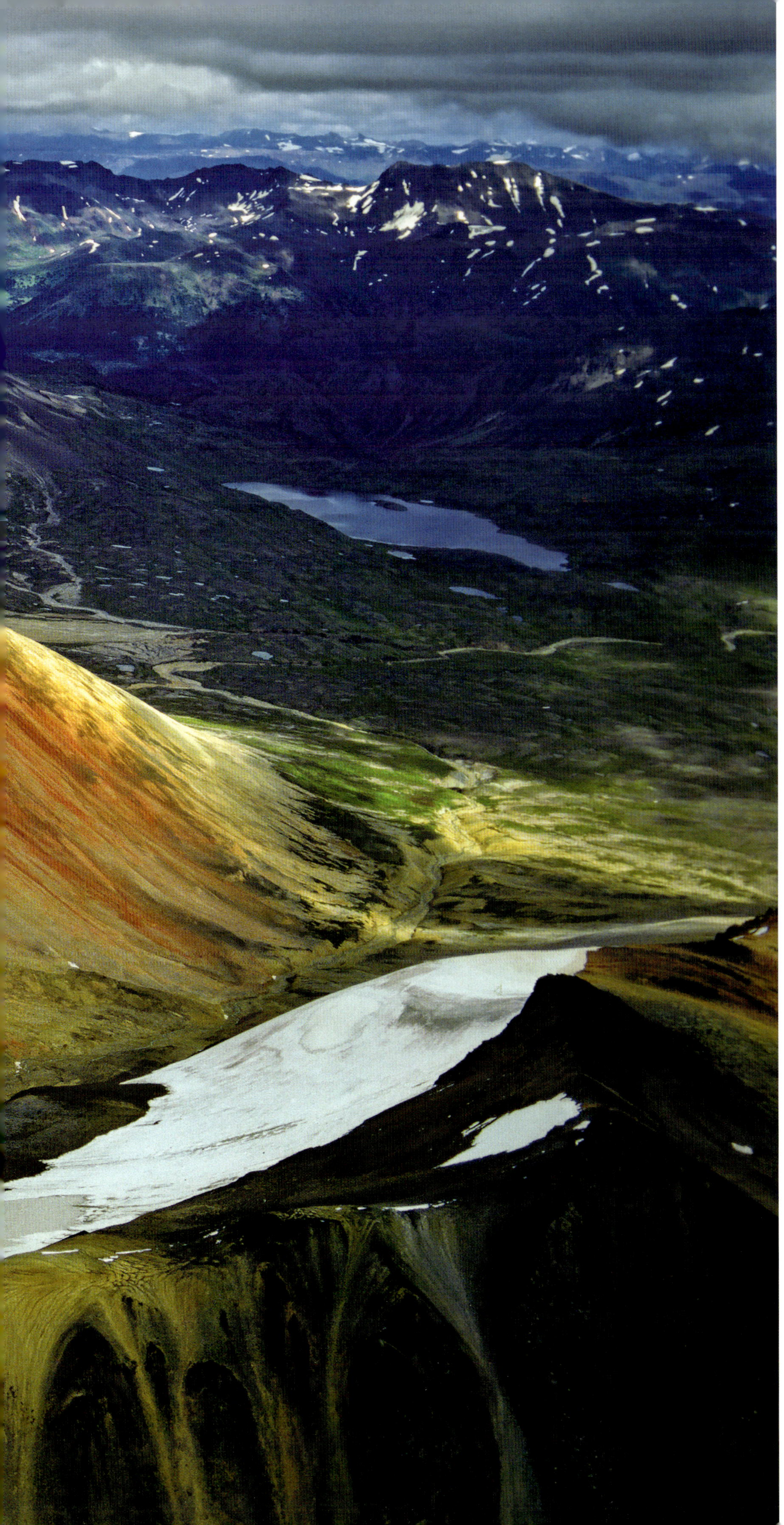

# CANADA

## IMAGES OF THE LAND

J.A. KRAULIS

INTRODUCTION BY ROY MACGREGOR

FIREFLY BOOKS

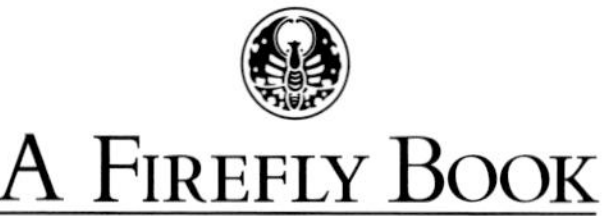

# A Firefly Book

Published by Firefly Books Ltd. 2015
Copyright © 2015 Firefly Books Ltd.
Individual photographs copyright © 2015 J. A. Kraulis

All rights reserved. No part of this publication may be reproduced,
stored in a retrieval system, or transmitted in any form or by any means,
electronic, mechanical, photocopying, recording or otherwise, without
the prior written permission of the Publisher.

First printing

**Publisher Cataloging-in-Publication Data (U.S.)**

Kraulis, J.A., 1949– .
Canada: images of the land / J. A. Kraulis; introduction by Roy MacGregor.
[224] pages: color photographs ; cm.
Includes index.
Summary: Photographer J. A. Kraulis captures the majesty and grandeur
of the vast and staggeringly diverse Canadian landscape.
ISBN-13: 978-1-77085-624-0
1. Canada – Pictorial works. I. Title.
971.0222          dc23          FC59.K738          2015

**Library and Archives Canada Cataloguing in Publication**

Kraulis, J. A., 1949– , photographer, writer of added text
Canada : images of the land / J. A. Kraulis ; introduction by Roy MacGregor.
ISBN 978-1-77085-624-0 (bound)
Canada — Pictorial works. I. MacGregor, Roy, 1948– , writer of supplementary
textual content II. Title.
FC59.K727 2015          971.0022'2          C2015-901173-6

Published in the United States by
Firefly Books (U.S.) Inc.
P.O. Box 1338, Ellicott Station
Buffalo, New York  14205

Published in Canada by
Firefly Books Ltd.
50 Staples Avenue, Unit 1
Richmond Hill, Ontario  L4B 0A7

Cover and interior design: Counterpunch Inc. / Linda Gustafson

Printed in China

The publisher gratefully acknowledges the financial support for our publishing
program by the Government of Canada through the Canada Book Fund as
administered by the Department of Canadian Heritage.

**Half Title:** Autumn in all its colours, the Laurentians, Morin-Heights, Quebec.
**Title Page:** Aerial view of the Spectrum Range, Mount Edziza Provincial Park, British Columbia.
**Dedication:** Victoria Falls below Glacier Peak and Mount Ringrose, Yoho National Park, British Columbia.
**Acknowledgements:** Sunrise over farm fields in autumn next to Island View Road, Saanich Peninsula, British Columbia.
**Page 8–9:** The Richardson Mountains in far northern Yukon in late August.

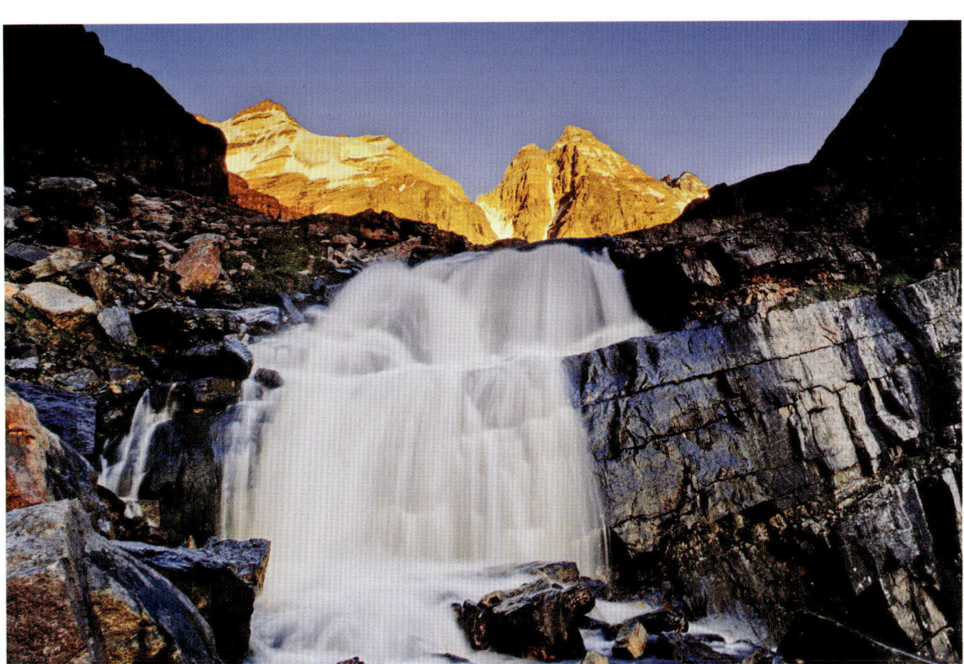

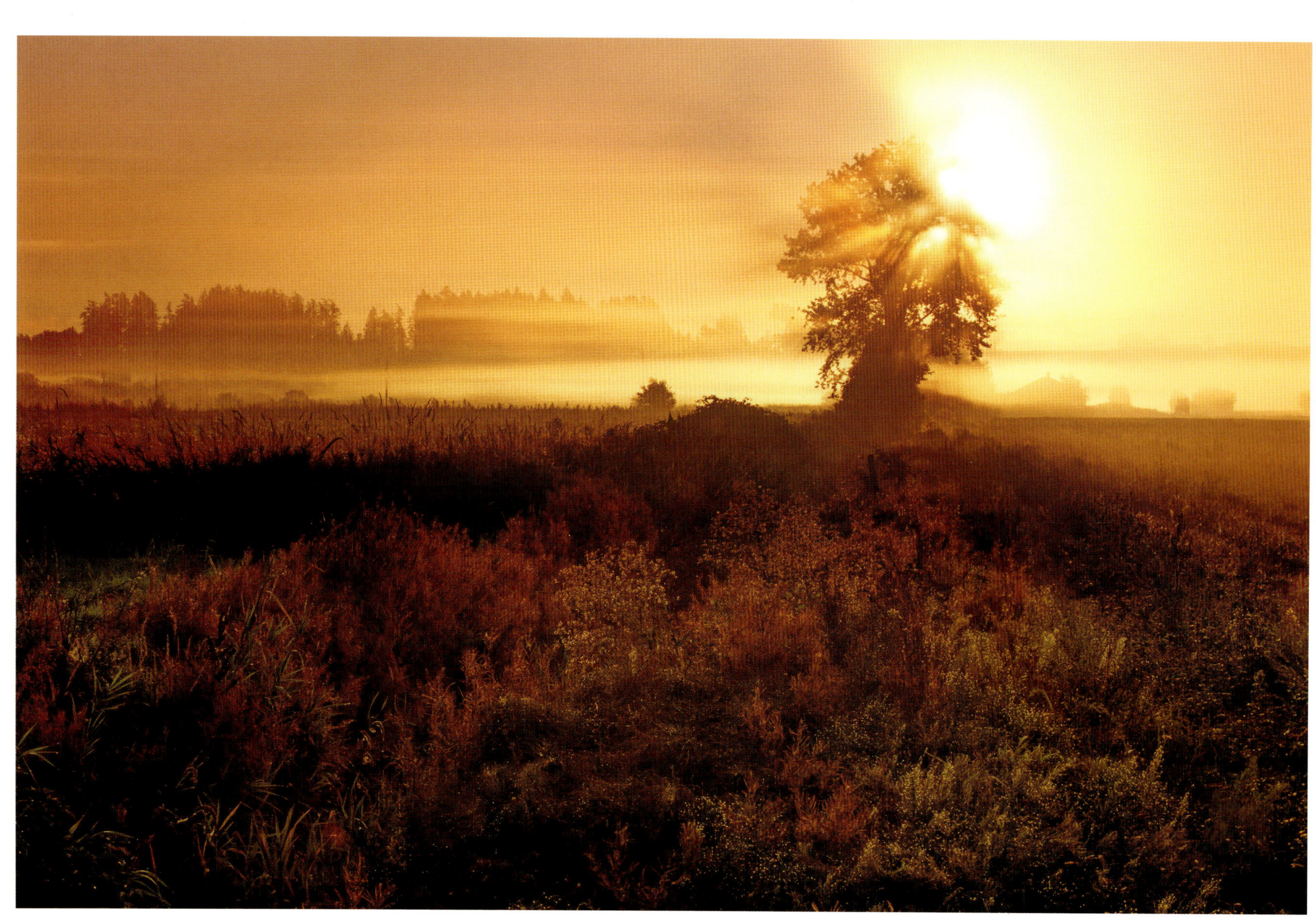

## Acknowledgements

I must first give credit and much thanks to publisher Lionel Koffler for proposing this project and for giving me the opportunity to realize it in a difficult and declining market, and to others at Firefly Books involved, including Michael Worek, Pippa Kennard and Hartley Millson. This is the second time I have collaborated on a book with Linda Gustafson, who apart from being a superb designer is a terrific person to work with. As one moves through the book, the photographs can be thought of as a script that cumulatively tells a visual story, and Linda, along with her colleague Peter Ross, is the director, the one who has brought it all together.

Almost none of the photographs would exist were it not for many who have enabled me to earn a living from photography, but to two parties in particular I will always be indebted. Mel Hurtig launched my career and published my first books and Steve Pigeon, along with his staff at Masterfile, more than anyone else has sustained my career over the decades.

Immeasurable also is the thanks I owe to my family, to my late parents, to my sister Ilze (who inspired me to become a photographer), to my wife, Linda Kuttis, to our daughter Anna and to our son Theo. They have contributed to the book in many ways, including taking part and assisting on the many trips represented herein.

Over the years many of my photos included were taken on solo excursions, but most are the result of shared journeys and shared efforts. I only credit a fraction who have so helped me by listing those who were involved with the photos which chance to be included in this book: Andra Leimanis, Nick Drager, Dale Wilson, Ron Watts, Ellen Lazare, Johny van Nieuwkerk, Pat and Baiba Morrow, (the late) Uldis Auders, Ingrid Prouty, Brian Finnie, Bernice Slotnick, Cheri Deal, John Tucker, Robyn Tucker, Alan Benckhuysen, Jason Puddifoot and Theresa Duynstee, Amy Teper, Greg Phillips, Jerry Kobalenko, and my niece, Marie-Anne Grassino.

It would not be proper for me to take exclusive creative credit for every photograph. There are some four dozen aerial images in the book, and for each one the role of the pilot in placing the aircraft in the right position in the sky was significantly more critical than that of the photographer pressing the shutter release. The late Philip Upton flew the Heliocourier from which the photos on pages 209, 211, 212 and 213 were taken and Colin Jackson was the pilot for page 65.

But this book would be much the poorer, if indeed it would have been possible without the contribution of my longtime friends, Bo Curtis and Cathy Young. Bo flew the plane and in effect created the composition for the photos on pages 2–3, 30, 48, 49, 64, 66, 67, 68, 69, 74, 78, 79,88, 89, 98, 99, 108, 109, 110, 111, 124, 125, 131, 133, 134, 135, 136, 137, 138, 143, 160, 161, 168, 169, 170, 171, 201, 204, 205, 215, and 216.

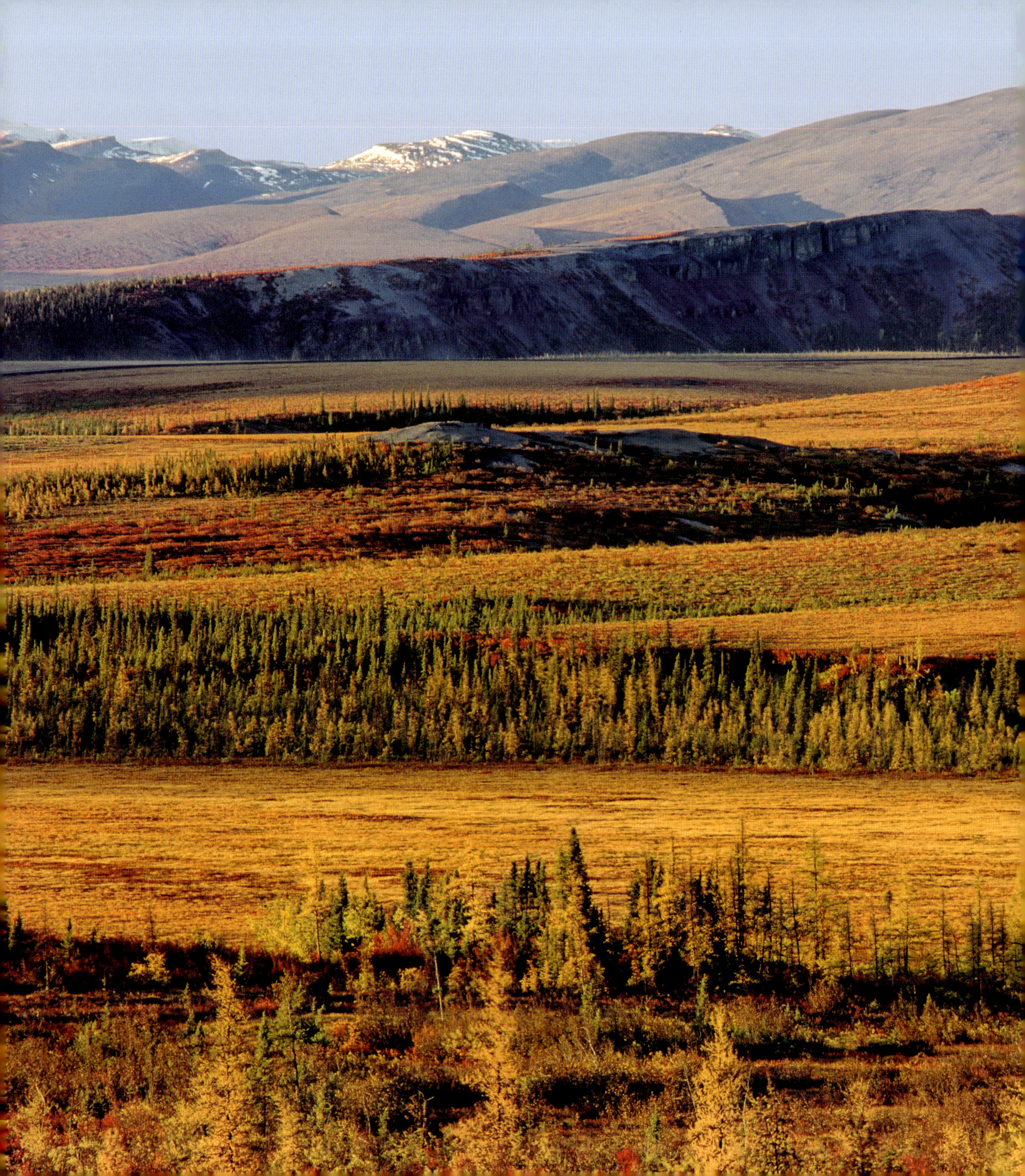

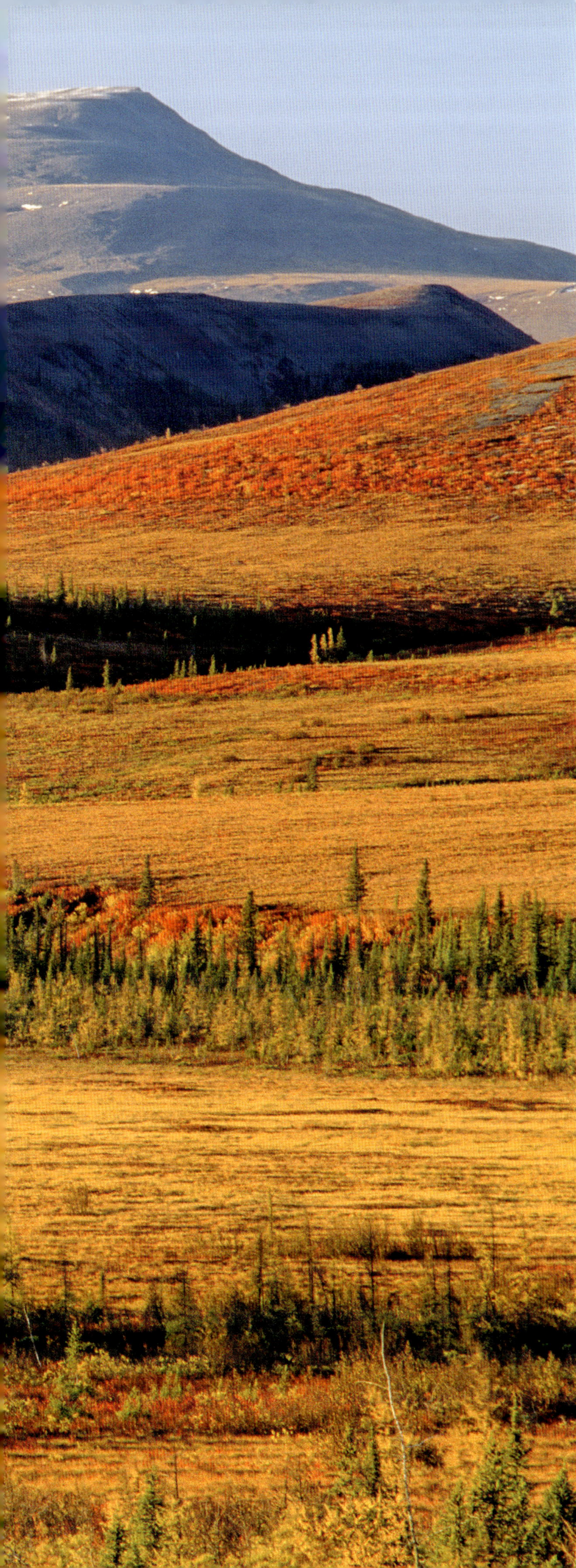



For all the accomplishments of Canada's authors, from Thomas C. Haliburton's *Sam Slick* tales to Alice Munro's Nobel Prize, no writer has ever been able to capture all of this extraordinary land in words.

Perhaps the alphabet is just not big enough for so large a country.

Instead, we have left the task of capturing just what this country really is to our painters and photographers — and even here it has not been an easy task. The very painters we today credit with "discovering" the Canadian landscape in their oils, Tom Thomson and the Group of Seven, were dismissed early on for using too much colour and painting with too much exaggerated flair. "Those who believe that pictures should be seen and not heard," the critic for the magazine *Saturday Night* wrote of a 1916 exhibition, "are likely to have their sensibilities shocked."

The snob meant it is a knock, of course, but failed to realize the truth in his statement. In fact, the very essence of the Canadian landscape is precisely that: a shock to the senses, a feeling of wonder, of sheer *awe* over the vastness of the land, the size of its mountains and the reach of the North. So sprawling is this land called "Canada" that there has never been a full and accurate count of its lakes, their number merely rounded off to three million or so.

When it comes to countries, size matters.

Fully embracing this huge landscape and its harsh climate was slow in coming. For much of the European settlement of this attic of North America, various governments pretended reality was something else altogether. When trying to attract immigrants from Europe at the turn of the 20th century, government officials forbade any use of the word "cold" and insisted on replacing it with the less-chilling "buoyant." Posters sent across the Atlantic to solicit settlers to the prairies showed a lightly clad nymph lifting a curtain of thick wheat to reveal a bucolic English-style countryside complete with trimmed hedgerows.

It took a while, but Canadians, both generational and brand new, eventually accepted their land for what it is, not what it isn't. The land, in fact, *is* the country, something first noted by the late, great Blair Fraser, then Ottawa editor of *Maclean's* magazine. In his centennial book, *The Search for Identity*, he put forward the notion that "What held such people [Canadians] together was not love for each other, but love for the land itself, the vast, empty land."

A decade or so ago, my newspaper, *The Globe and Mail*, launched a series of articles called "New Canada" by commissioning a survey that asked Canadians from all generations and regions what best symbolized their country. We had no idea what they would choose and anticipated a fractured response that would include such disparate ingredients as hockey, moose, maple syrup and saying "Sorry" too often. Much to our surprise, 89 percent, nearly nine out of every 10 Canadians, said that it was "the vastness of the land" that symbolized the country.

Janis Kraulis needed no such newspaper poll to tell him that. He had known since the early 1960s when he was growing up in Montreal. His sister returned from a summer job at Lake Louise with slides she had taken during hikes around Banff National Park. Using an old projector, 14-year-old Janis viewed them on the wall of his room. "That was my first experience with the power of photography," he remembers. "Mountains had been transported to my bedroom. Or I had been transported to the mountains, no distinction need be made there."

Janis himself soon went west, working four summers in British Columbia's Yoho National Park. He had studied architecture, but it was in the western mountains that he found what he wanted to do for a living: take pictures of what he saw all around him. Forty years later, J. A. Kraulis is the most-renowned landscape photographer of his generation. As Tom Thomson and the Group of Seven were to painting, Janis has been to photography. It is a comparison he denies.

"I don't regard my photos as 'art.'" Janis once wrote. "I think of them as discoveries, the fruits of exploration."

In fact, Janis is quick to give as much credit to the camera in his hand or the pilot of the single-engine plane that has taken him to such remarkable spots. He claims he has no particular "vision" apart from the literal sense of the word. The pilot takes him there, the eyes see the shot, the camera takes it. "To imagine that one is thereby creating art," he argues, "is a bit like a backhoe operator thinking that he is a champion weightlifter." In fact, he *is* a champion landscape photographer, as this breathtakingly beautiful book instantly proves.

"When I was a child," Janis says, "I wanted to be an African explorer when I grew up. I didn't know that there were no career openings in that field anymore, that Africa has had more than enough of colonizing explorers and that it wasn't all jungle inhabited mainly by lions and elephants. But as for the explorer part, I guess that is where I ended up."

Janis became a discoverer of great natural wonders. He vividly recalls the first time he flew in a small plane low over Niagara Falls. "I remember thinking, this must be what Father [Louis] Hennepin thought back in the 17th century when he came through the forest and first saw the falls." The effect was overwhelming, leaving one small human in awe at the power and grandeur of nature. It is a feeling he has never lost. One small human in a country too large to grasp, to paint, to photograph — and much too large for any one person to know entirely.

Over the span of my own career in journalism, I have been fortunate to stand at Cape Spear as the sun rose on the 21st century. I have waded into the Pacific Ocean at Tofino. I have stood at the end of the runway at Alert and stared across the broken ice in search of Russia. For more than 40 years I have travelled this country — as a reporter covering federal and provincial elections, Royal tours, northern adventures and hockey tournaments, and on canoe trips and family vacations — so much so that some have said, though it's impossible to know for sure, that I've seen more of Canada than anyone. Yet I feel no different than David Thompson, the great mapmaker, who spent a lifetime travelling across this country by canoe, horse and foot — and claimed, near the end, that he had seen but a small fraction of the country he had mapped.

To pass one's eyes through this remarkable and beautiful book, you would think that Janis, if anyone, had seen it all — but he would never make any such claim. What he has done is stare endlessly in wonder, and

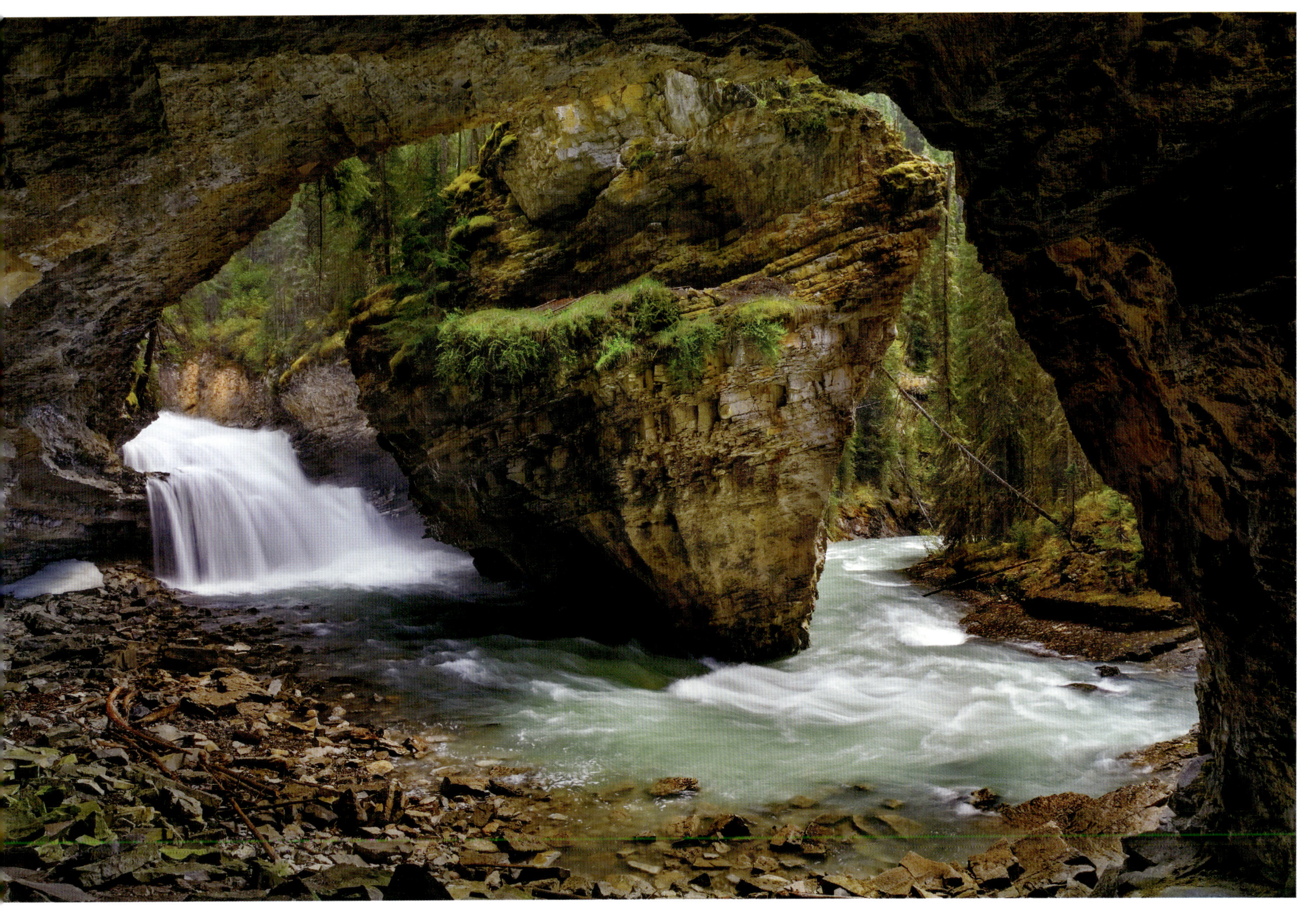

Grotto and waterfall, Johnston Canyon,
Banff National Park, Alberta.

where possible record what he has seen. His own great "discovery"—what truly makes Janis an explorer in his own right—was an epiphany he had early on while photographing the wide prairies and the impossibly big sky above it. "I realized," he says, "that on the ground I had in effect been looking along the surface of a painting that could only be properly appreciated from above." By photographing the land from above, he has shown us a beauty in the flat prairie unknowable while standing on it, and in so doing has especially captured my admiration for his work.

The spectacular mountain vistas and breathtaking skies are what one would expect in a book celebrating the natural beauties of this country—and, frankly, no one does this better—but there is also great surprise to be found here. Prairie fields such as those on pages 66–67 and 78–79 reveal designs unknowable to those who merely pass by in cars at street level or fly over them at 35,000 feet. Wetlands seen from a small low-flying aircraft, on pages 134-35, feel like Impressionist paintings by a master. But then, he is a modern master. When I look at his photograph of the swirling waters on page 93, I feel that they are a magnet drawing me into the scene. Though readers will find their own roots on other pages, the entire book, in fact, is home to all of us: Canada.

Janis believes that if he were blindfolded and taken far away and the blindfold removed, he could tell if he were still in Canada even if he had never been in that place before. There is, he argues, "a distinct 'Canadian landscape.' It's not something in the imagination—it is as firm and real as bare bedrock."

When you think that there are more than 30,000 islands in Georgian Bay and that this is but a single bay of the far larger Lake Huron, you begin to grasp the scale of Canada. When you know that there are vast mountains in the far North you have likely never heard of—the United States Range and the British Empire Range, for example—you begin to understand why Canadian travel writer Edward McCourt would eventually conclude: "In Canada there is too much of everything. Too much rock, too much prairie, too much tundra, too much mountain, too much forest."

Many of us would disagree, but all would agree that while you can *see* England and *tour* Europe, you cannot do that here. You can *experience* Canada, and you can *imagine* Canada, and you can *feel* that incredible awe of Canada captured through the lens of J. A. Kraulis' camera.

In 1872, five years after Confederation, Sandford Fleming—who would later give the world time zones—decided to lead a grand expedition across the new country to see what had been assembled from such far-flung and profoundly different parts. The Fleming expedition went from Halifax to Victoria and calculated they covered 2,715 kilometres by steamer, 3,516 kilometres by horses, including coaches, wagons, packs and saddle-horses, nearly 1,609 kilometres by train and 780 kilometres by canoe or rowboats.

They saw nothing of the North, nothing of Newfoundland and Labrador, nothing beyond their own sight lines as the pencil mark of their journey traced across the map. But they saw enough that George M. Grant, who was assigned to keep a record of the journey, noted that the country "rolled out before us like a panorama, varied and magnificent enough to stir the dullest spirit into patriotic emotion." Such is the experience of anyone fortunate enough to begin a journey through Canada by turning these pages.

"I have never abandoned the habit of looking at photographs and dreaming," Janis says.

Nor have we. Let the dreaming begin.

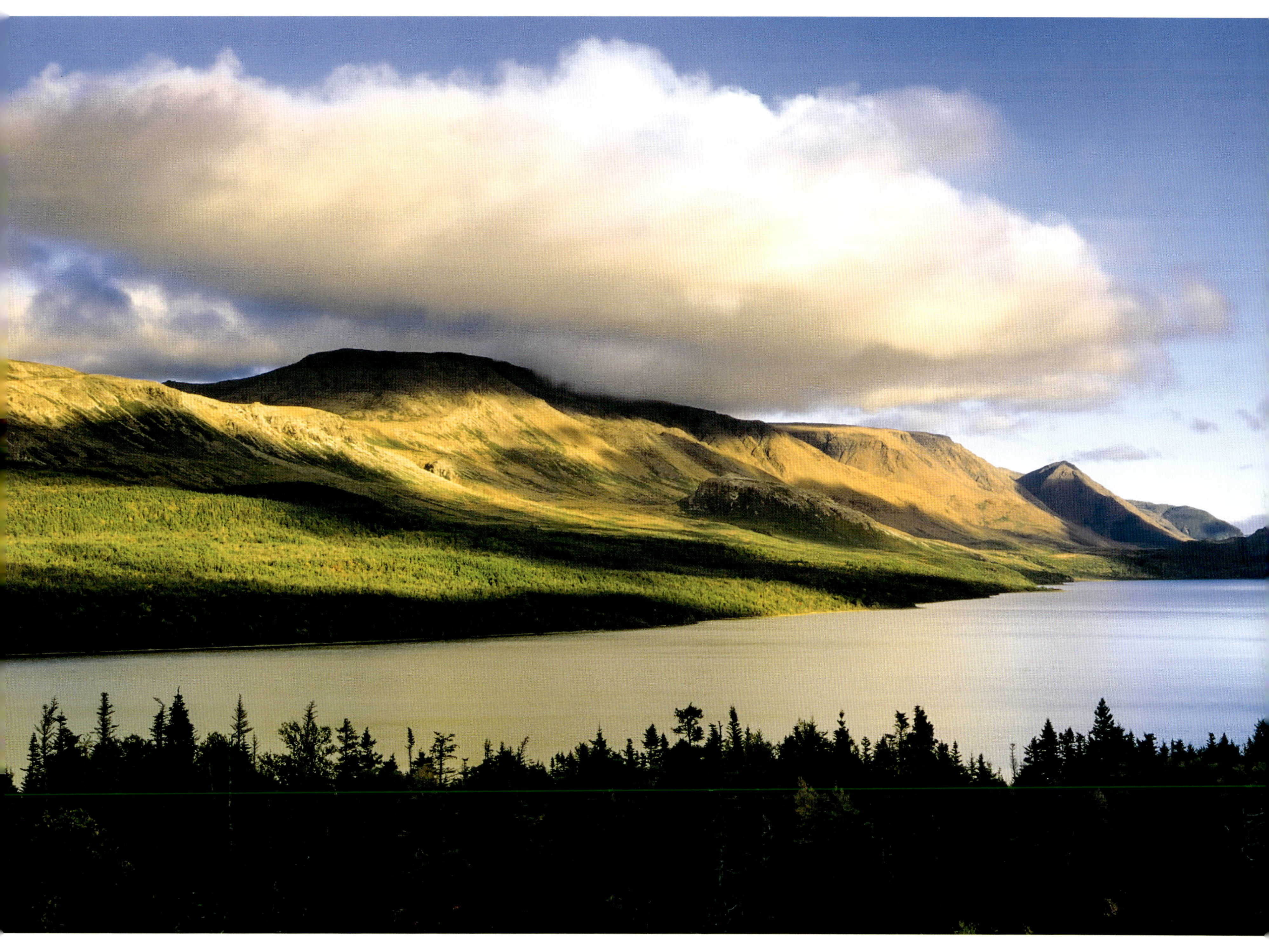

Cloud shadows on the Tablelands above Trout River Pond,
Gros Morne National Park, Newfoundland.

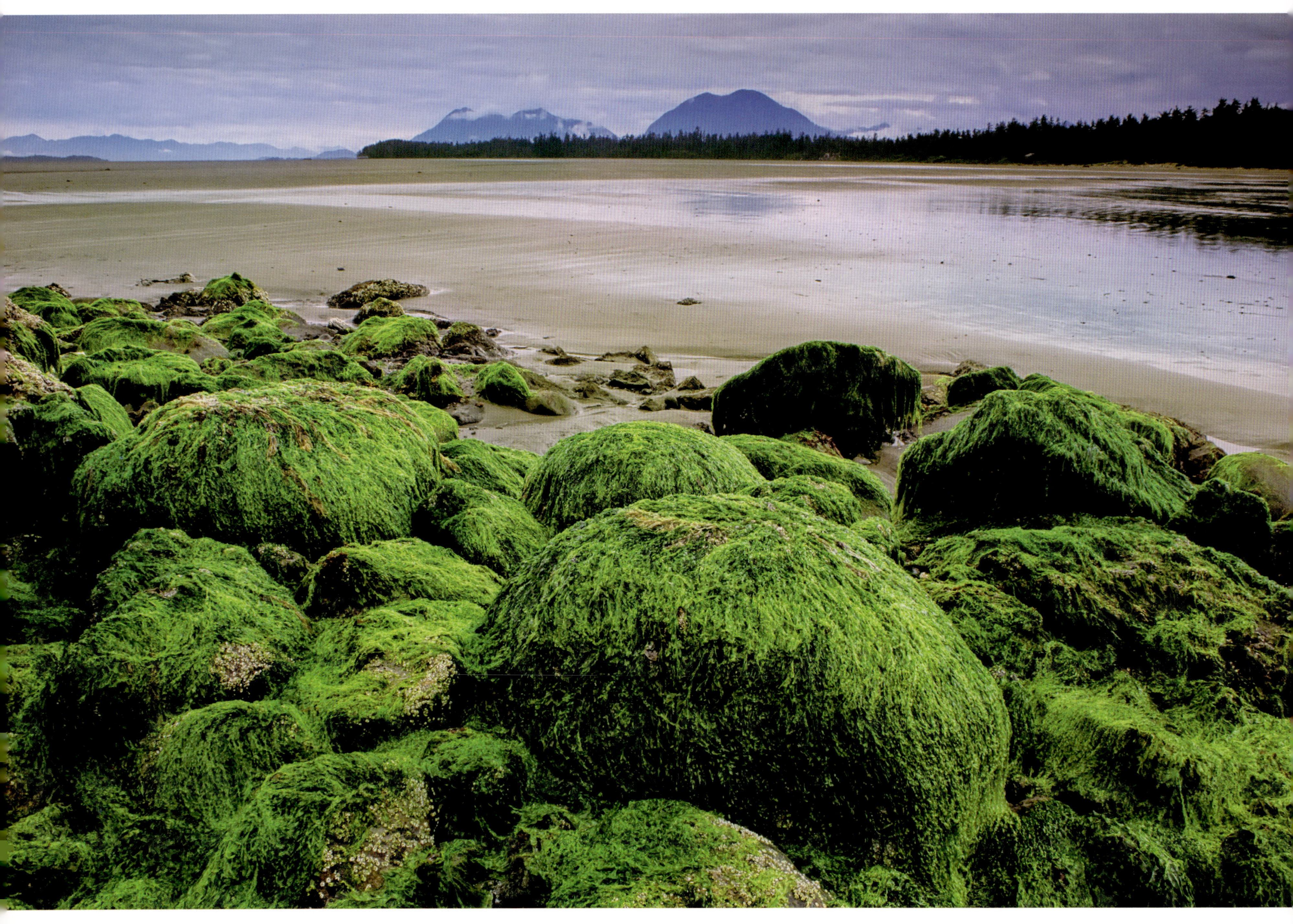

Rocks exposed at low tide at Chesterman Beach
near Tofino (above) and at Carmanah Beach
along the West Coast Trail, Pacific Rim National
Park Reserve, both on Vancouver Island, British
Columbia.

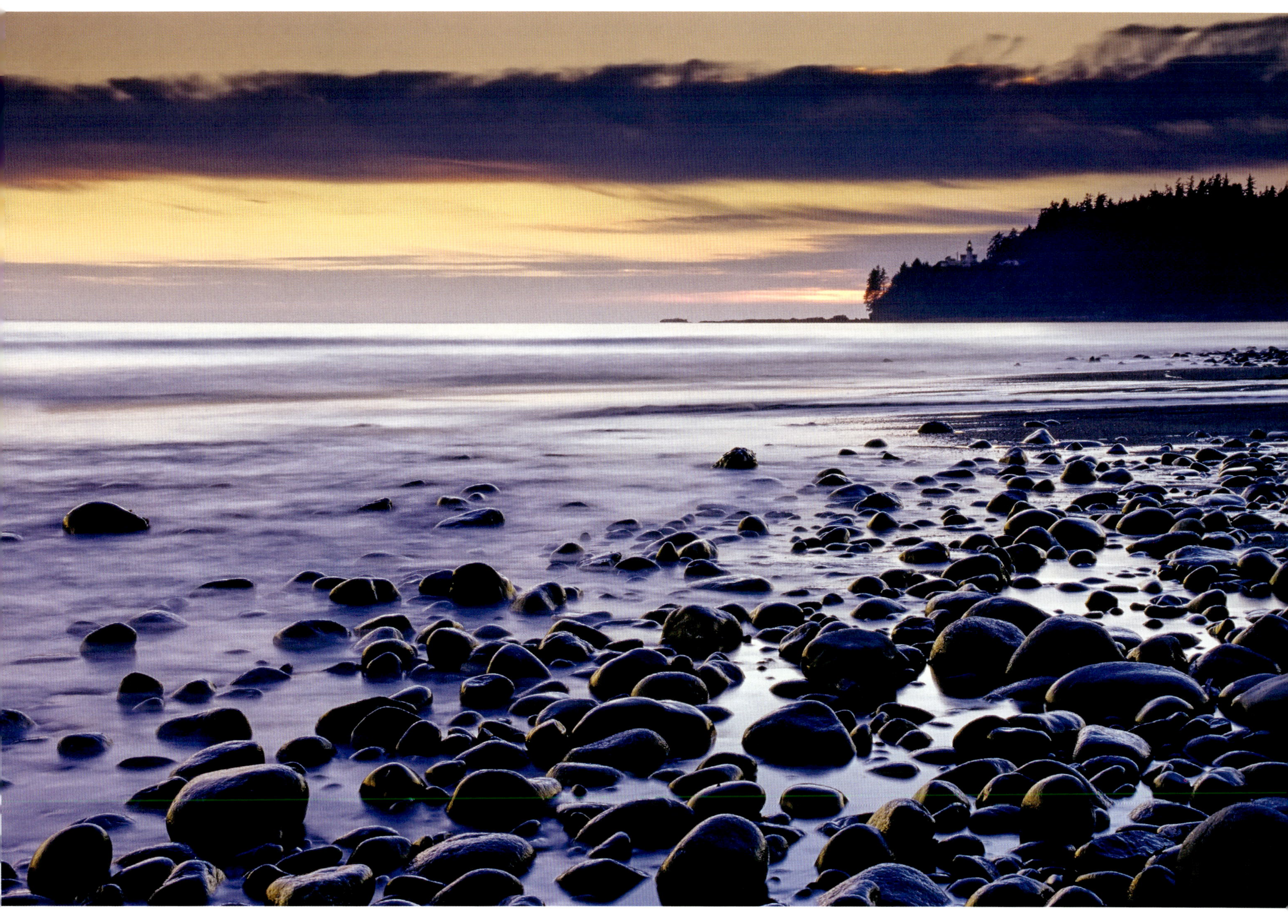

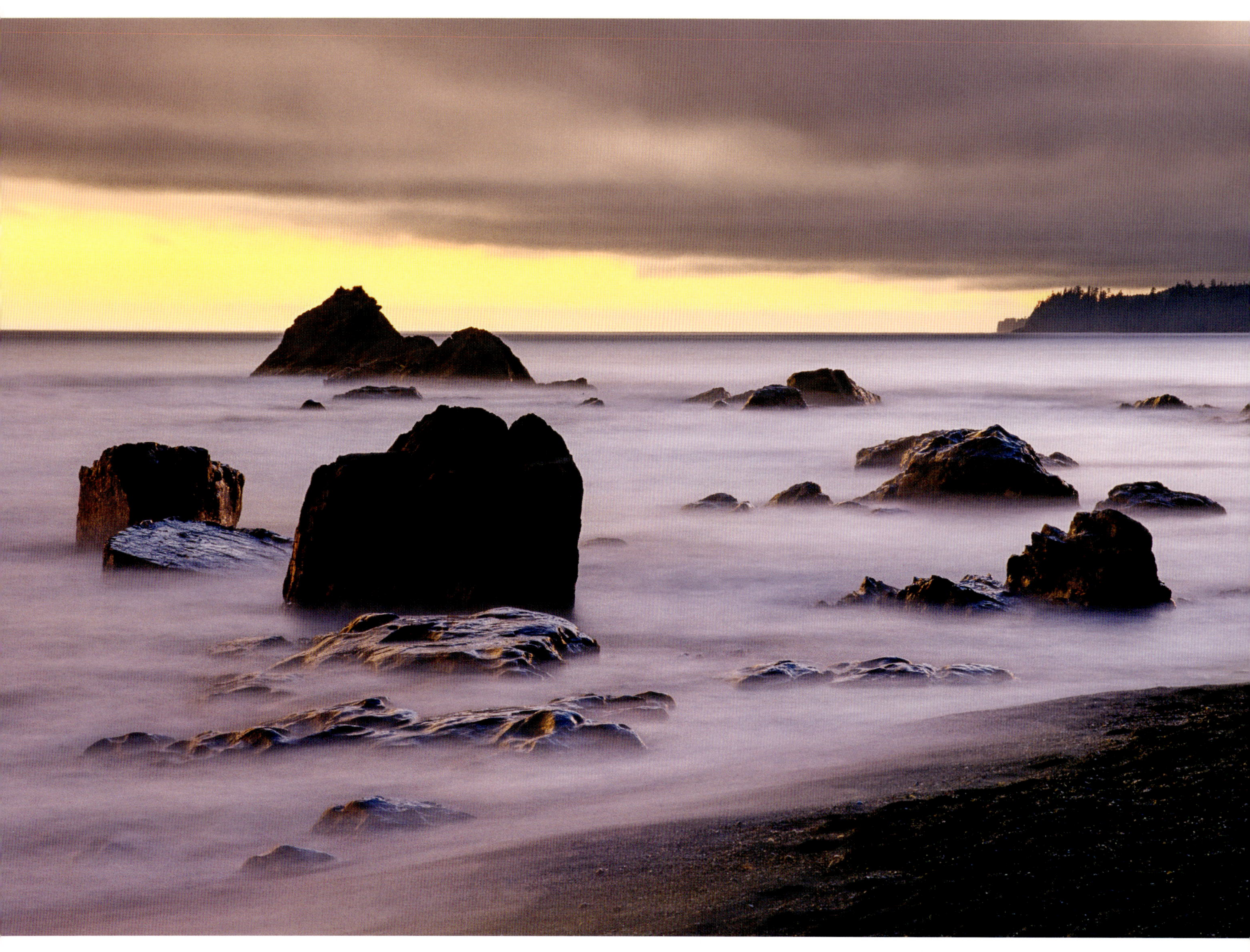

Evening on Sombrio Beach along
the Juan de Fuca Trail (above) and at
Chesterman Beach, Vancouver Island,
British Columbia.

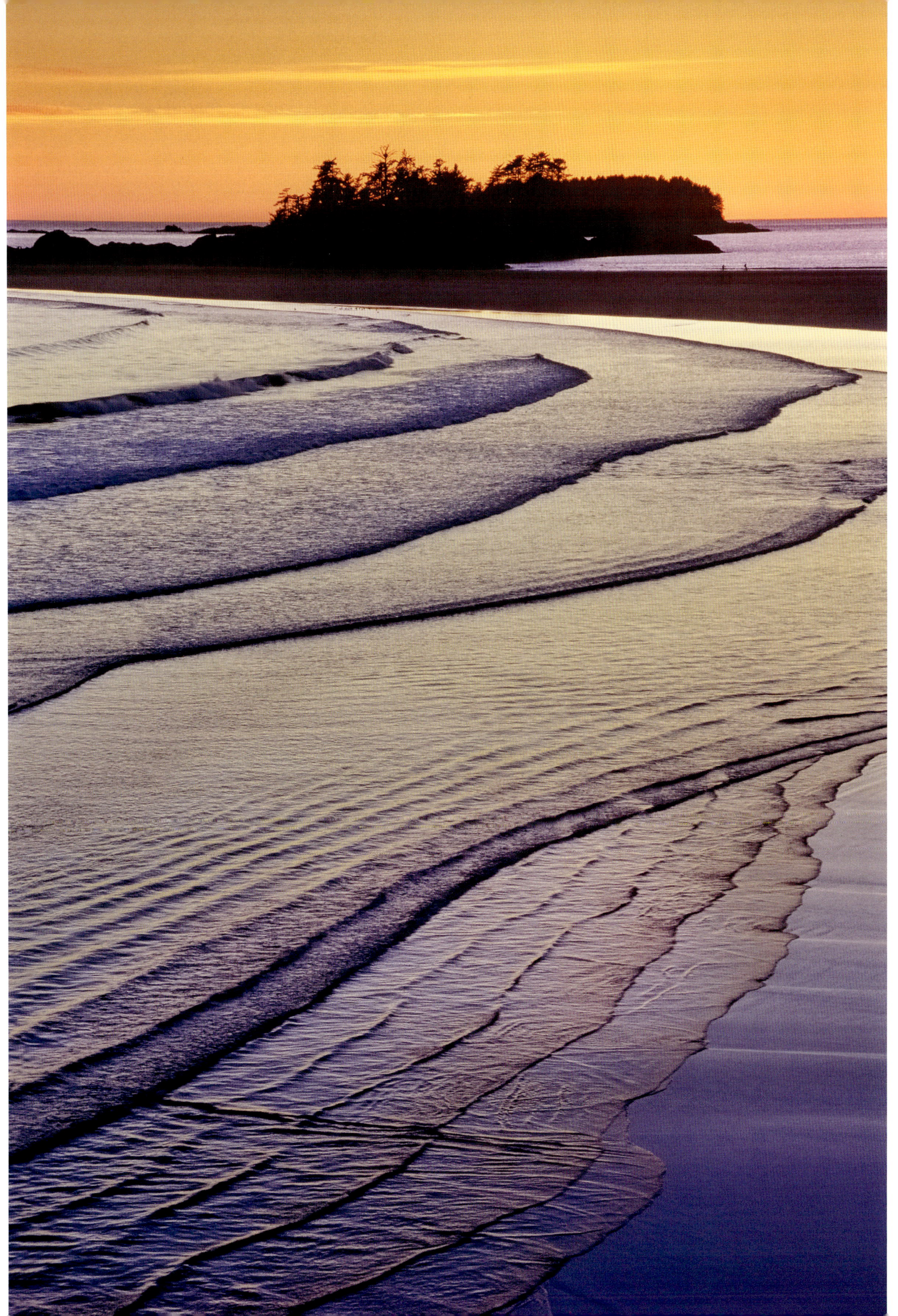

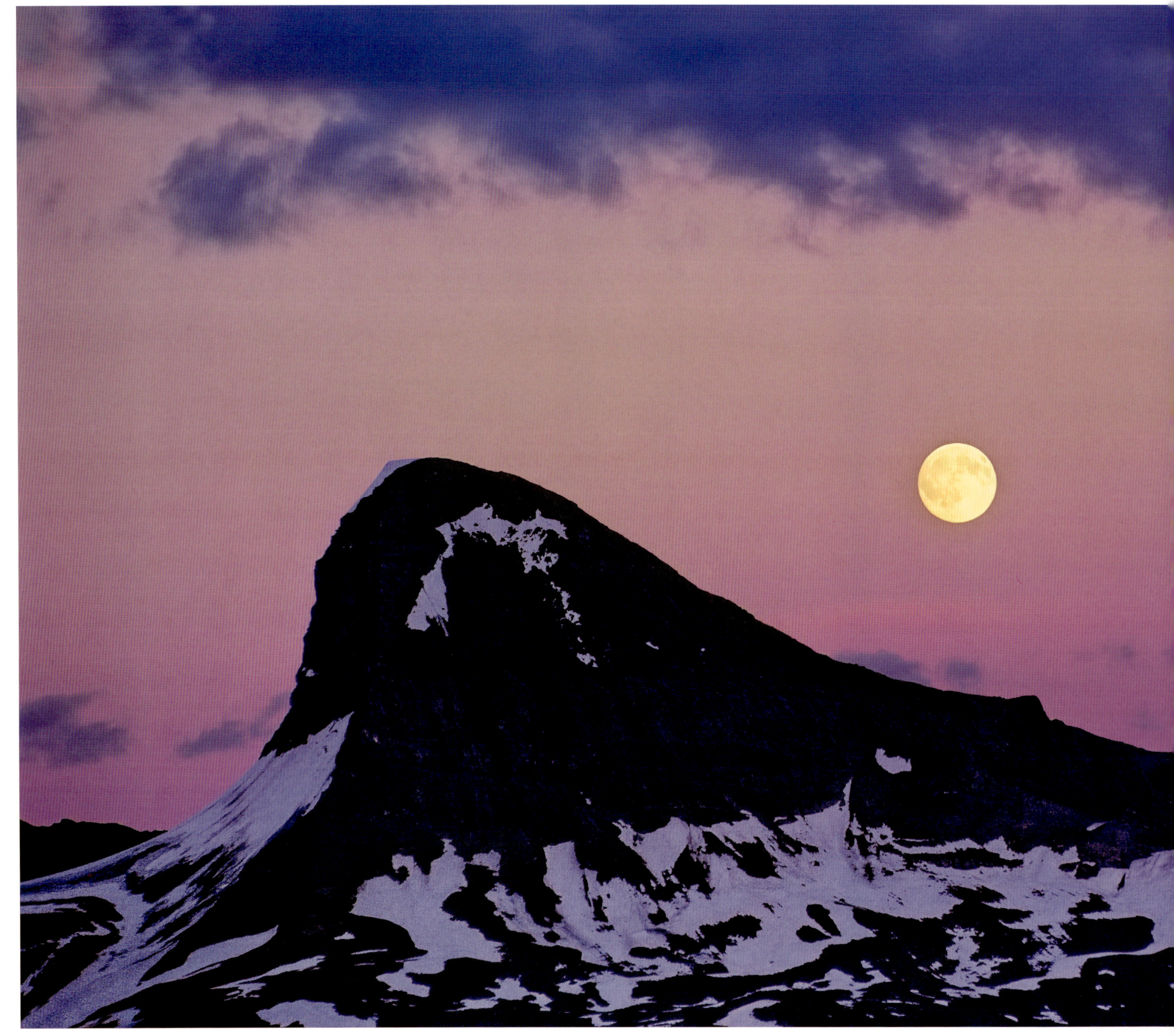

The full moon rises at dusk over Mount Niles, Yoho National Park (above) and an evening crescent moon hangs over the Inside Passage just south of Prince Rupert, British Columbia.

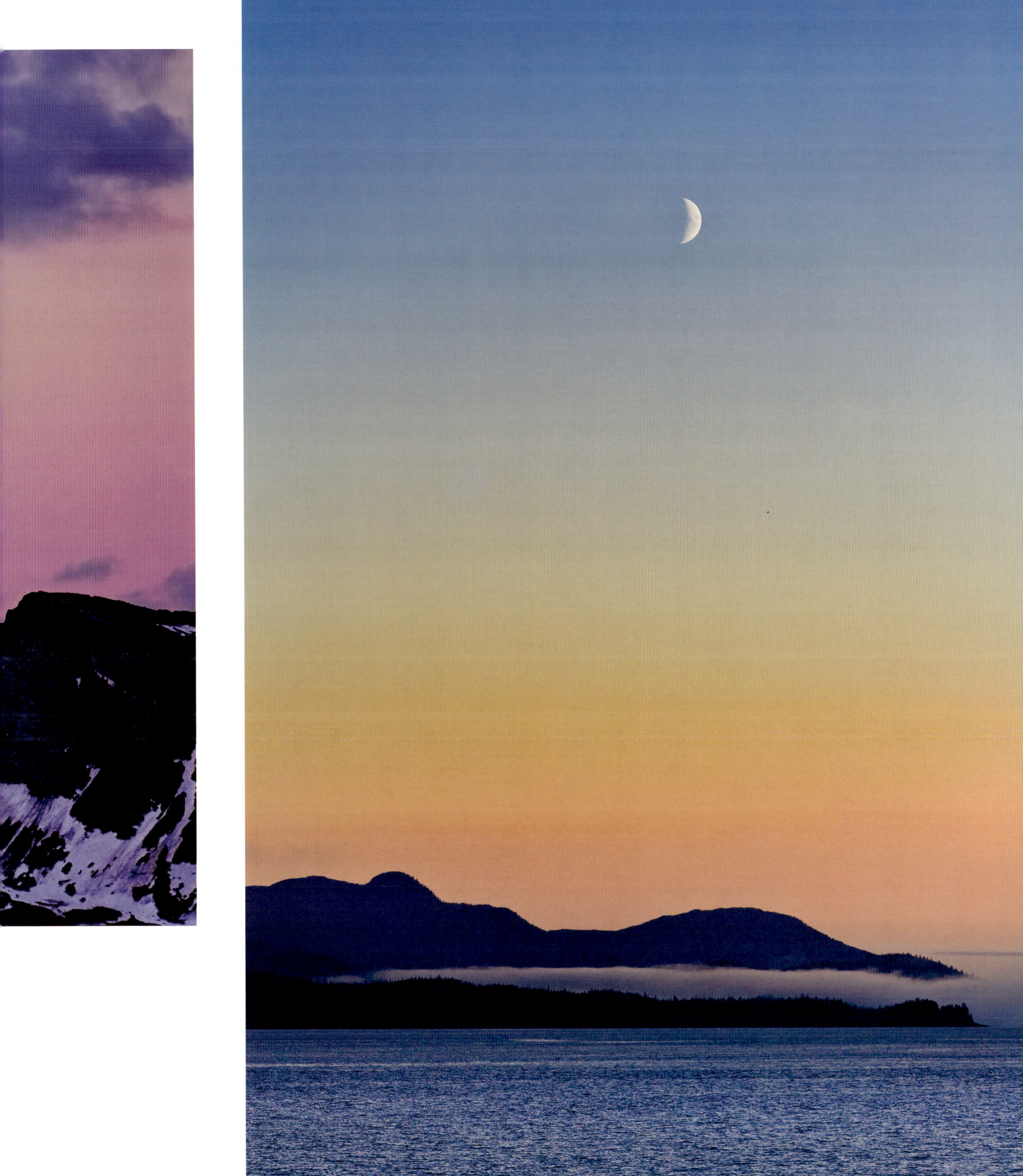

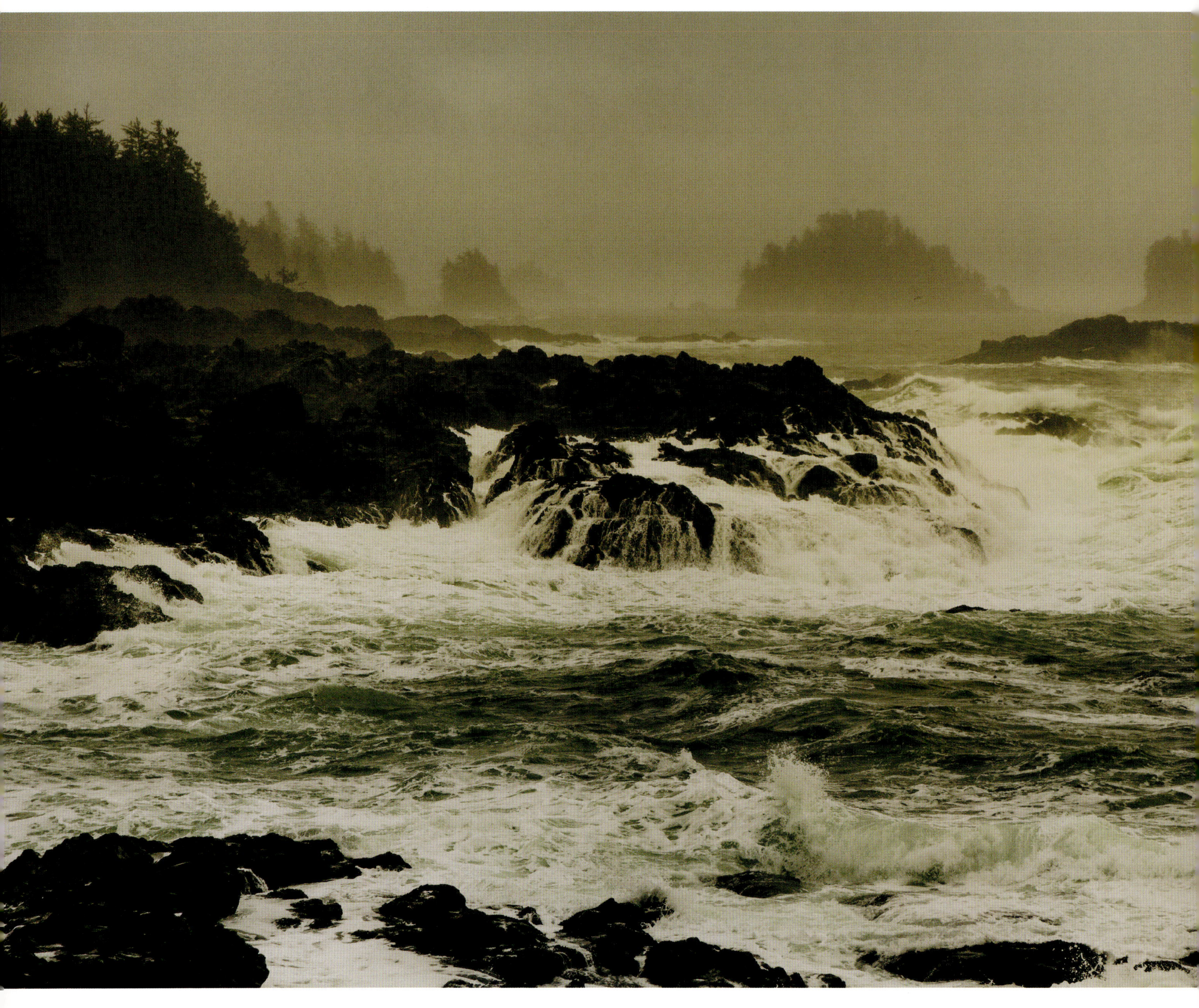

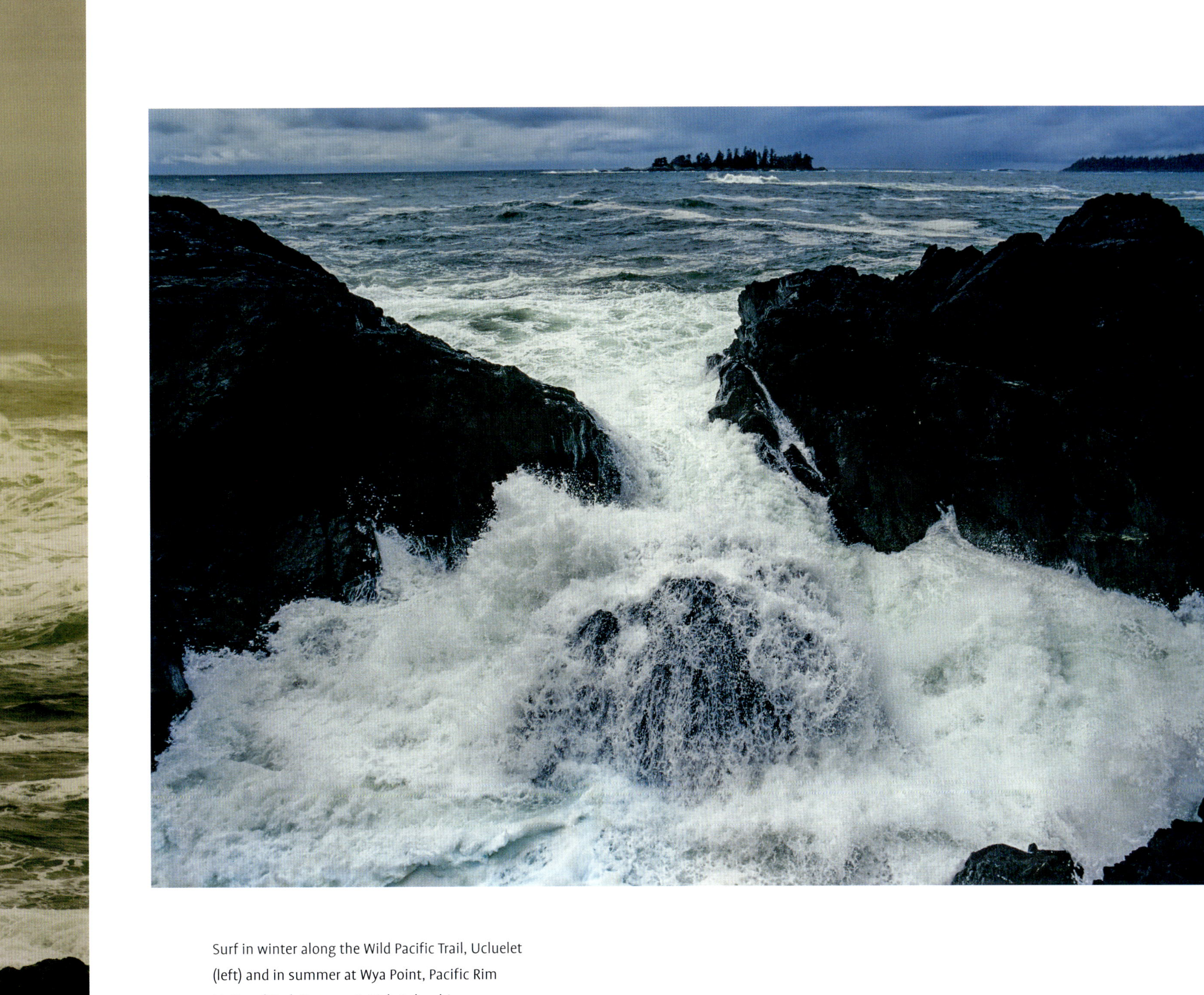

Surf in winter along the Wild Pacific Trail, Ucluelet
(left) and in summer at Wya Point, Pacific Rim
National Park Reserve, British Columbia.

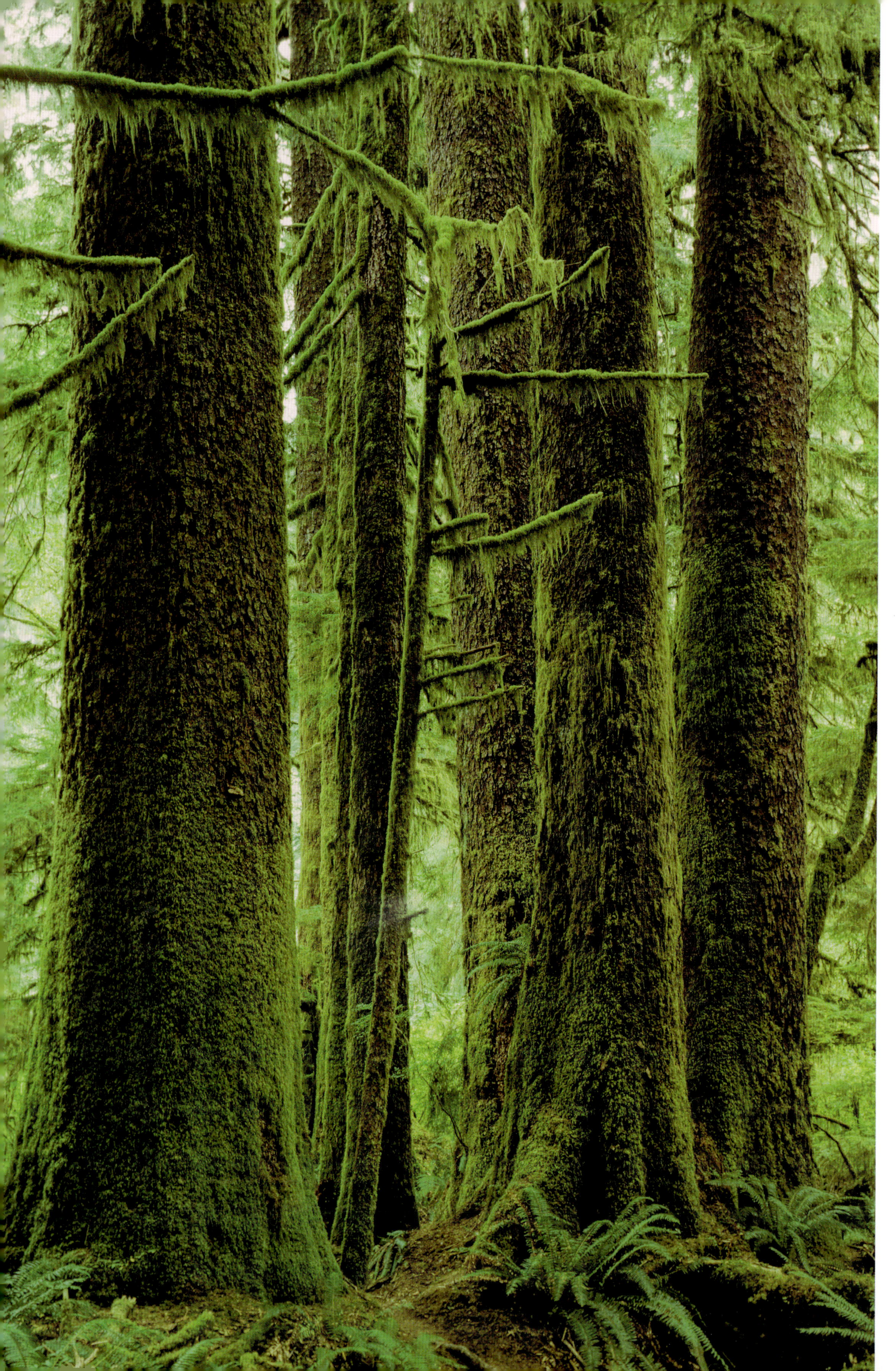

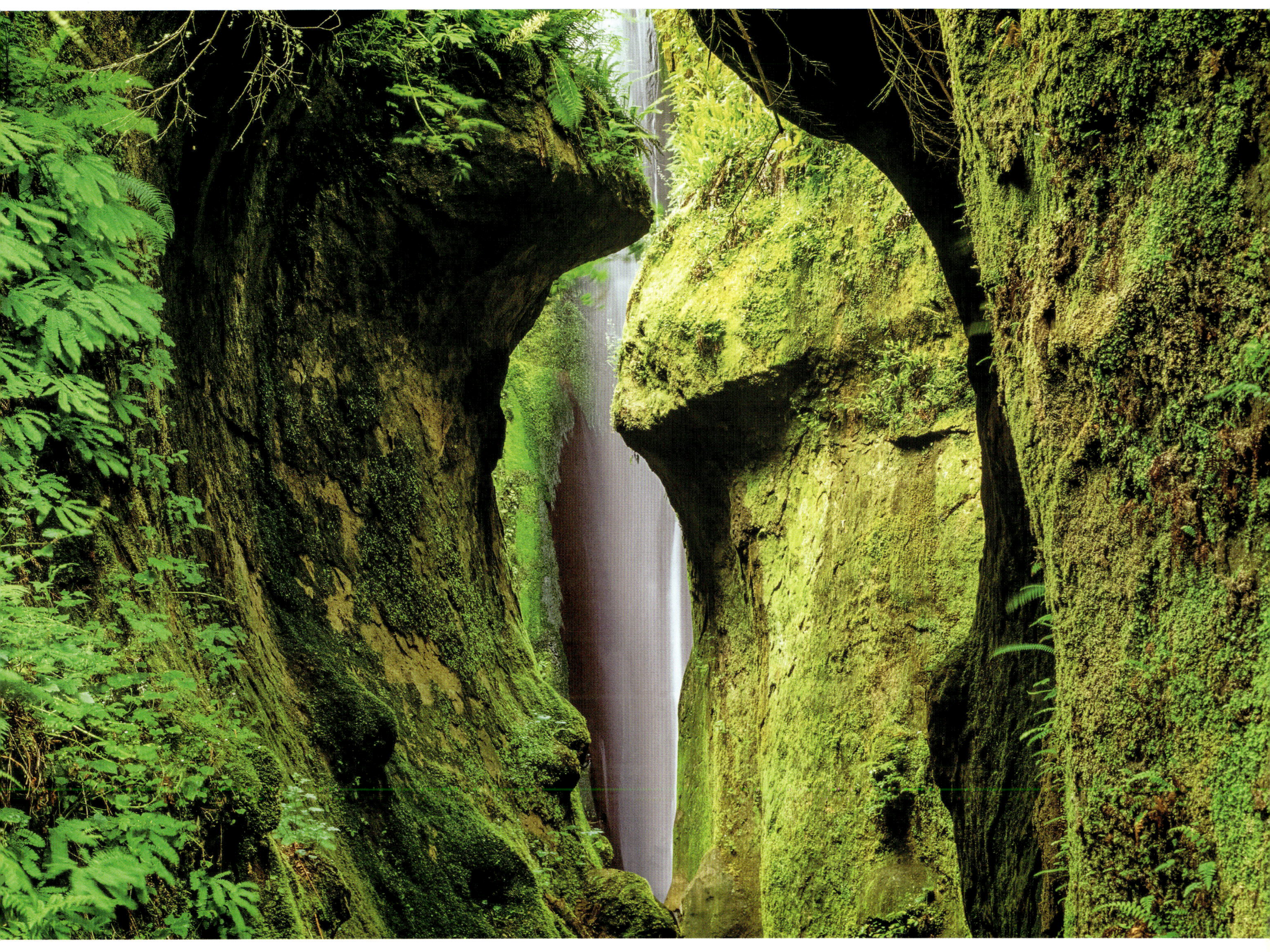

One of numerous groves of towering Sitka spruce
protected in Carmanah Walbran Provincial Park (left)
and a waterfall in a hidden grotto off Sombrio Beach
in Juan de Fuca Provincial Park, both on Vancouver
Island, British Columbia.

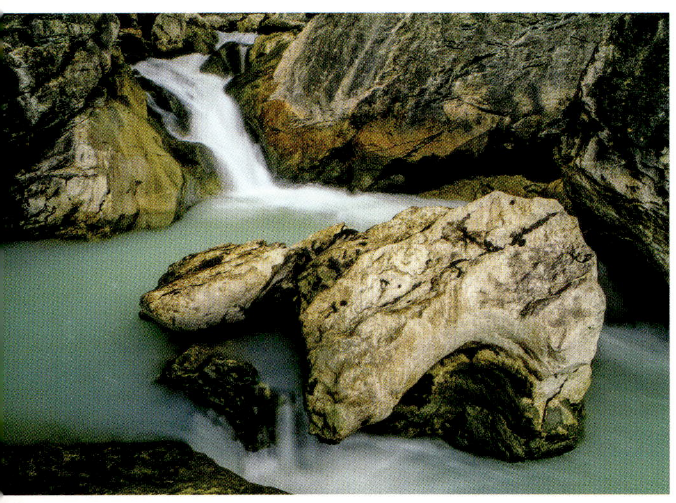

A cascade at the base of Takakkaw Falls (above)
and Lake Oesa from Mount Yukness, Yoho
National Park, British Columbia.

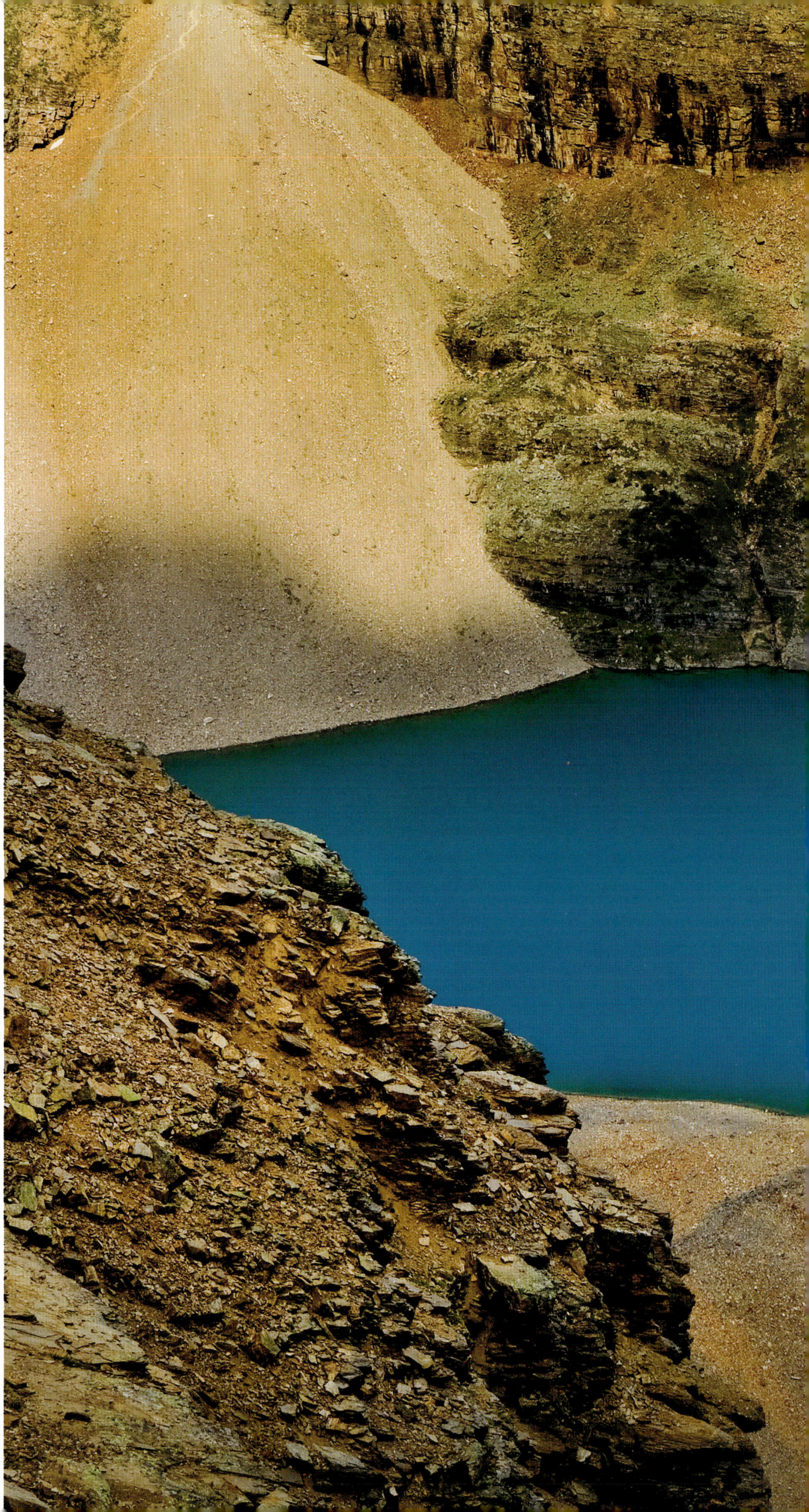

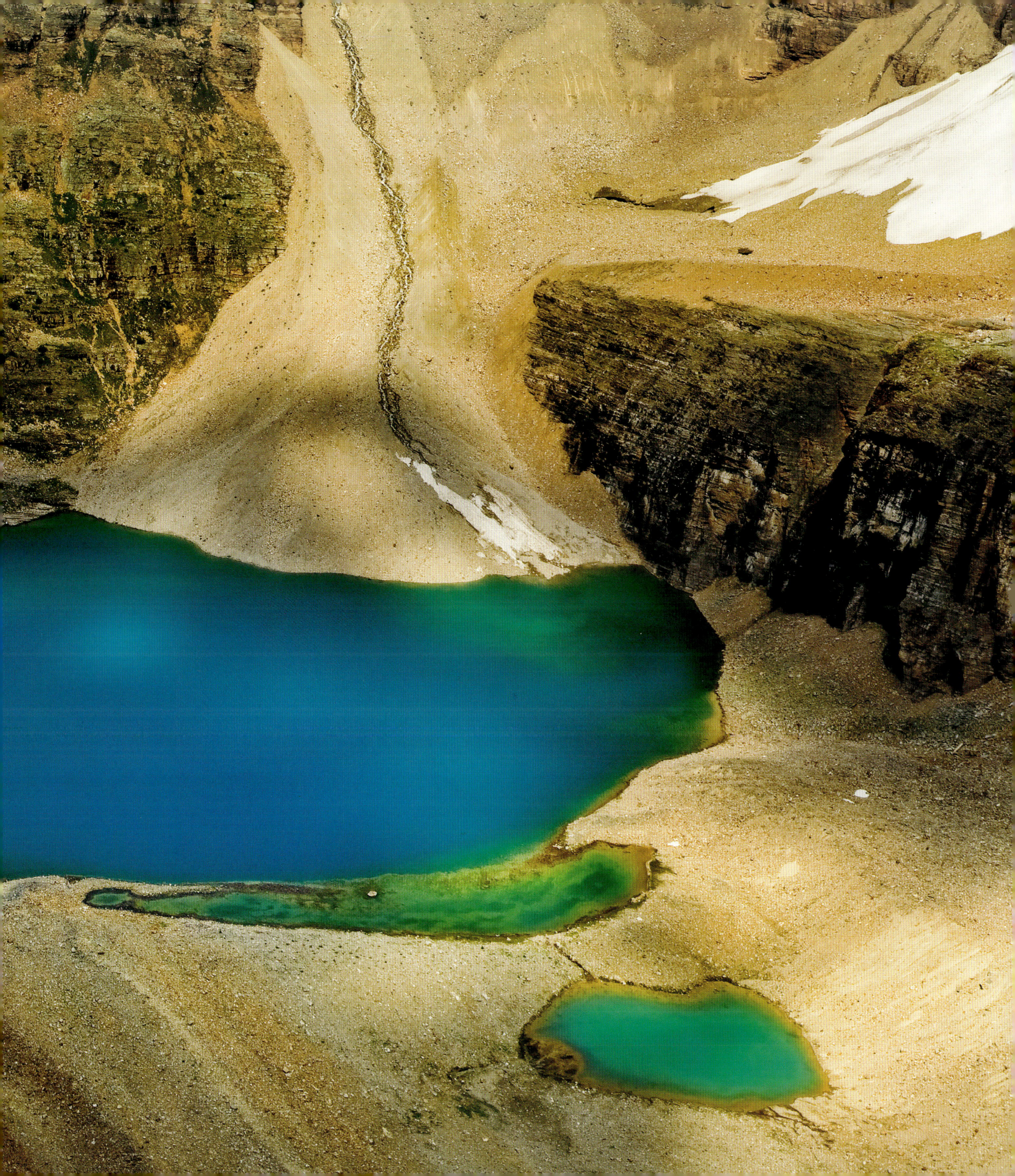

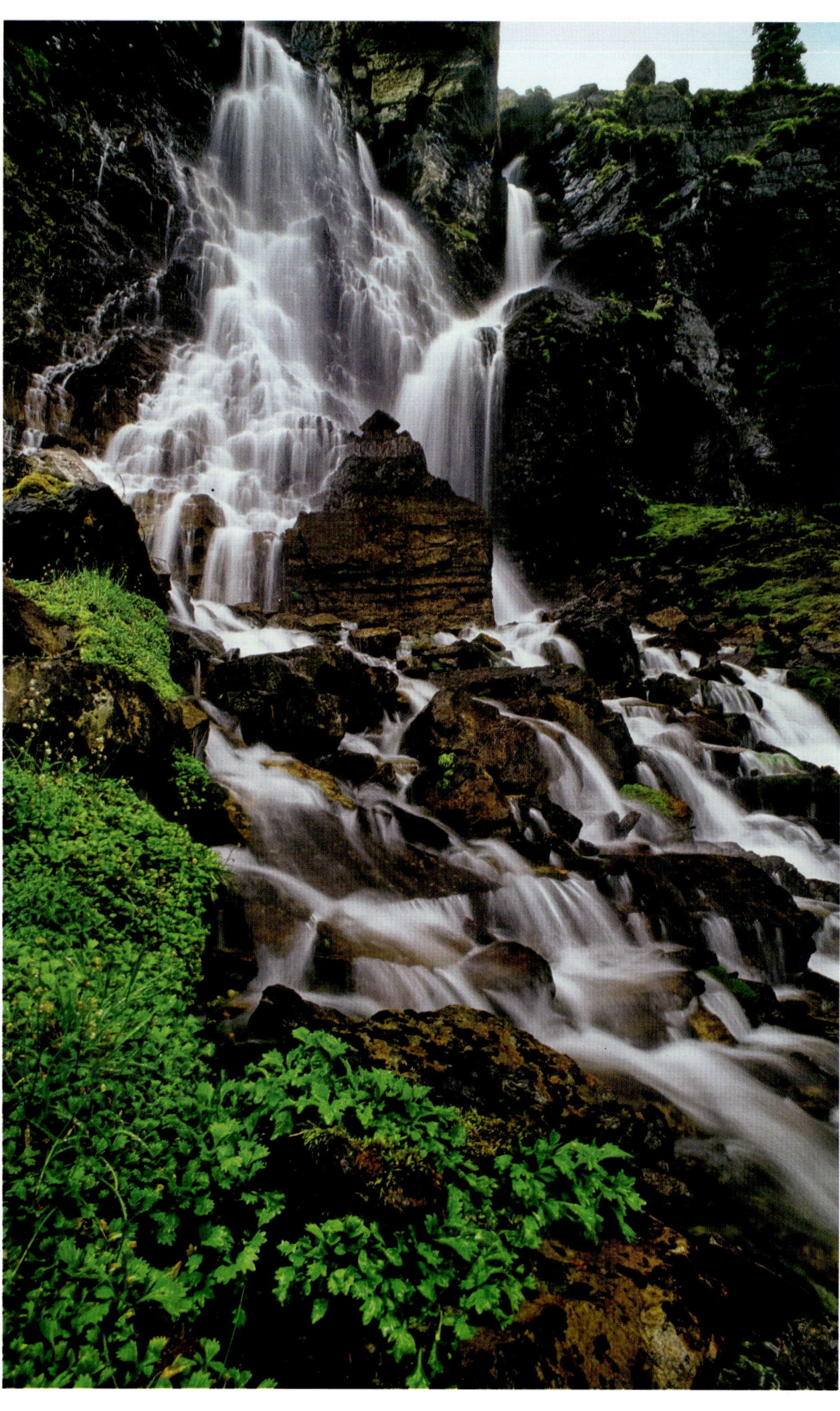

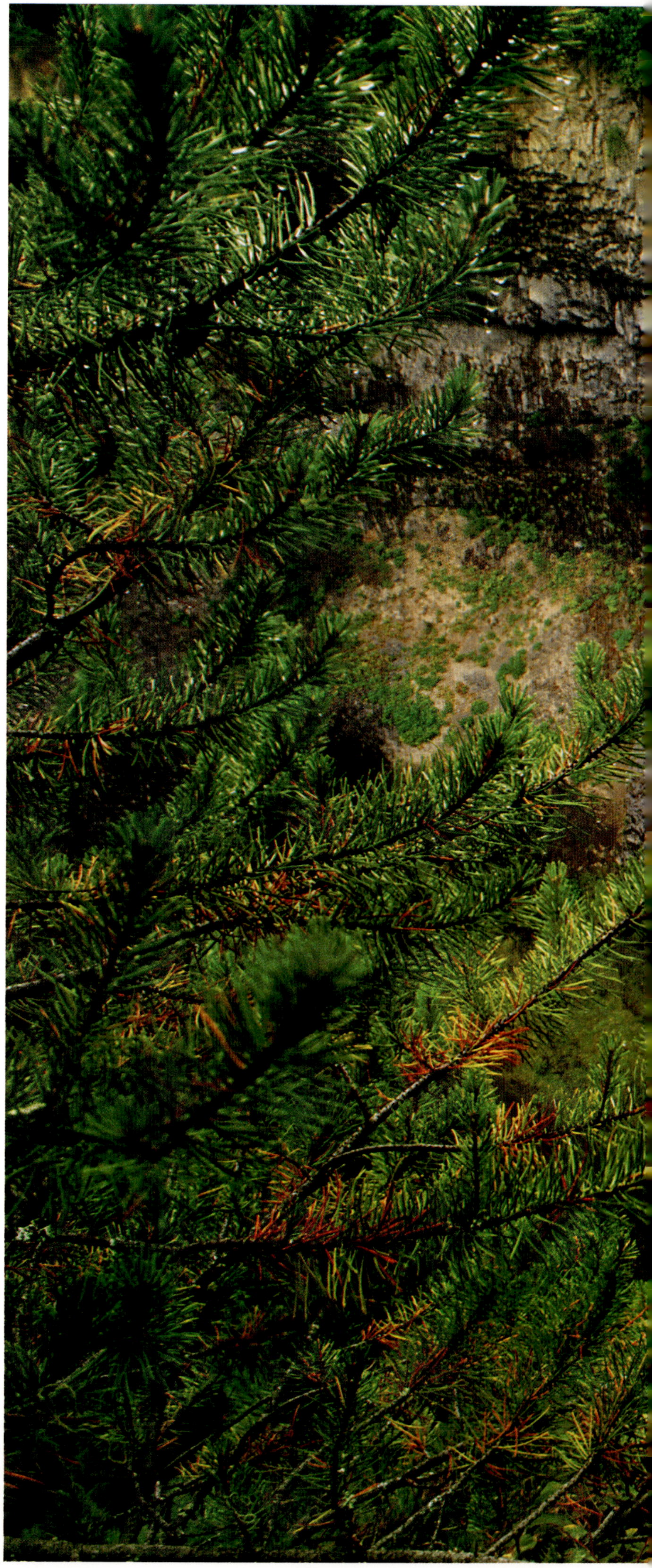

A portion of Seven Veils Falls above Lake O'Hara,
Yoho National Park (above) and 66-metre
high Brandywine Falls south of Whistler,
British Columbia.

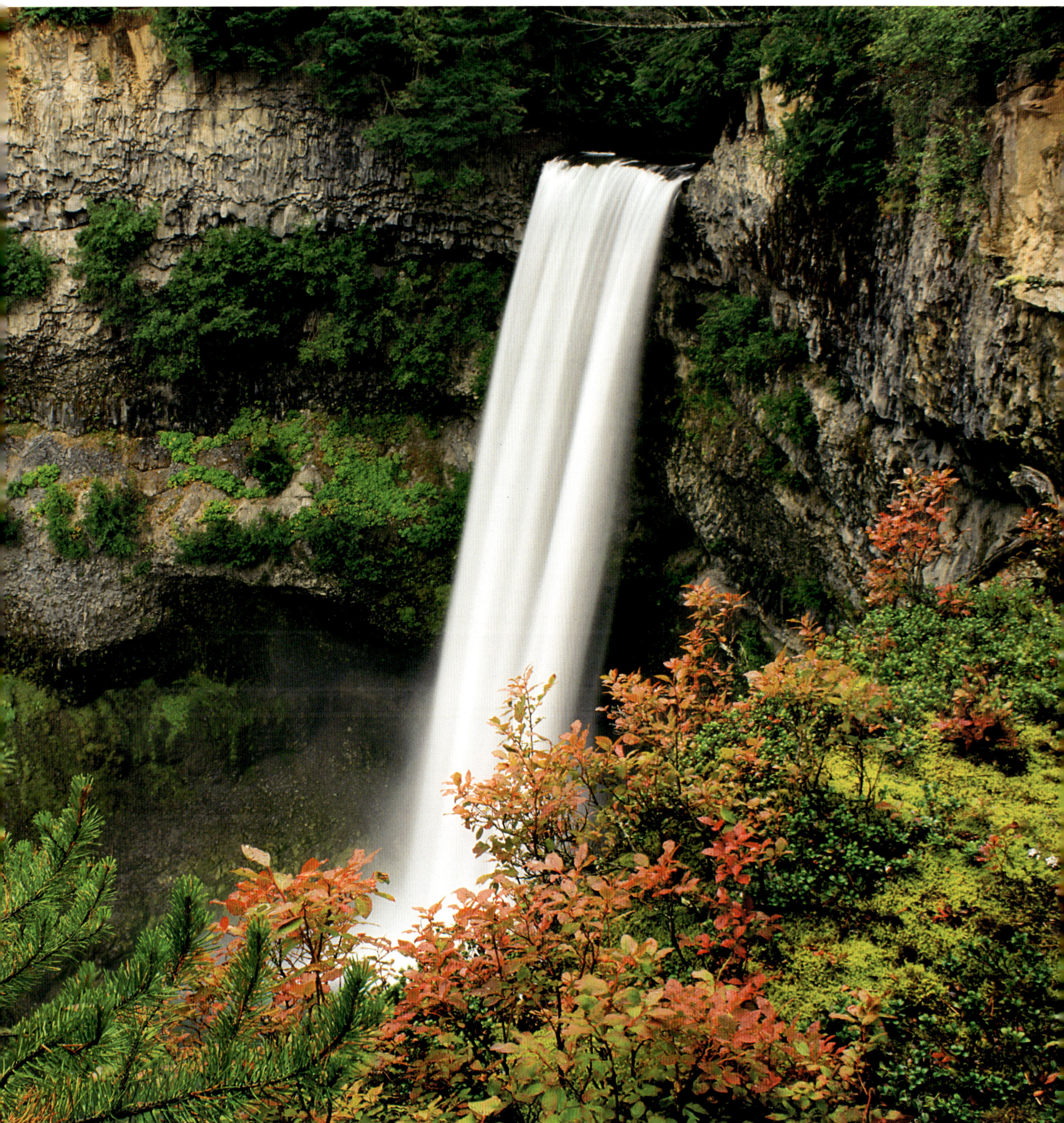

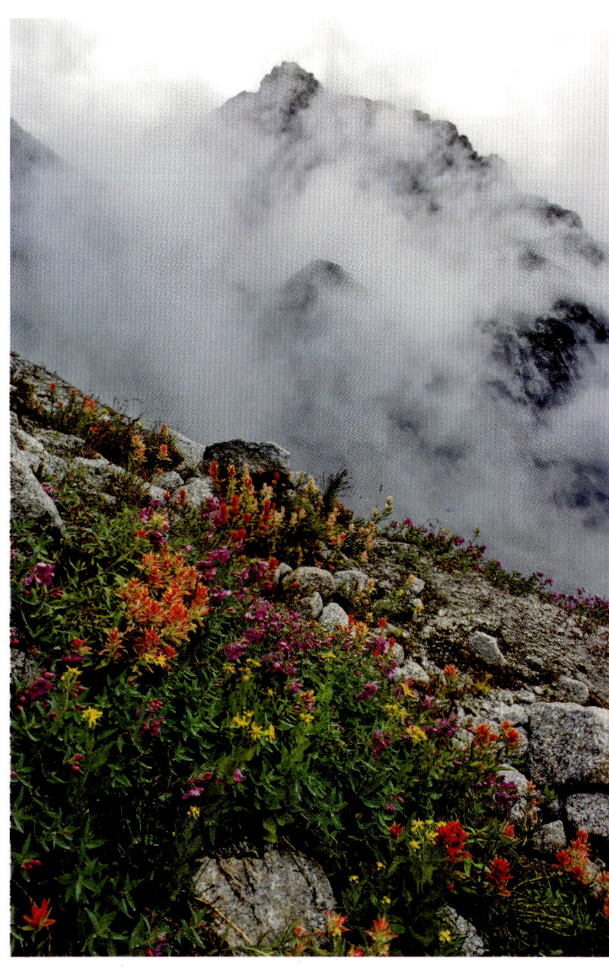

Alpine wildflowers (Indian paintbrush, arnica and willow herb) below Eastpost Spire, the Bugaboos, Bugaboo Provincial Park, Purcell Mountains (above). Ferns, broad-leaved willow herb and pearly everlasting on an alpine slope overlooking the Salmon Glacier in the Boundary Ranges, Coast Mountains, British Columbia.

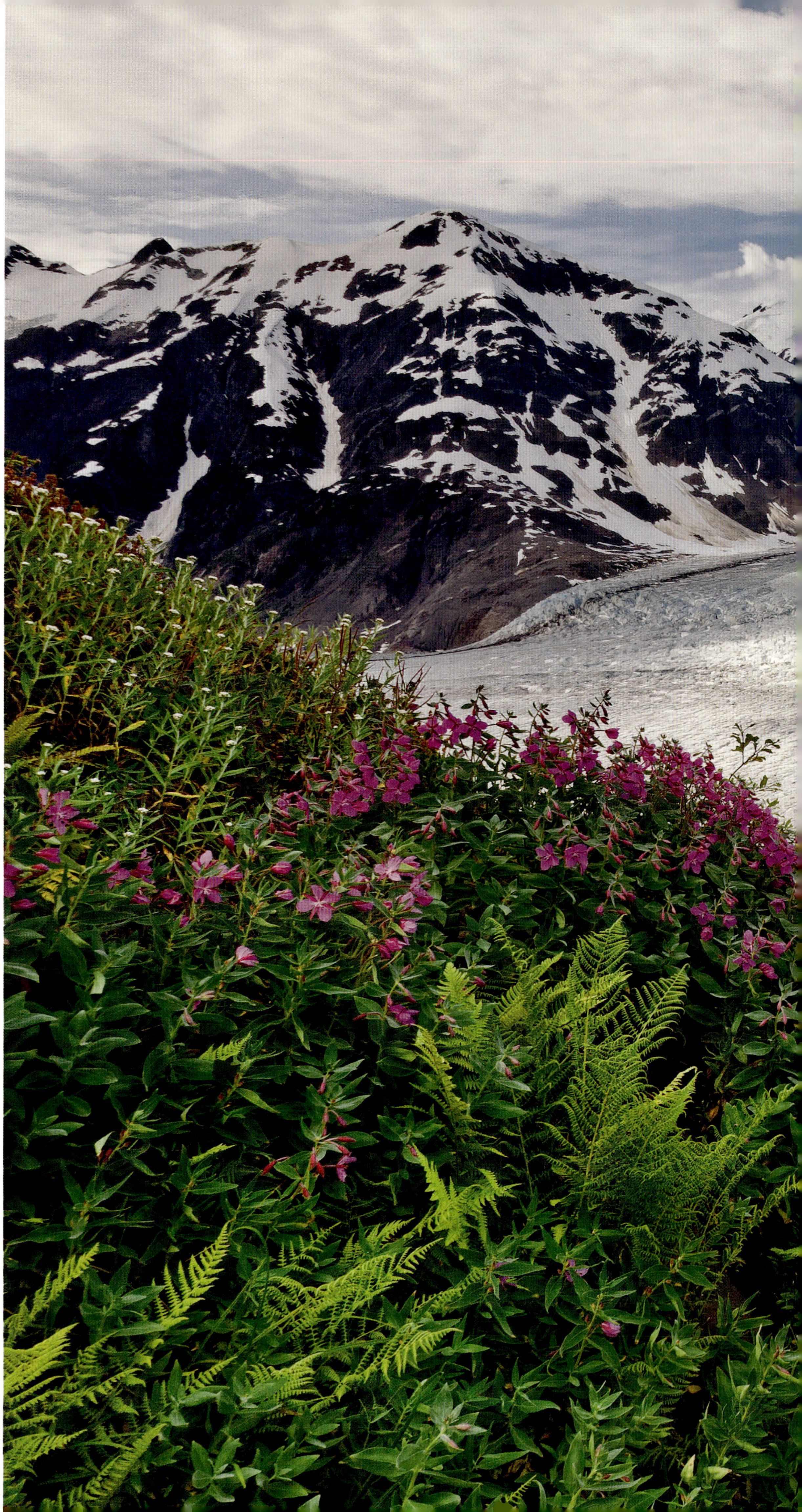

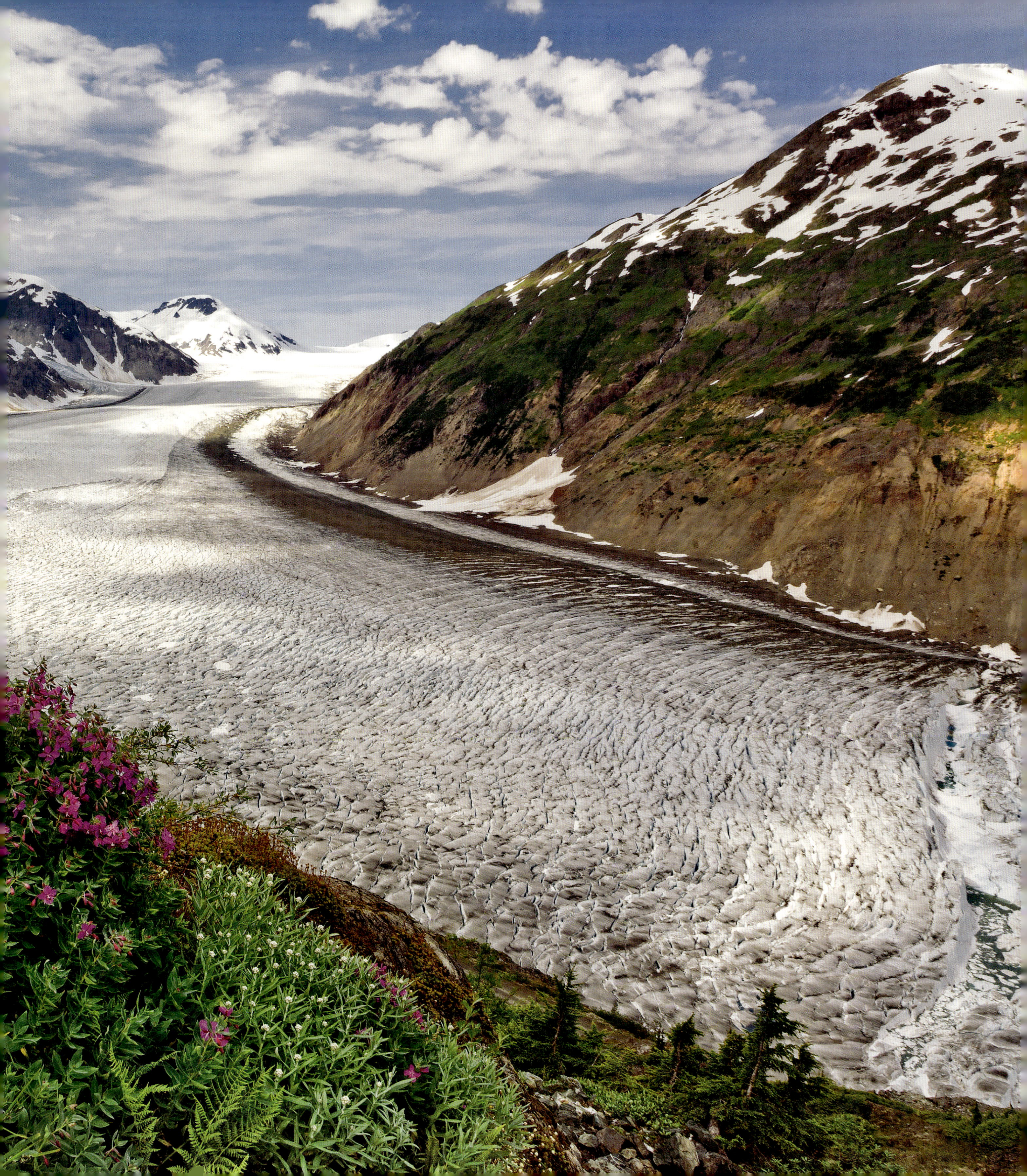

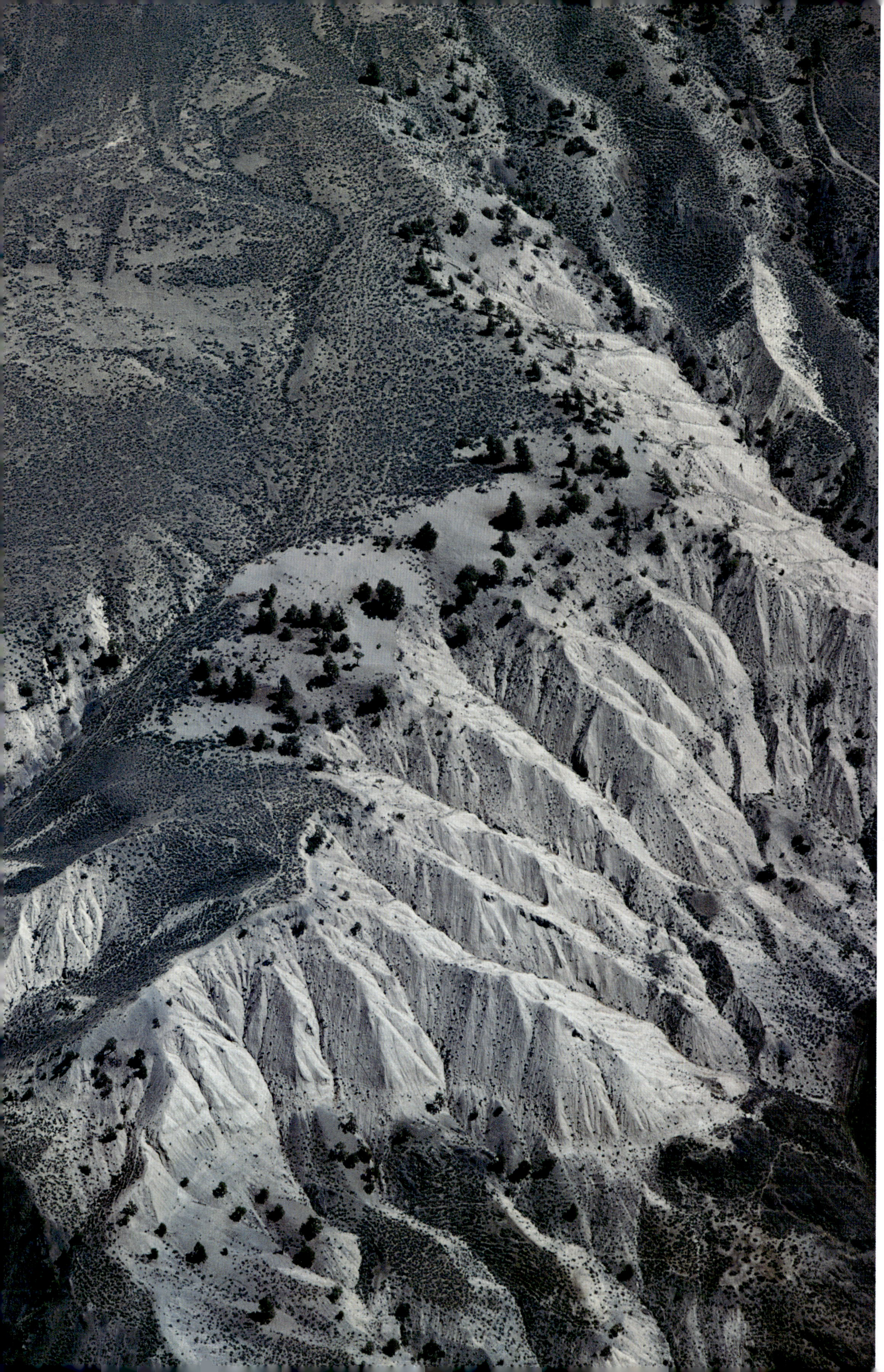

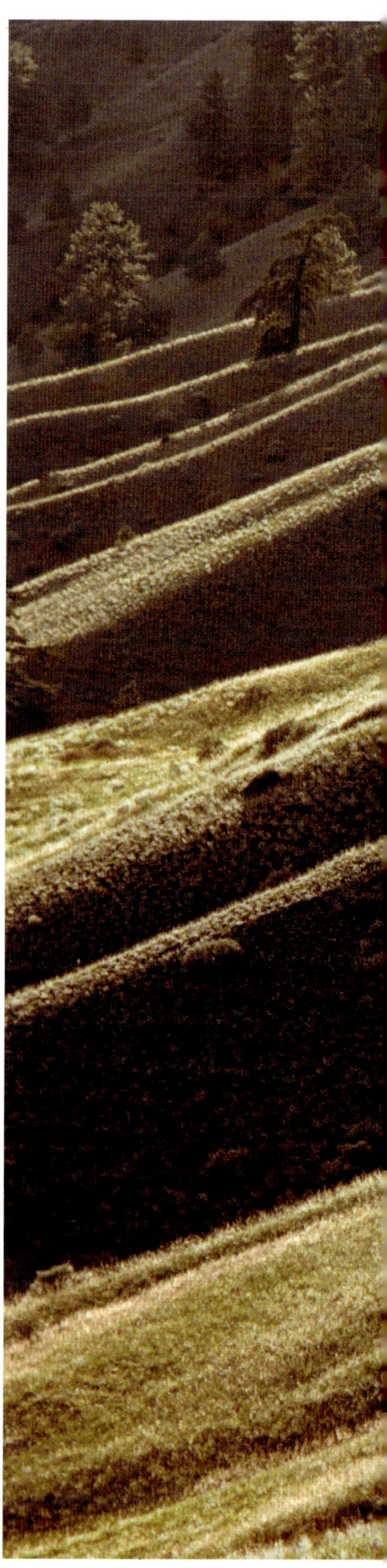

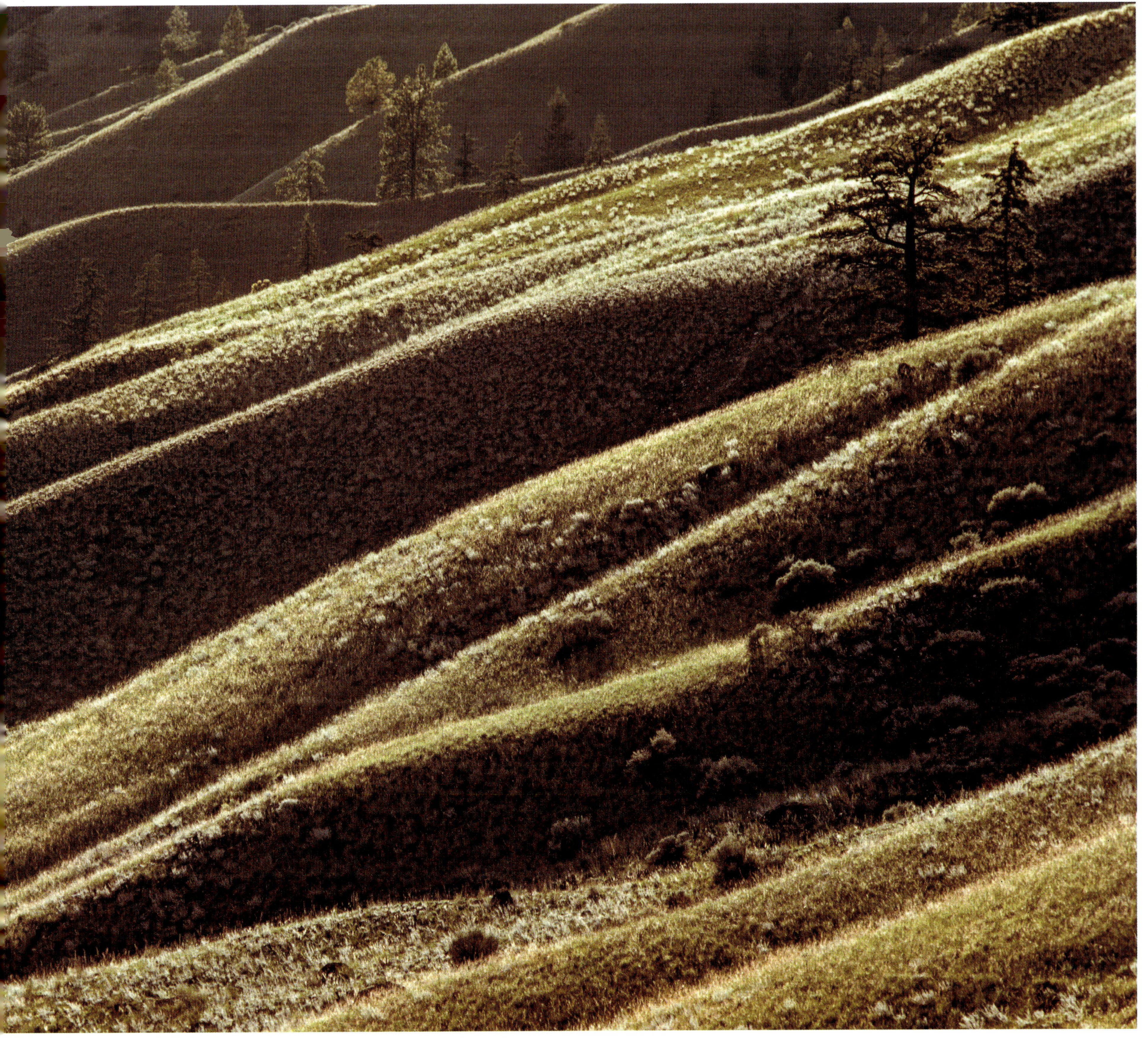

Dry lands of the British Columbia interior. An aerial view
of a mountainside near Spences Bridge studded with pine,
juniper and sage (left) and afternoon light grazes across a
hillside above Canoe Creek south of Gang Ranch.

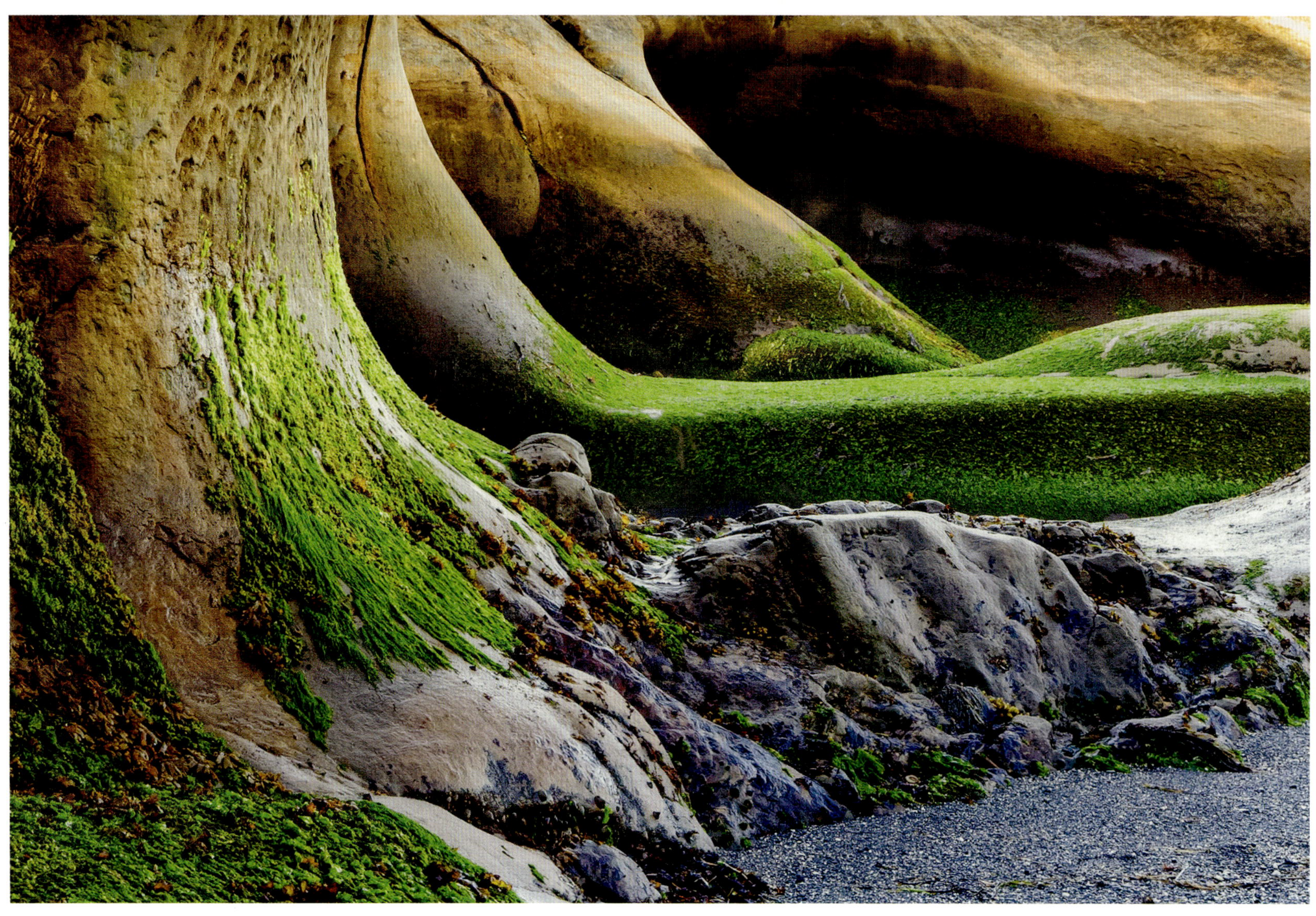

Wave-carved sandstone in the tidal zone at
Botanical Beach, Juan de Fuca Provincial Park,
British Columbia.

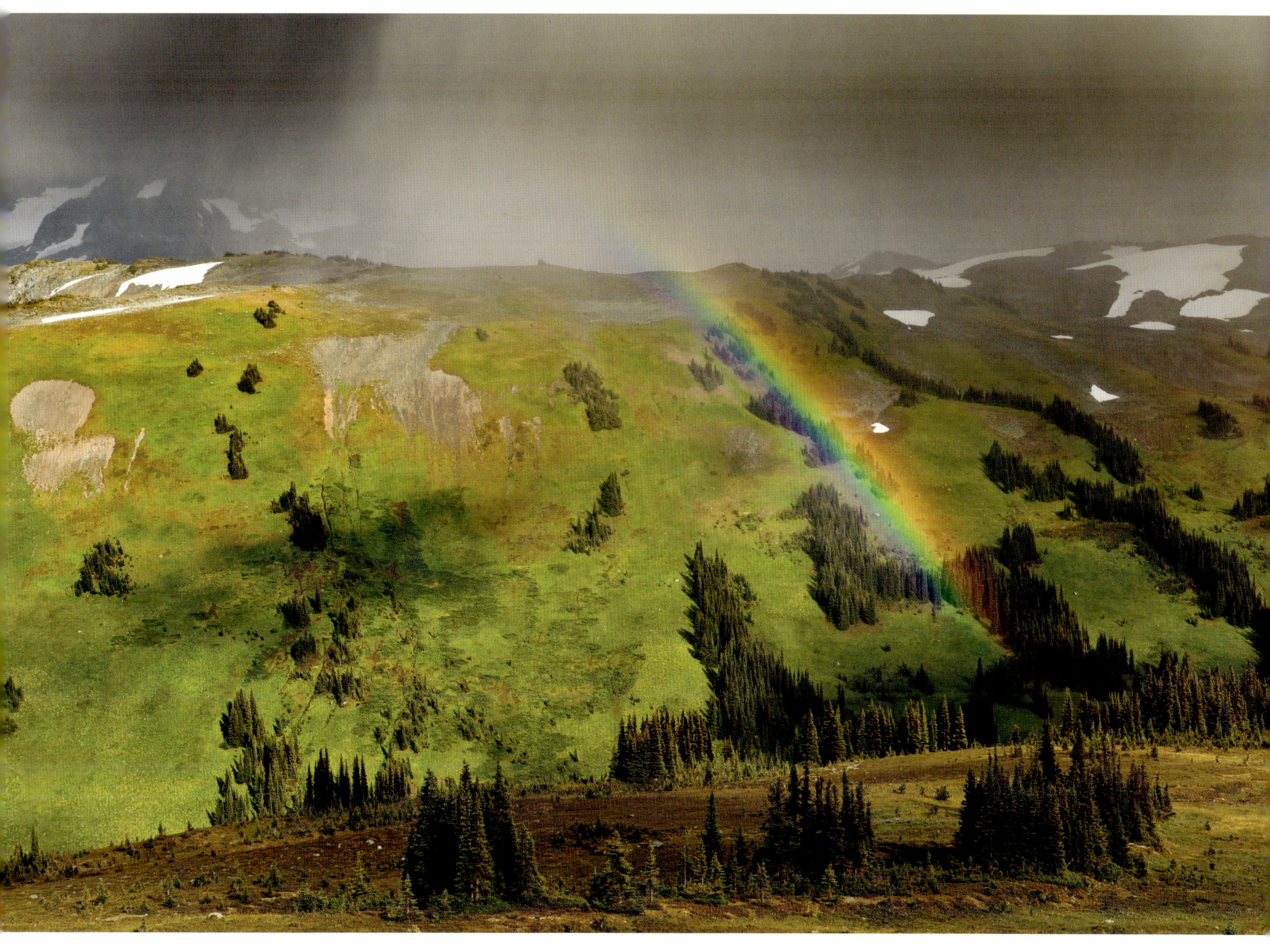

A passing rain shower leaves a rainbow at Singing
Pass in the Fitzsimmons Range, Garibaldi Provincial
Park, British Columbia.

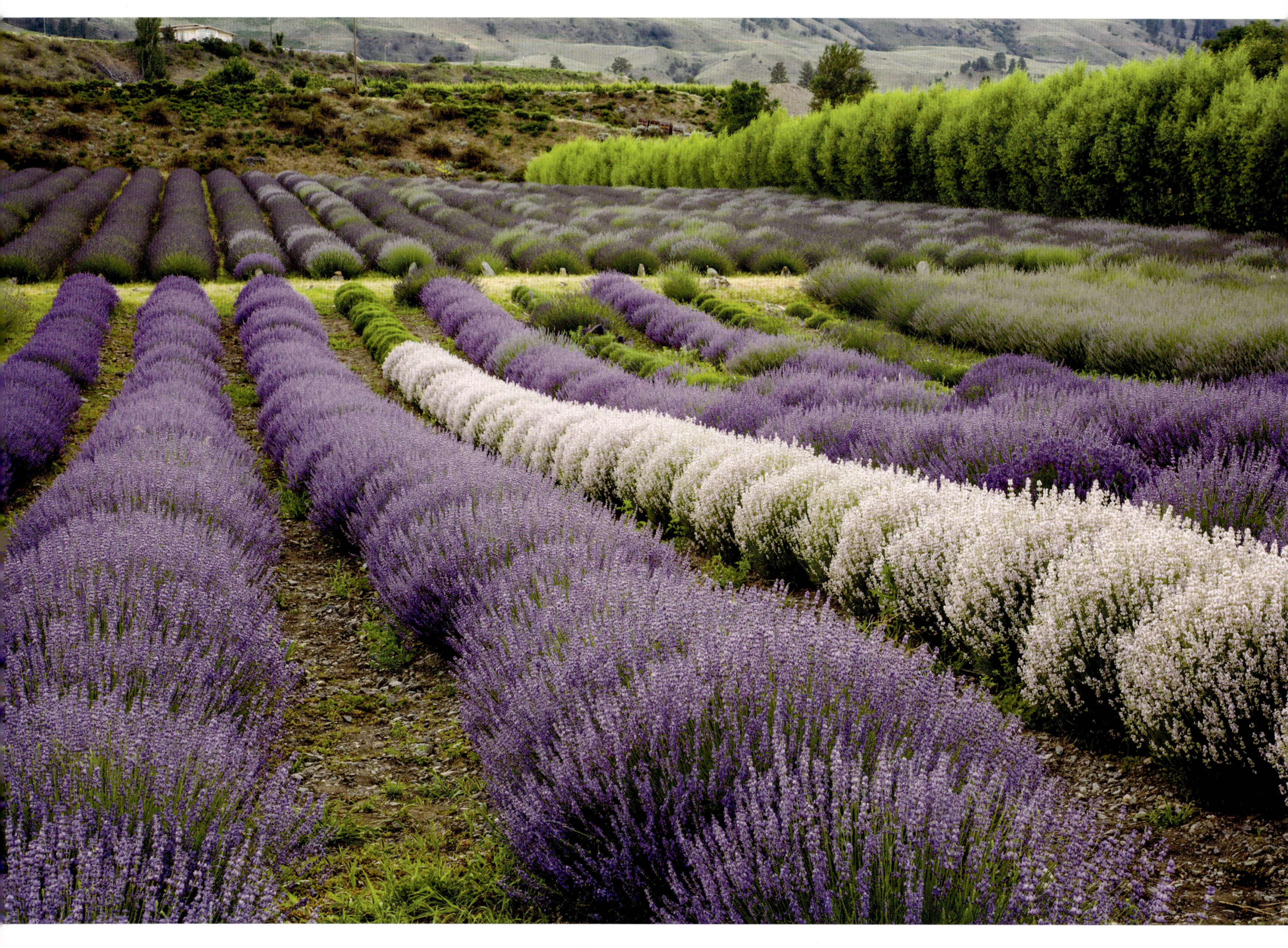

Rows of varied lavender cultivars near Oliver (above) and a vineyard outside of Osoyoos in the Okanagan Valley, British Columbia.

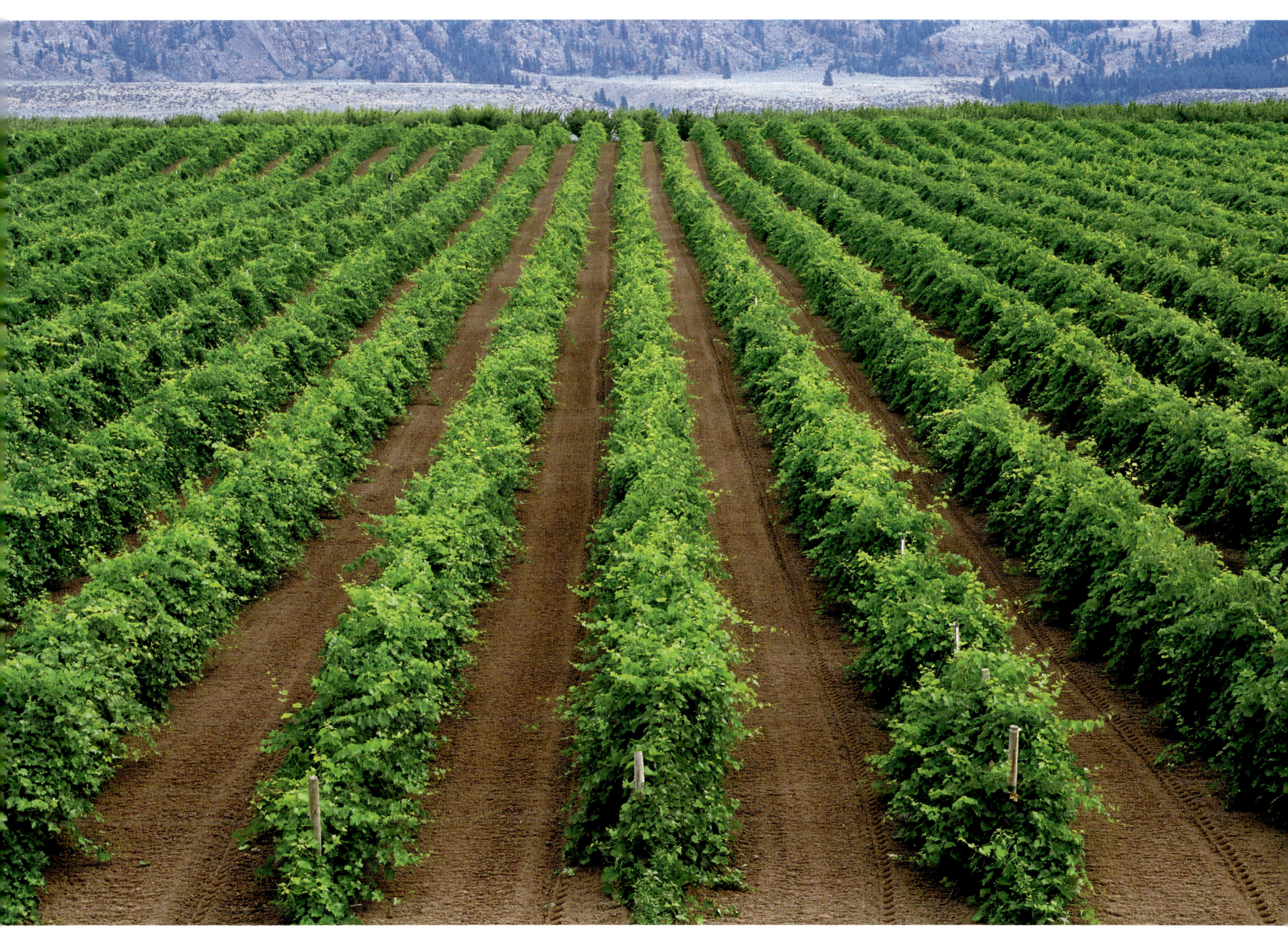

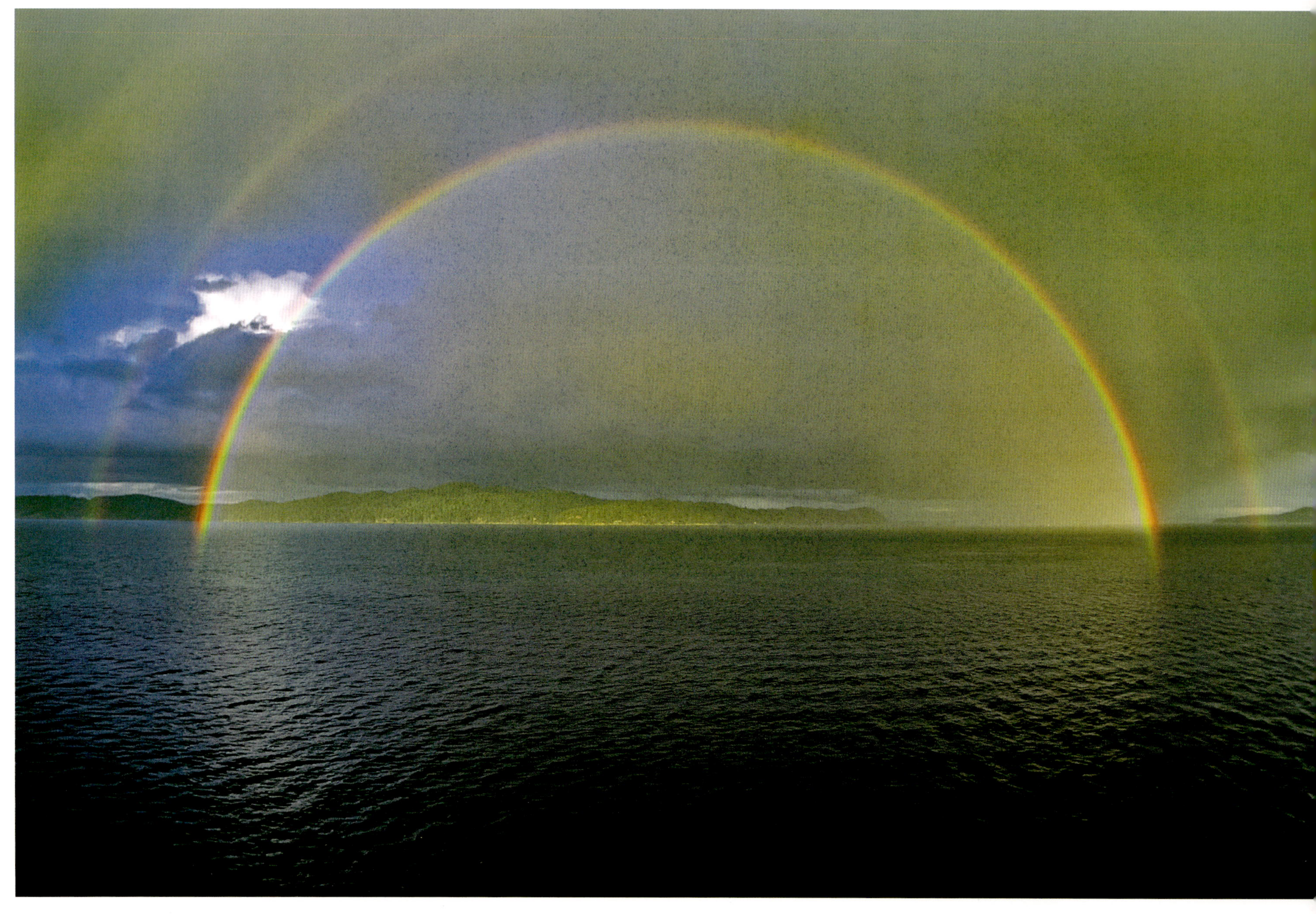

A complete double rainbow over Swanson Channel
and Pender Island in the Southern Gulf Islands,
British Columbia.

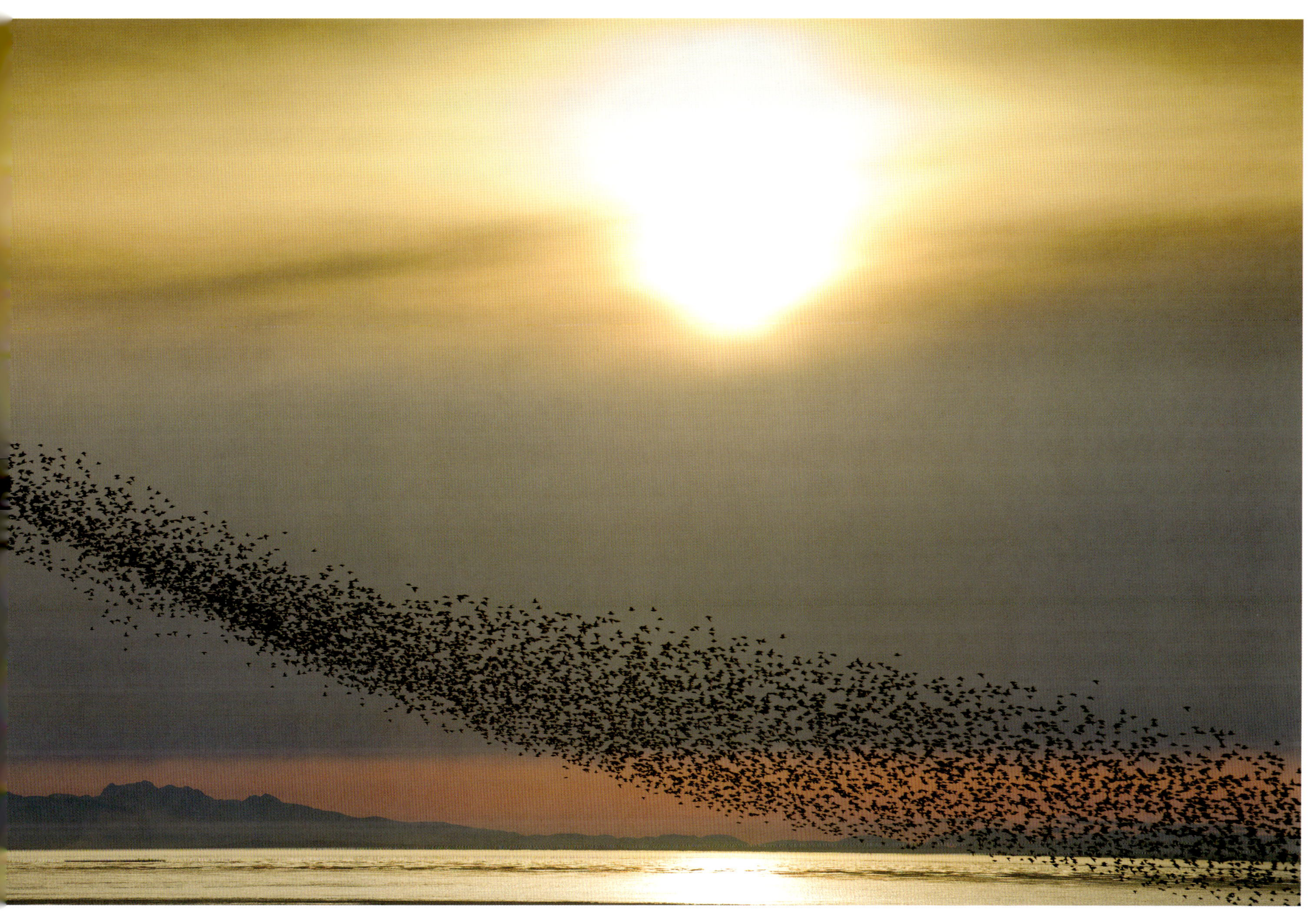

A formation of western sandpipers flying in unison
arcs against the setting sun above Roberts Bank at
the mouth of the Fraser River, British Columbia.

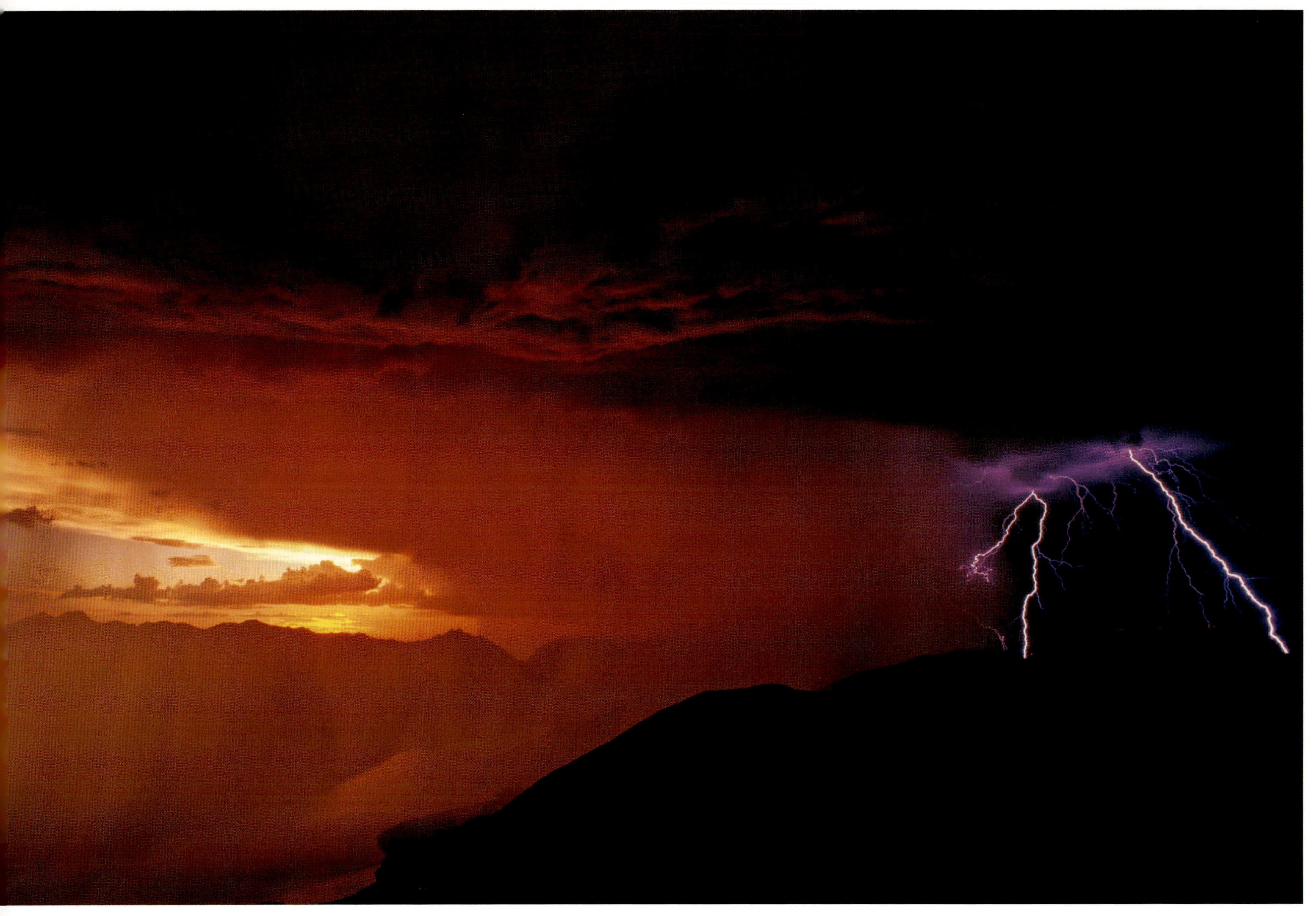

Lightning at sunset from the summit of Idaho
Peak in the Selkirk Mountains, British Columbia,
high above Slocan Lake below.

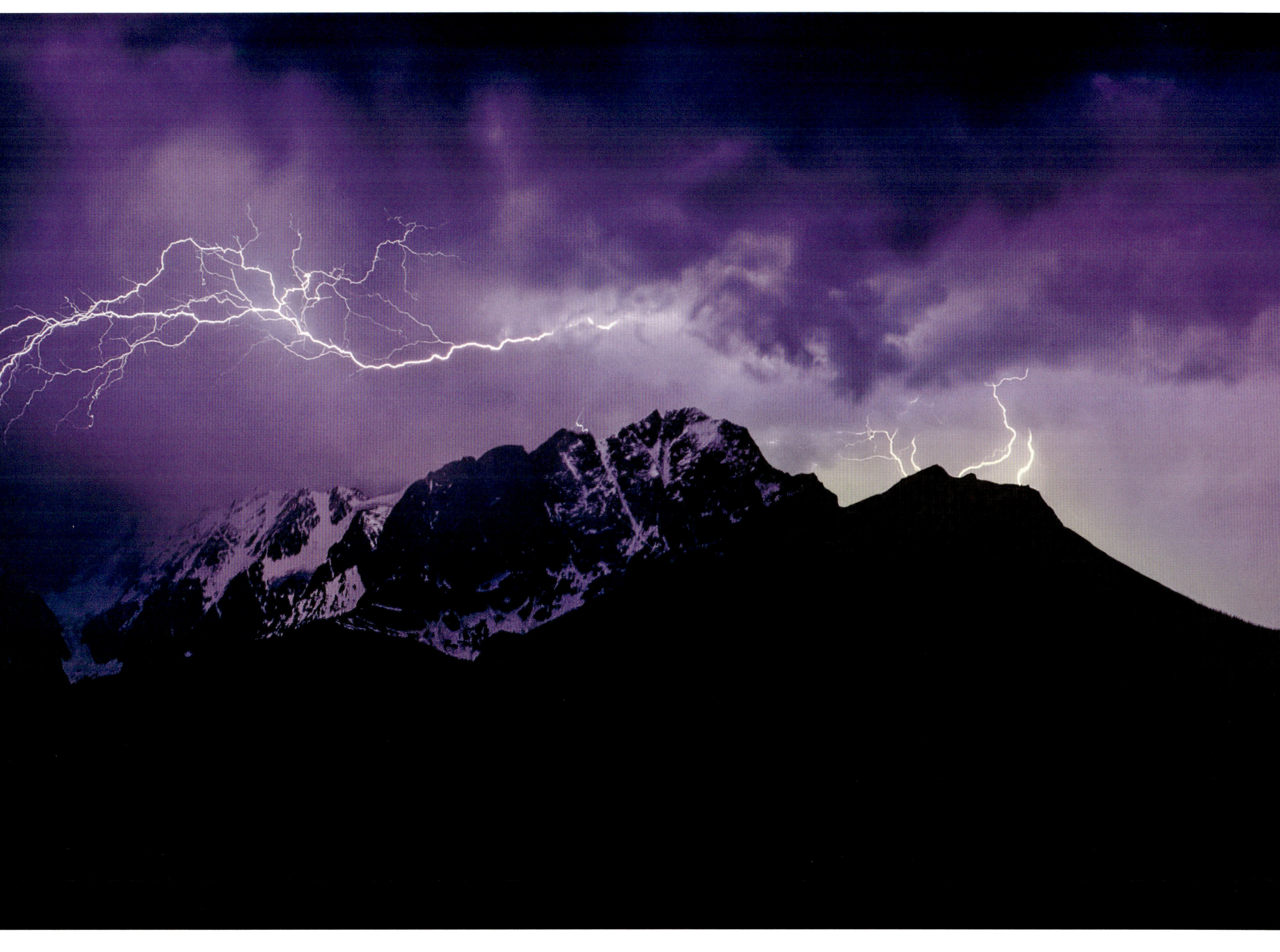

Lightning at night over Mount Hurd in the Canadian
Rockies, Yoho National Park, British Columbia.

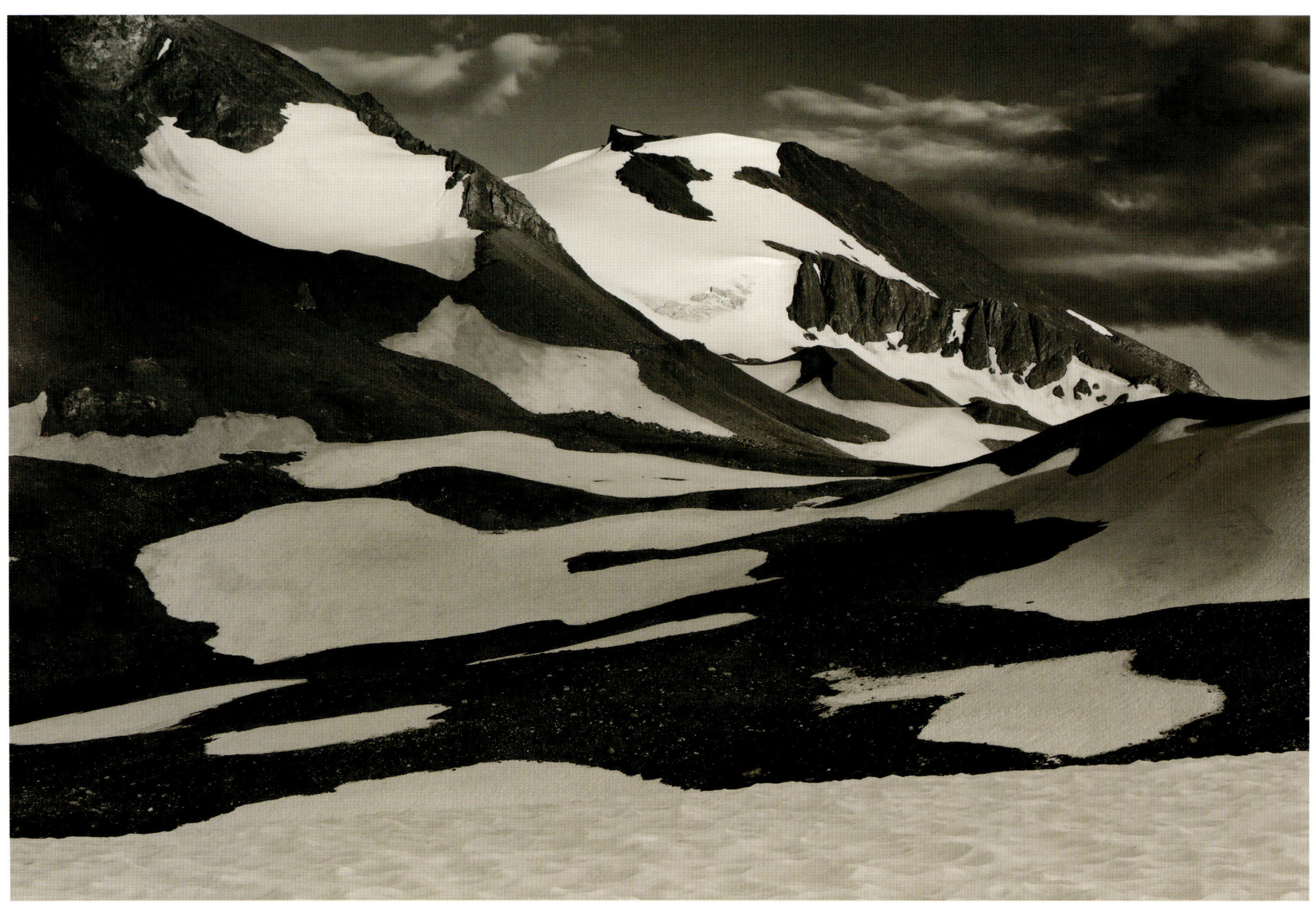

Snow patches from the preceding winter linger
unmelted in early September on the slopes of
Fissile Peak, Garibaldi Provincial Park (above).
Hikers pause in wonder overlooking the Salmon
Glacier north of Stewart. Both in the Coast
Mountains, British Columbia.

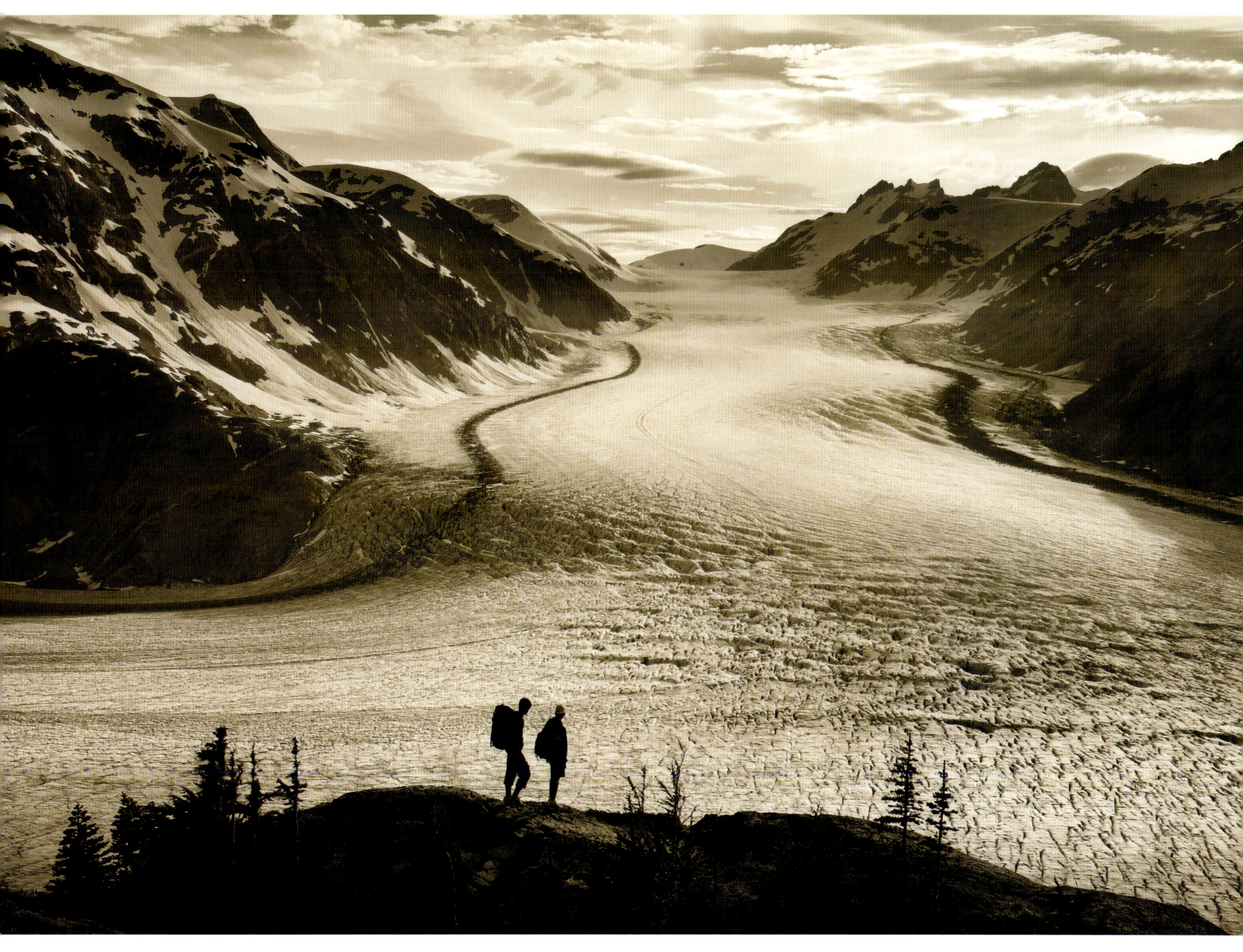

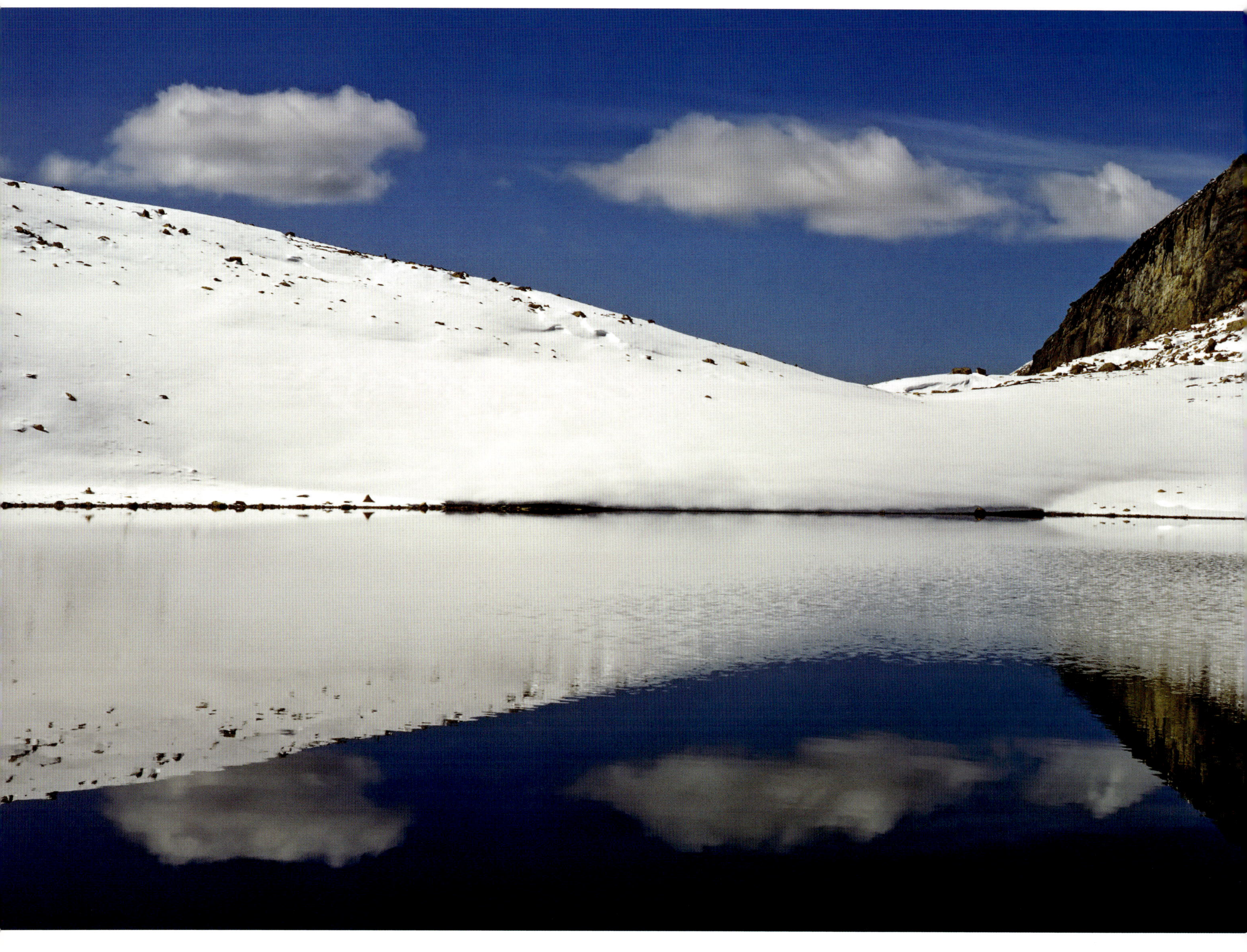

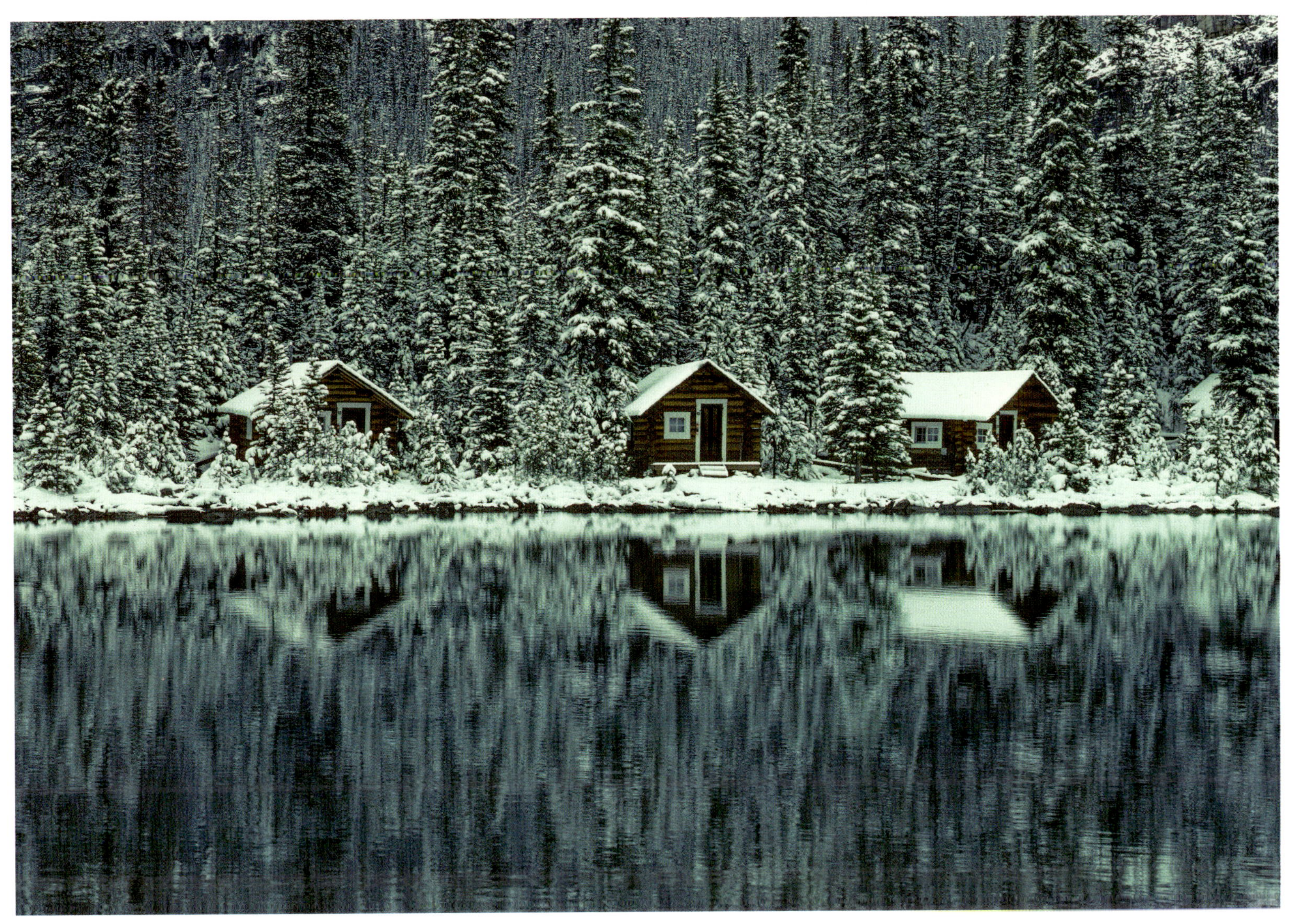

September snowfalls reflected in the unfrozen
still waters of Kiwetinok Lake, one of the highest
in Canada (left) and at Lake O'Hara, both in Yoho
National Park, British Columbia.

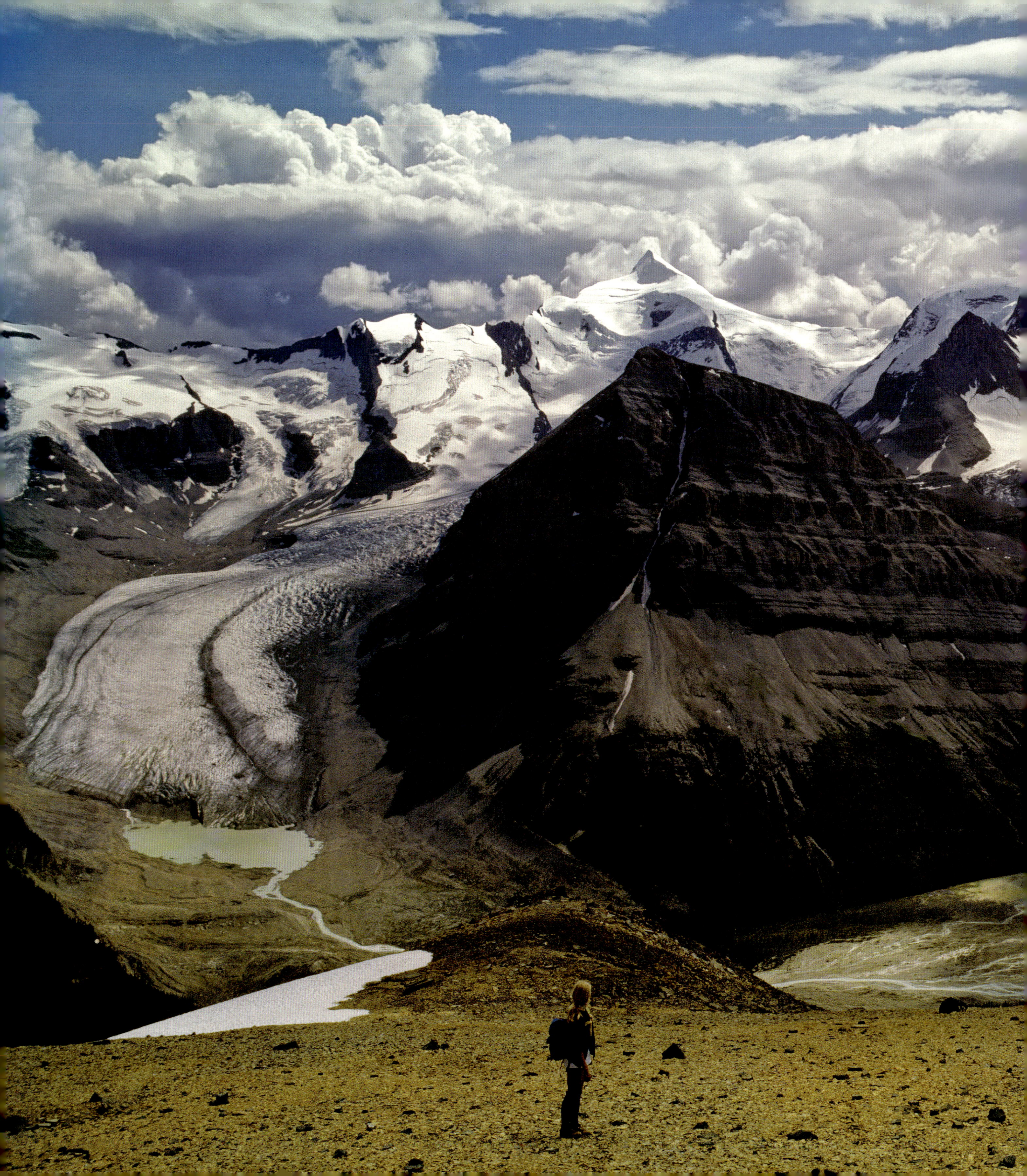

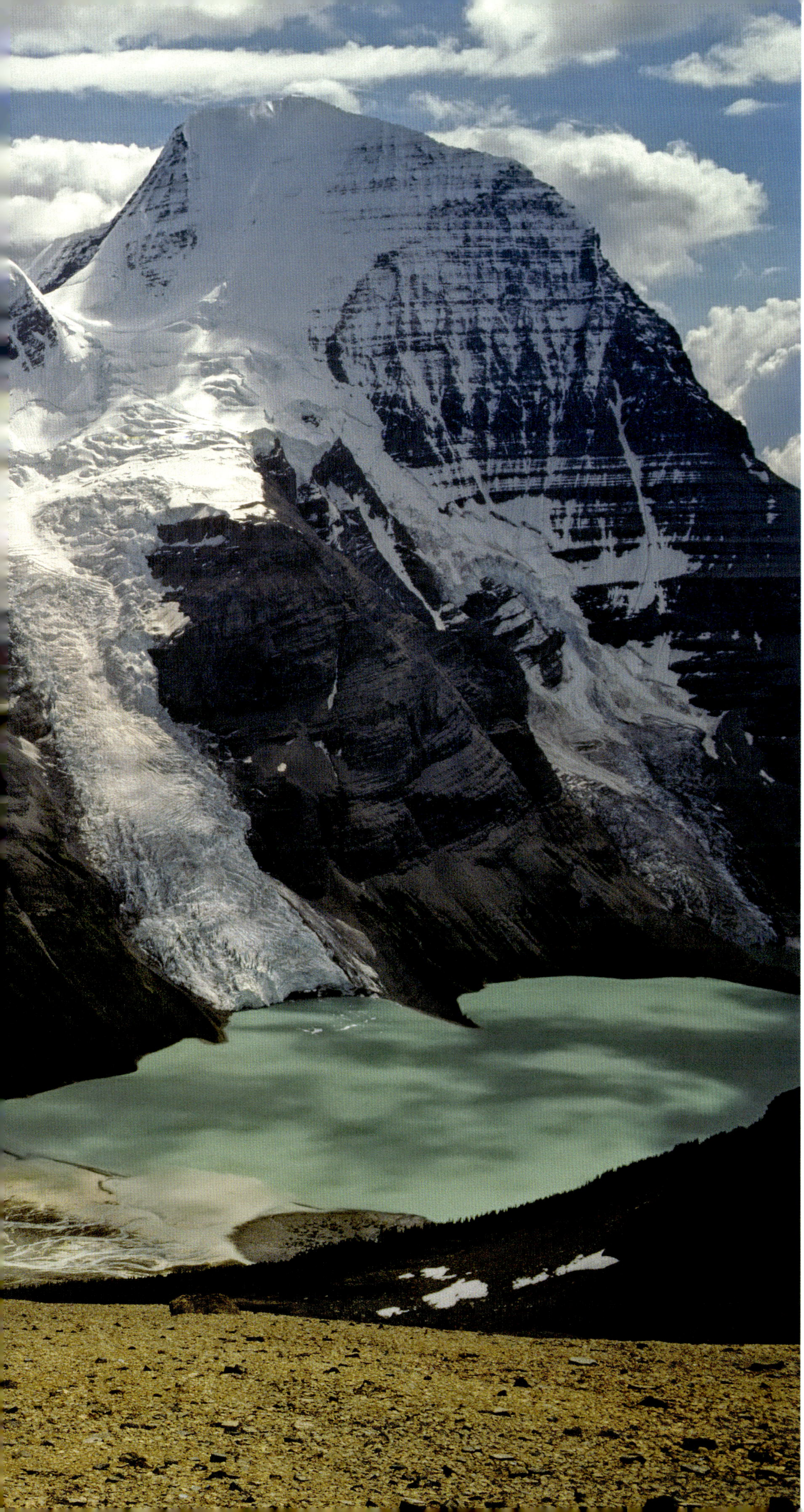

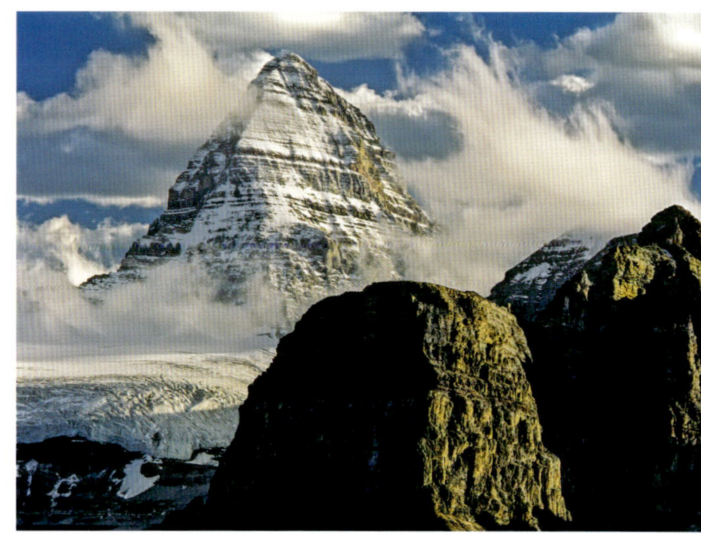

The slopes of Mumm Peak offer a tremendous view
of Berg Lake and Mount Robson, the highest and
greatest peak in the Canadian Rockies (left).
Mount Assiniboine is the highest summit in
the southern Rockies.

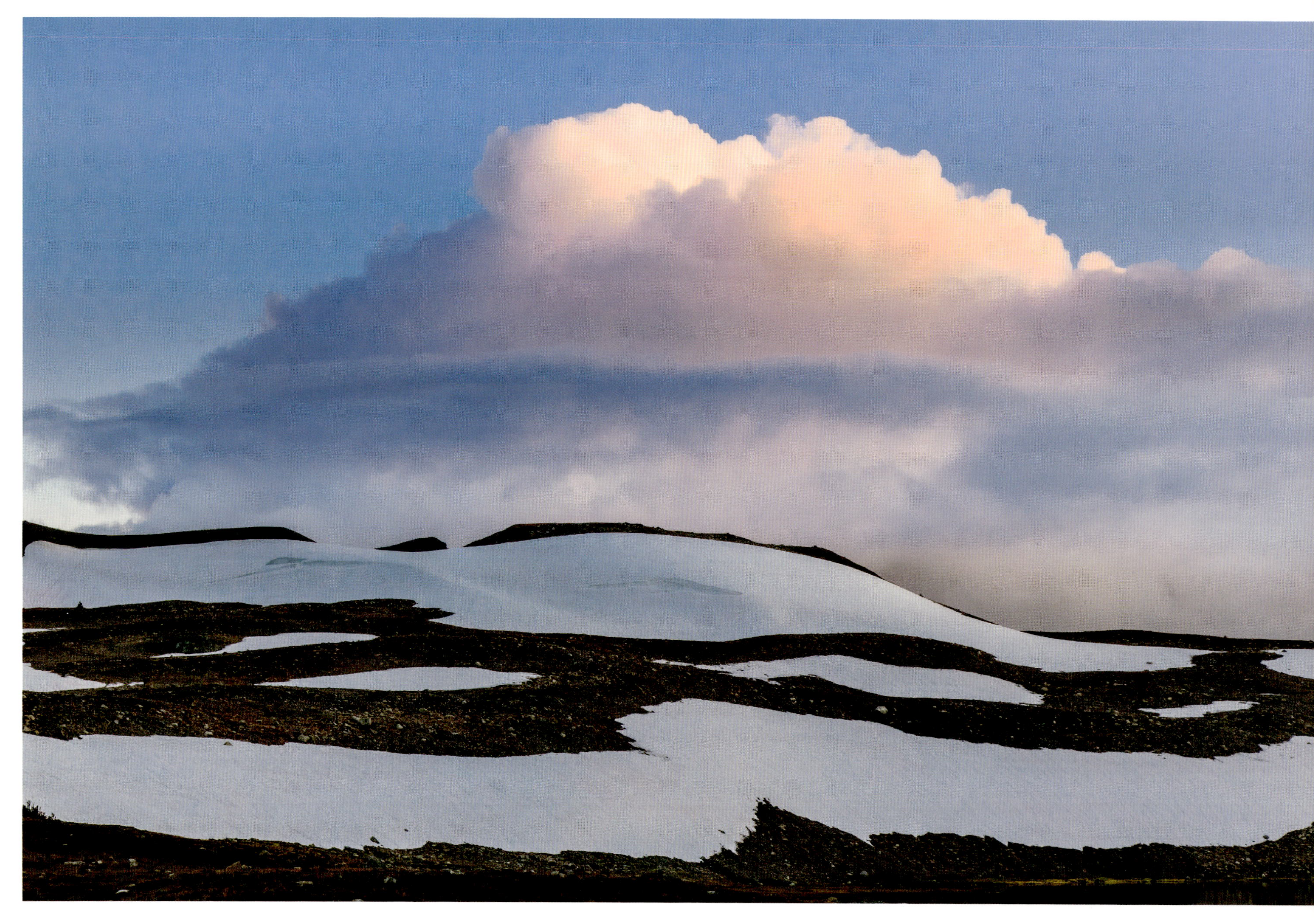

Lingering snowpack above Russet Lake (above)
and on the upper slopes of The Black Tusk
(with the Tantalus Range in the distance), both
in Garibaldi Provincial Park, British Columbia.

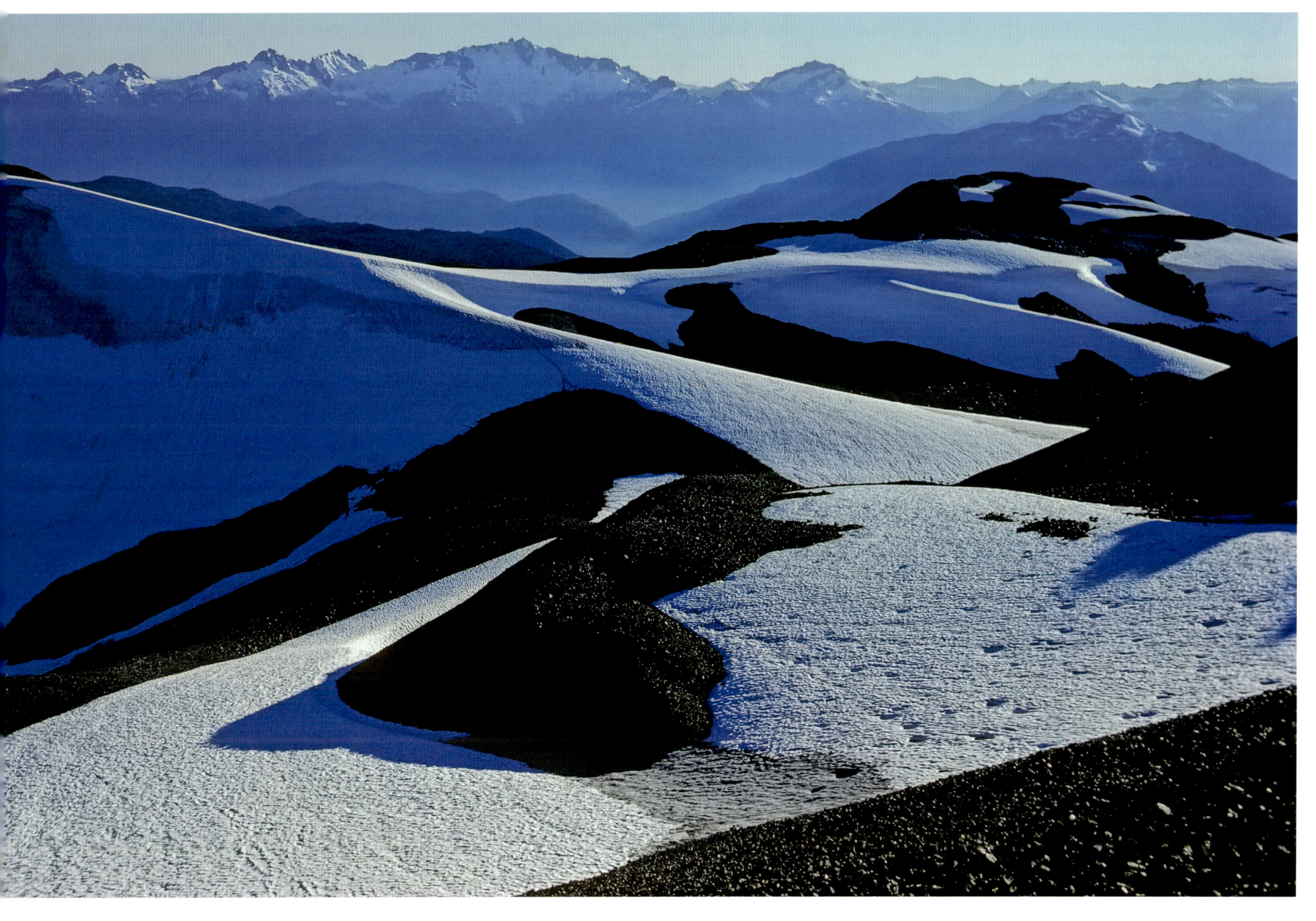

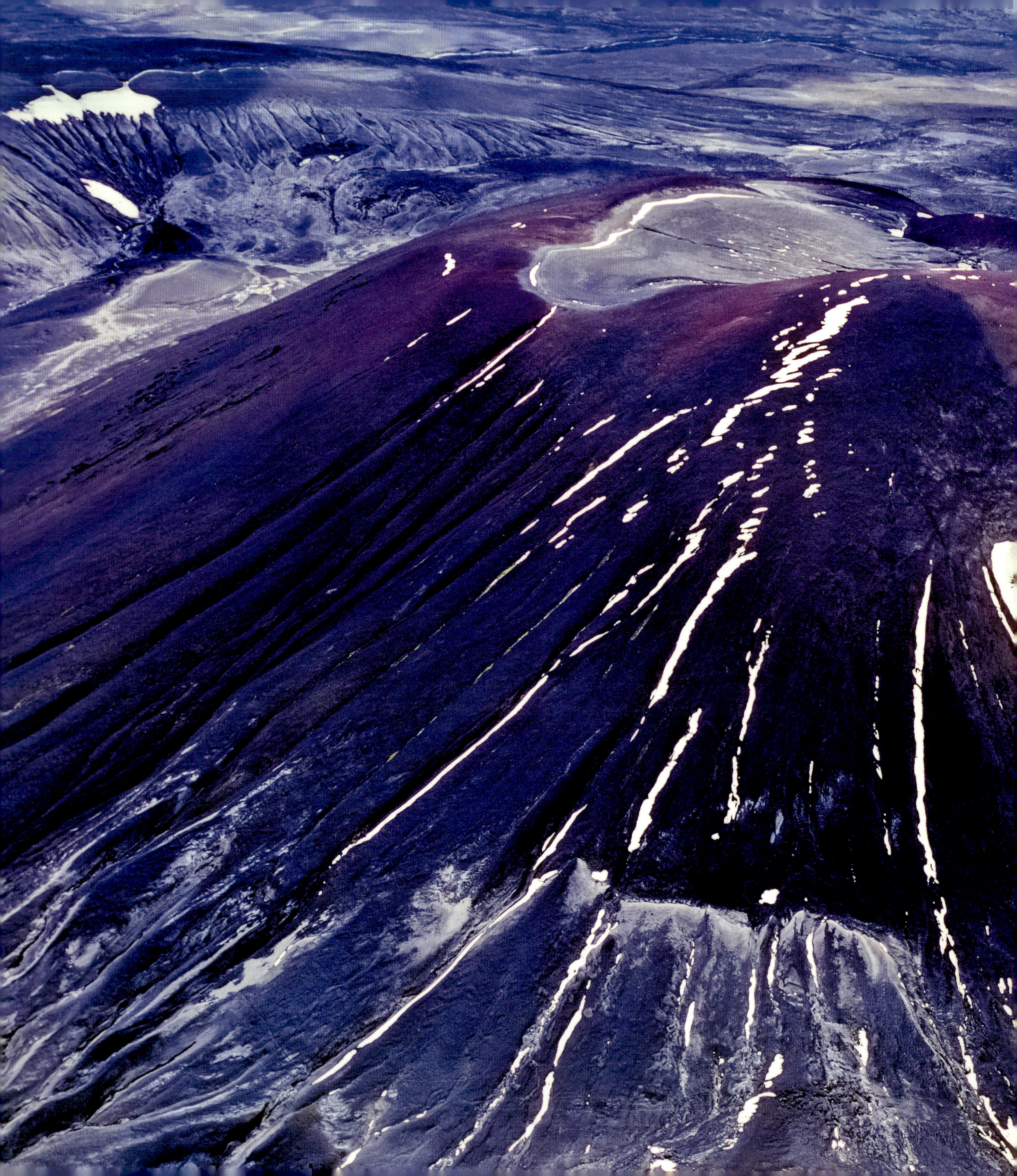

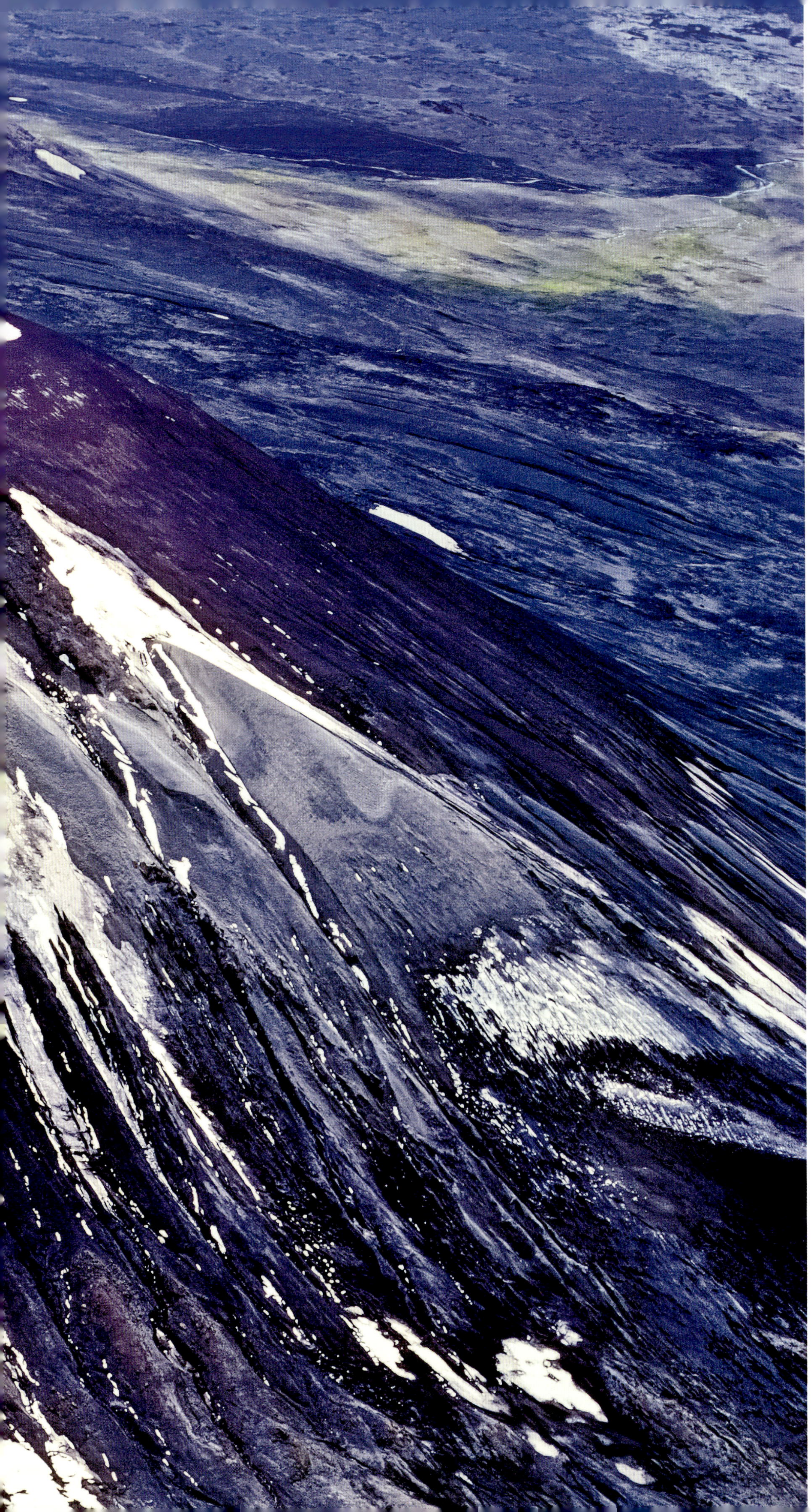

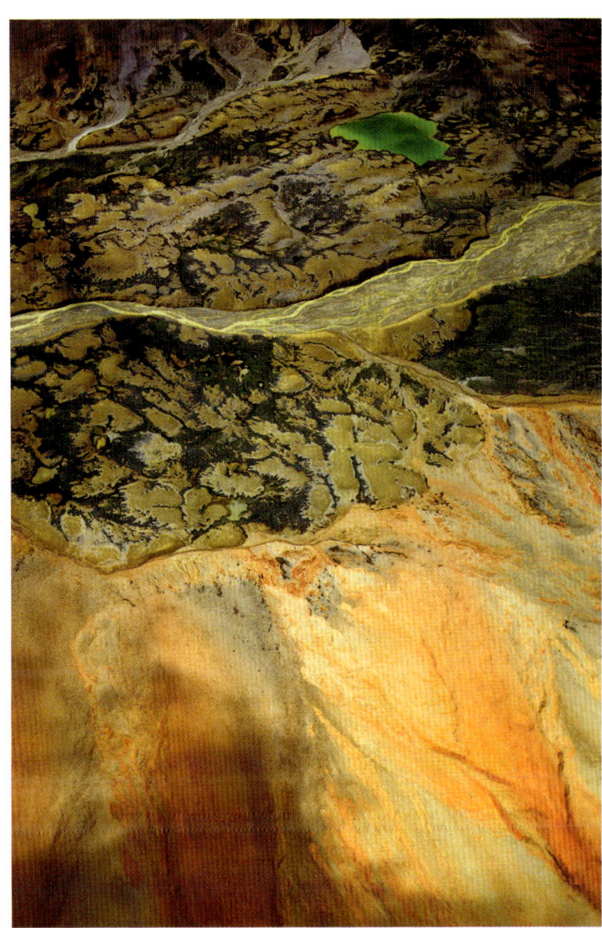

Aerial views of a cinder cone on Big Raven Plateau (left) and of the headwaters of Ball Creek in the Spectrum Range, where heavy mineralization has coloured the rocky slopes, ponds and streams. Both in Mount Edziza Provincial Park, British Columbia.

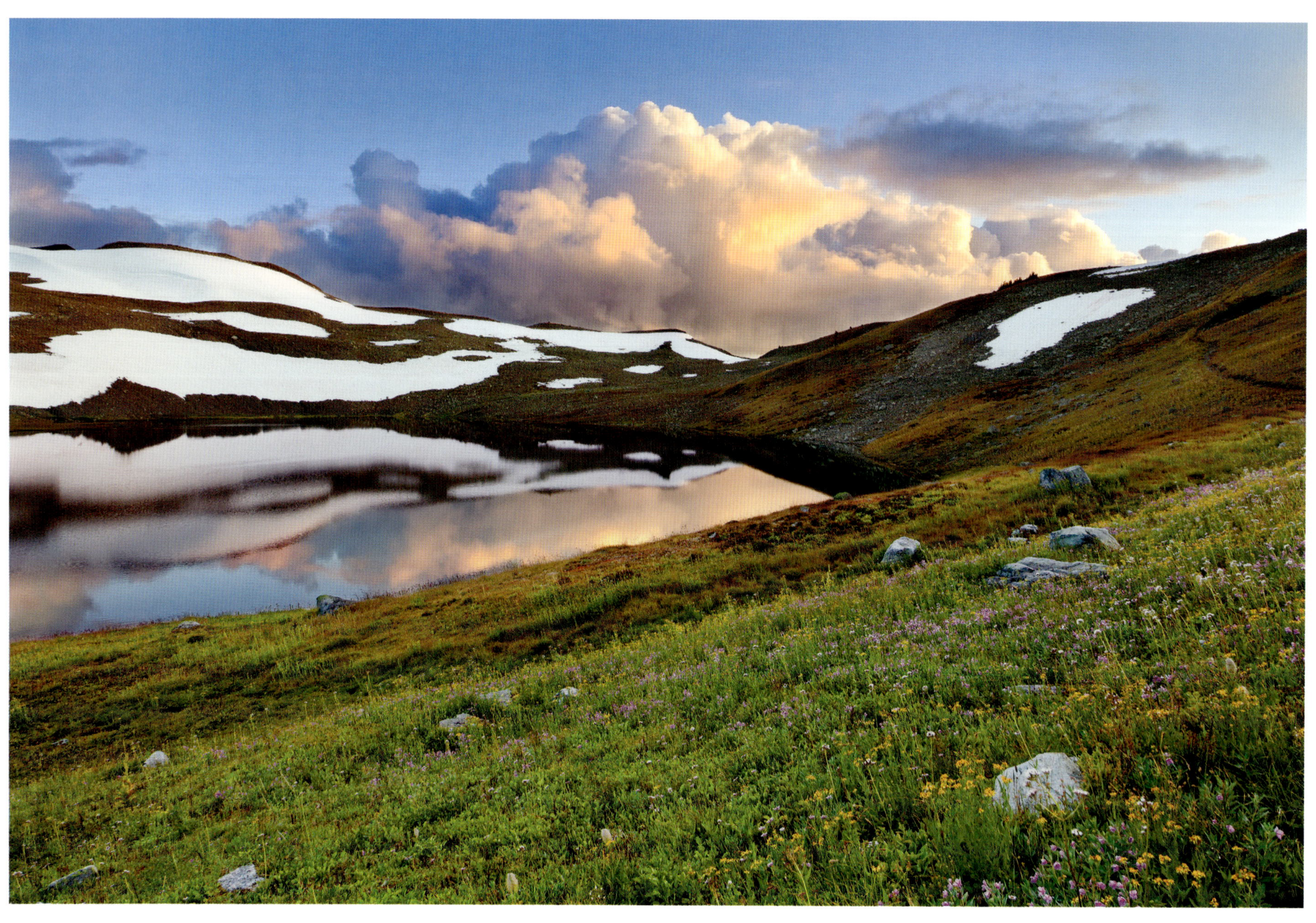

Summer is short in high alpine regions.
Wildflowers in bloom on Labour Day at Russet
Lake in Garibaldi Provincial Park (above), and in
August on the summit slope of Idaho Peak above
New Denver, British Columbia.

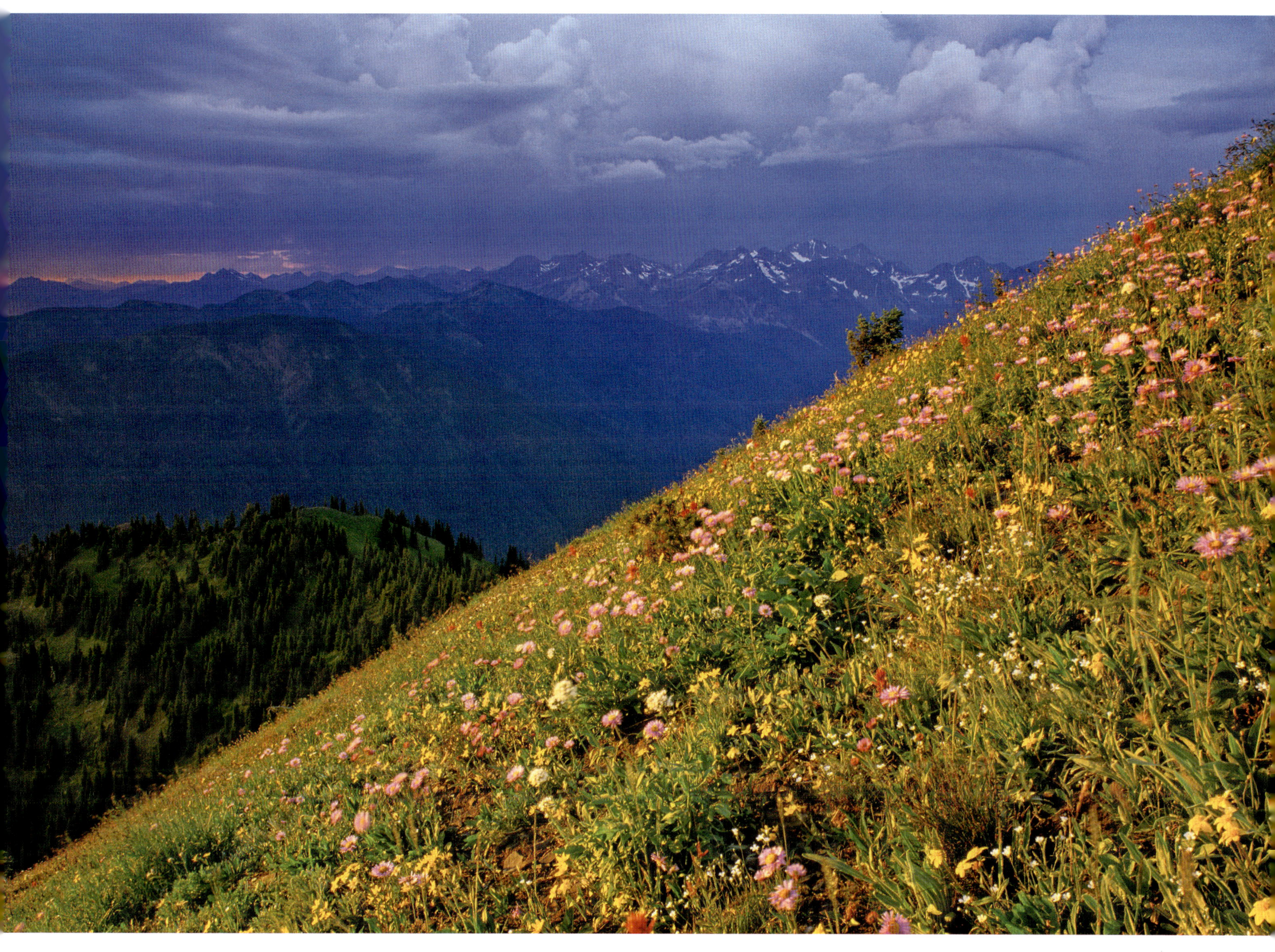

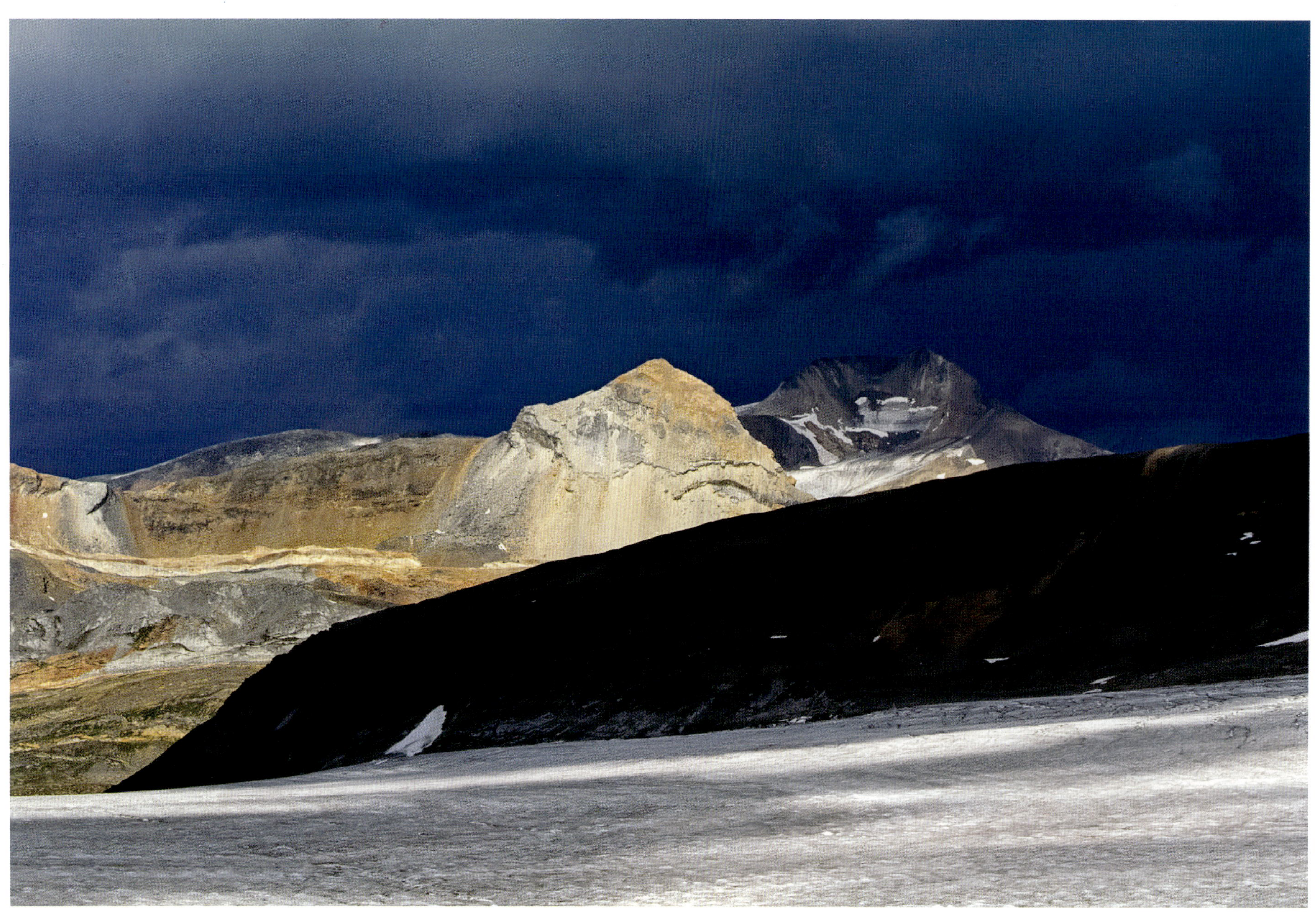

The view from Snowbird Pass, Mount Robson
Provincial Park, looks across the Reef Icefield In
Jasper National Park and towards peaks on the
Continental Divide, the boundary between Alberta
and British Columbia.

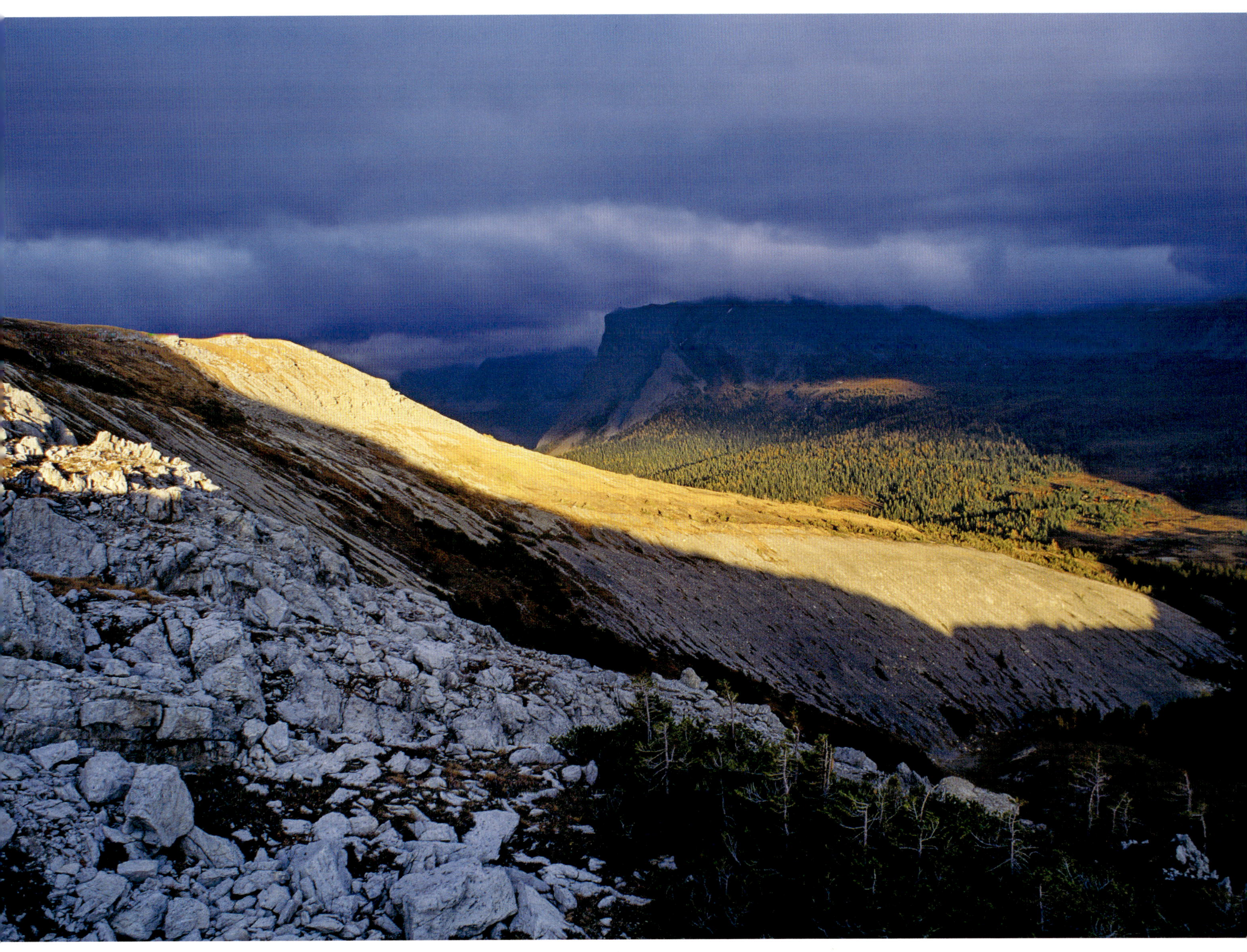

A slice of light on the ridge of Nub Peak in Mount
Assiniboine Provincial Park, looking towards
Assiniboine Pass and mountains in Banff National
Park in the distance.

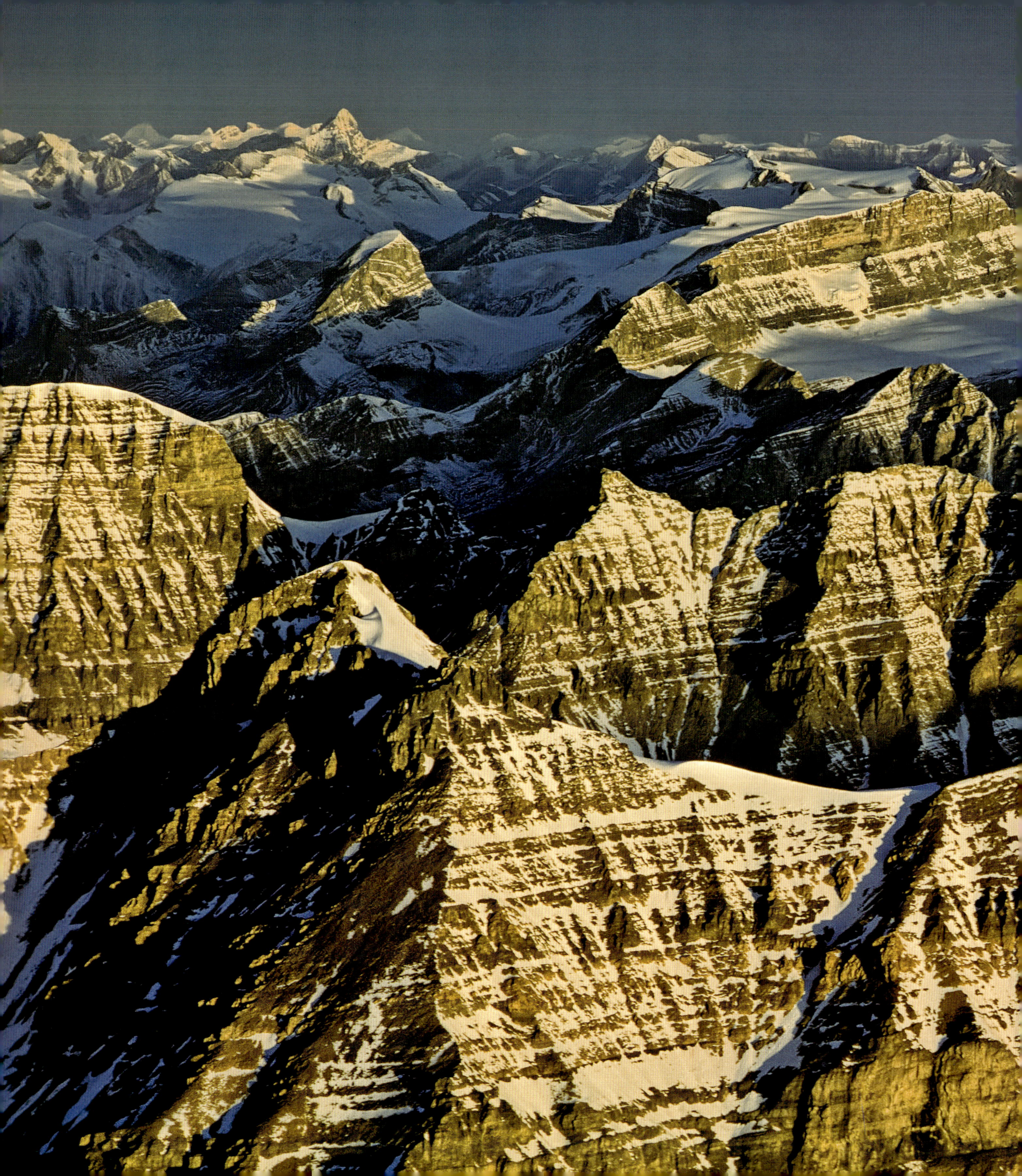

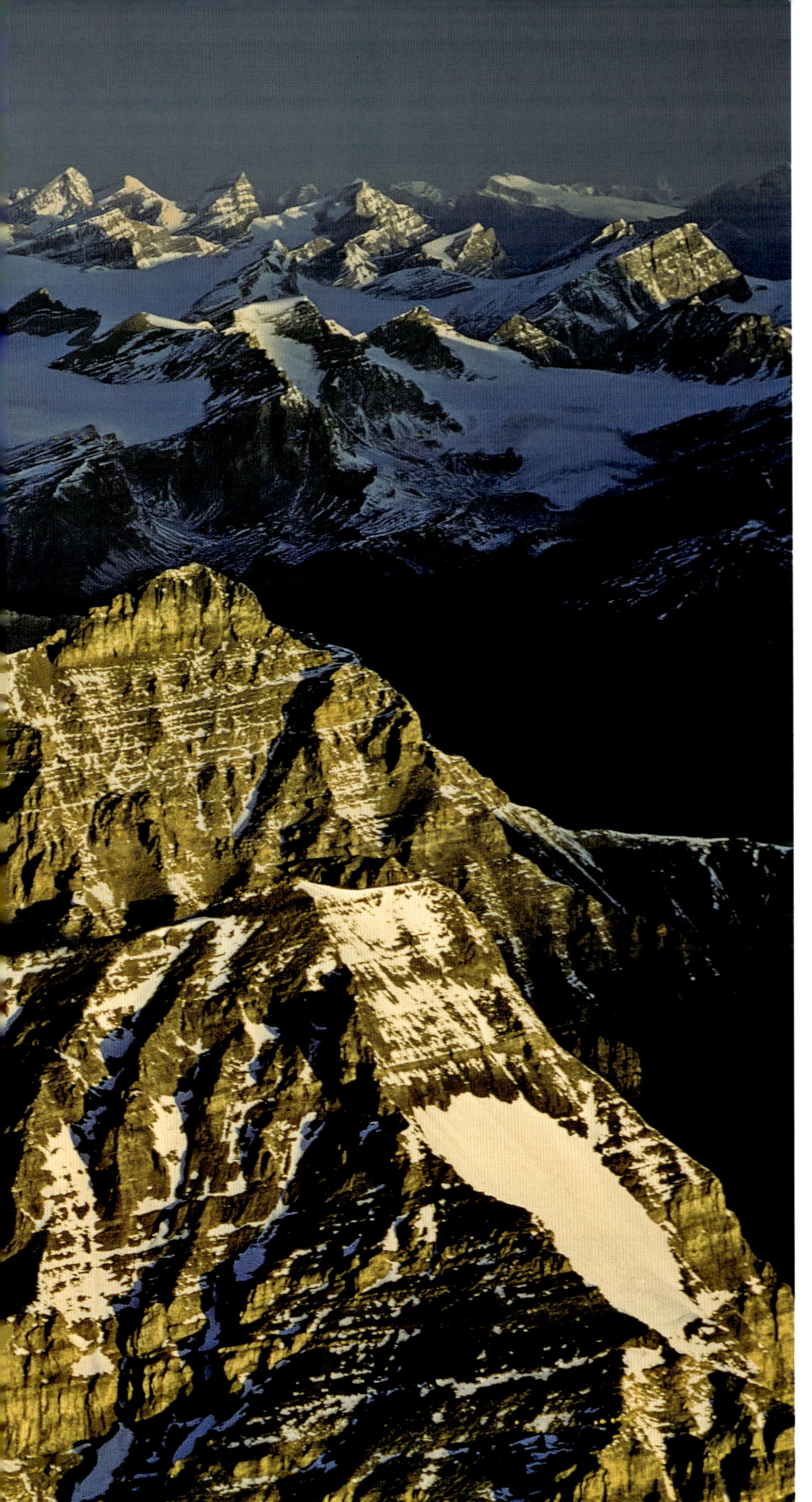

A small portion of the staggering summit view at
sunrise from Mount Temple, the highest mountain
in the Lake Louise vicinity, Banff National Park,
Alberta.

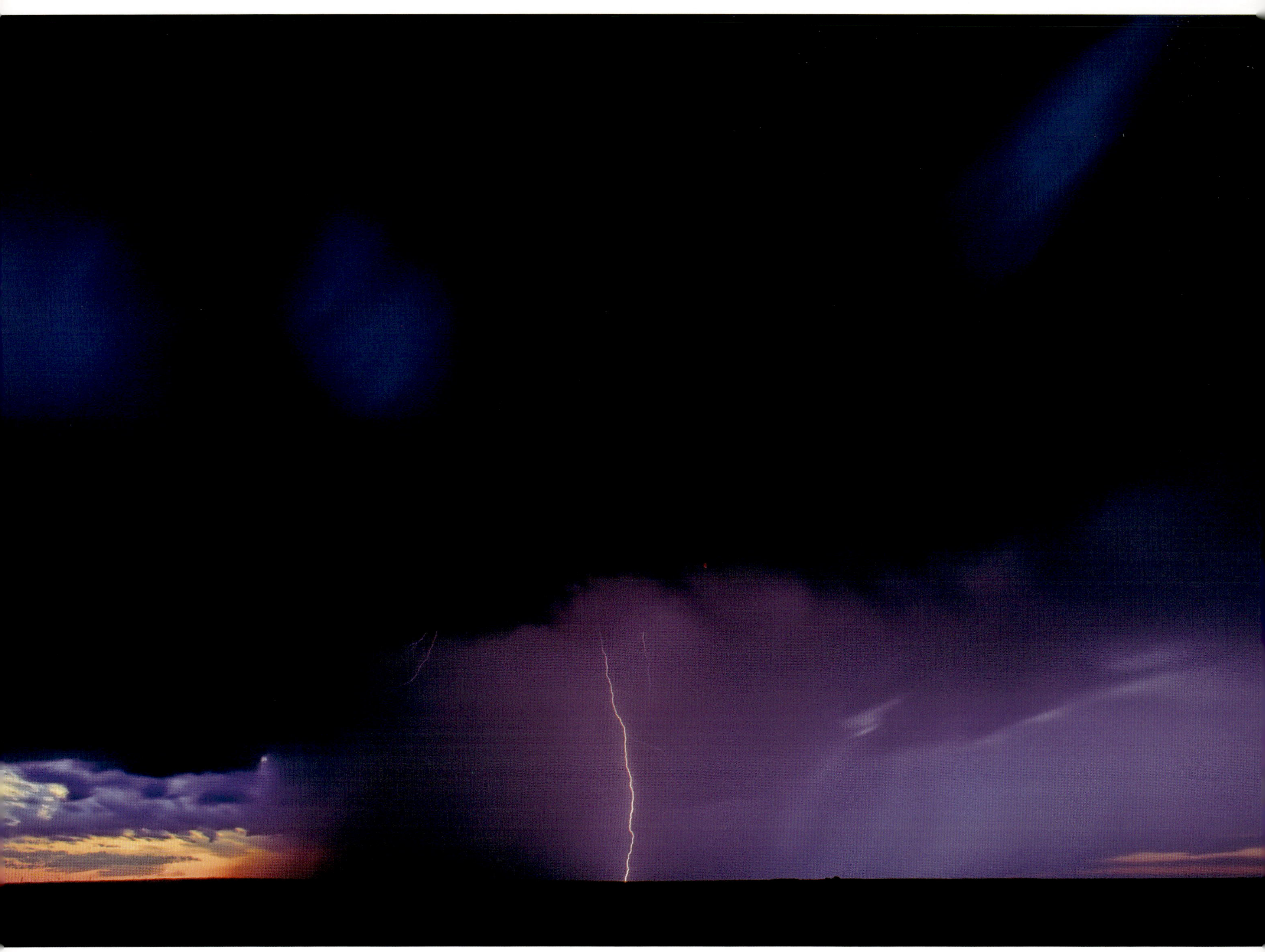

Lightning strikes within a violent cloudburst near
Youngstown, Alberta.

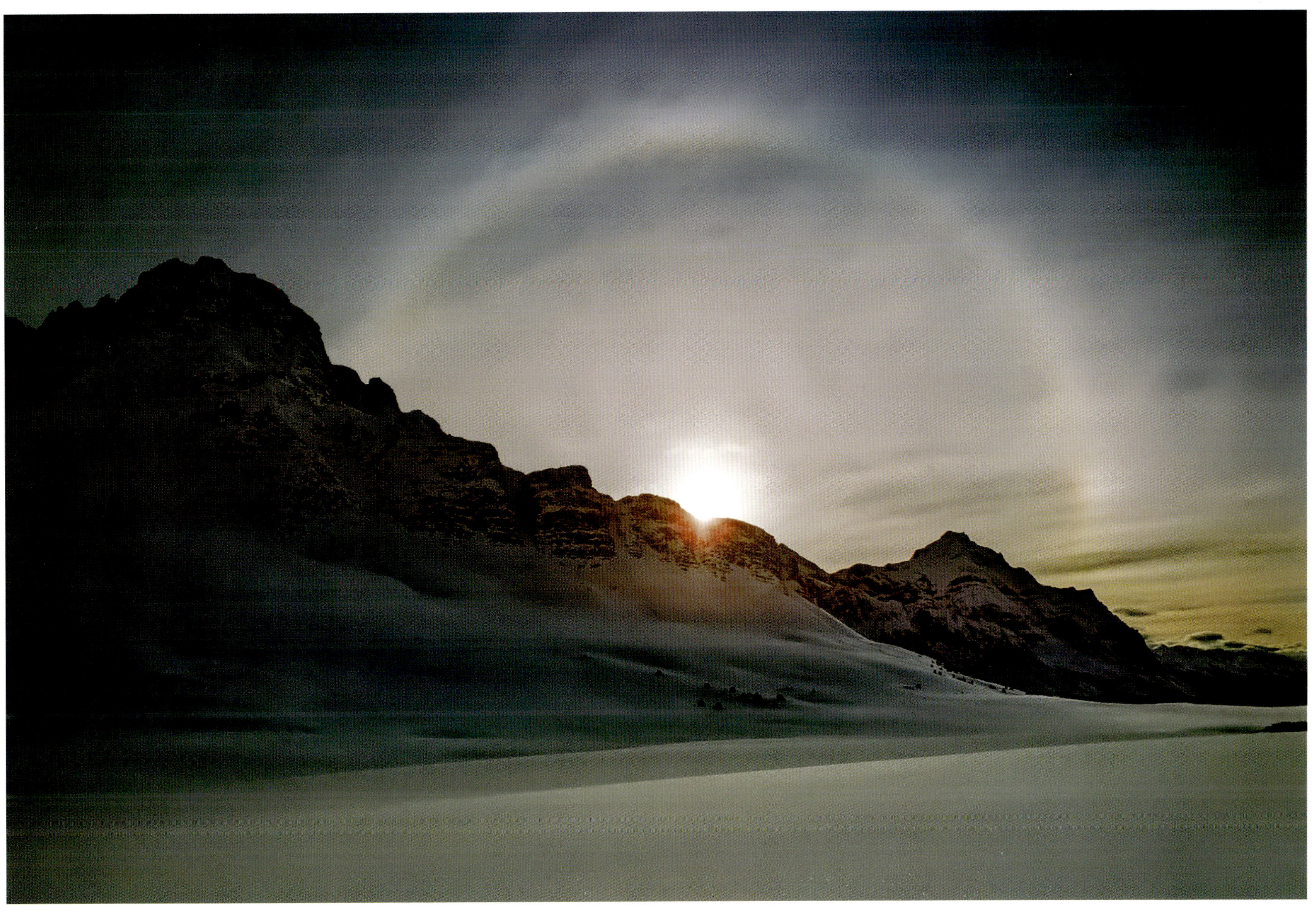

The refraction of sunlight through ice crystals in the
air causes a 22-degree halo at Jonas Pass in Jasper
National Park.

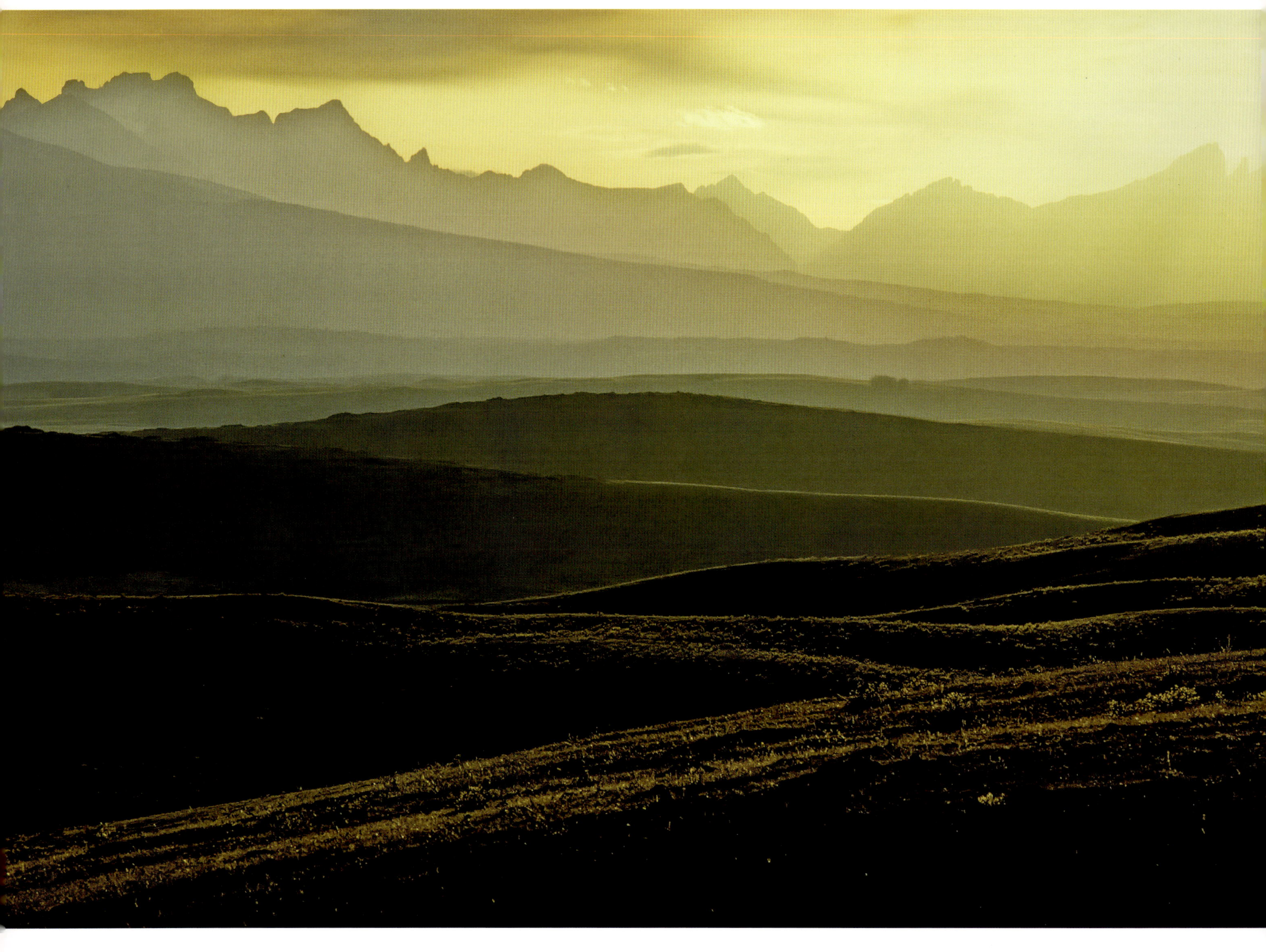

South of Cardston, Alberta, the ridges of the Rocky
Mountain Foothills and the peaks of the Rockies
in Waterton Lakes National Park are silhouetted in
the setting sun.

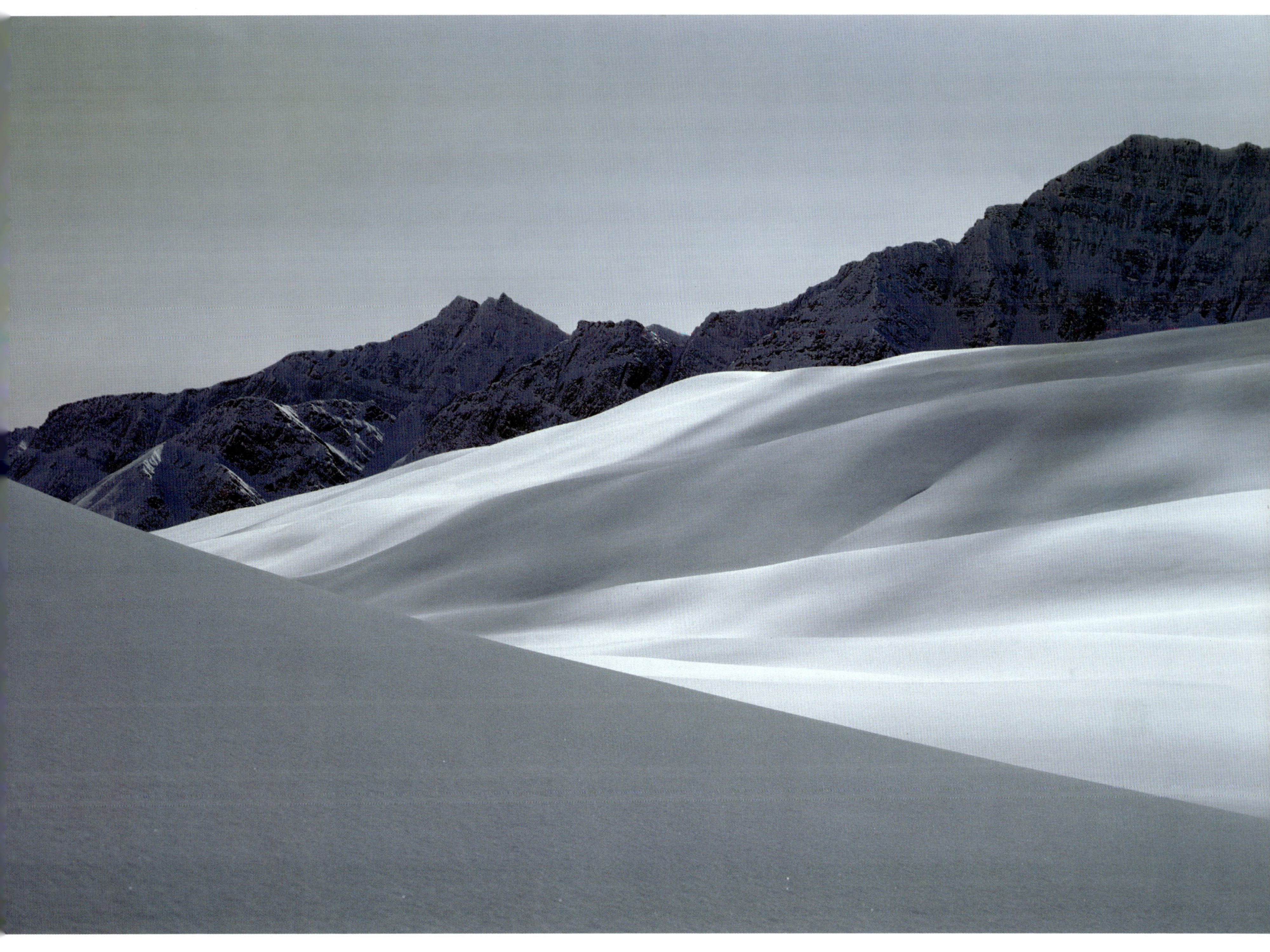

Part of the Endless Chain Ridge, Jasper National Park
from Maligne Pass, still snowbound in May, as is
typical of the alpine elevations.

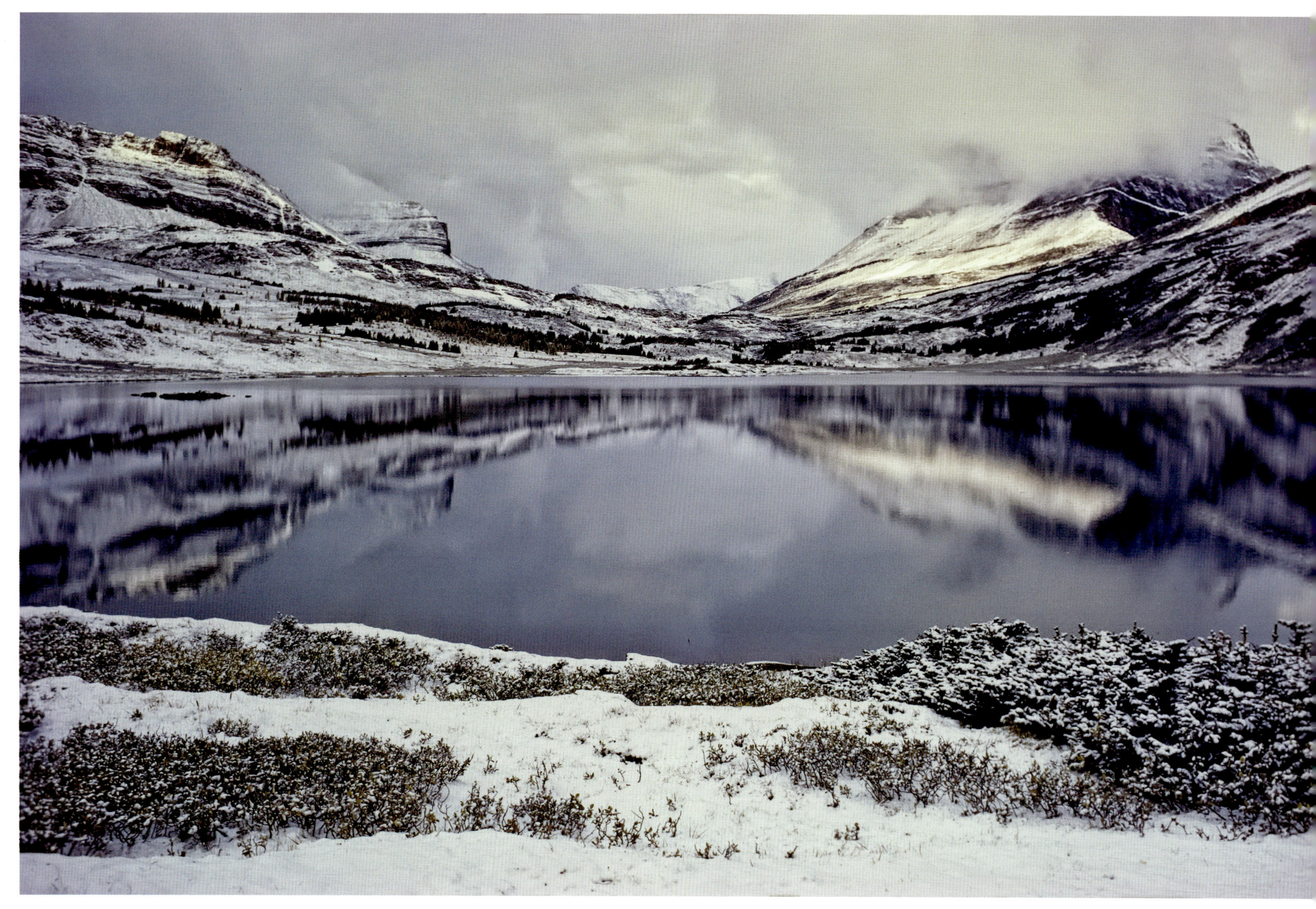

A September snowfall whitens the landscape
around Baker Lake in Banff National Park (above).

The lower of the two Headwall Lakes in the
Kananaskis Range, Peter Lougheed Provincial Park,
Alberta.

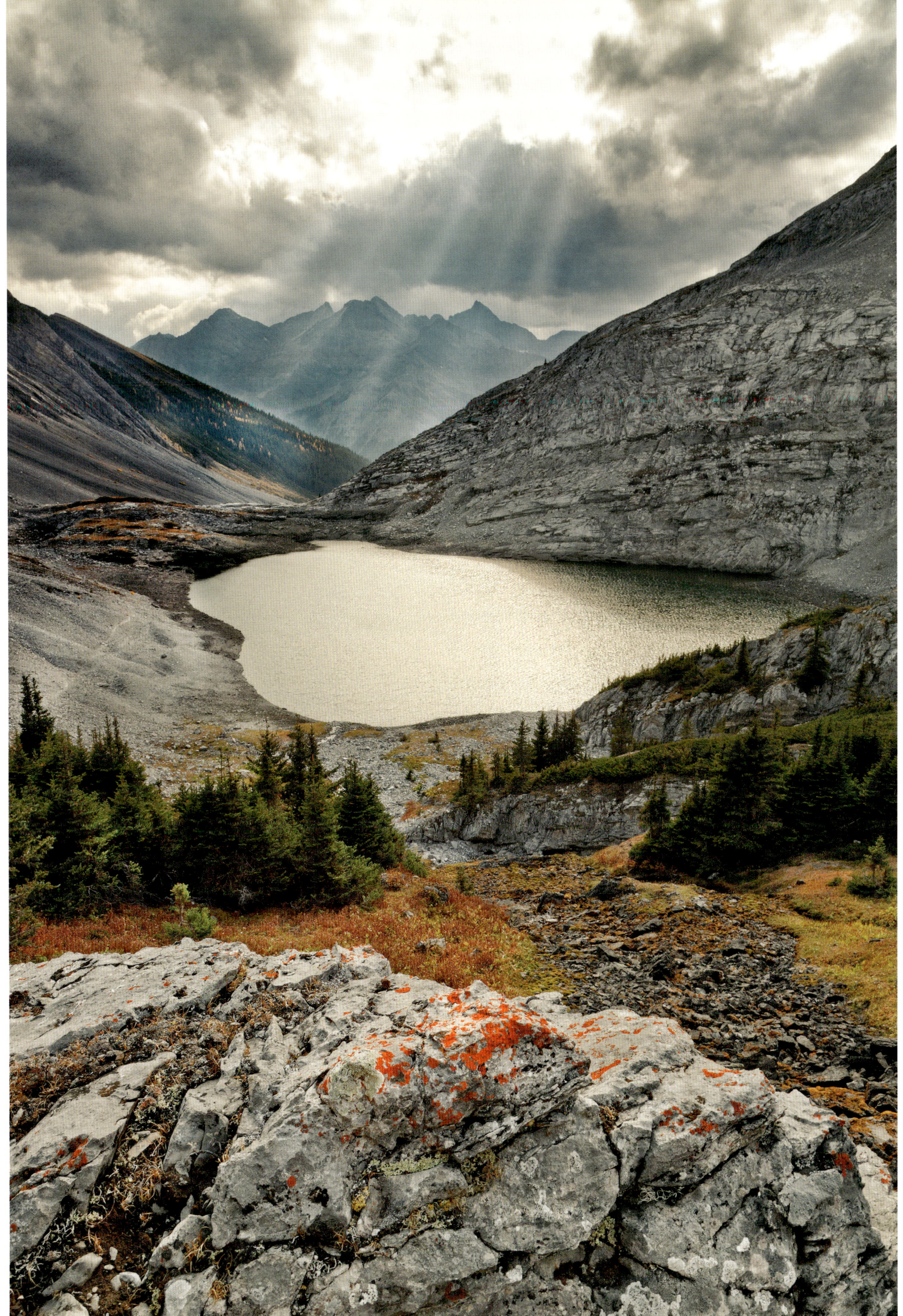

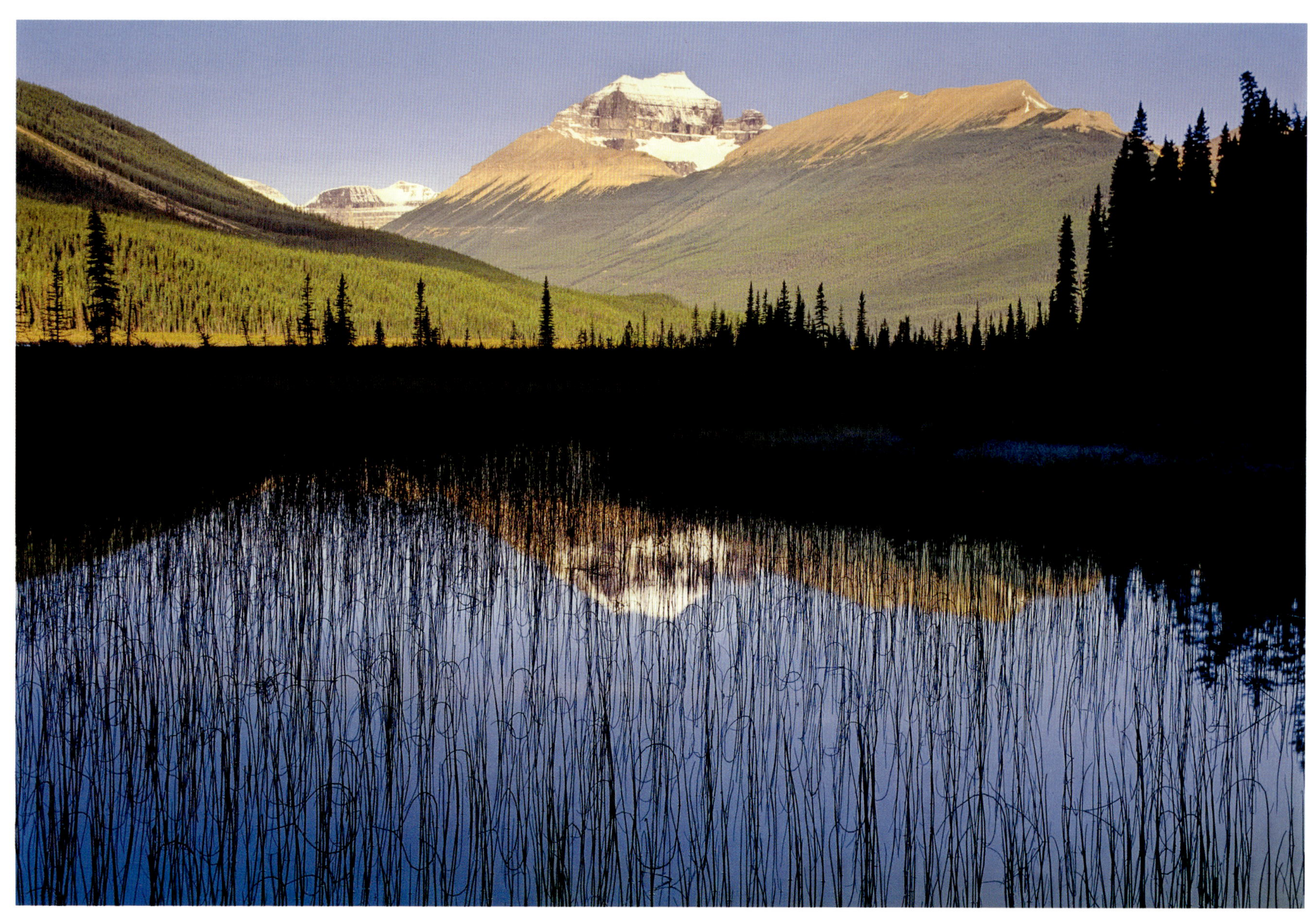

Mount Saskatchewan reflected in a reed-filled
pond in the flats of the North Saskatchewan River,
Banff National Park.

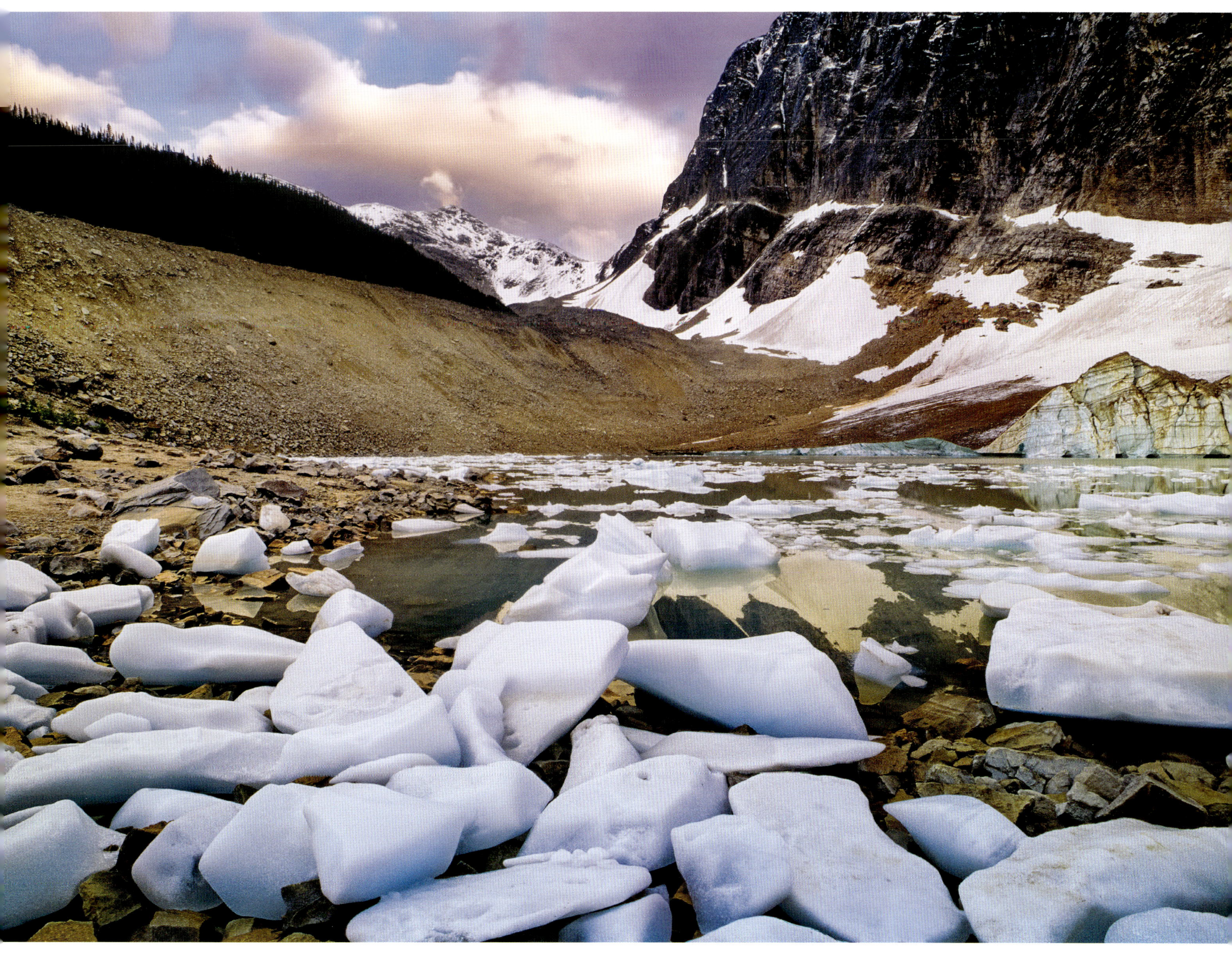

Bergs fill the meltwater pond of the Cavell Glacier
at the base of the north face of Mount Edith Cavell,
Jasper National Park, Alberta.

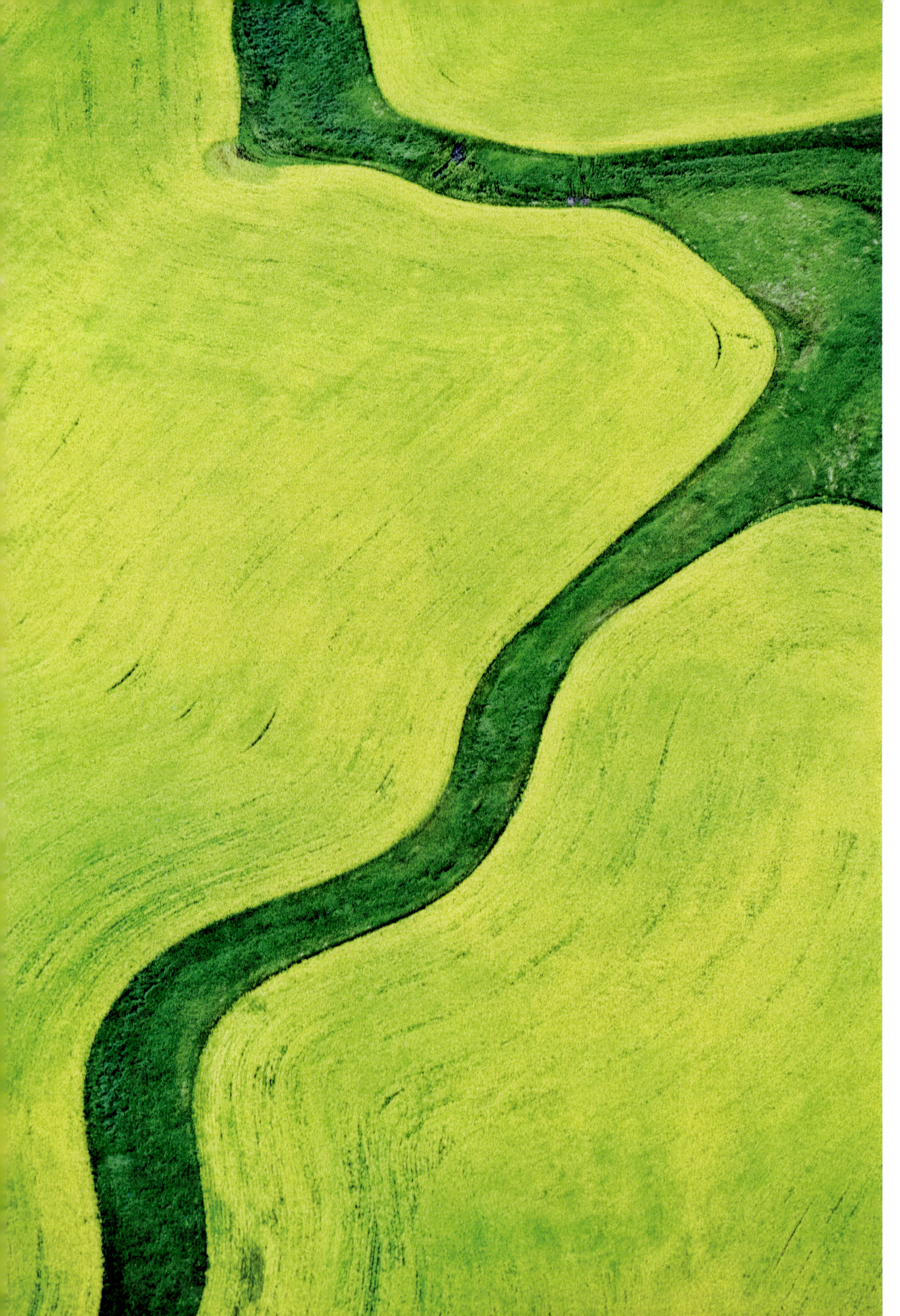

Green with weeds, grasses and bushes, an uncultivated drainage channel snakes through a field of canola in bloom, seen from the air southeast of Edmonton (left). The North Saskatchewan River cuts through hillsides yellow with aspen in the fall, east of Banff National Park, Alberta.

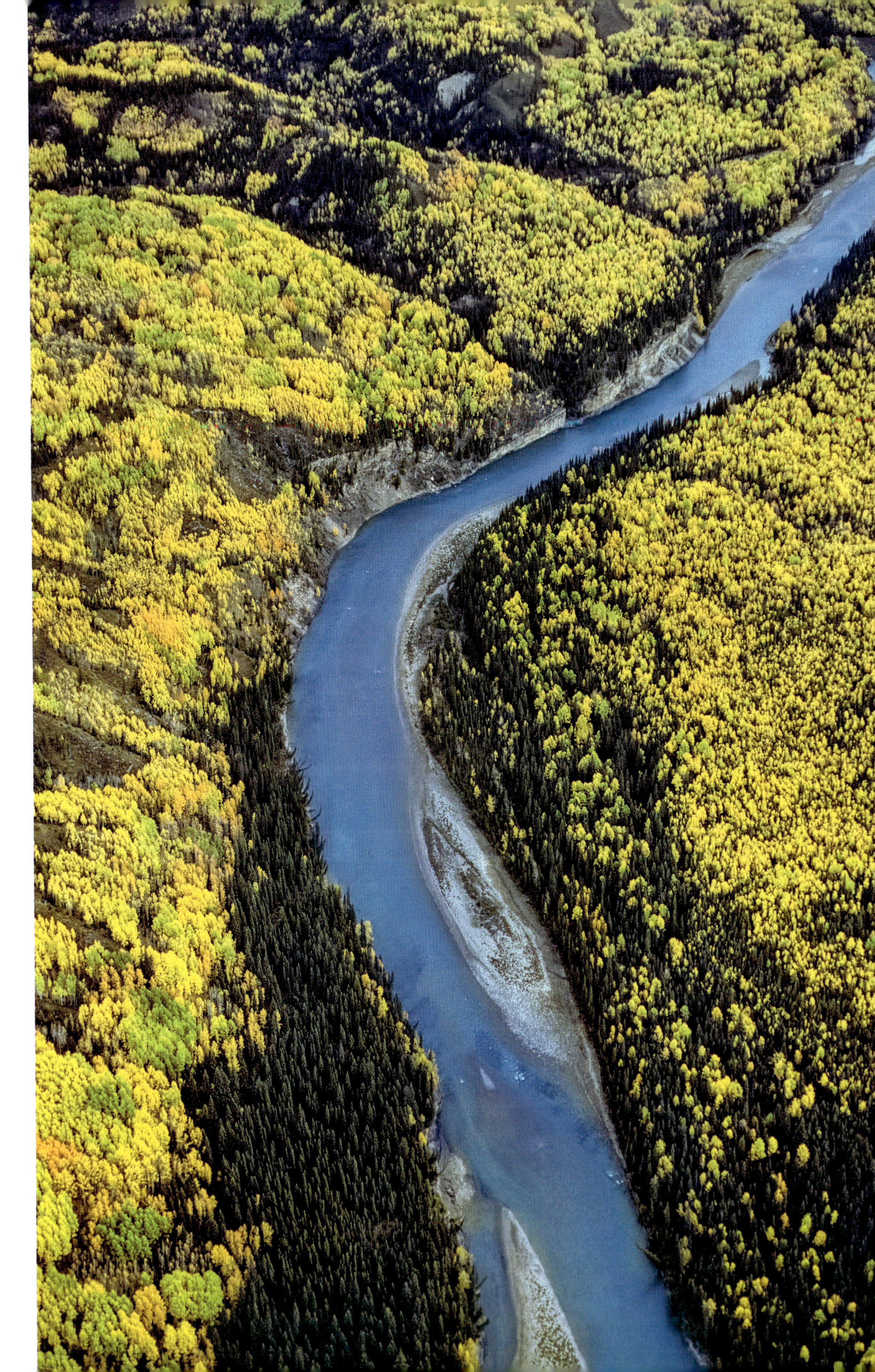

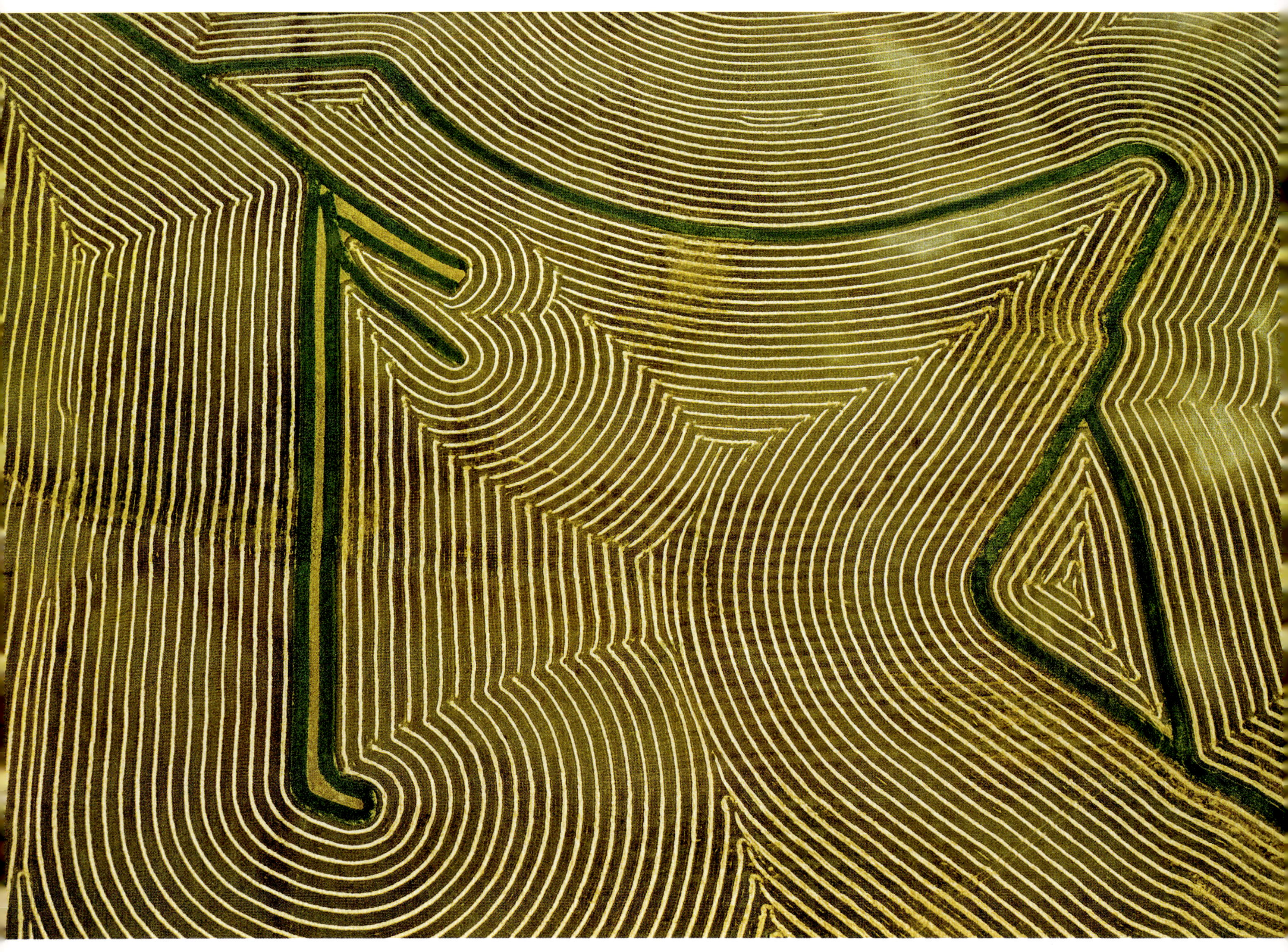

Near Drumheller, Alberta, untilled and unplanted
drainage channels have forced the reaping of
a wheat field into a pattern of swaths that is
optically mesmerizing when seen from above.

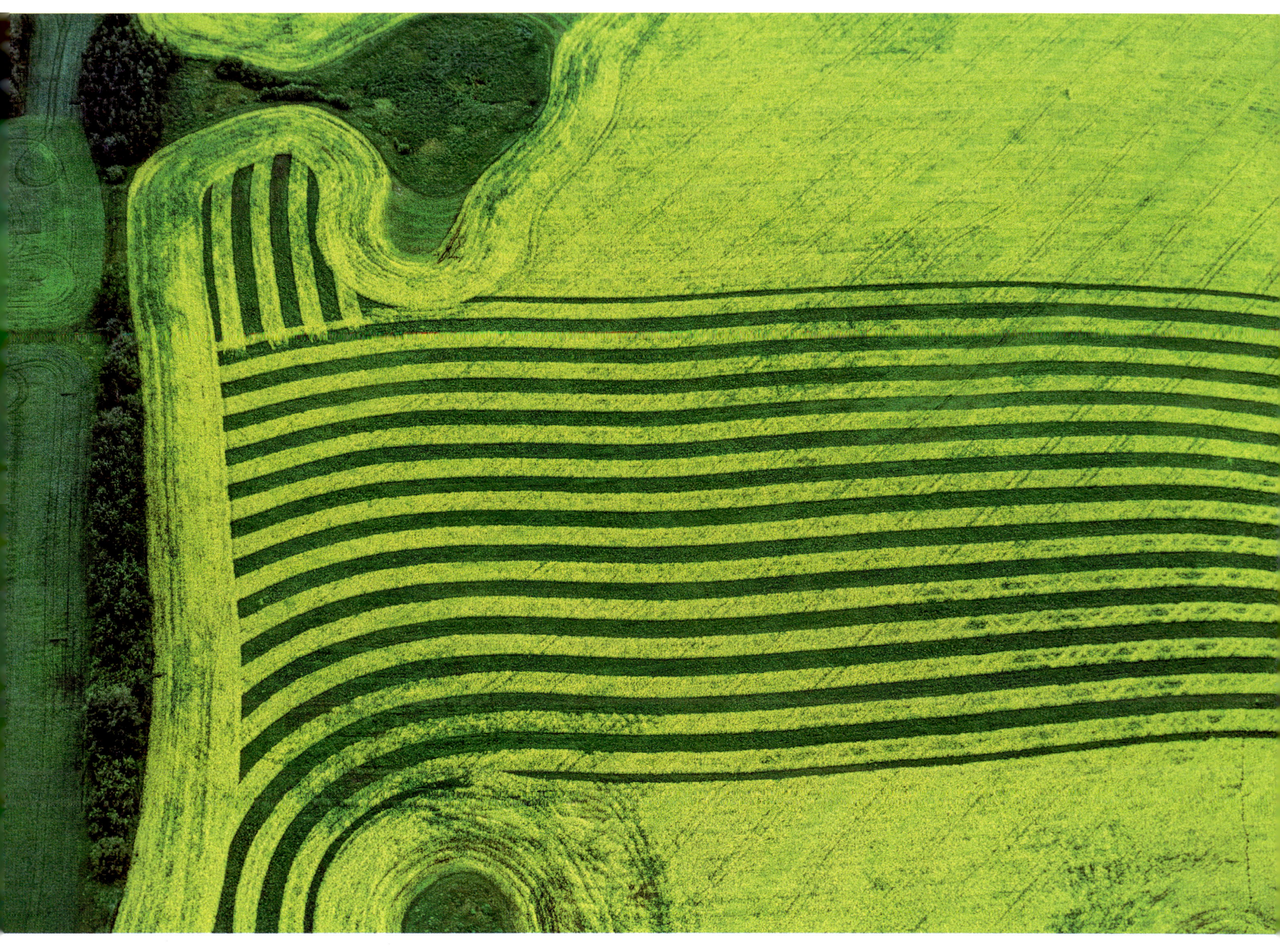

South of Edmonton, one half of a blocked tandem seed drill rig was blocked when this field of canola was planted, yielding alternate strips of weeds among the crop.

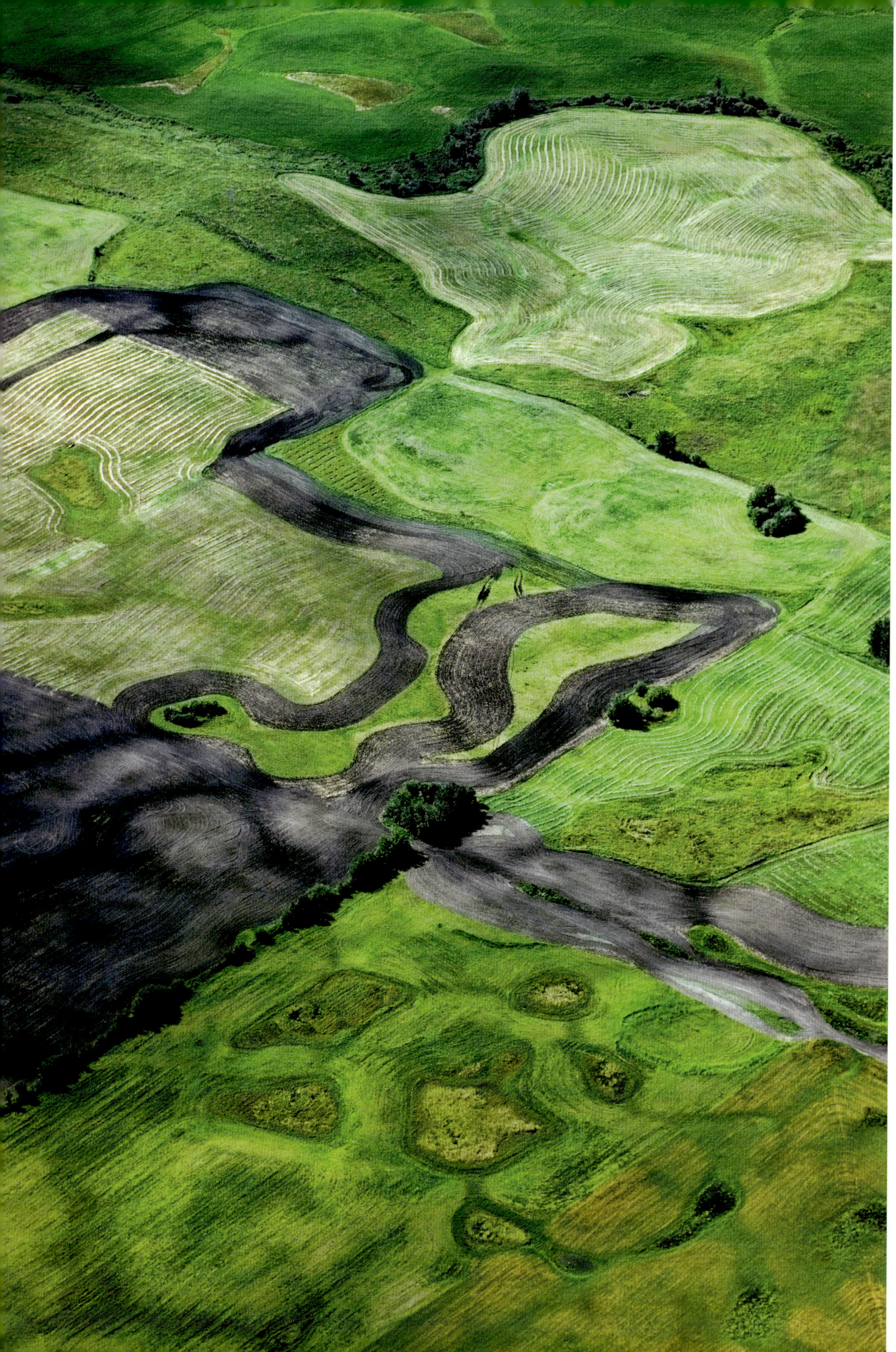

Aerial views of the Prairies supply an endle
variety of patterns. Plots in various stages
of planting, harvesting and tilling in rollin
prairie (left) and looping vehicle tracks acr
a field in summer fallow, both in Alberta.

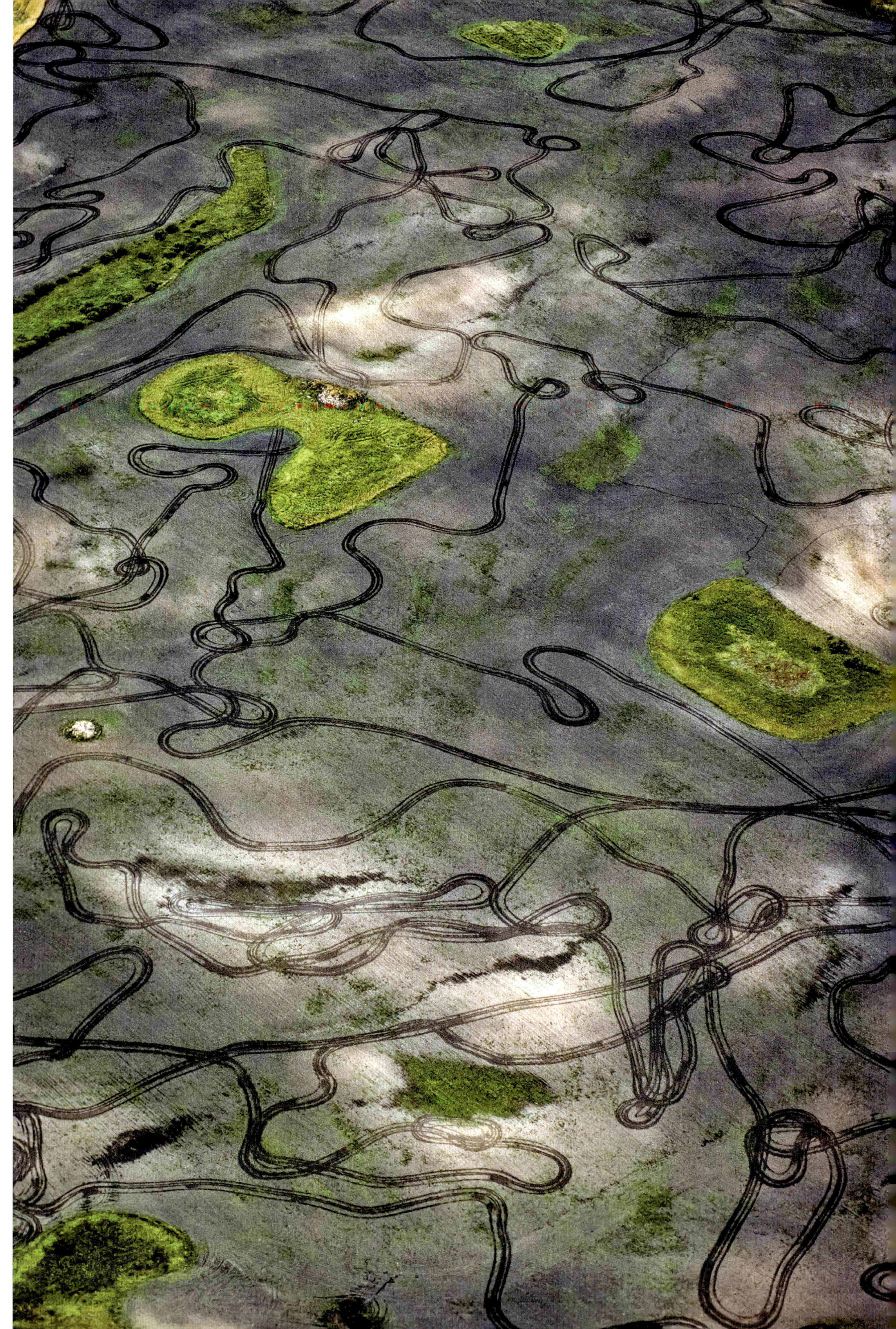

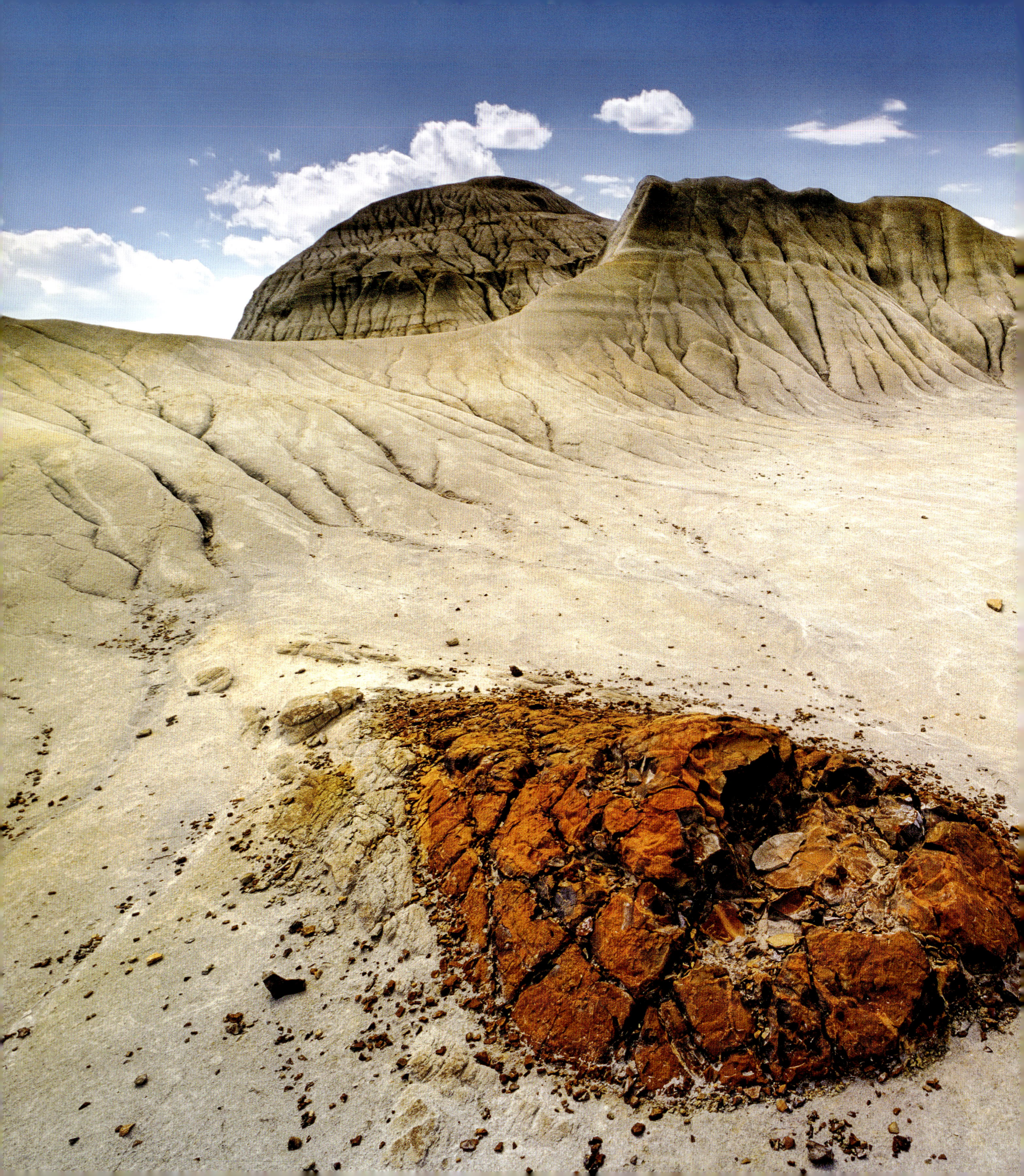

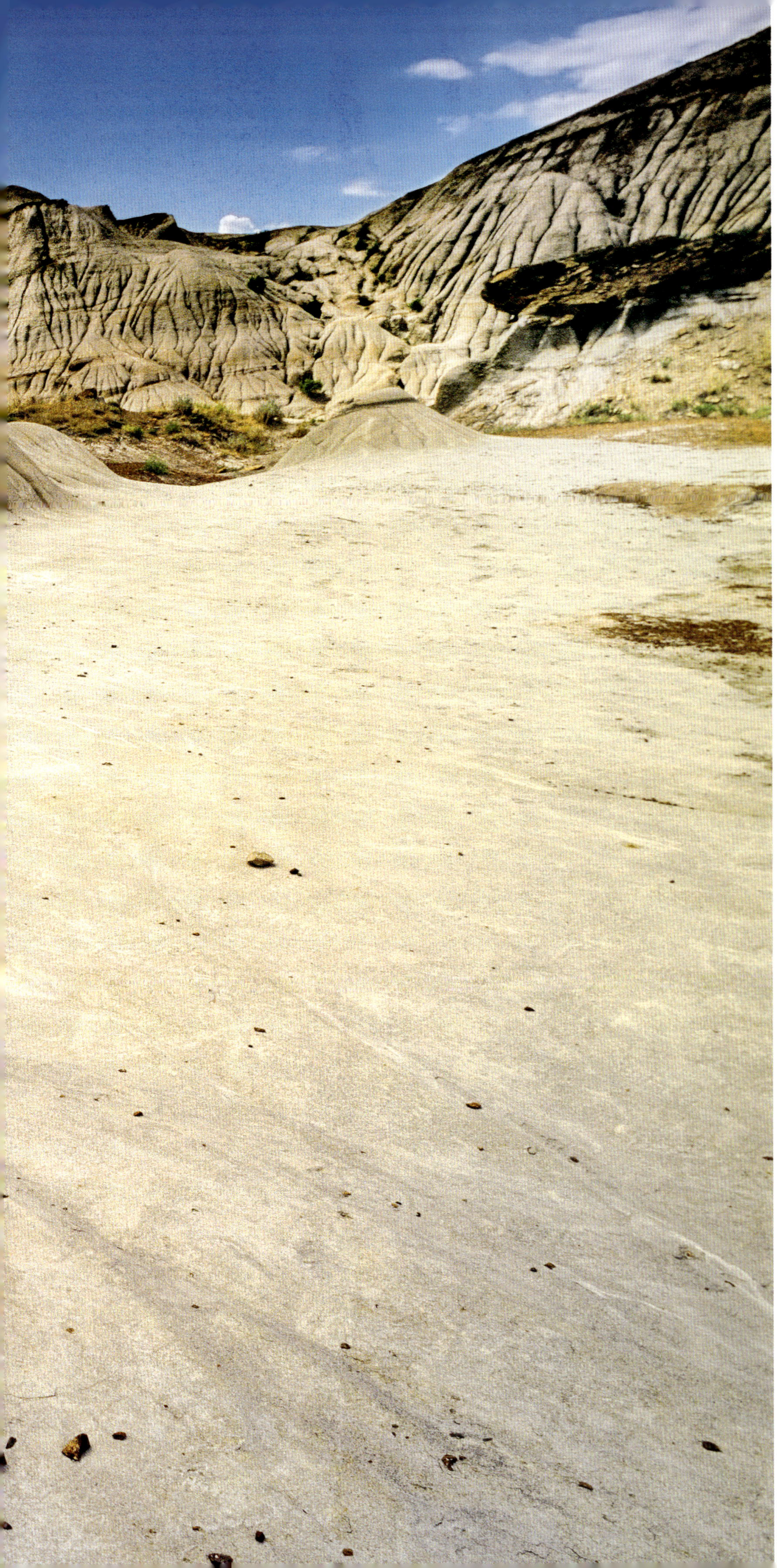

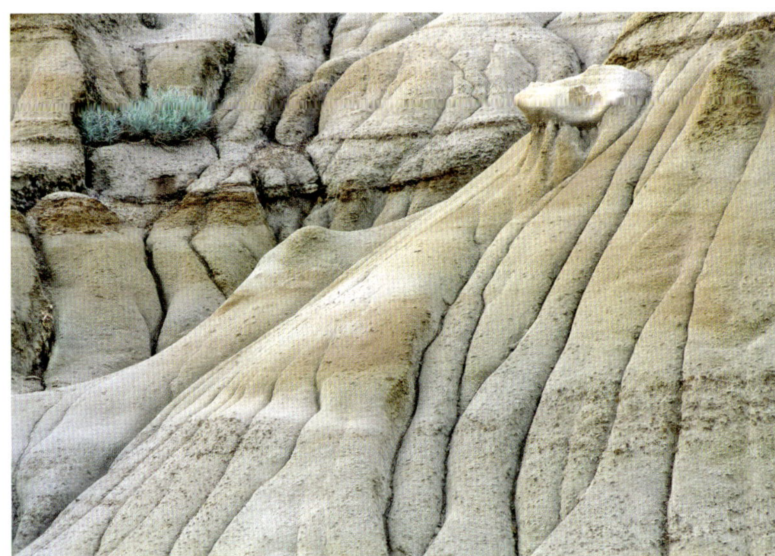

Not a fossil, a rock outcrop exposed in Dinosaur Provincial Park, Alberta, is suggestive of the carapace of some prehistoric creature in a landscape world-renown for its fossils (left). Badlands at the Hoodoos south of Drumheller, Alberta.

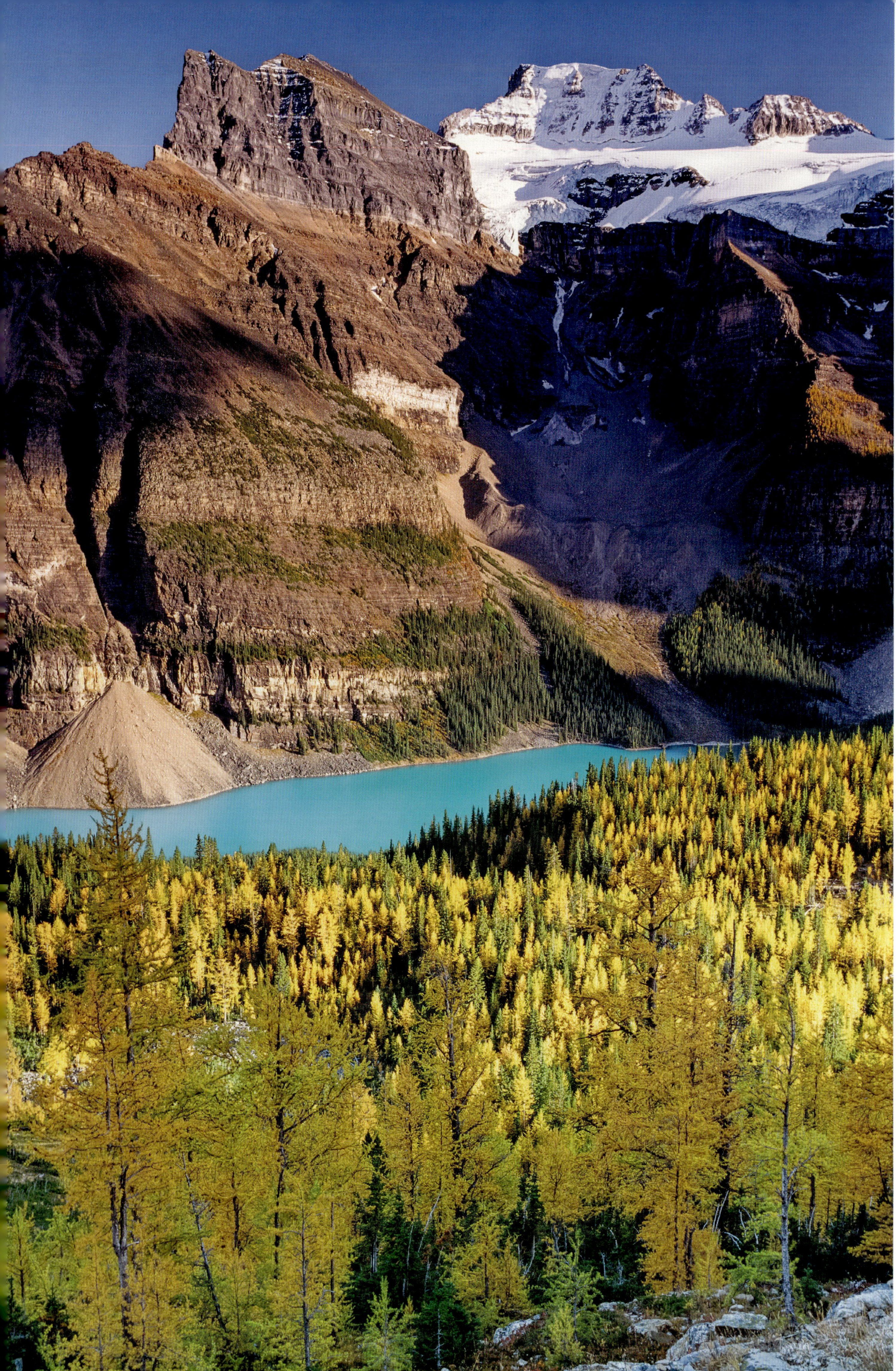

Mount Fay, Moraine Lake and alpine larch at peak fall colour from Larch Valley, Banff National Park (left). A patch of bearberry vivid in autumn with the Athabasca Glacier at the Columbia Icefields, Jasper National Park, Alberta.

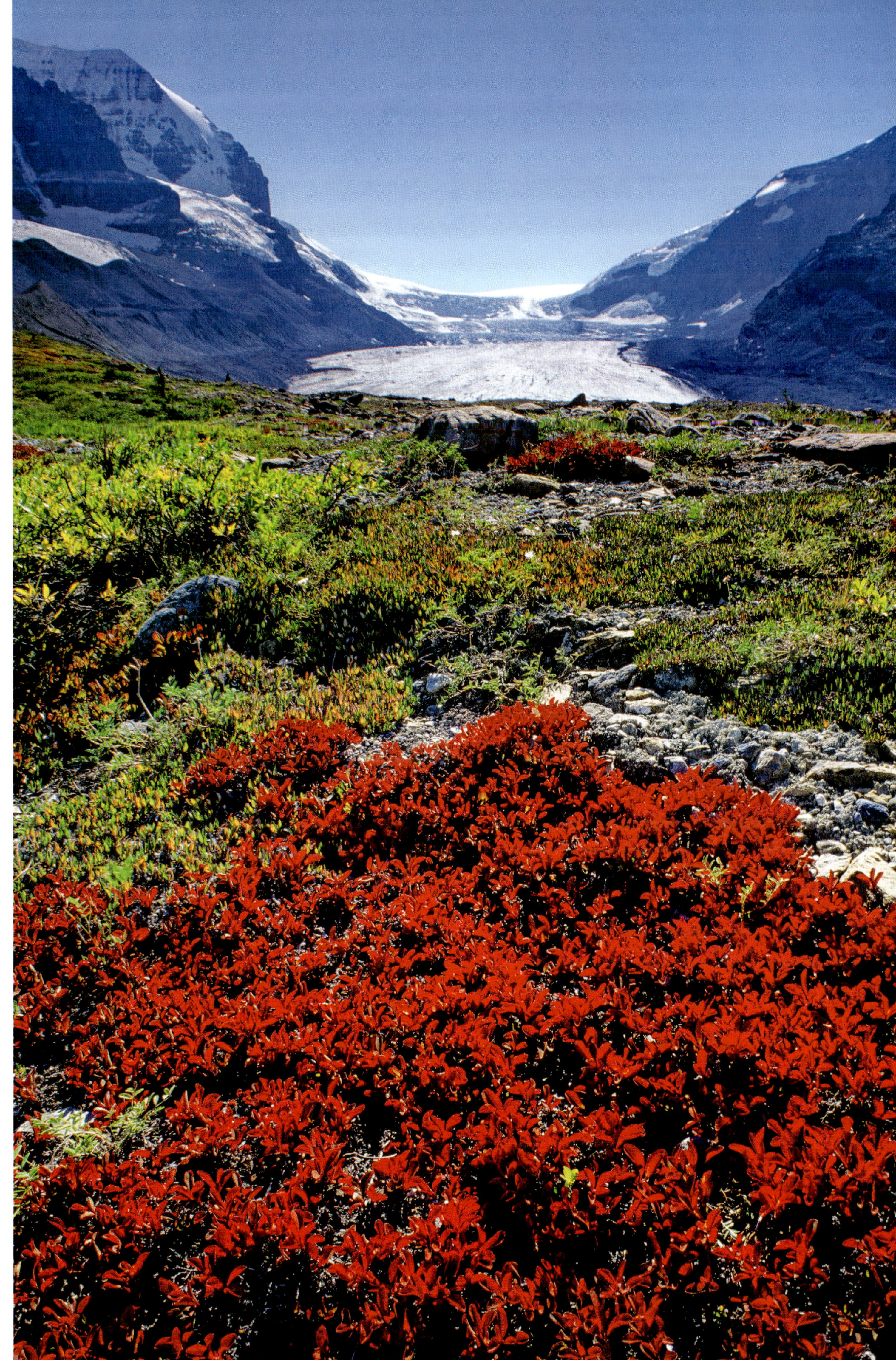

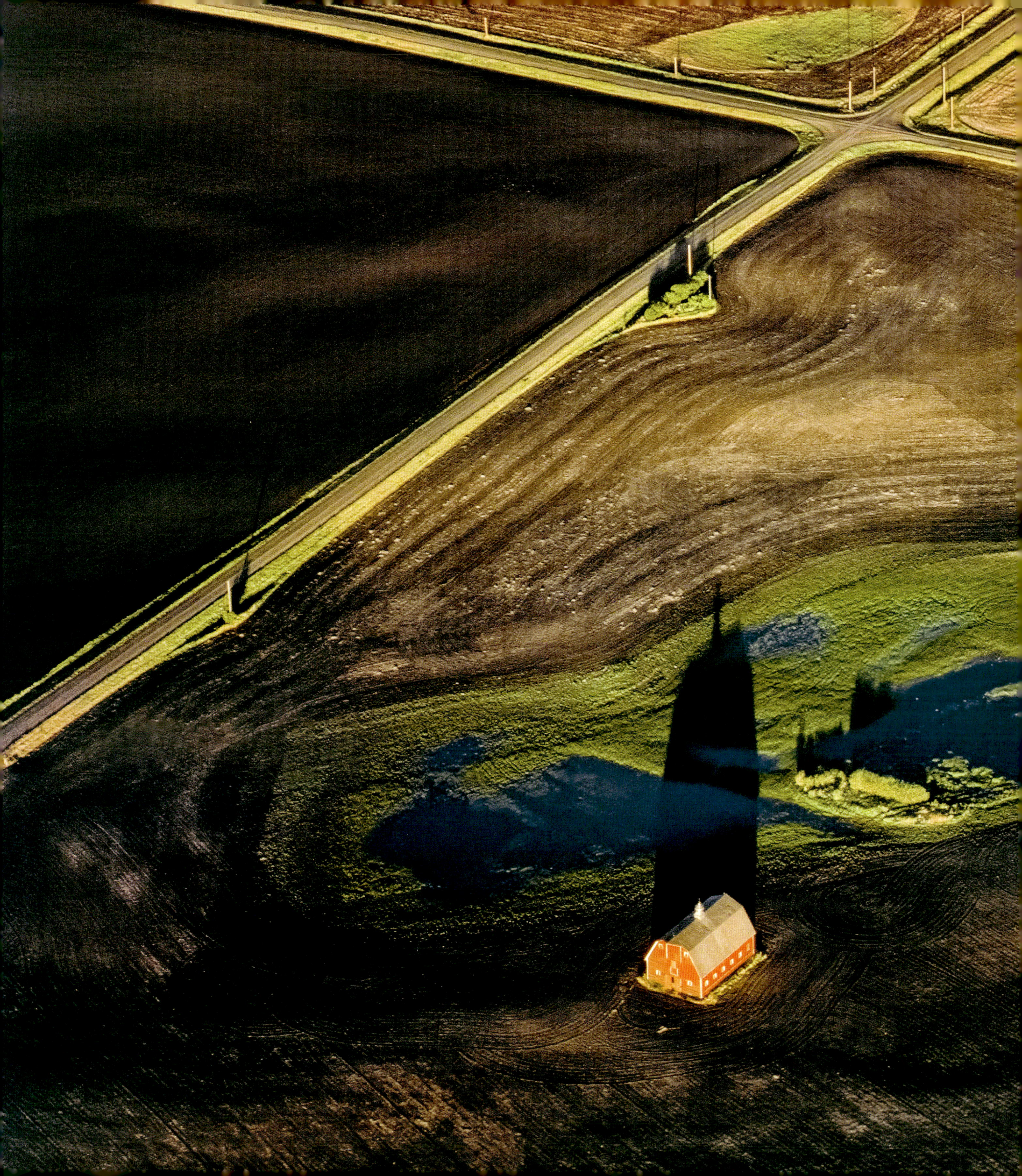

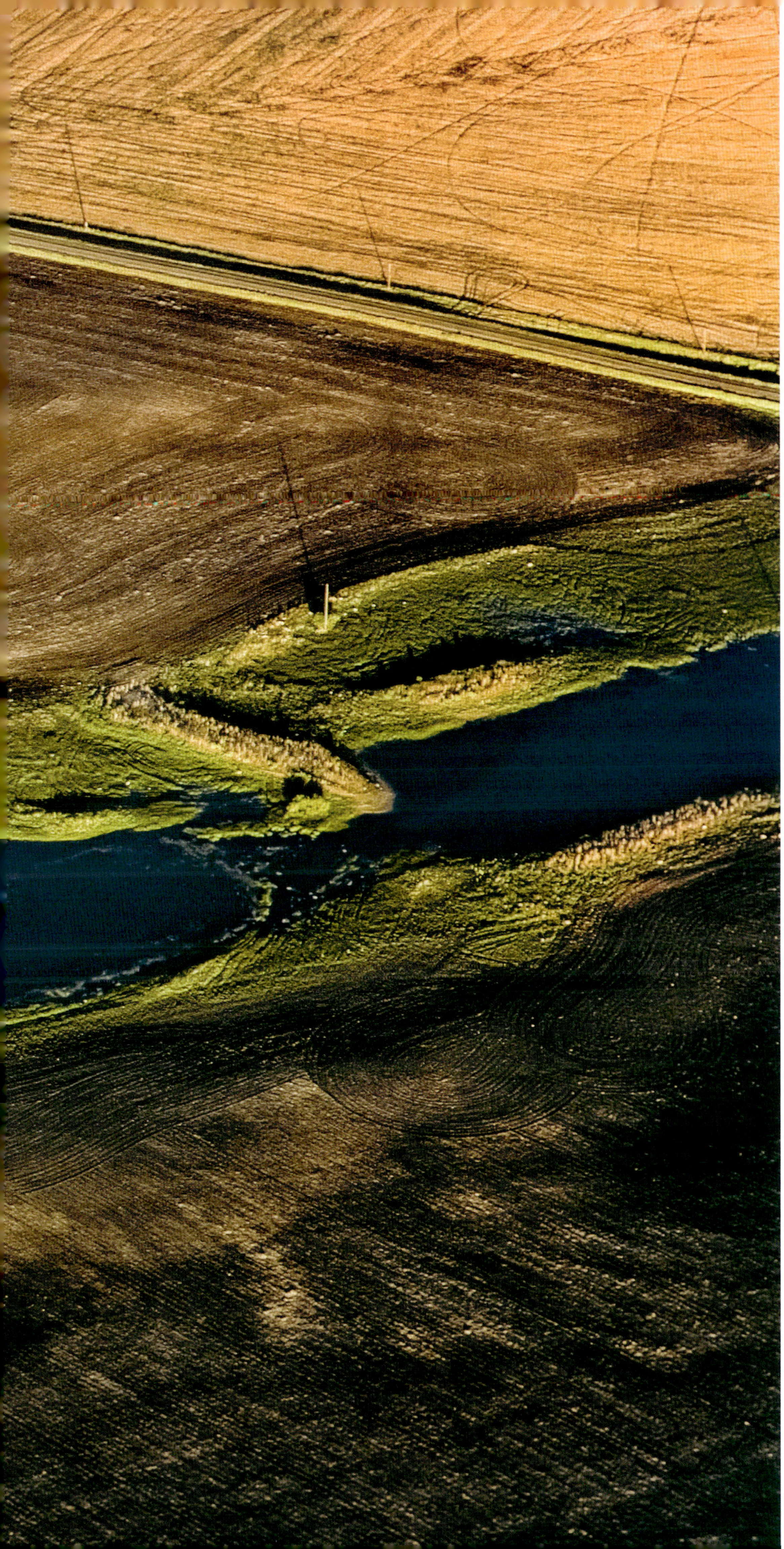

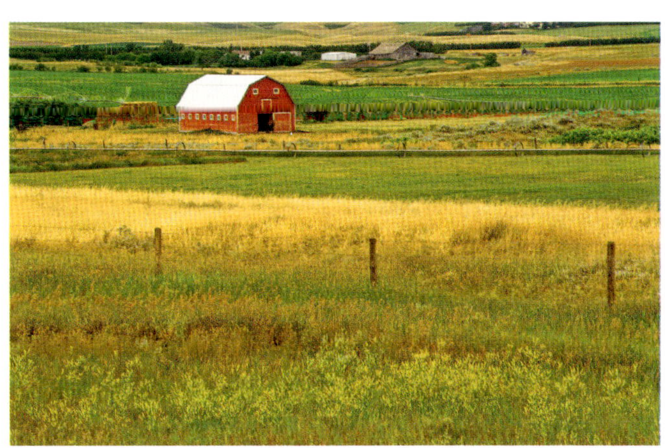

The late afternoon shadow of a barn
stretches across a prairie pothole (kettle)
and field in summer fallow in southern
Saskatchewan (left). A red barn in a
bucolic landscape west of Moose Jaw,
Saskatchewan.

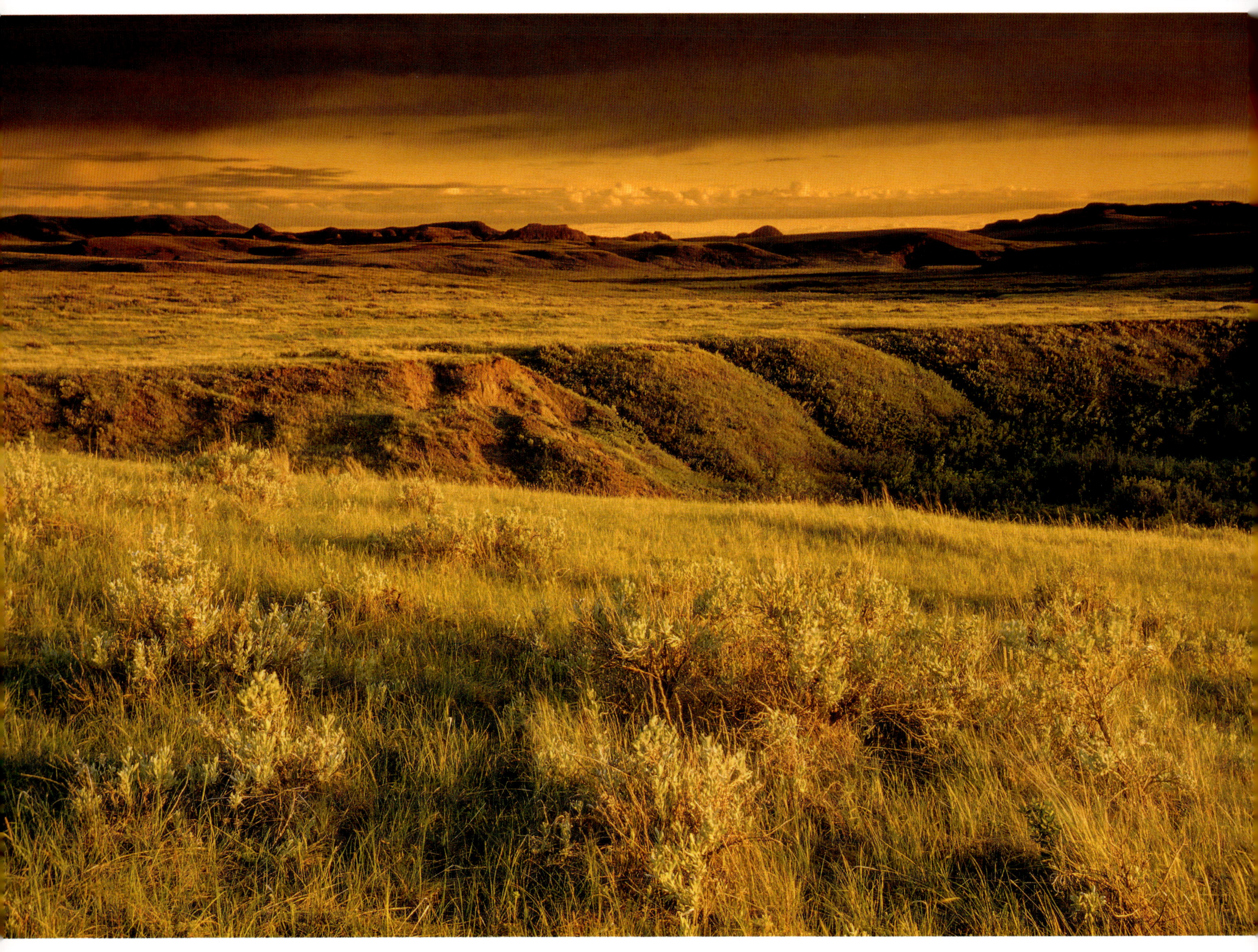

Late afternoon in the East Block of Grasslands
National Park, which preserves one of the few
remaining areas of the native mixed-grass prairie.

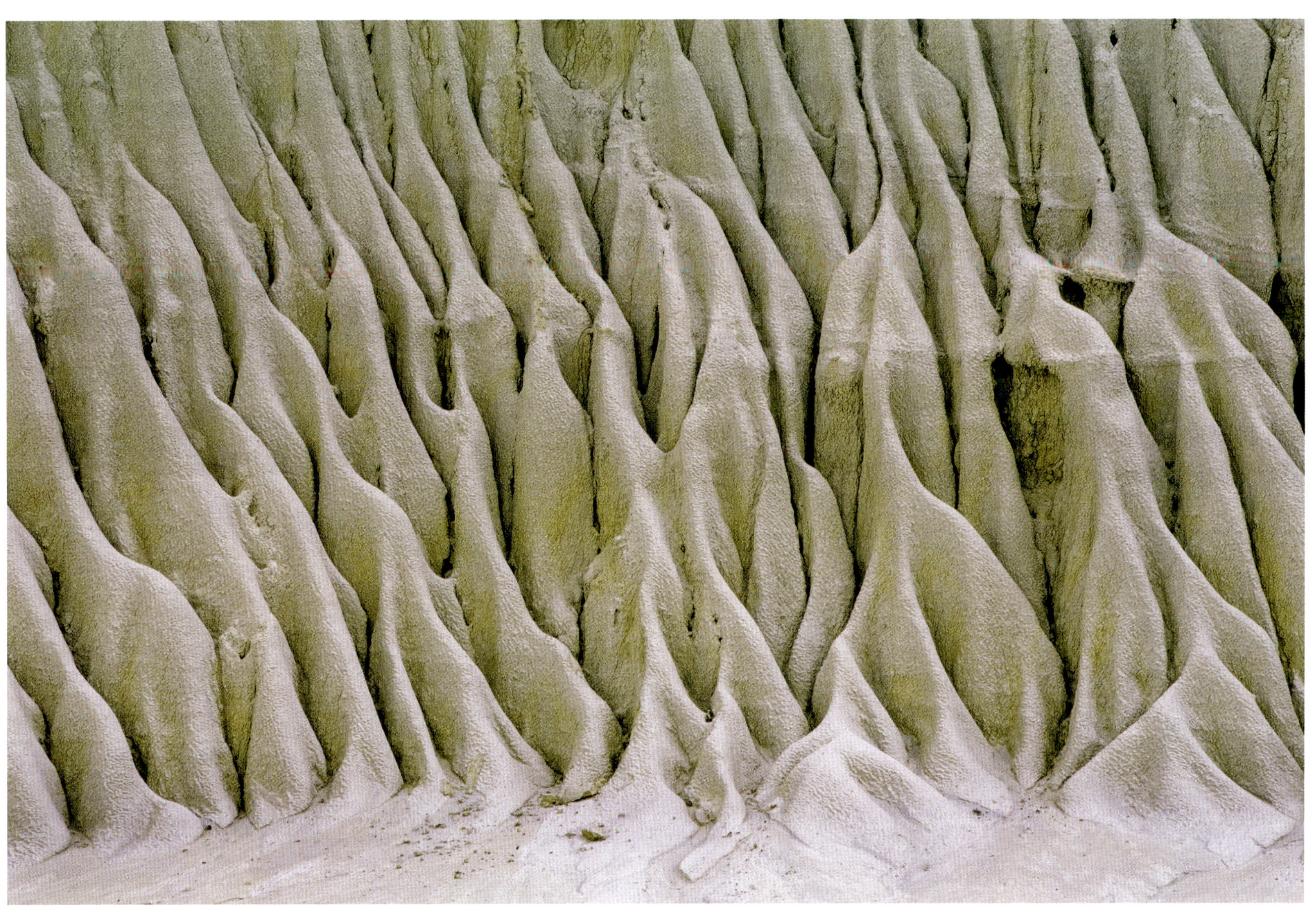

An exquisitely fluted butte at Big Muddy Badlands
near Bengough, Saskatchewan.

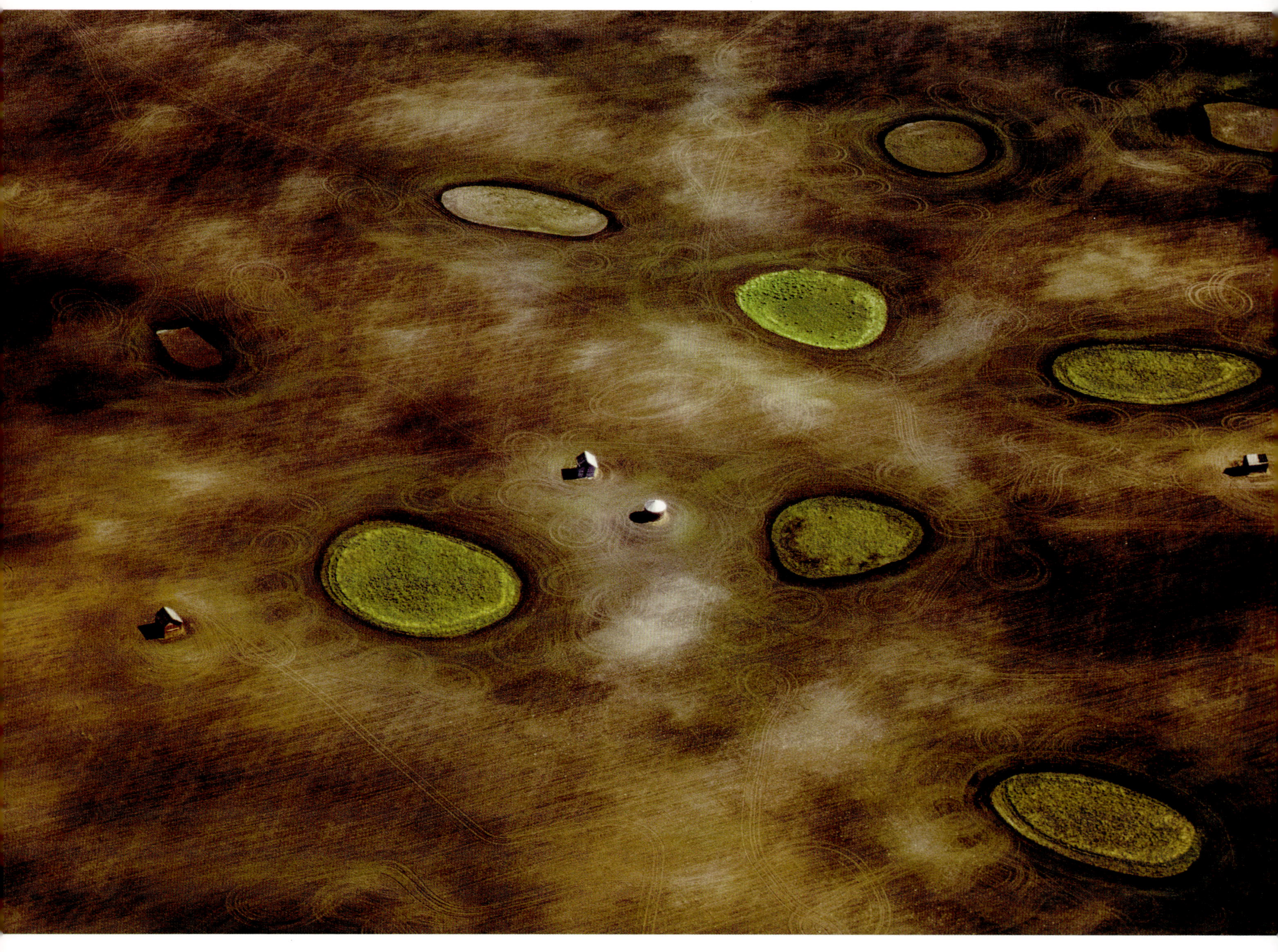

Saskatchewan farm patterns from the air. Former kettle ponds that have grown in but are too damp to till and plant leave round patches in a field in summer fallow.

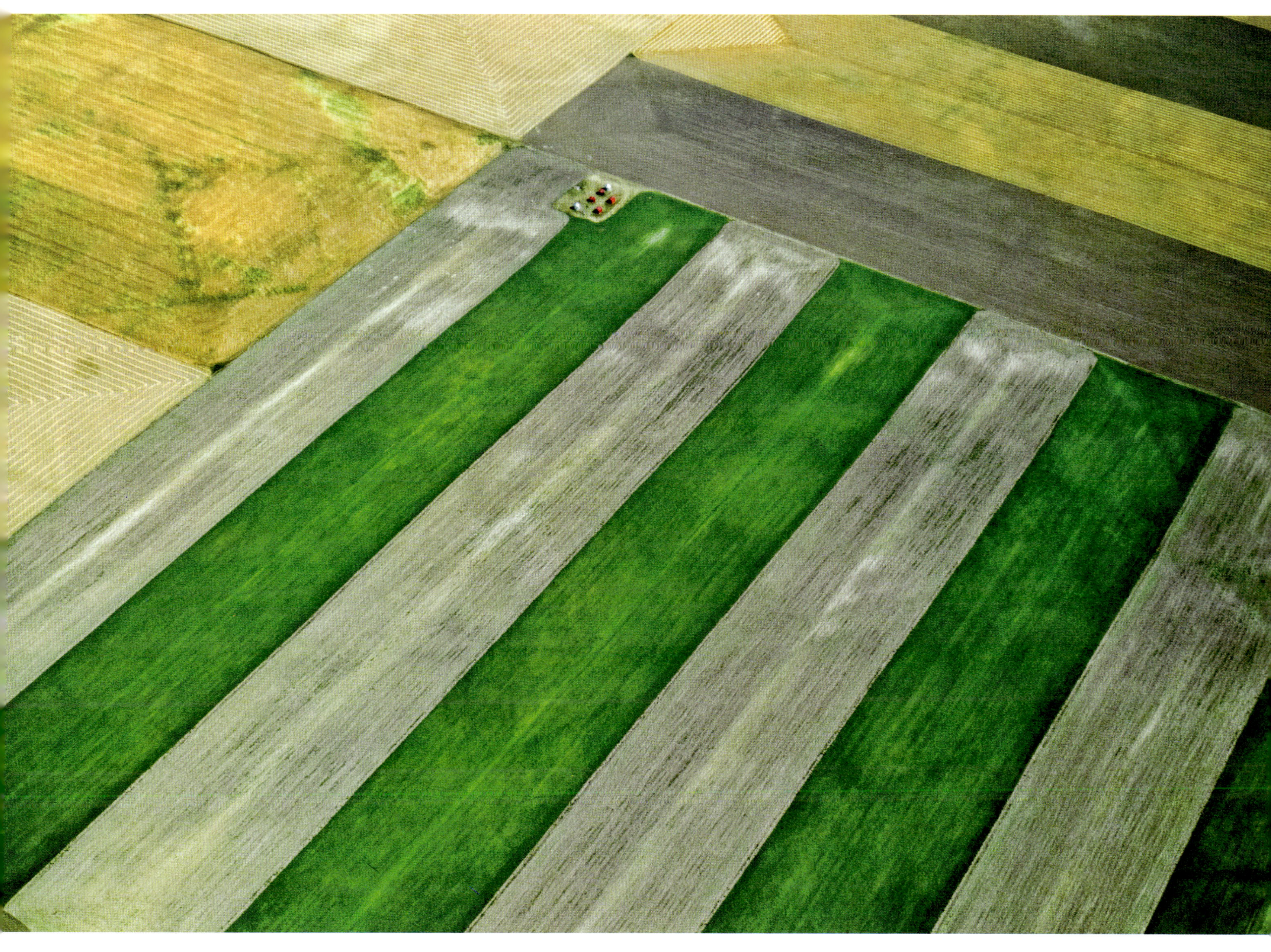

Dryland farming practice creates colourful geometries
where strips of green winter wheat alternating with
unplanted soil contrast with the yellow of mature grain
and of swathed harvested fields.

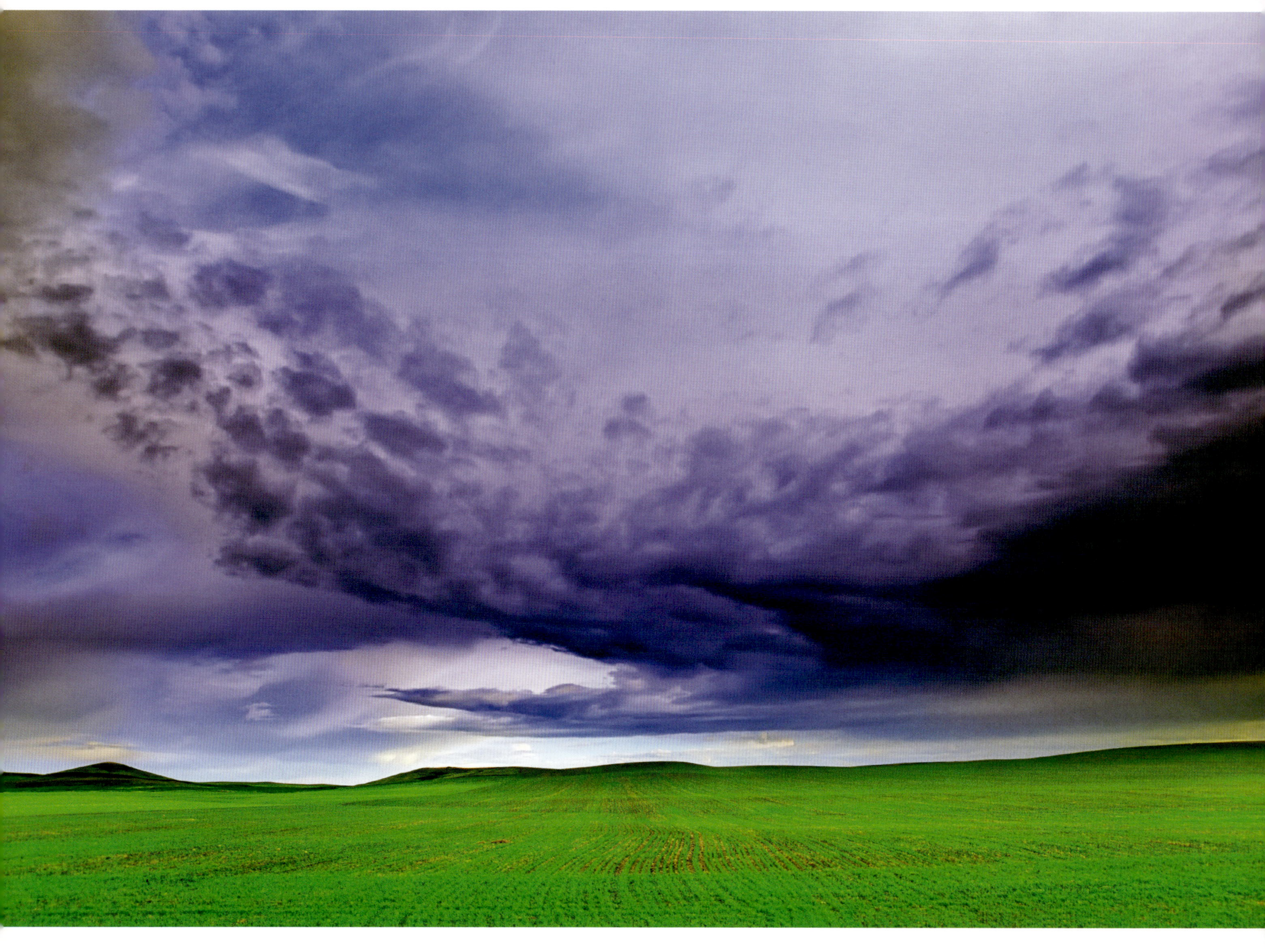

Prairie skies over a field of sprouting wheat north
of Grasslands National Park (above) and over the
Great Sand Hills near Leader, Saskatchewan.

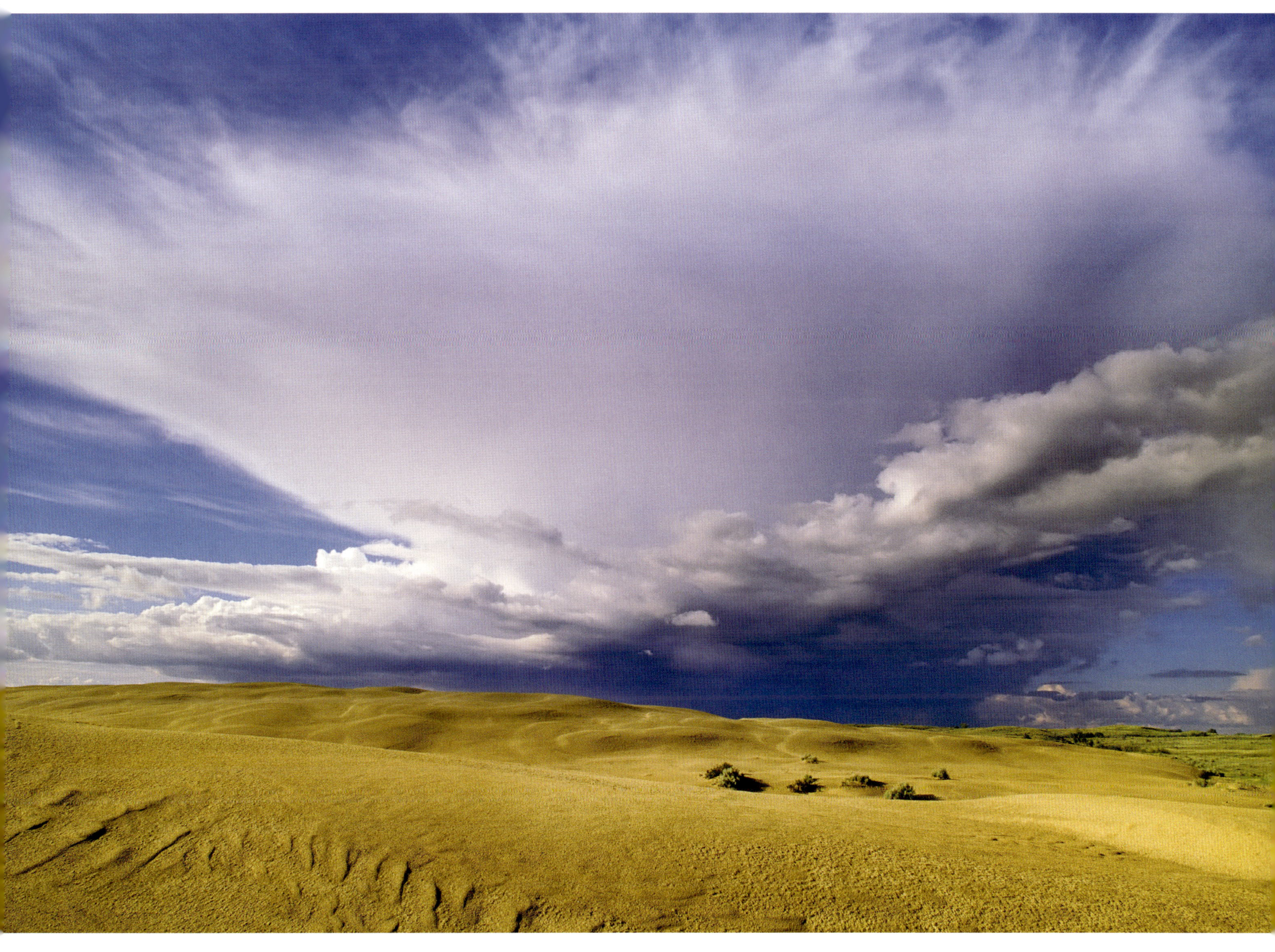

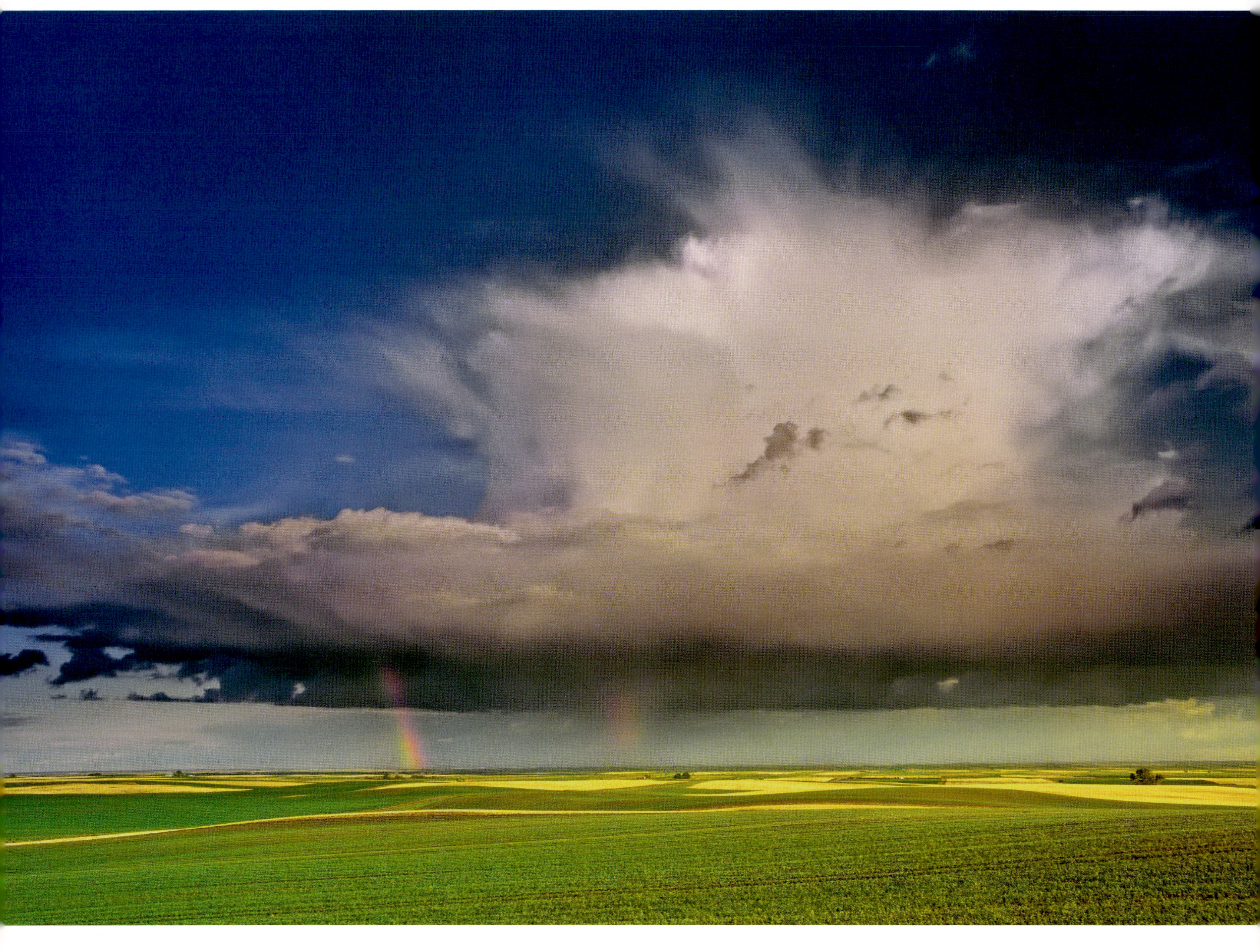

A thunderstorm trails a rainbow west of Liebenthal
(above) and a supercell dominates the view down a
rural road south of Rosetown, Saskatchewan.

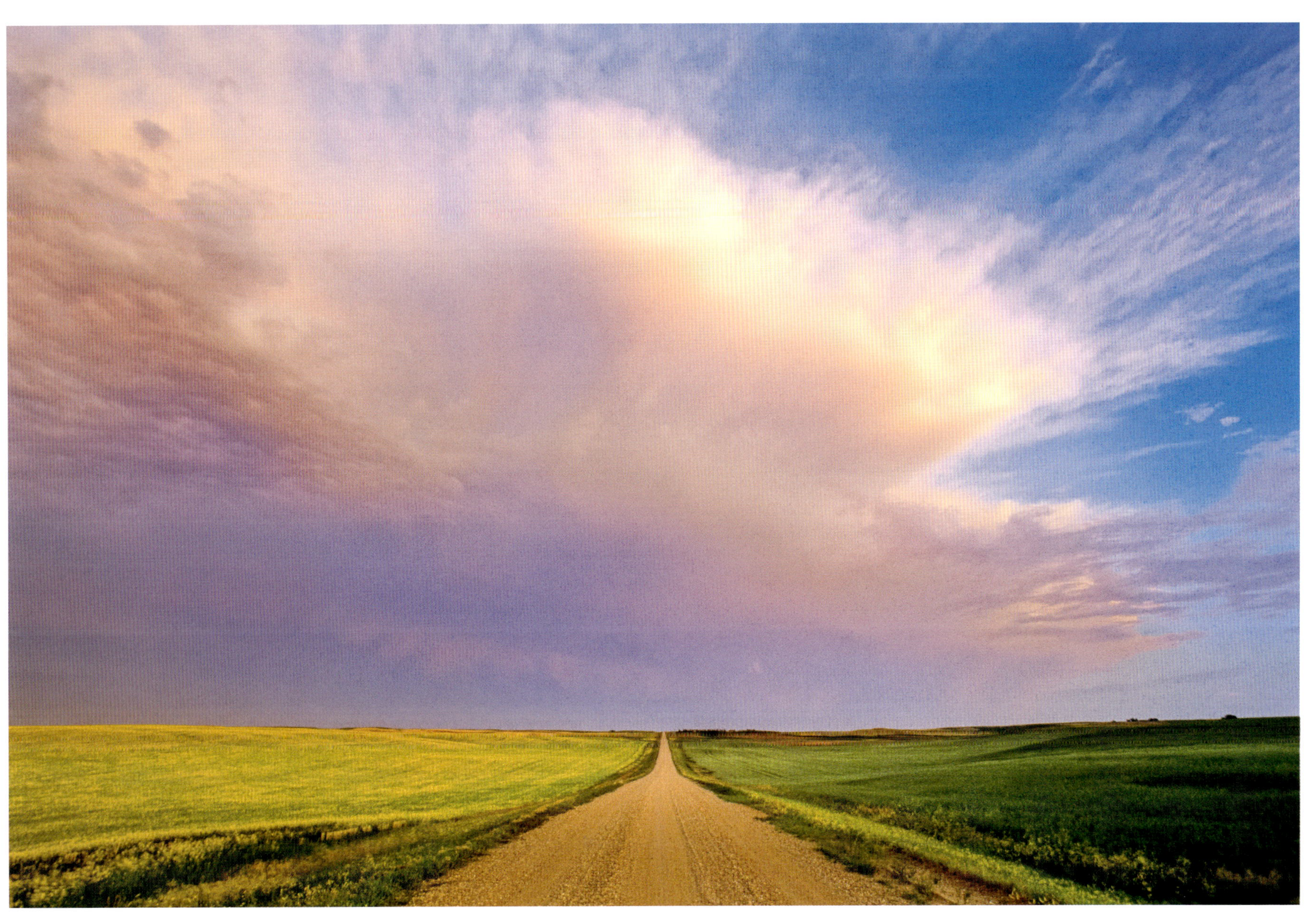

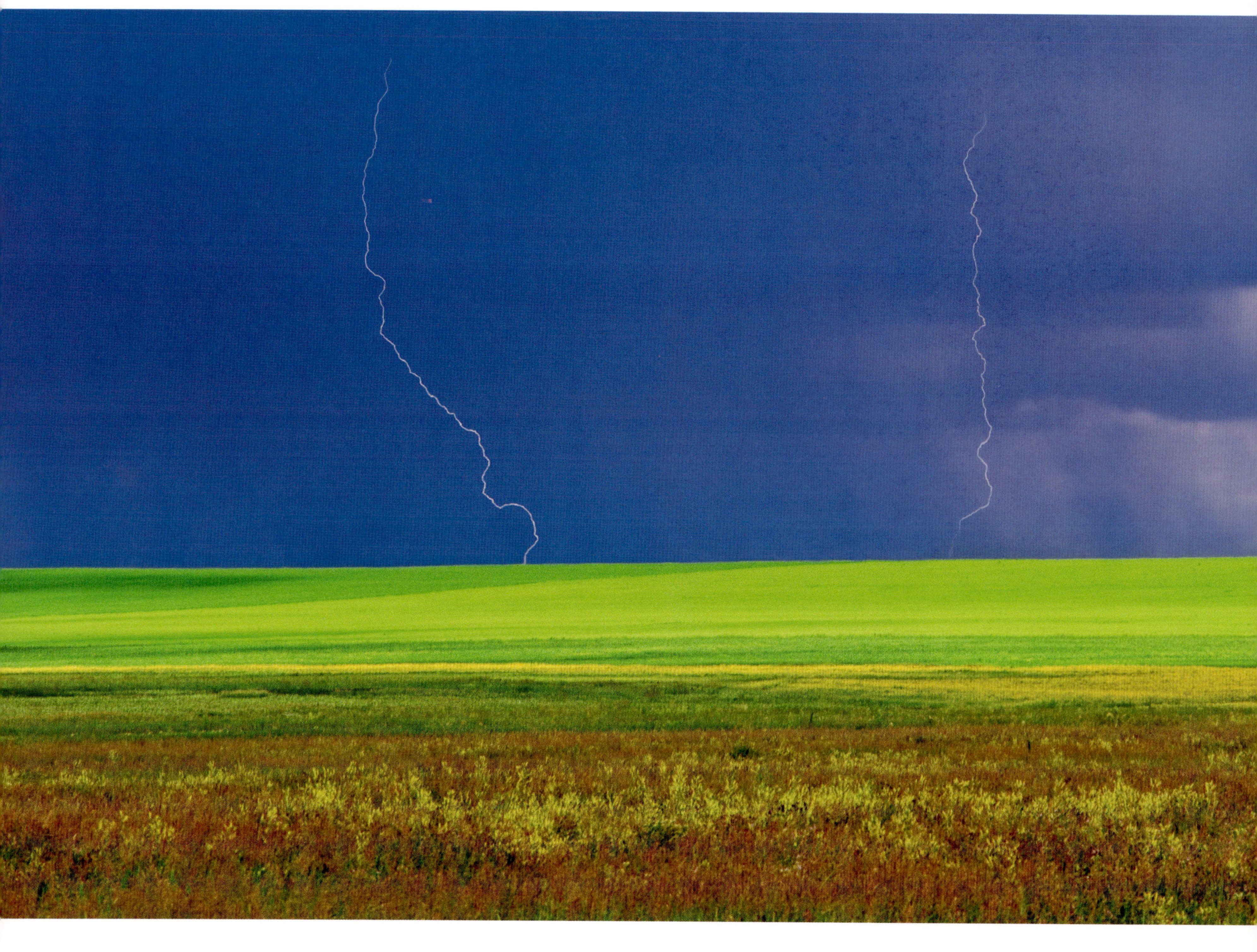

Bolts of lightning strike fields of canola and wheat
near Hanley, Saskatchewan.

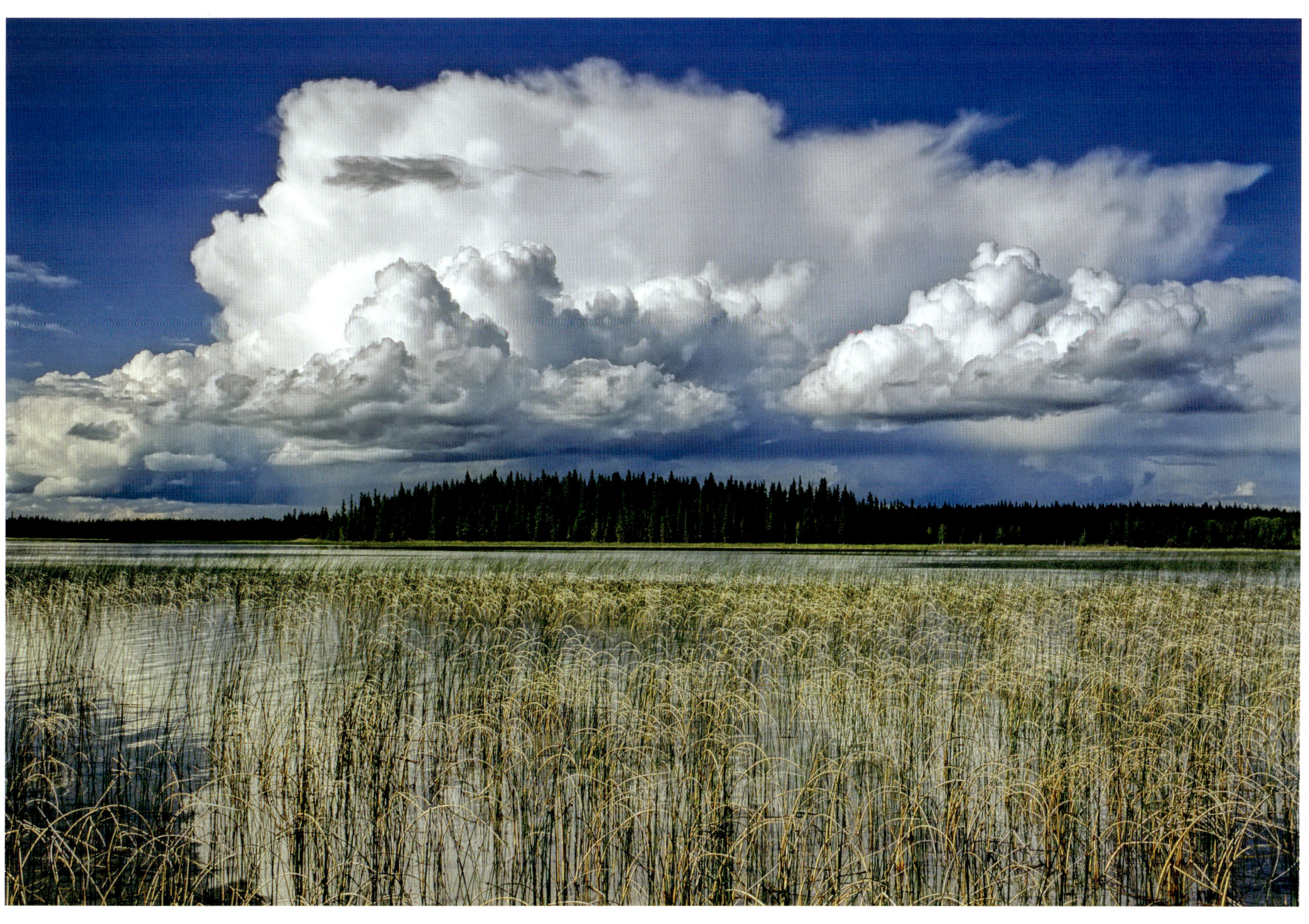

A thunderstorm brews over reed-fringed Trappers
Lake in Prince Albert National Park.

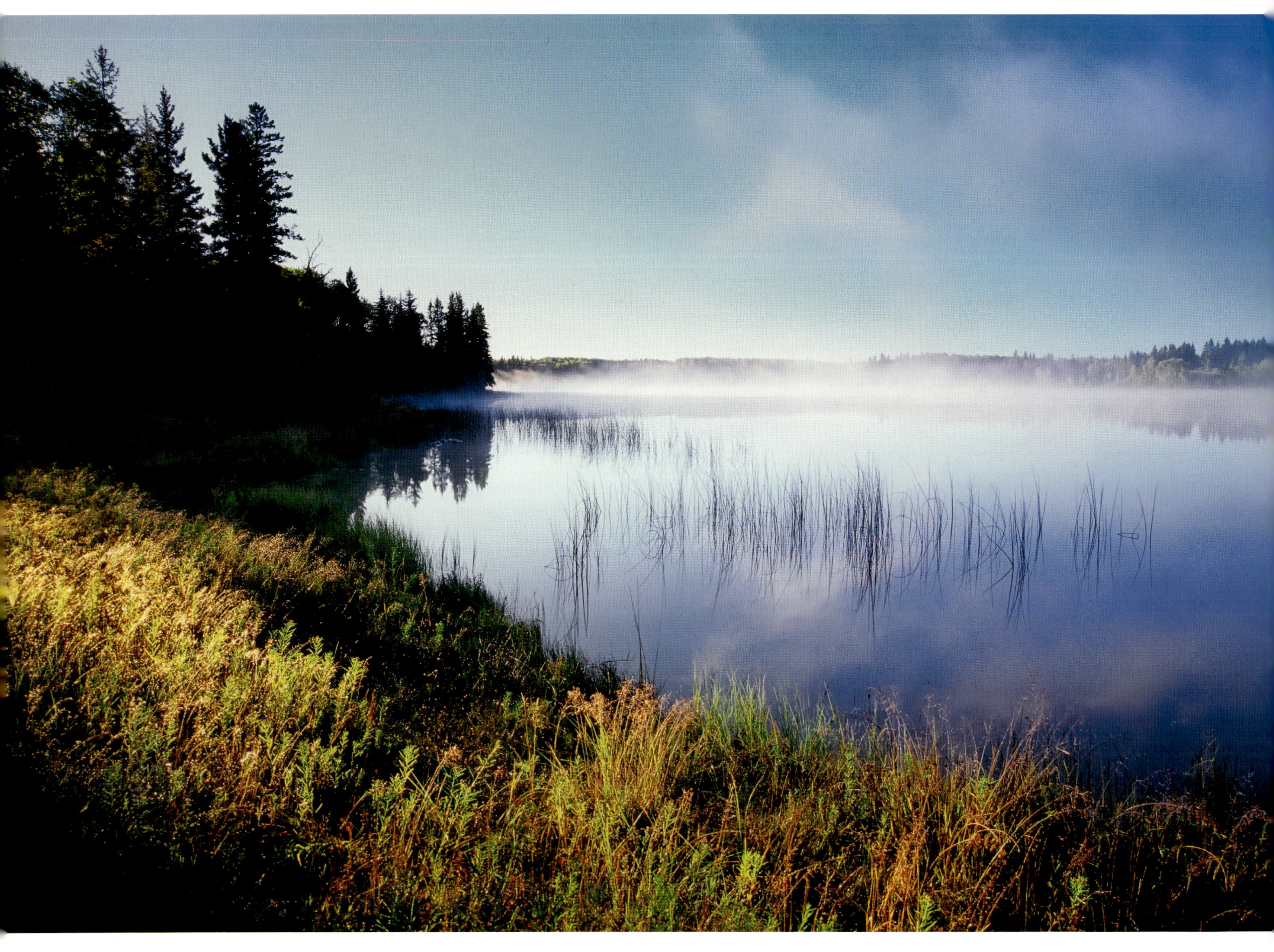

Morning mist clears off Katherine Lake in Riding
Mountain National Park, Manitoba.

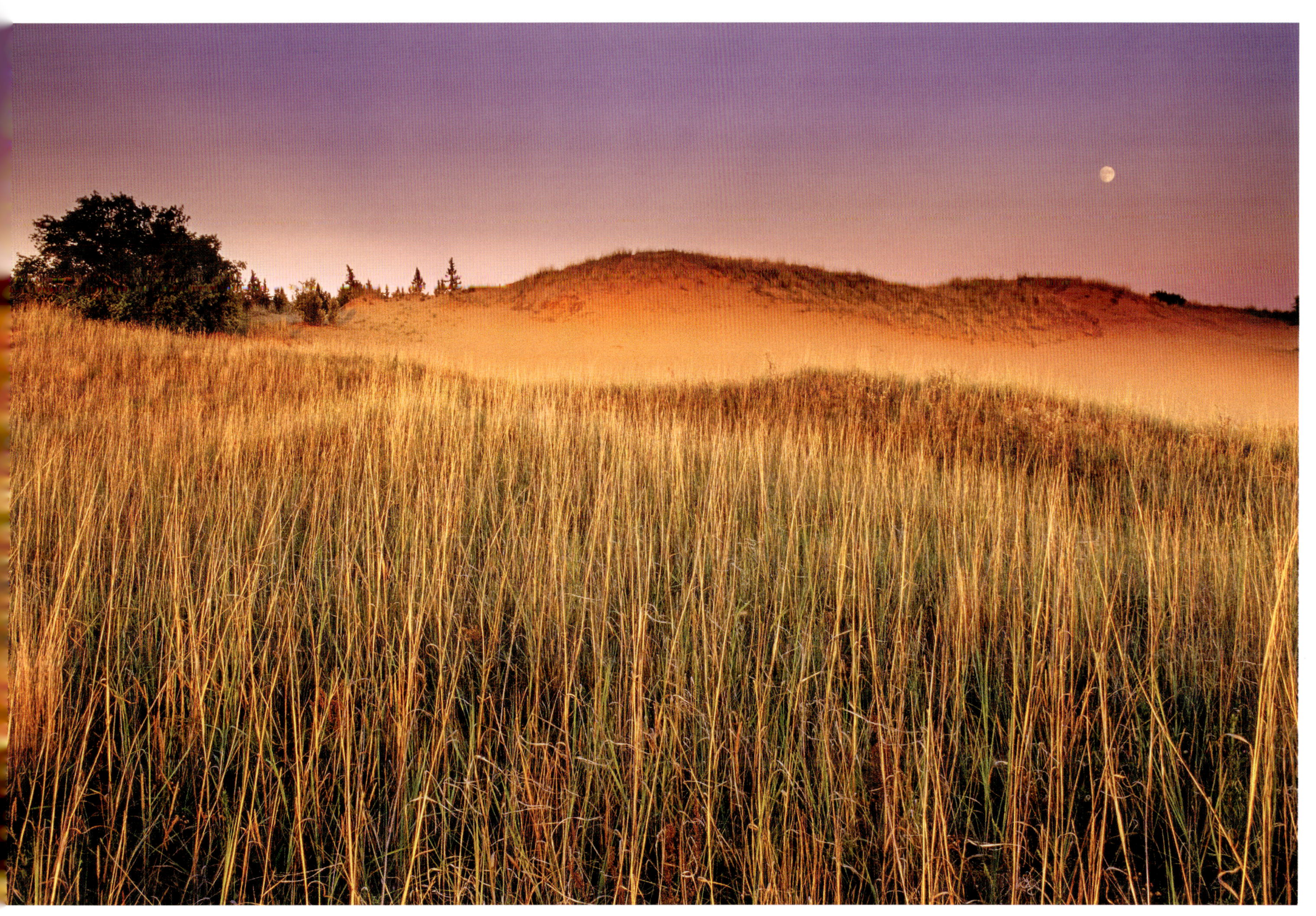

The moon rises at sundown over the Carberry sandhills, or
Spirit Sands in Spruce Woods Provincial Park, Manitoba.

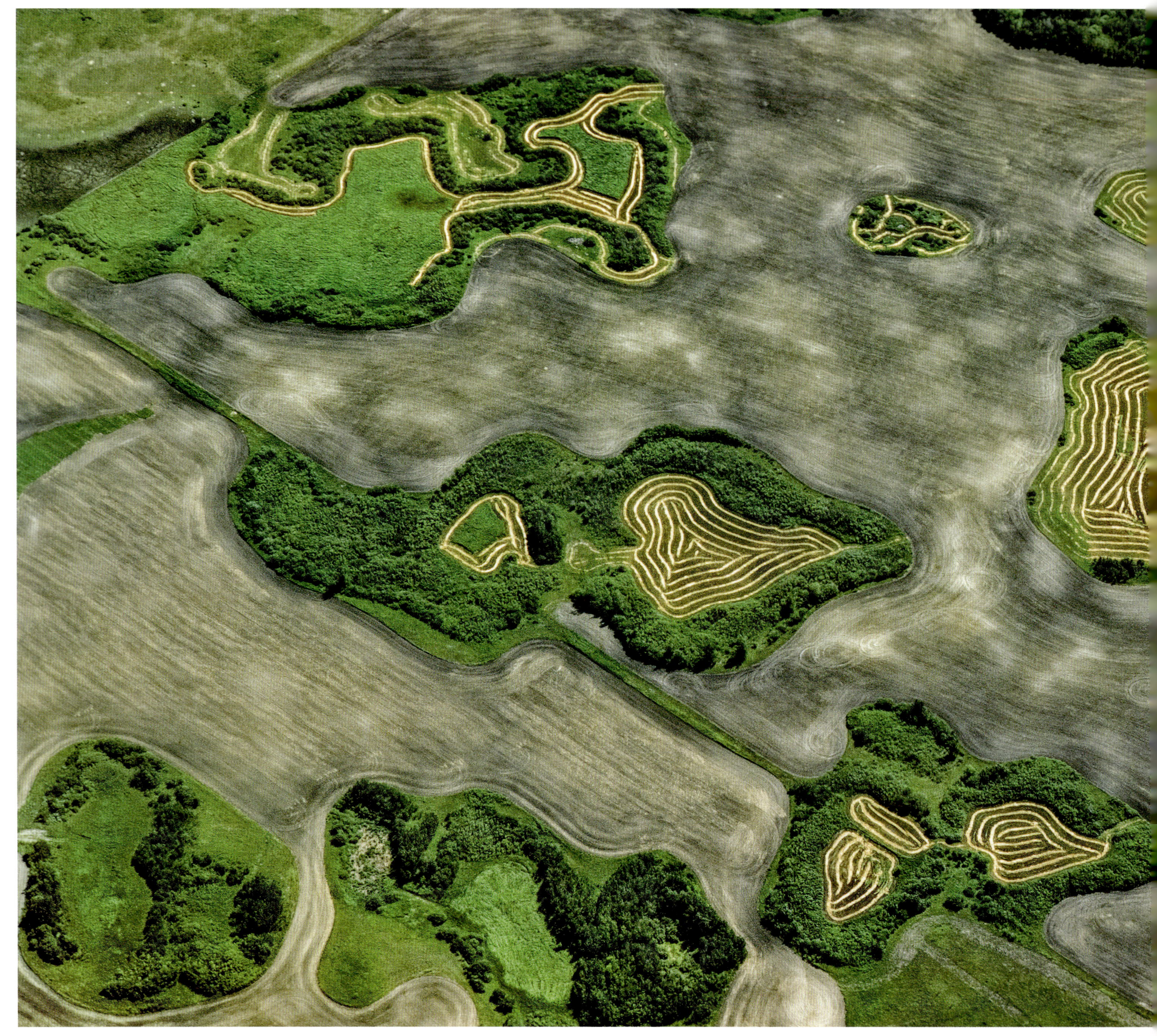

Swaths created by selective or incomplete mowing
create unconscious artwork in these aerial views of
farm fields west of Winnipeg, Manitoba.

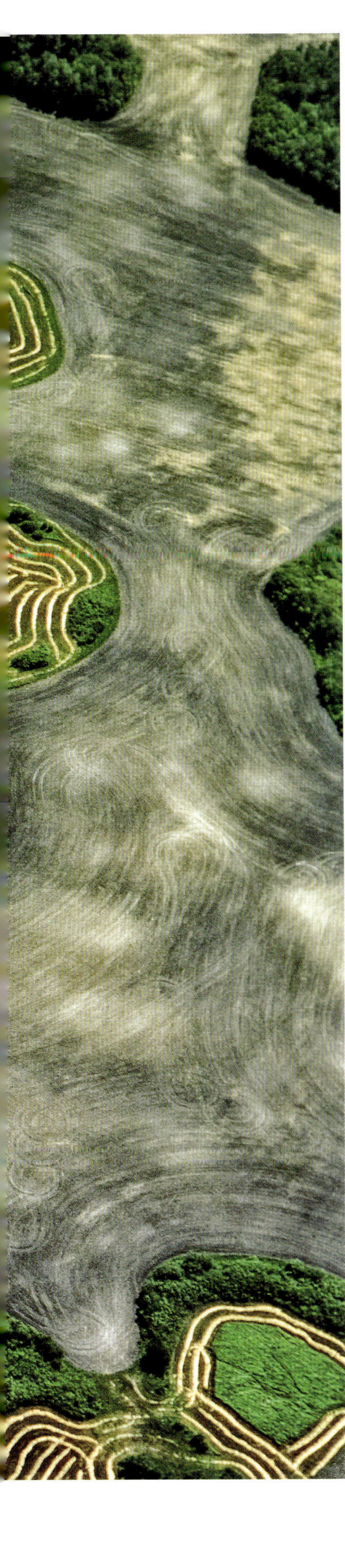

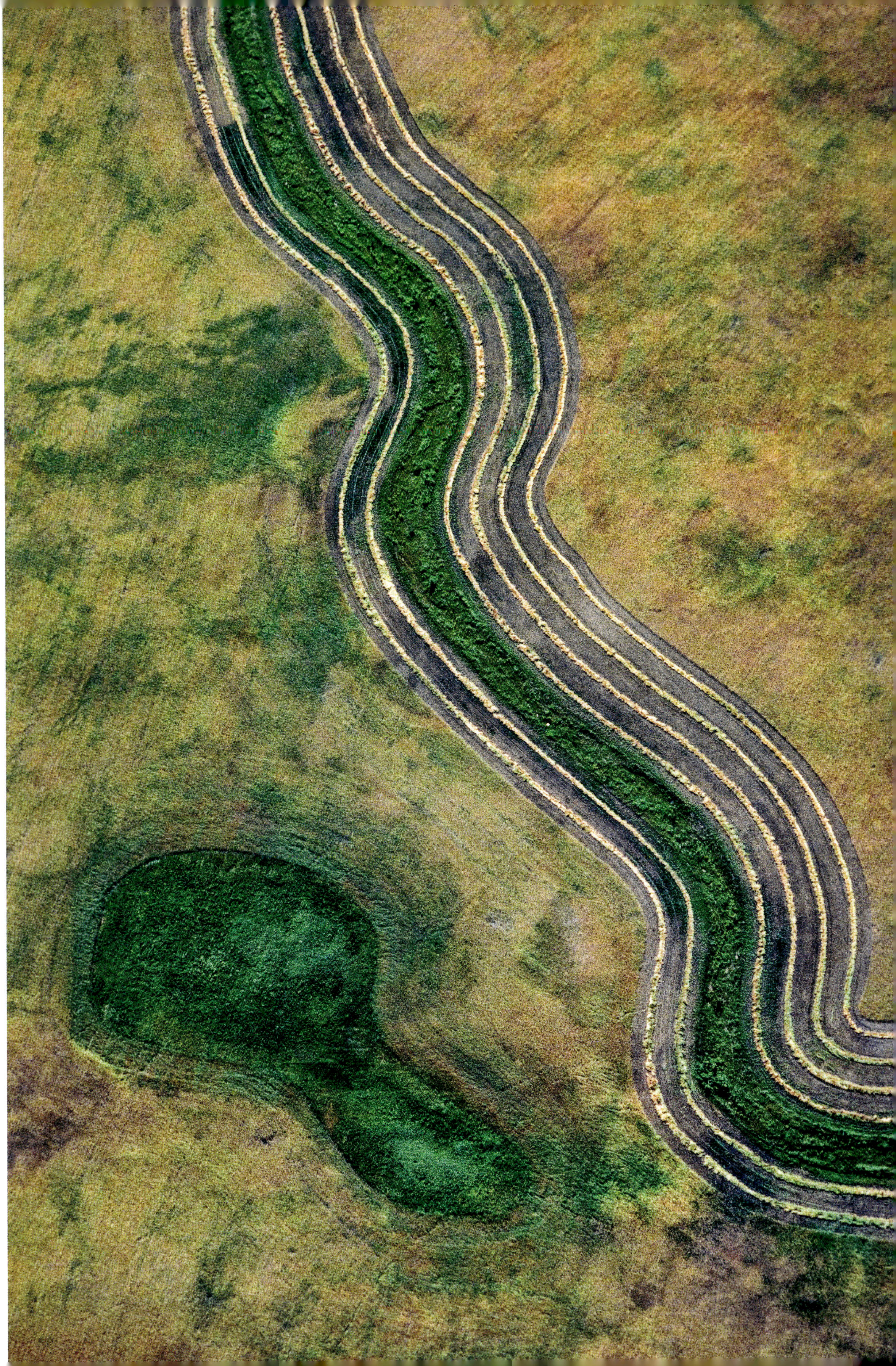

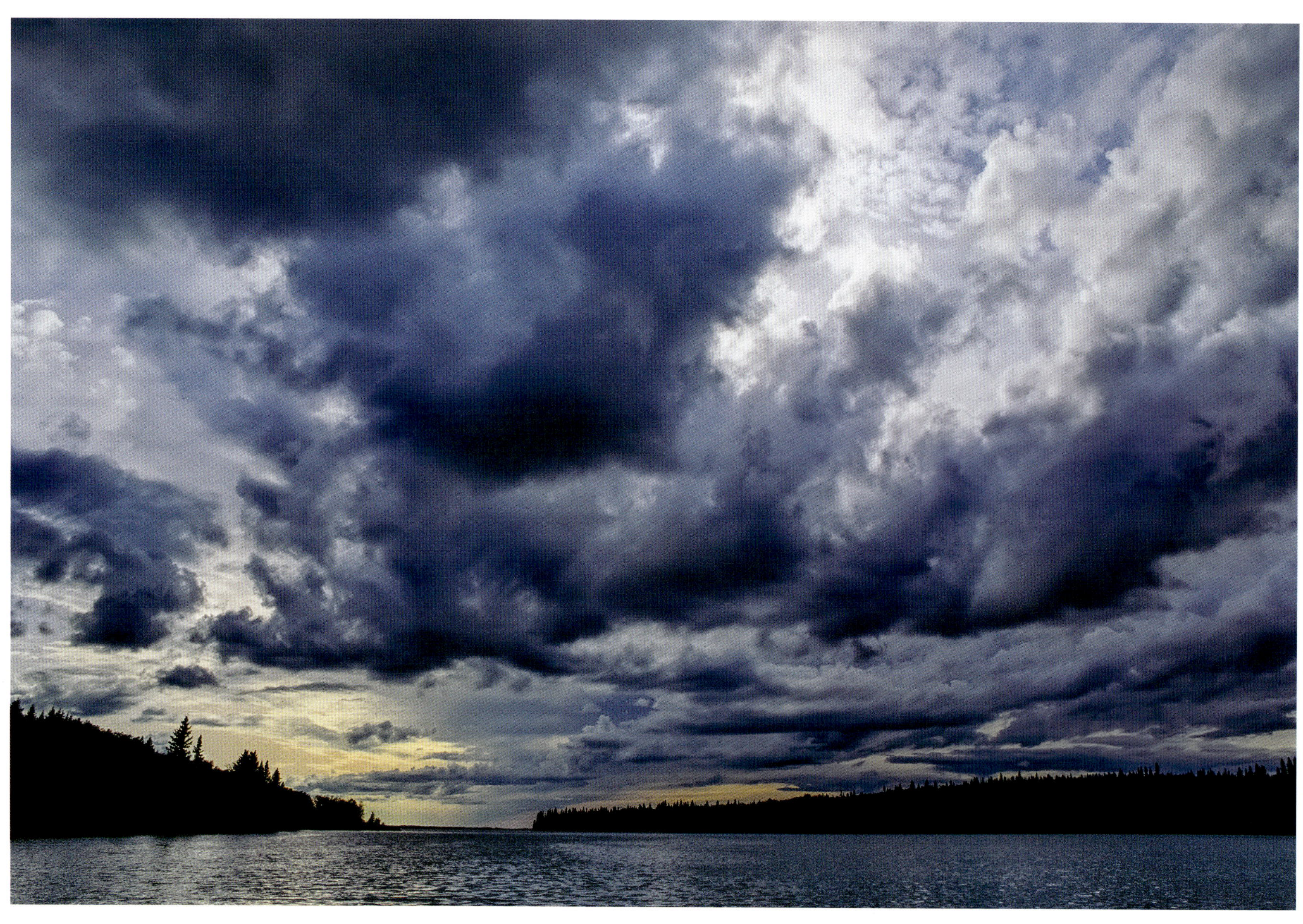

Stormy skies over Clear Lake, Riding Mountain
National Park, Manitoba.

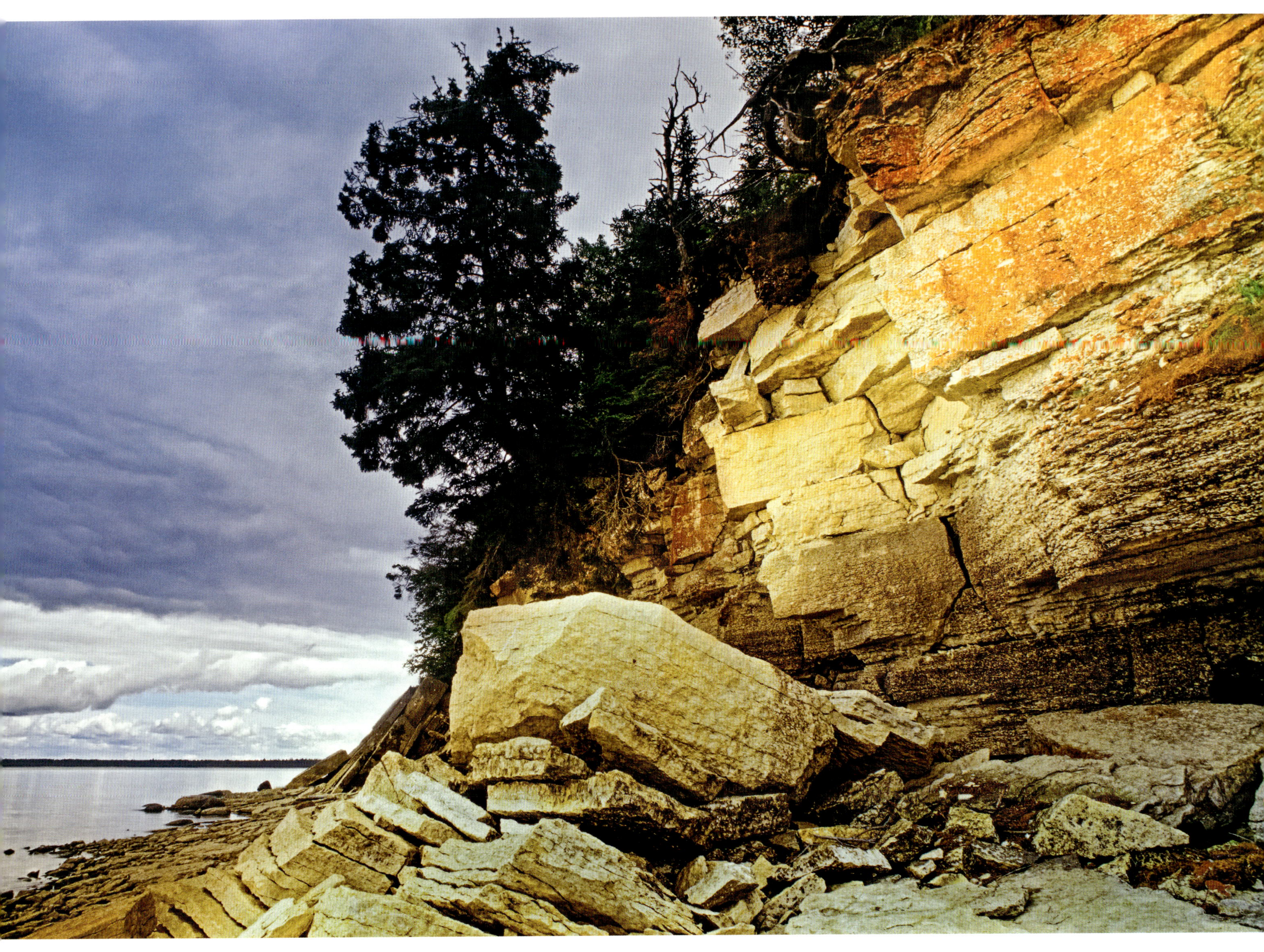

Bluffs of broken sedimentary rock along the
shore of Lake Winnipeg in Hecla/Grindstone
Provincial Park, Manitoba.

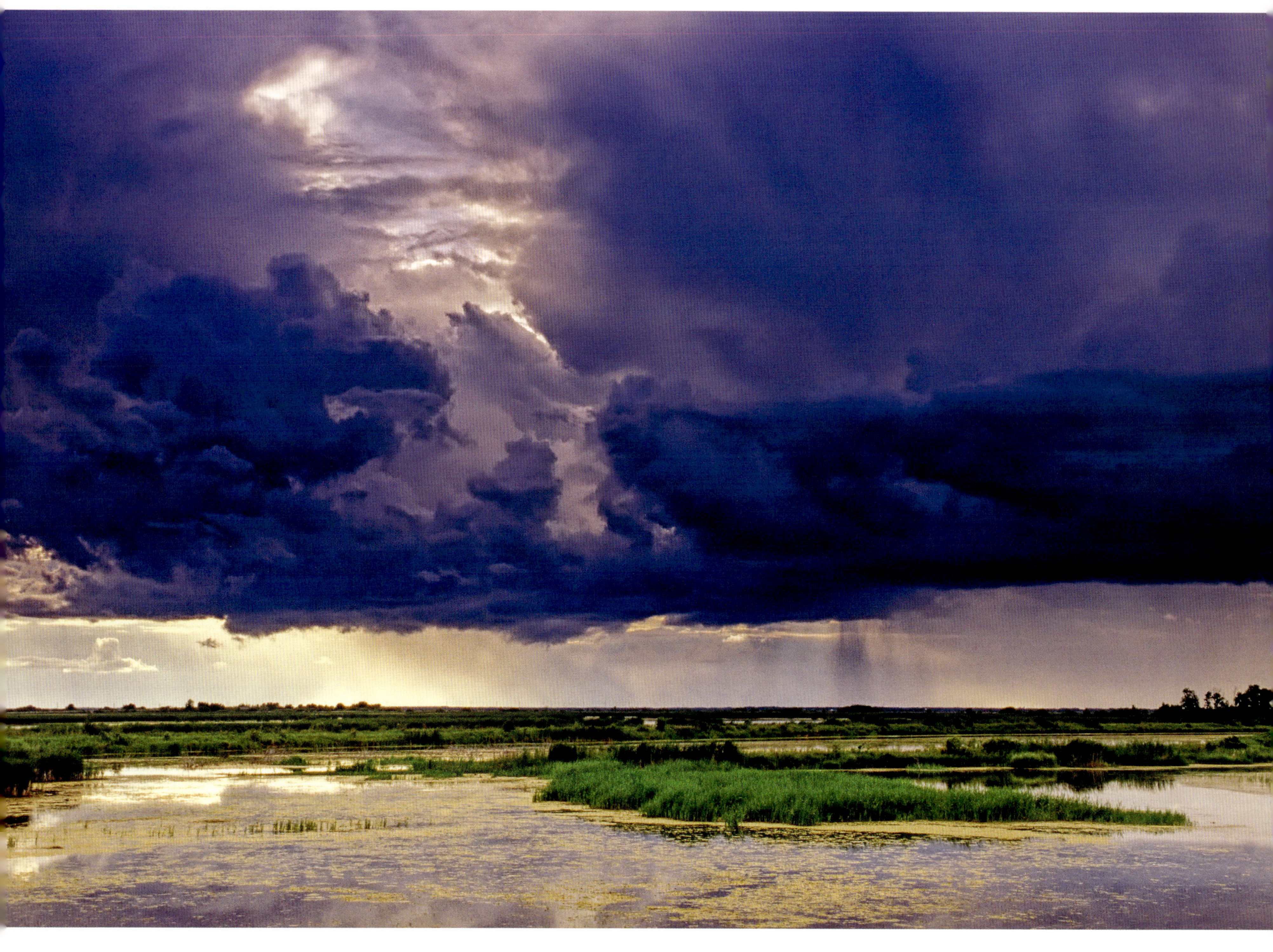

Turbulent skies over Grassy Narrows Marsh,
Hecla/Grindstone Provincial Park.

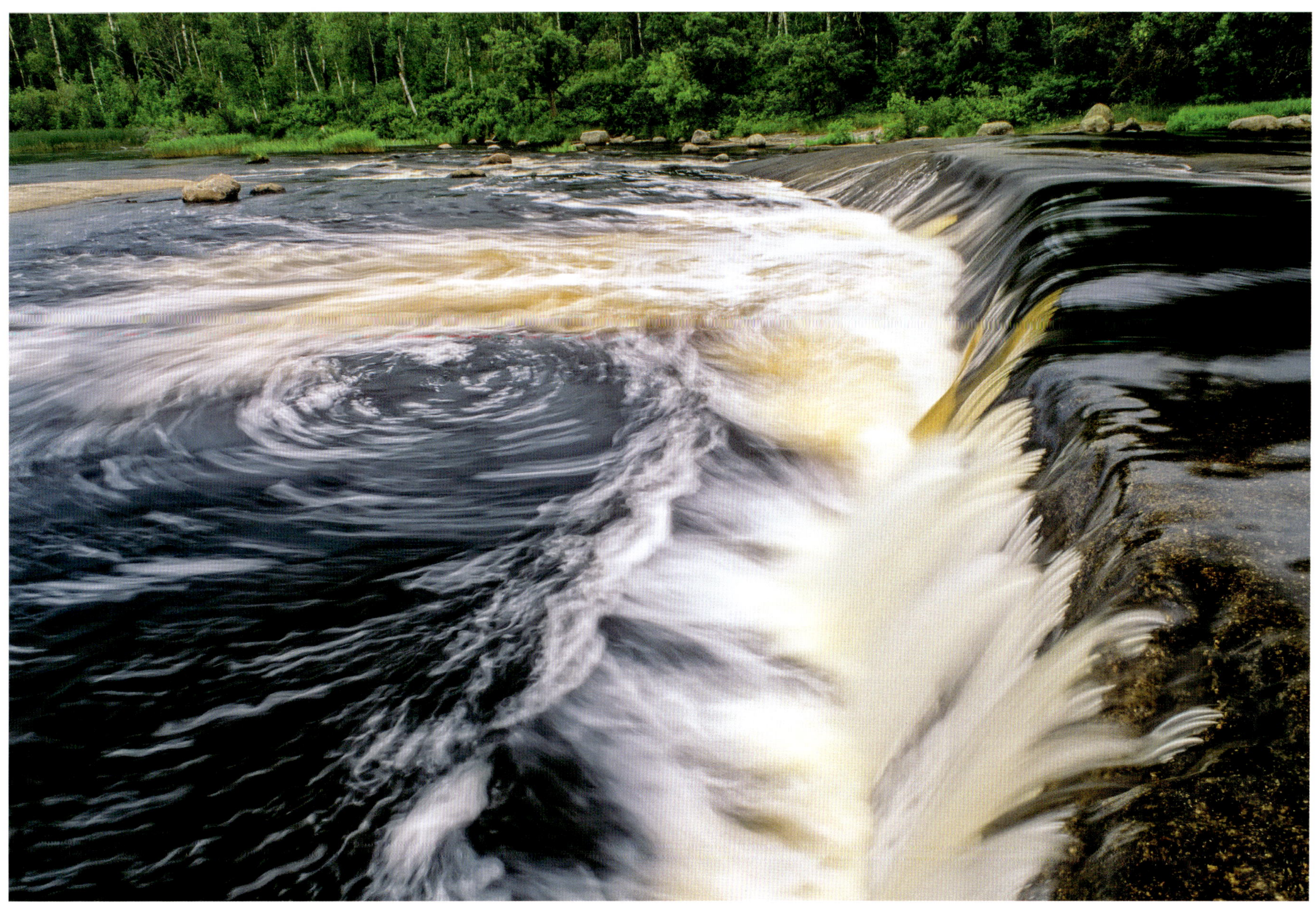

Rainbow Falls in Whiteshell Provincial Park,
Manitoba.

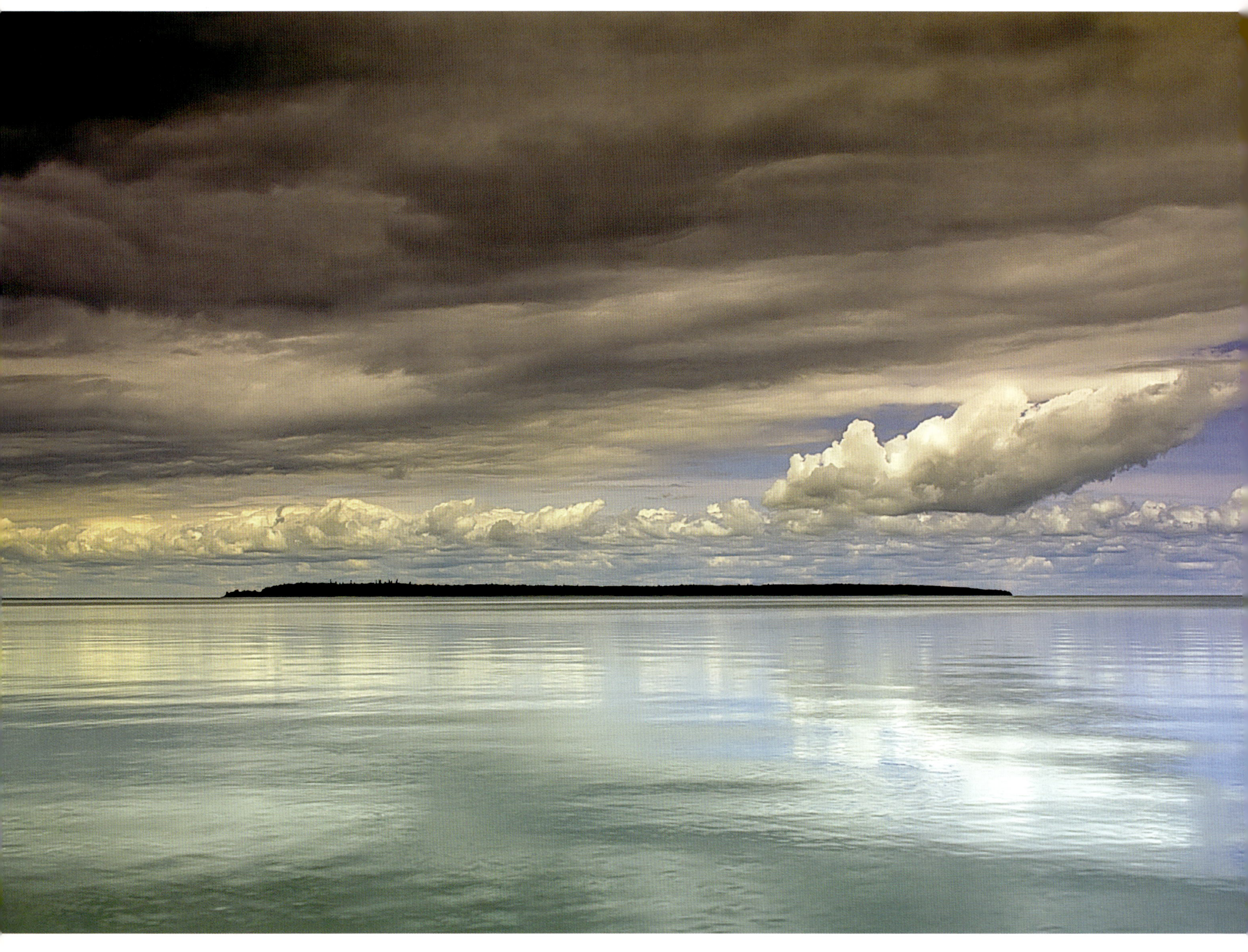

Punk Island in Lake Winnipeg, from the West
Quarry Trail on Hecla Island, Hecla/Grindstone
Provincial Park, Manitoba.

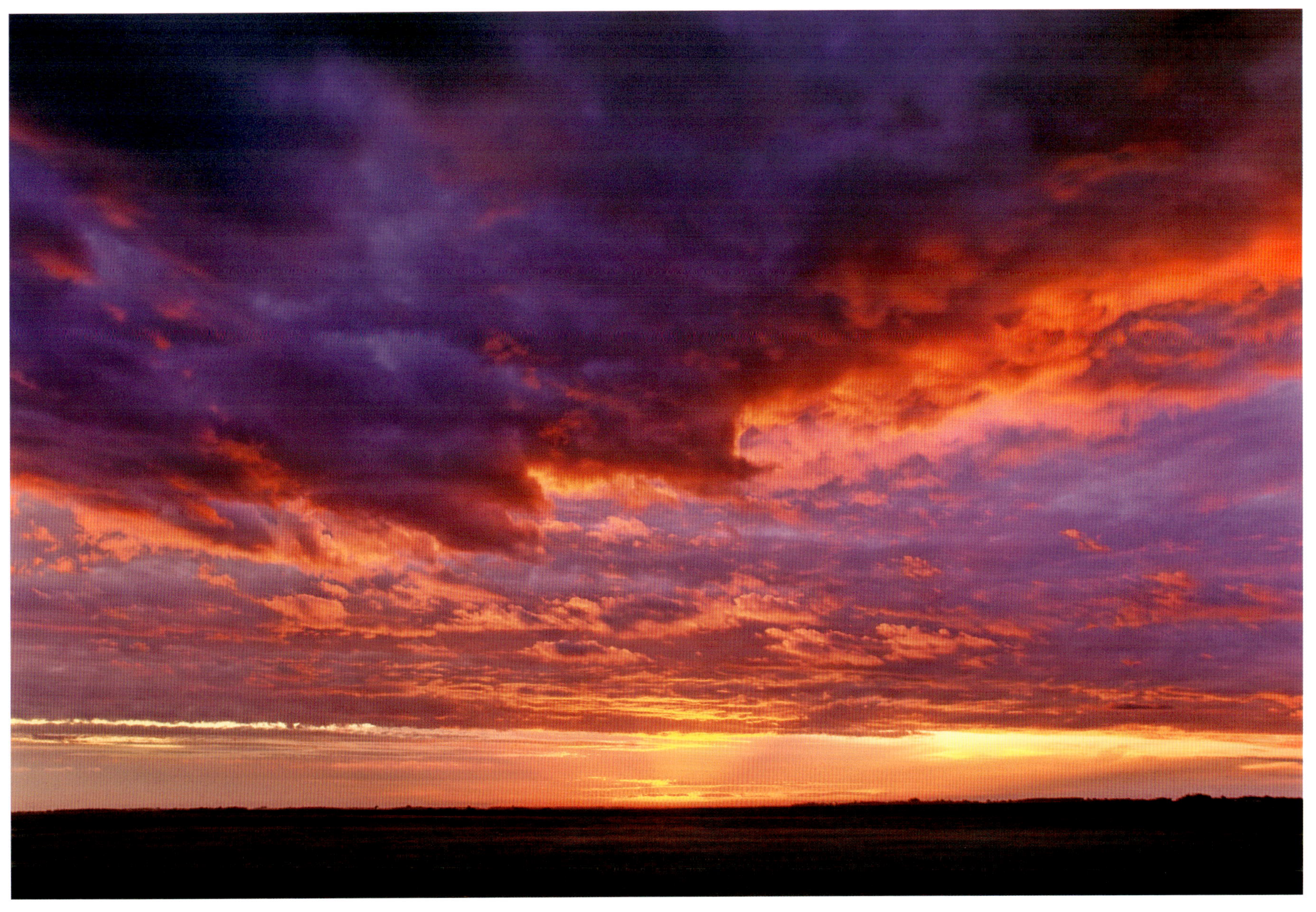

Sunset near Ste. Anne southeast of
Winnipeg, Manitoba.

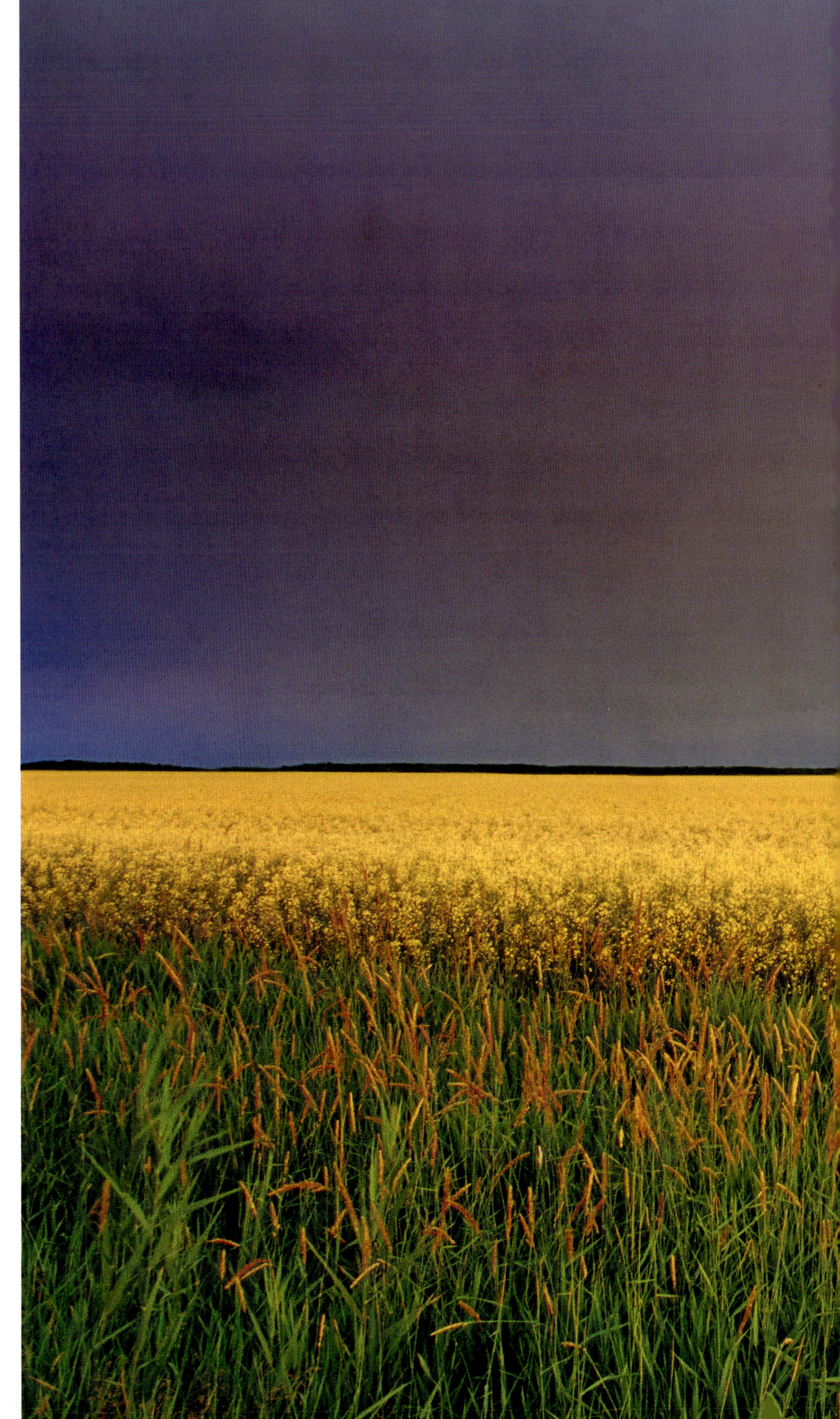

A rainbow over canola fields near Selkirk, Manitoba.

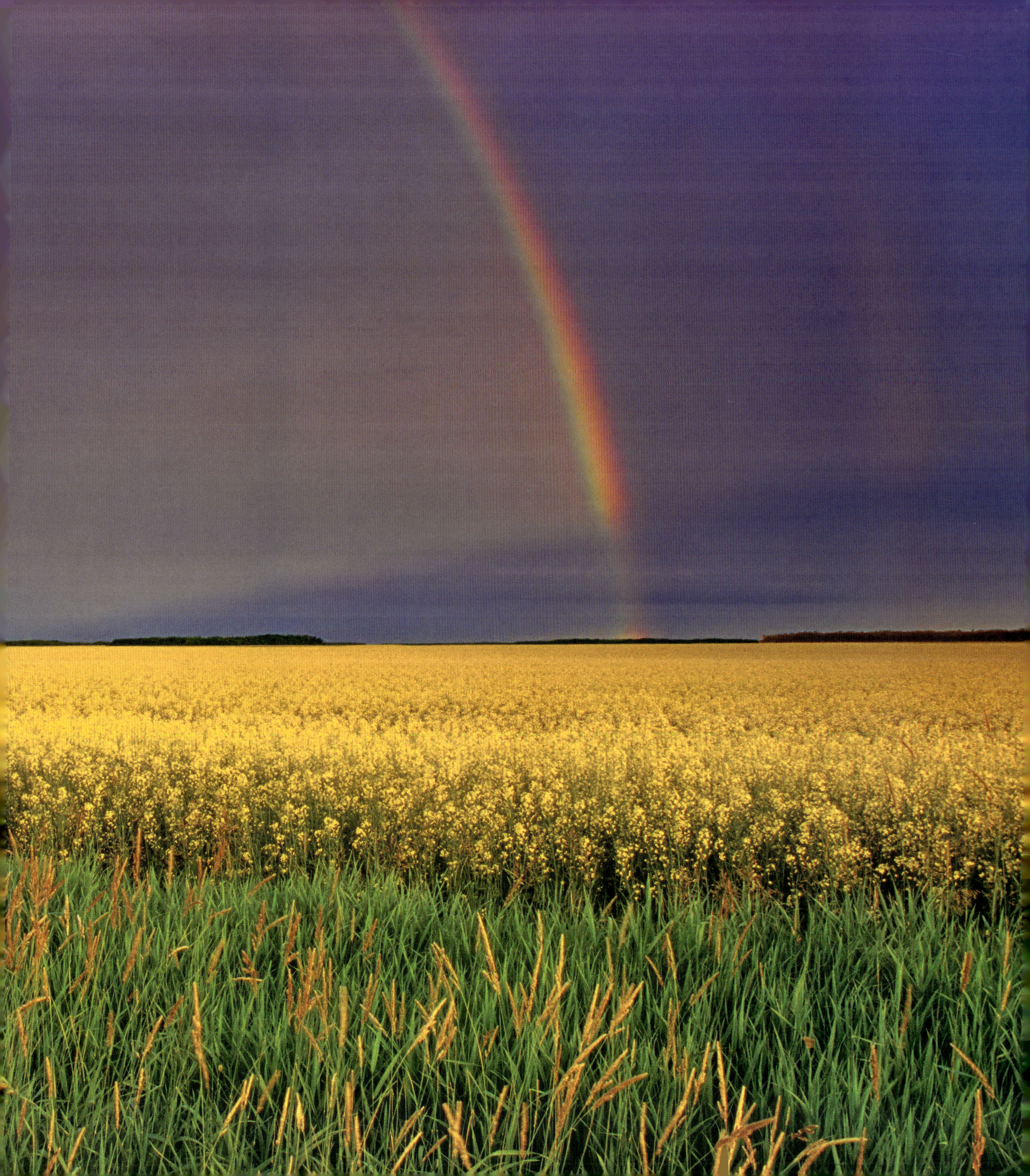

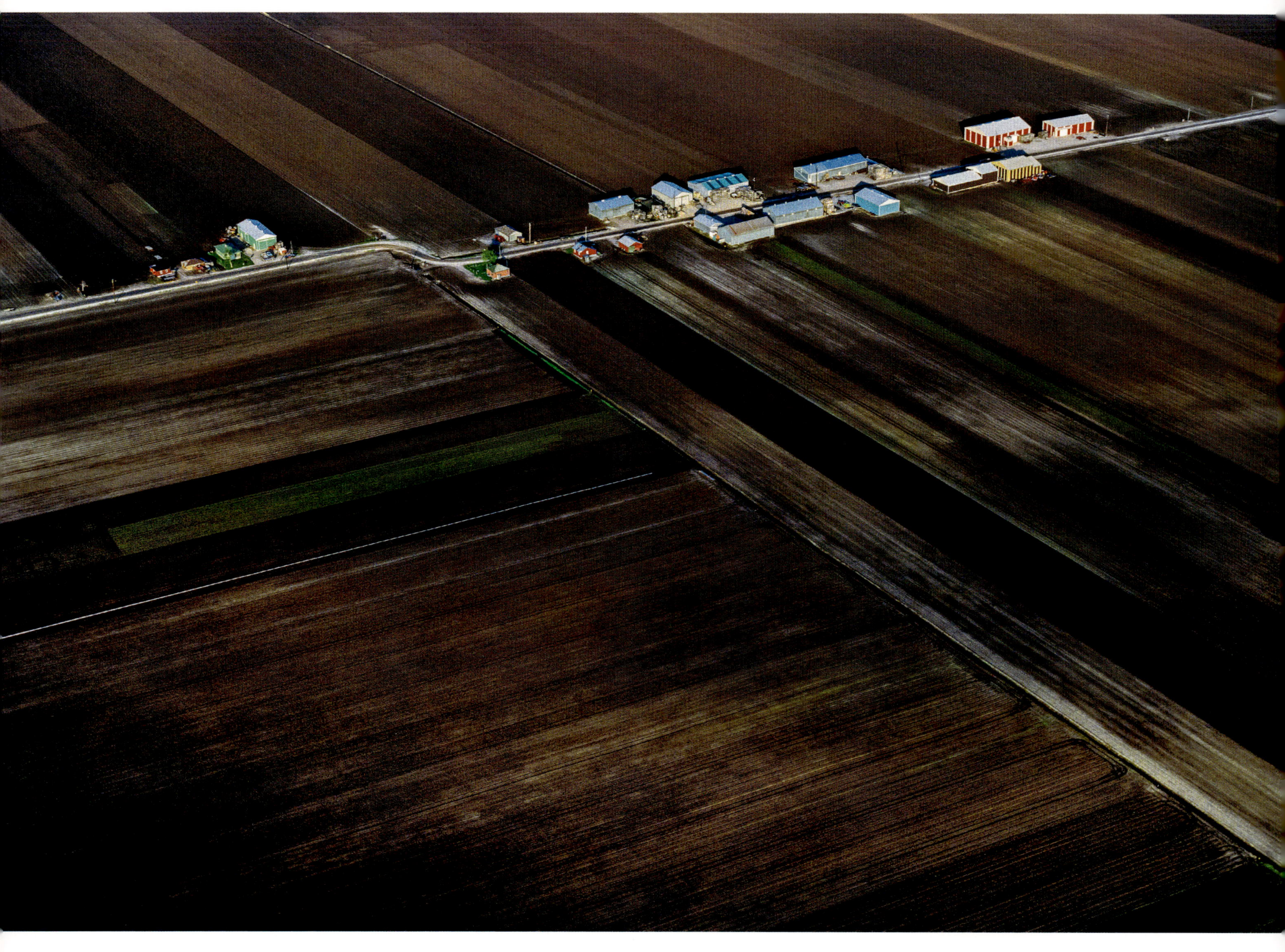

Aerial views in spring (above) and summer of market garden farming in the Holland Marsh between Toronto and Barrie, Ontario.

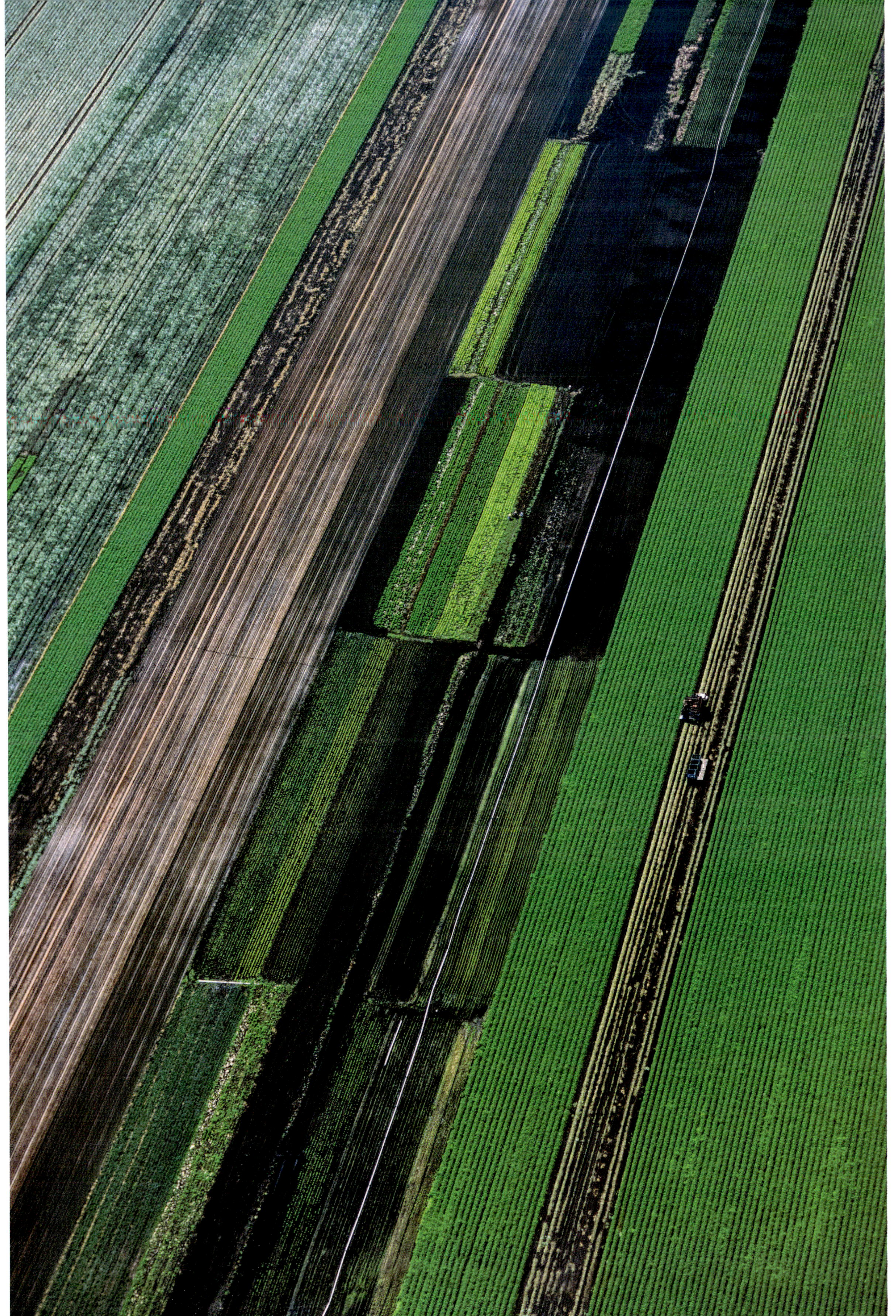

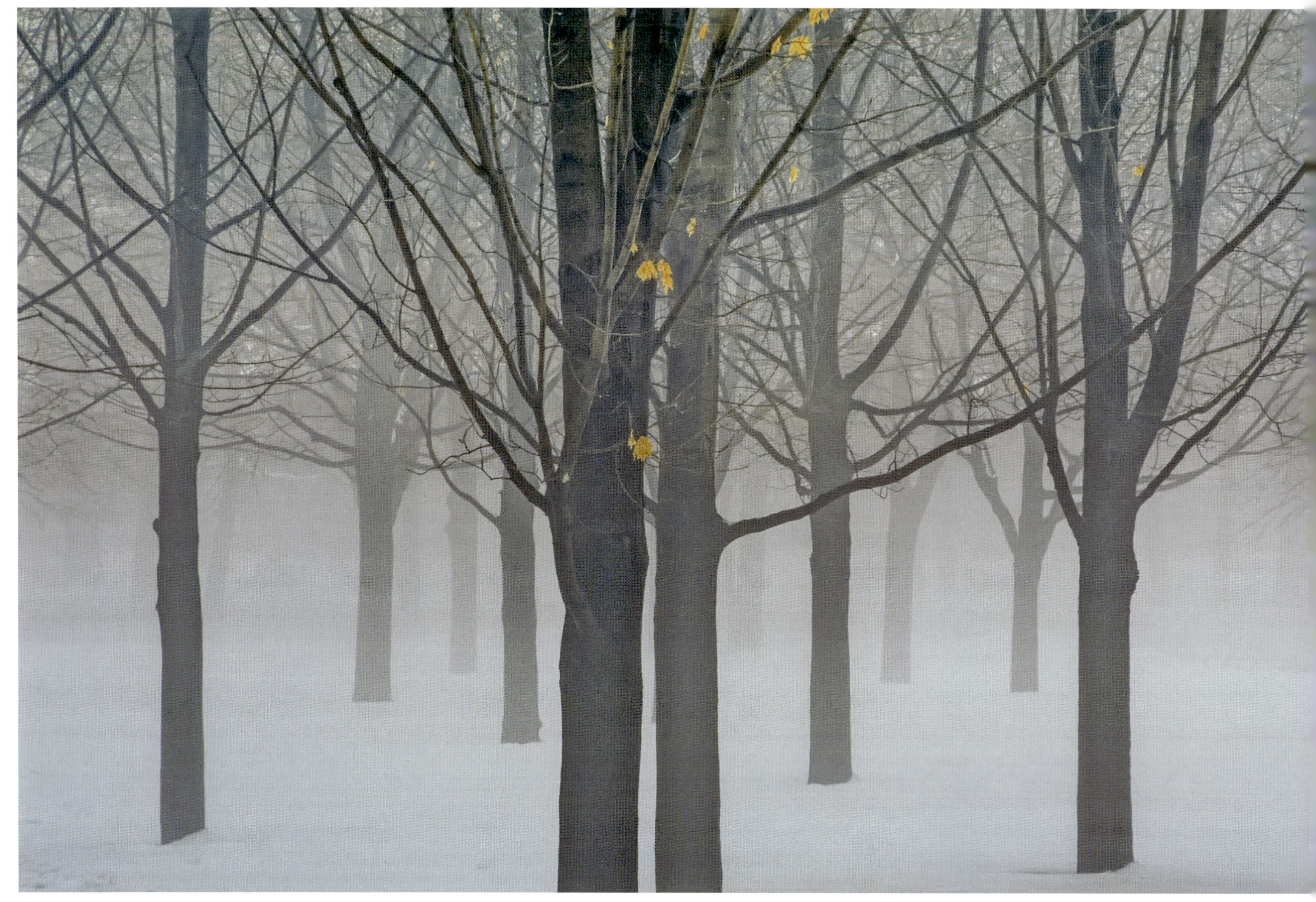

Mist on a winter's day in High Park, Toronto
(above).

Algae and autumn leaves float on a pond
reflecting tree trunks in Muskoka, Ontario.

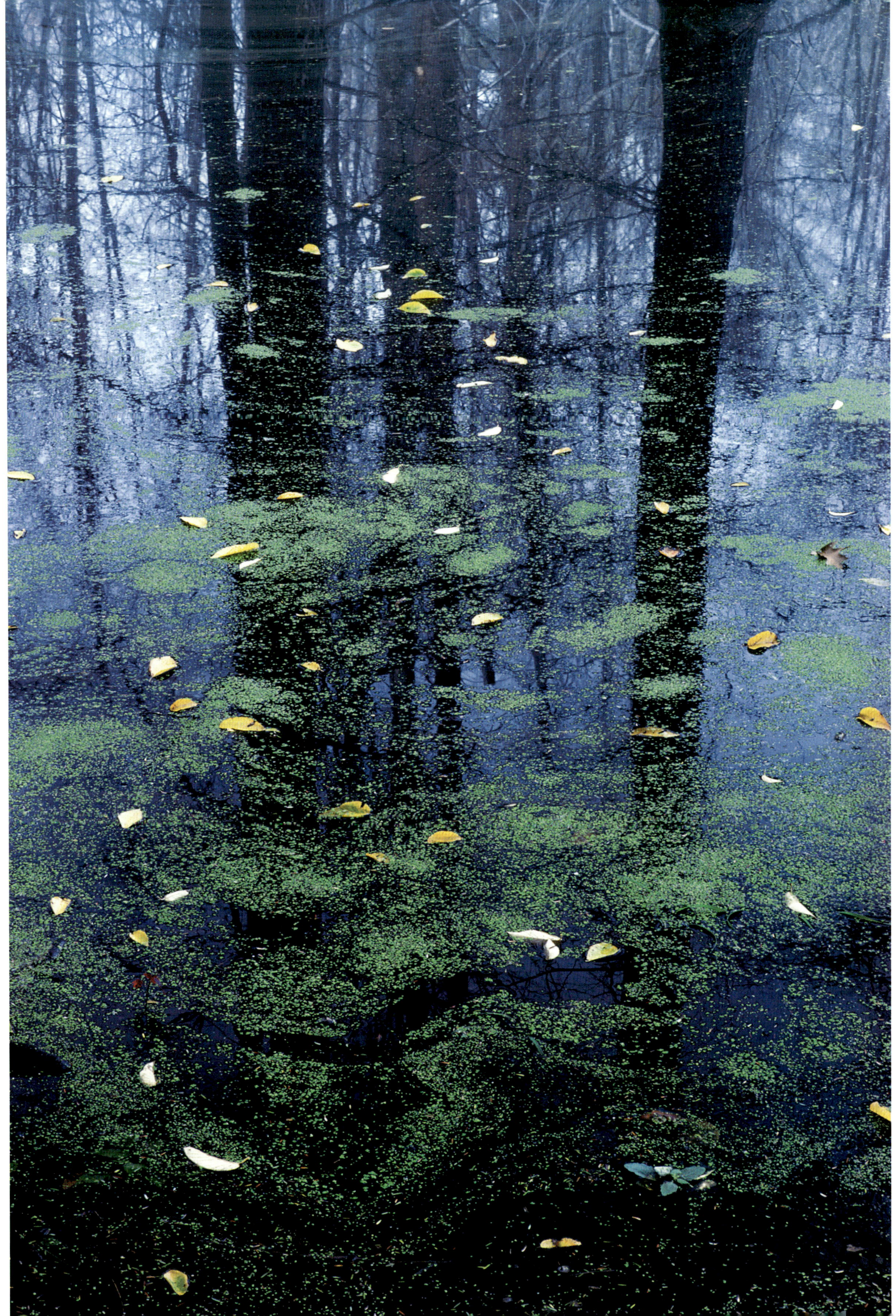

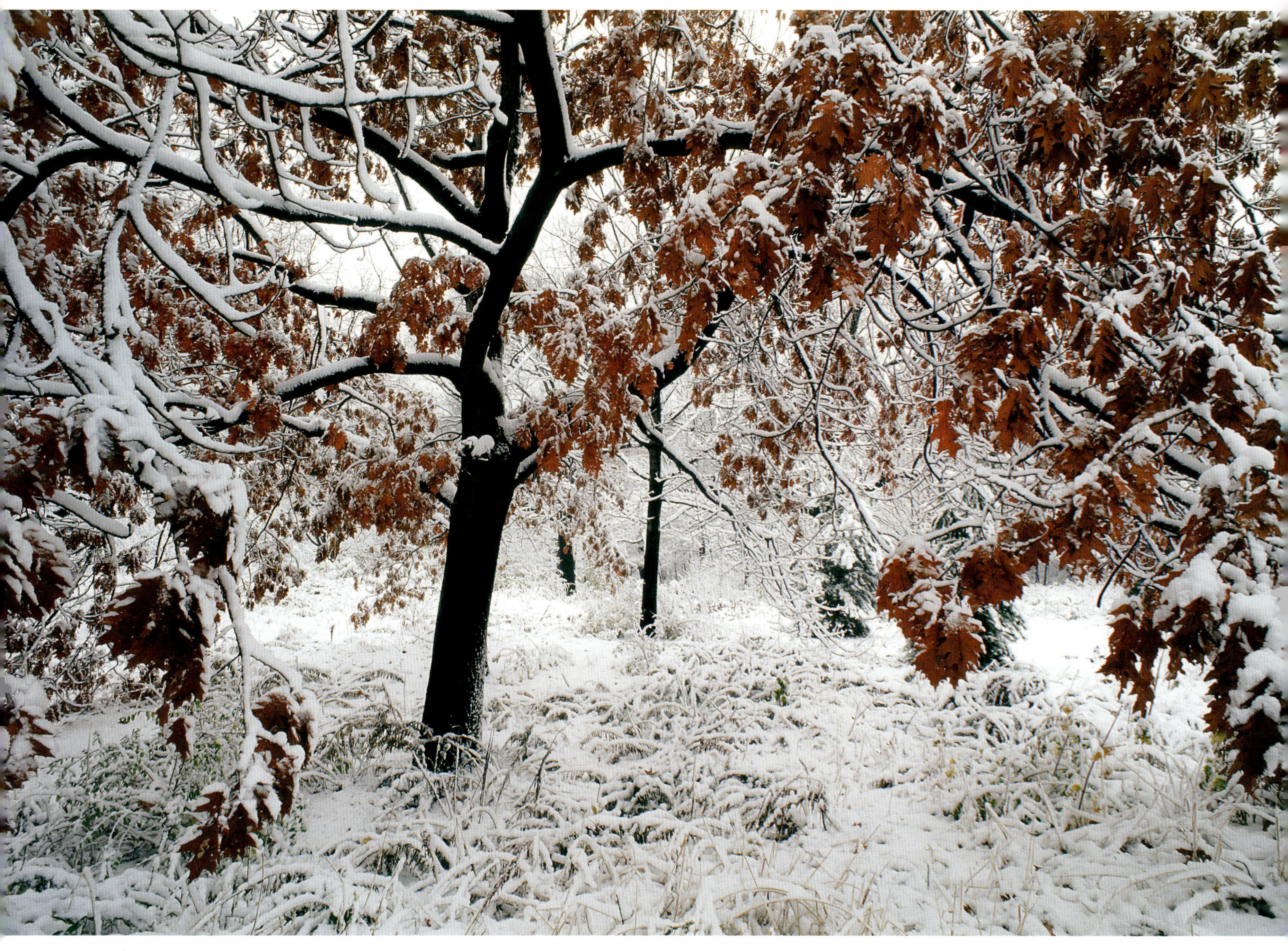

Lingering autumn leaves of oak (above) and maple
add colour to High Park, Toronto, freshly white
after an early winter snowfall.

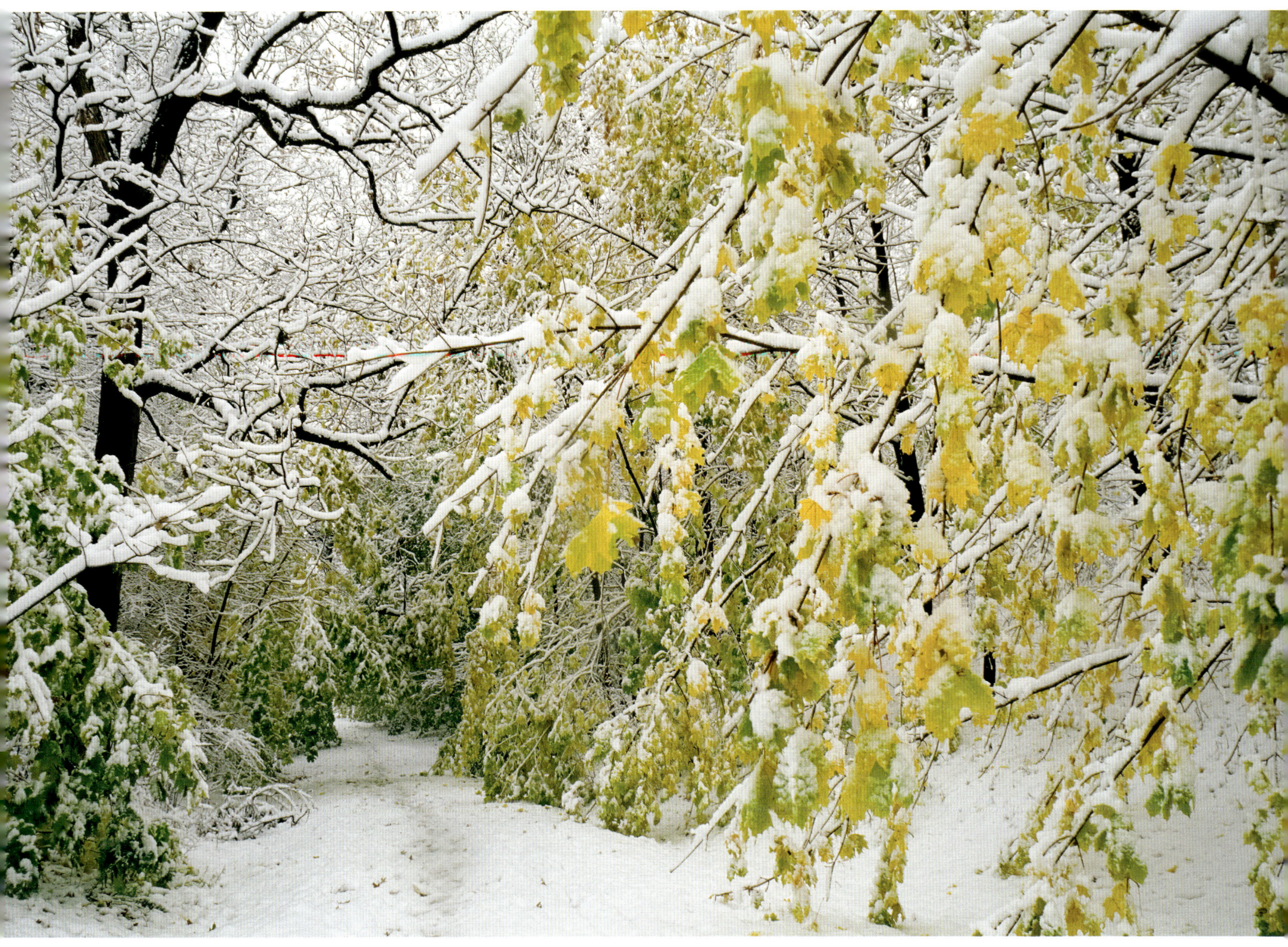

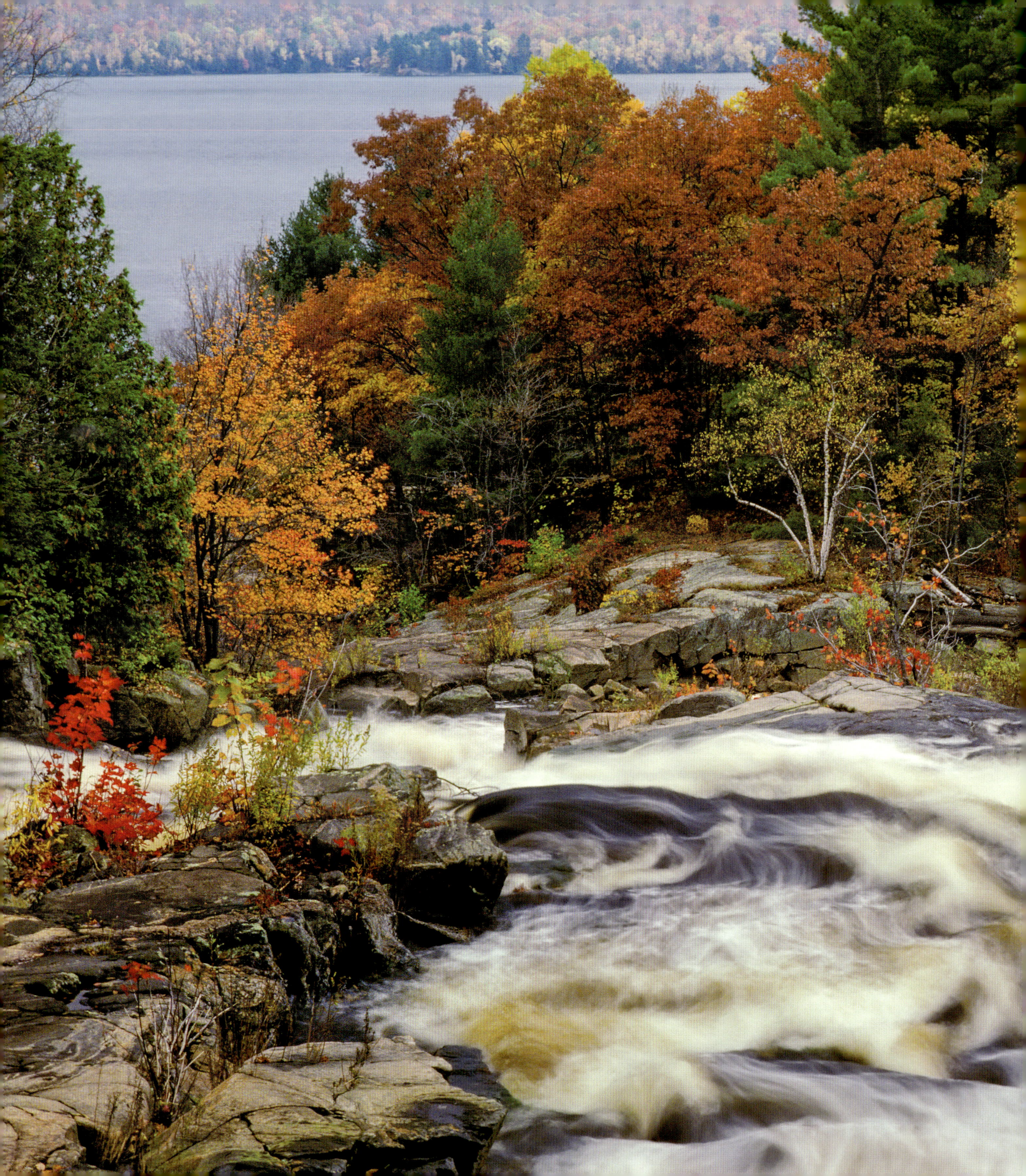

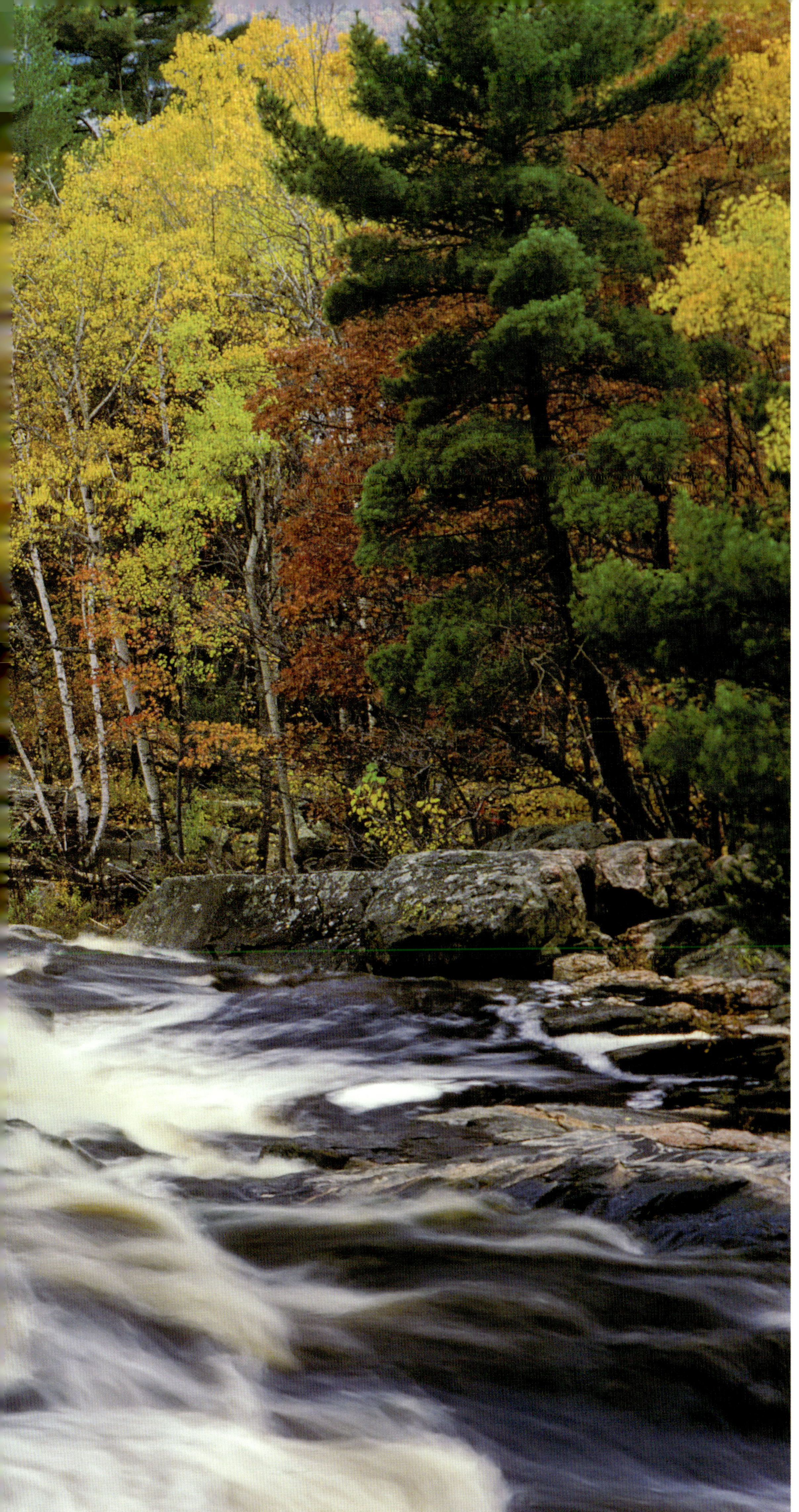

Rosseau Falls cascades into Lake Rosseau
in autumn, Muskoka, Ontario.

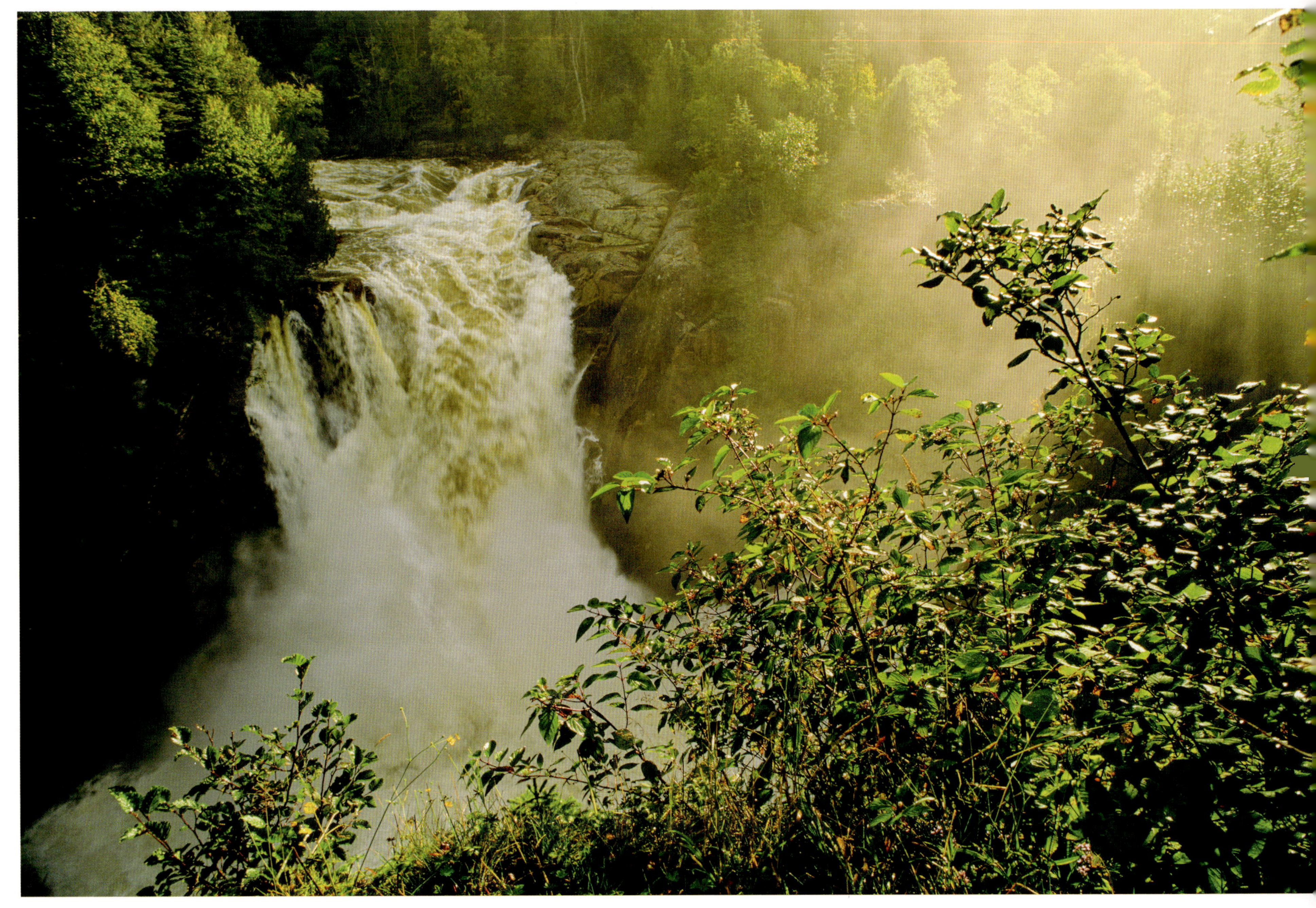

Following fractures in two-and-a-half-billion-
year-old bedrock, the Aguasabon River plunges 30
metres over Aguasabon Falls and into a deep gorge
near Terrace Bay, Ontario.

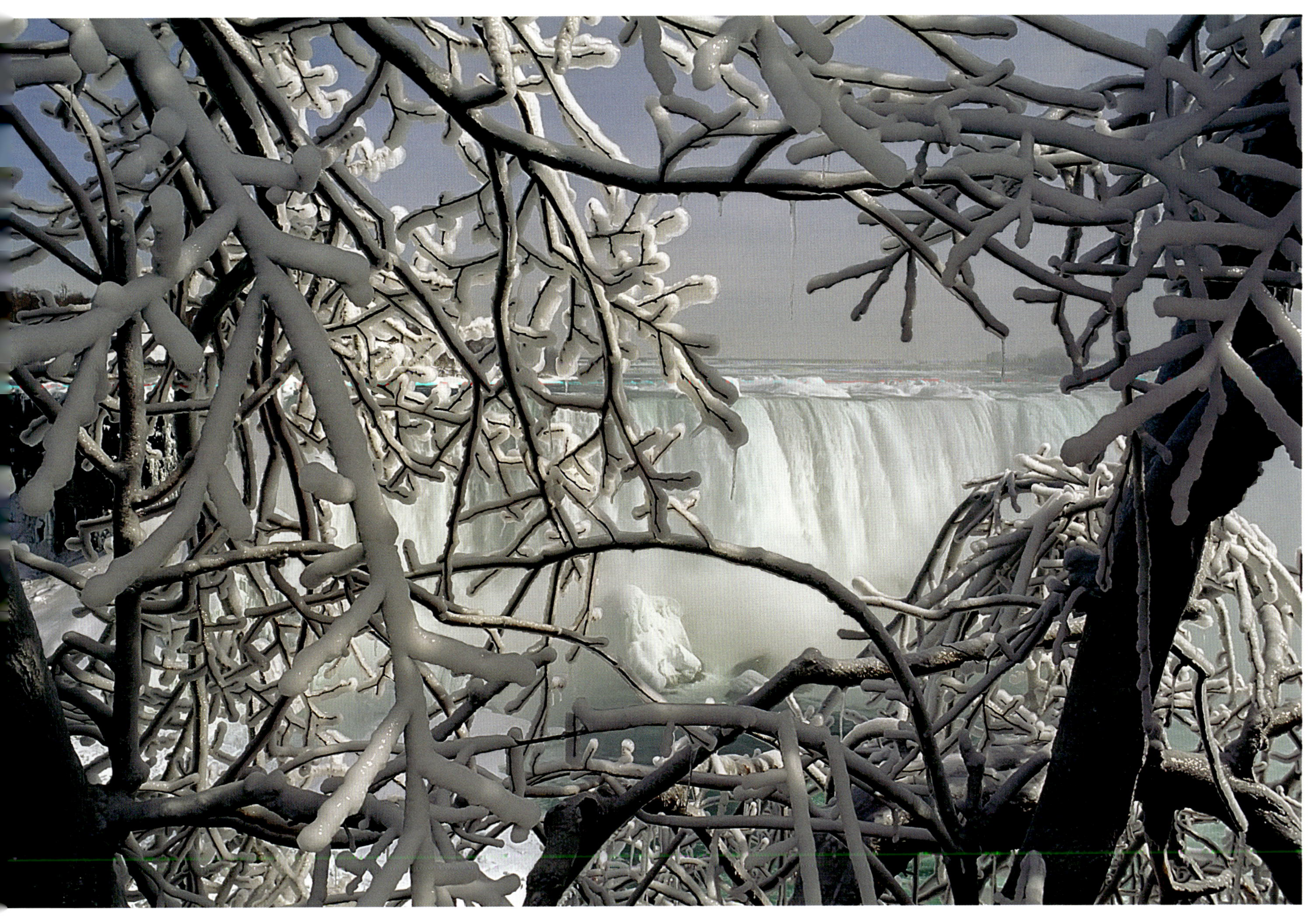

Trees rimed with ice from spray frame Horseshoe
Falls in winter, Niagara Falls, Ontario.

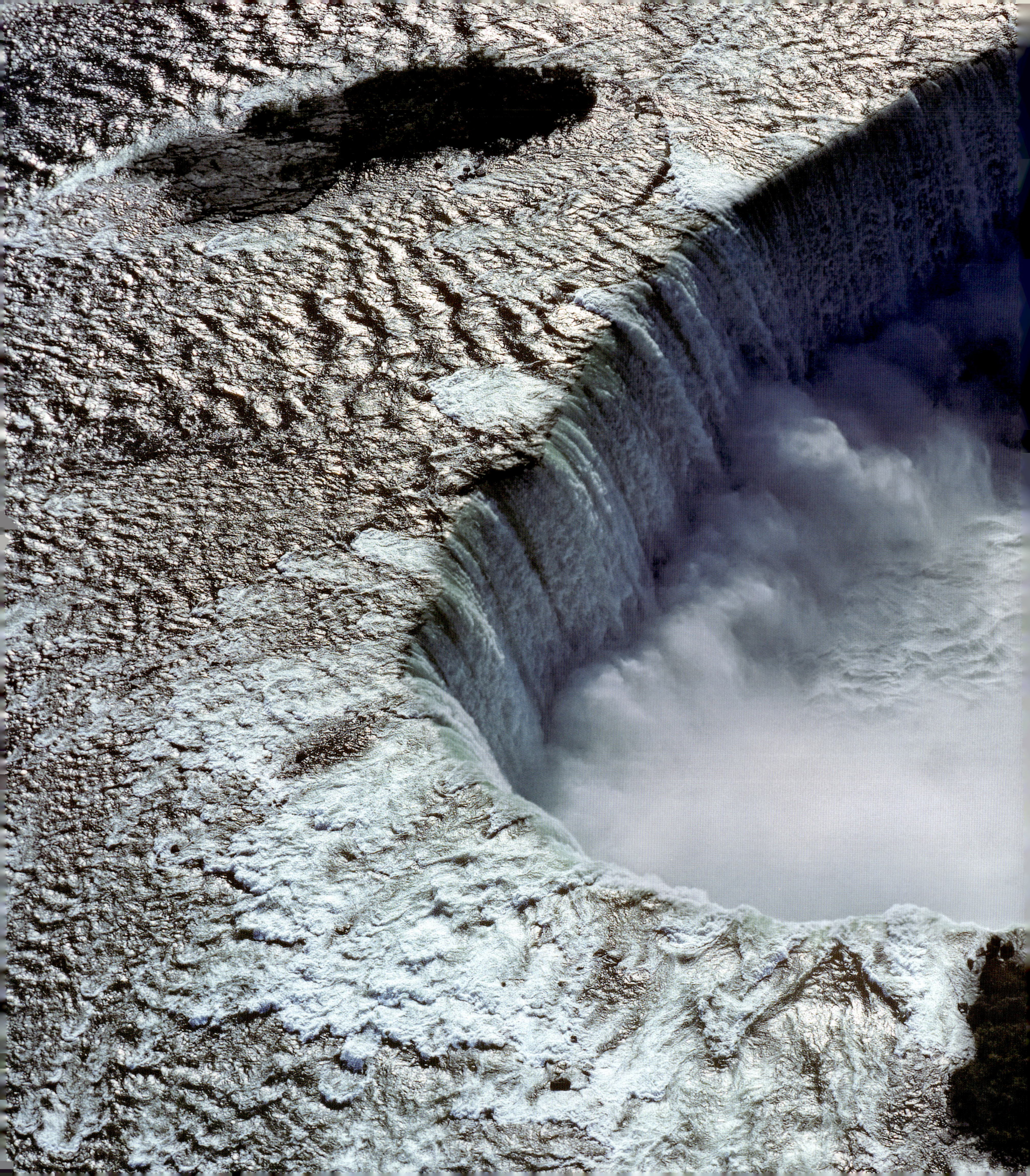

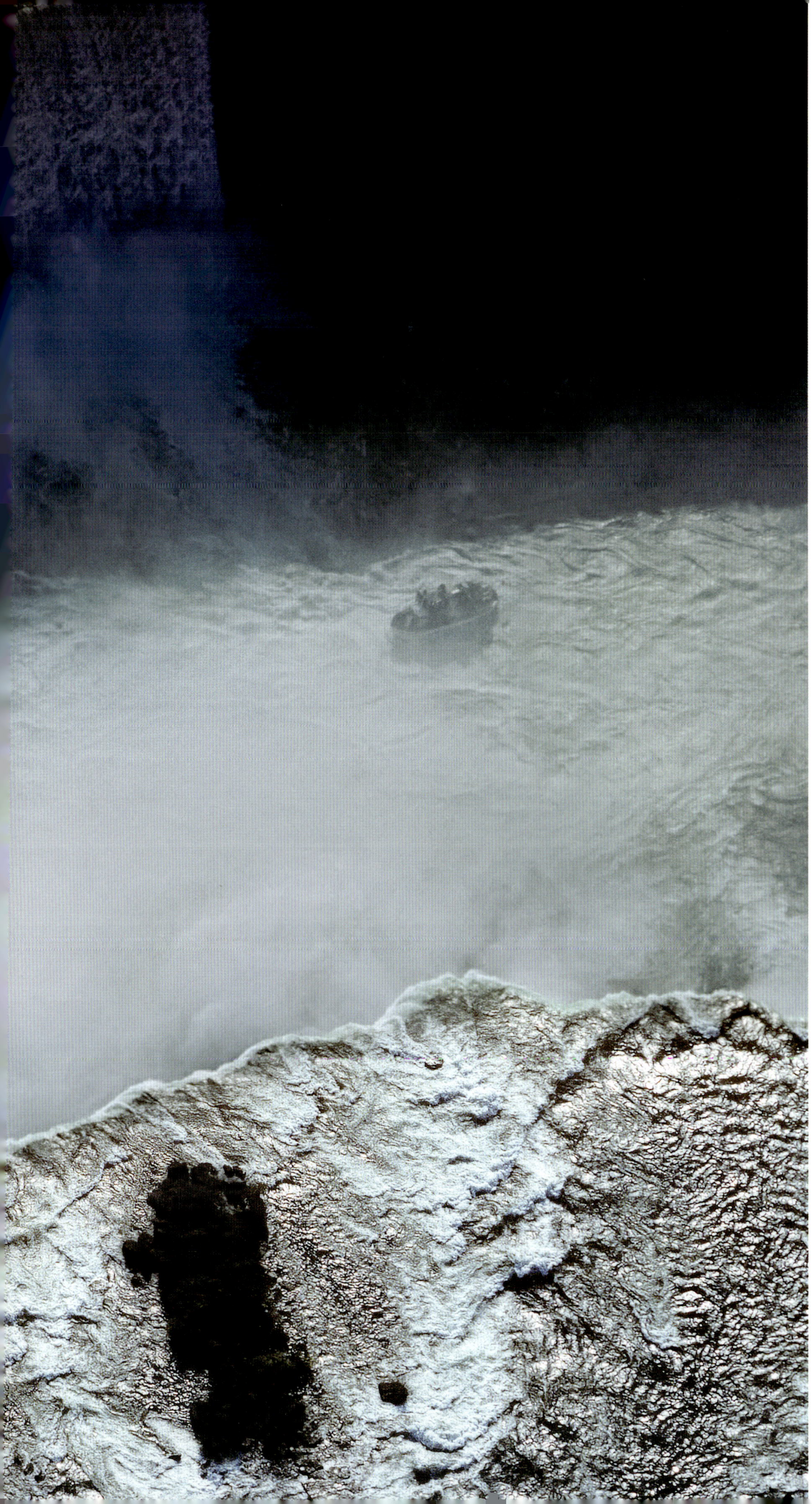

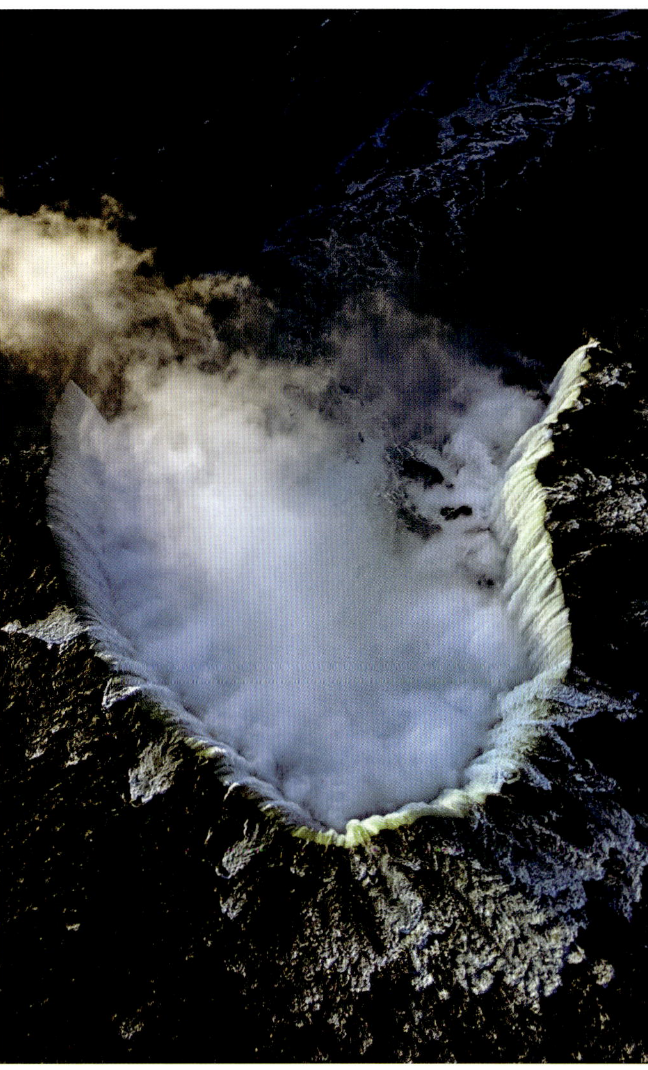

Horseshoe Falls from above, Niagara Falls, Ontario.

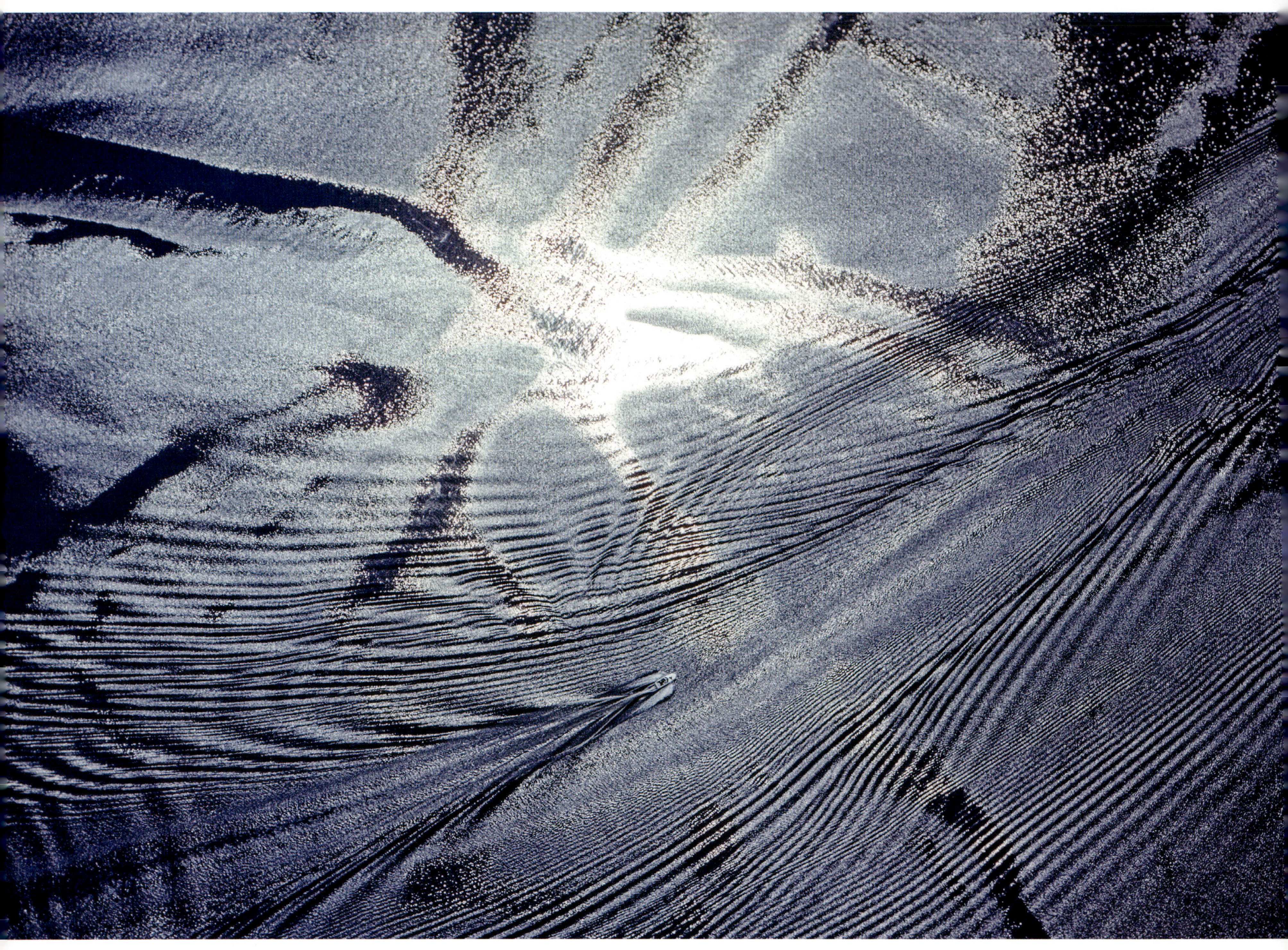

Aerial views of motorboat wakes in summer on the
Ottawa River (above) and in the Thirty Thousand
Islands, the world's largest freshwater archipelago
stretching for 150 kilometres along the east coast
of Georgian Bay, Lake Huron, Ontario.

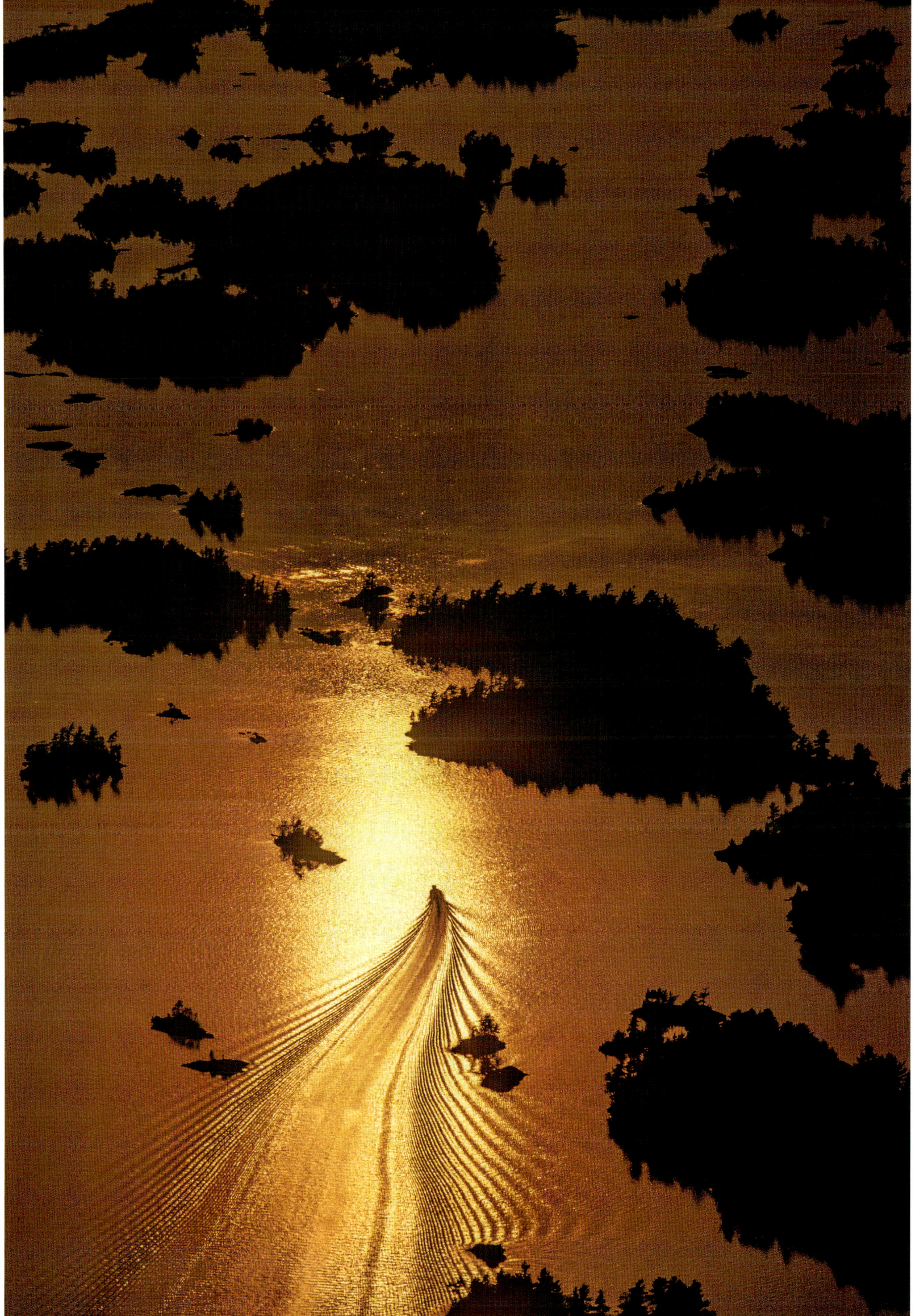

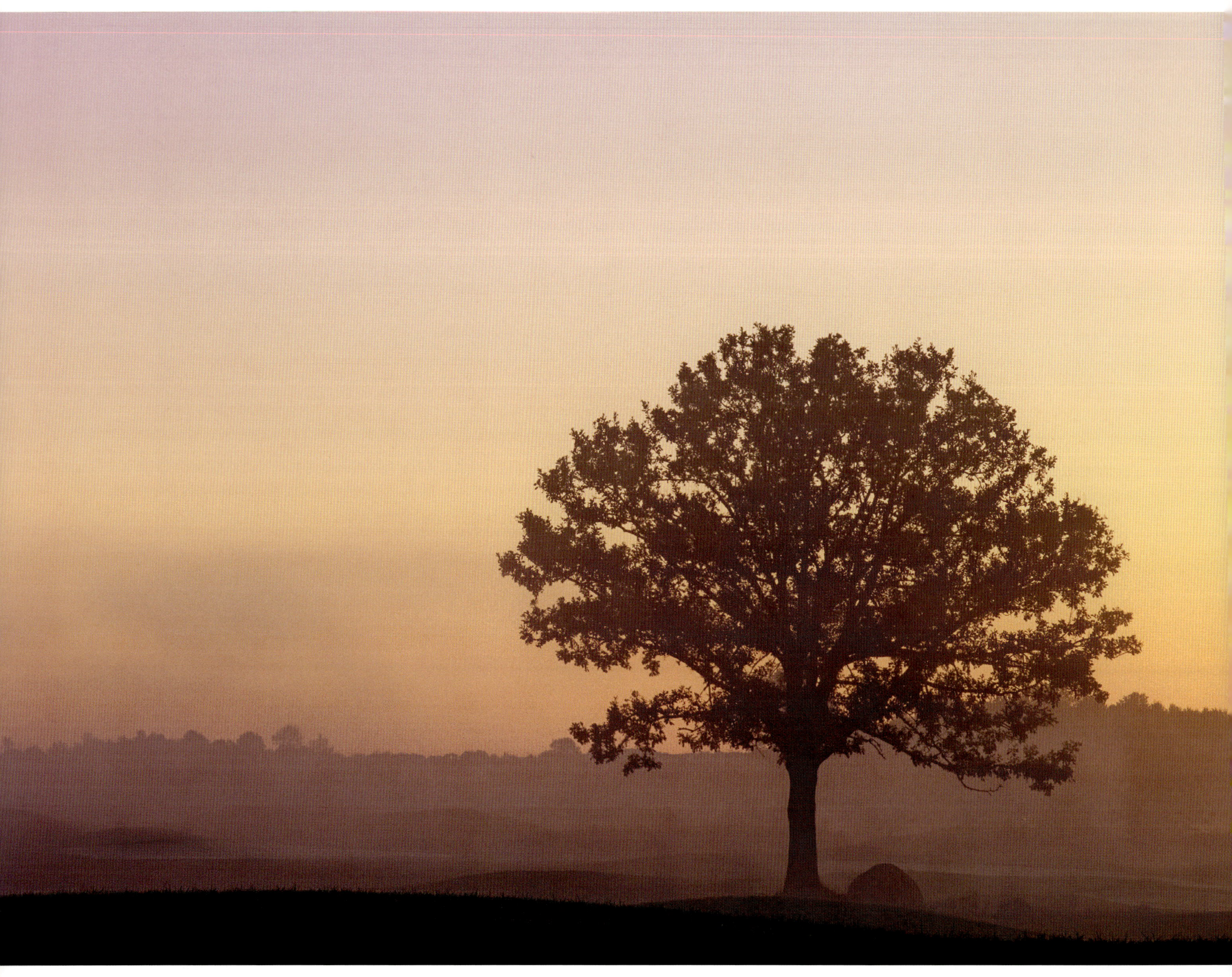

A lone tree early in the morning in the manicured
landscape of a golf course 10 kilometres south of
Barrie, Ontario.

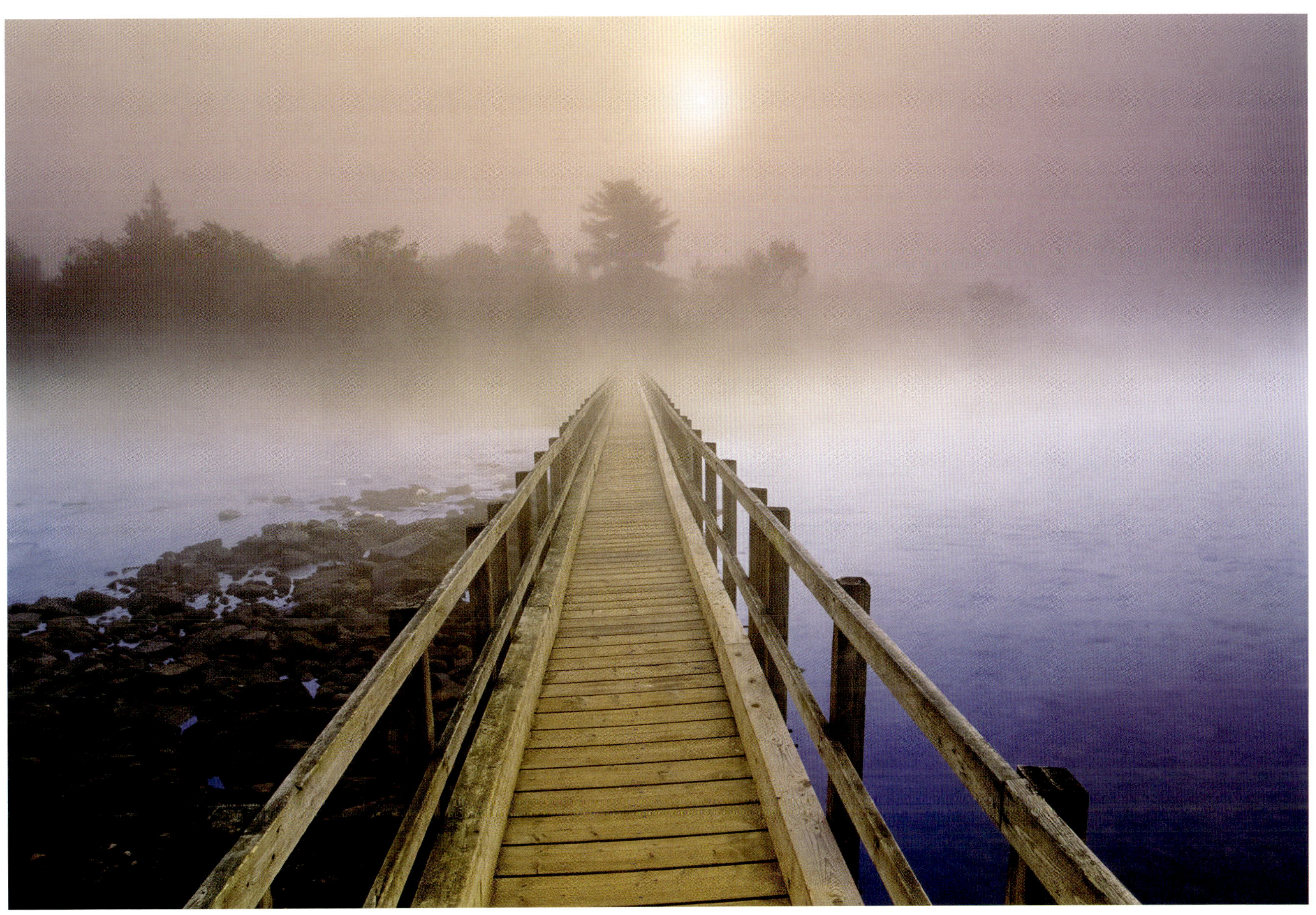

A walking bridge across the Du Fond River where
it leaves Moore Lake in Samuel de Champlain
Provincial Park, Ontario.

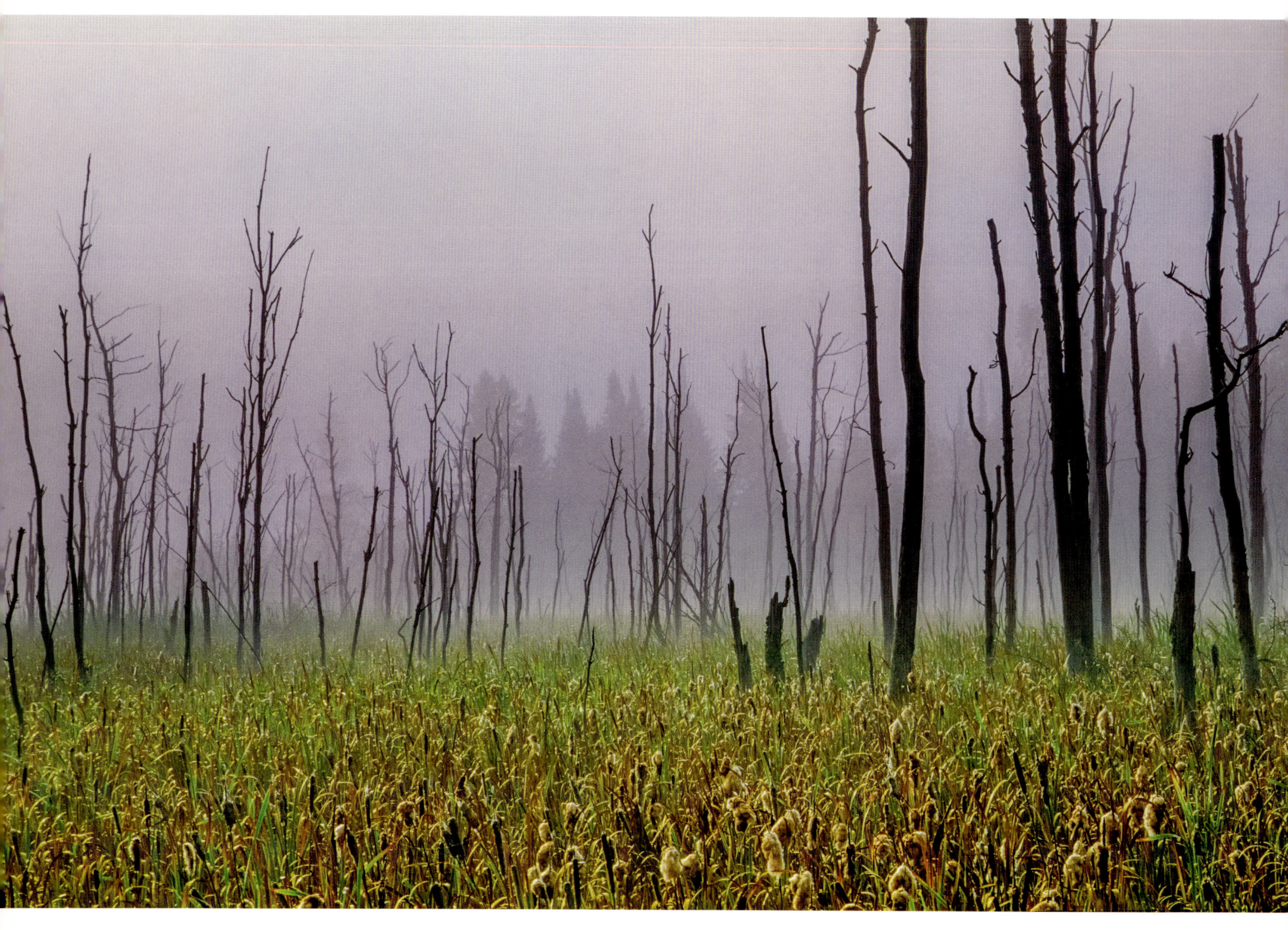

Tree snags and bullrushes in morning mist near
Mattawa, Ontario.

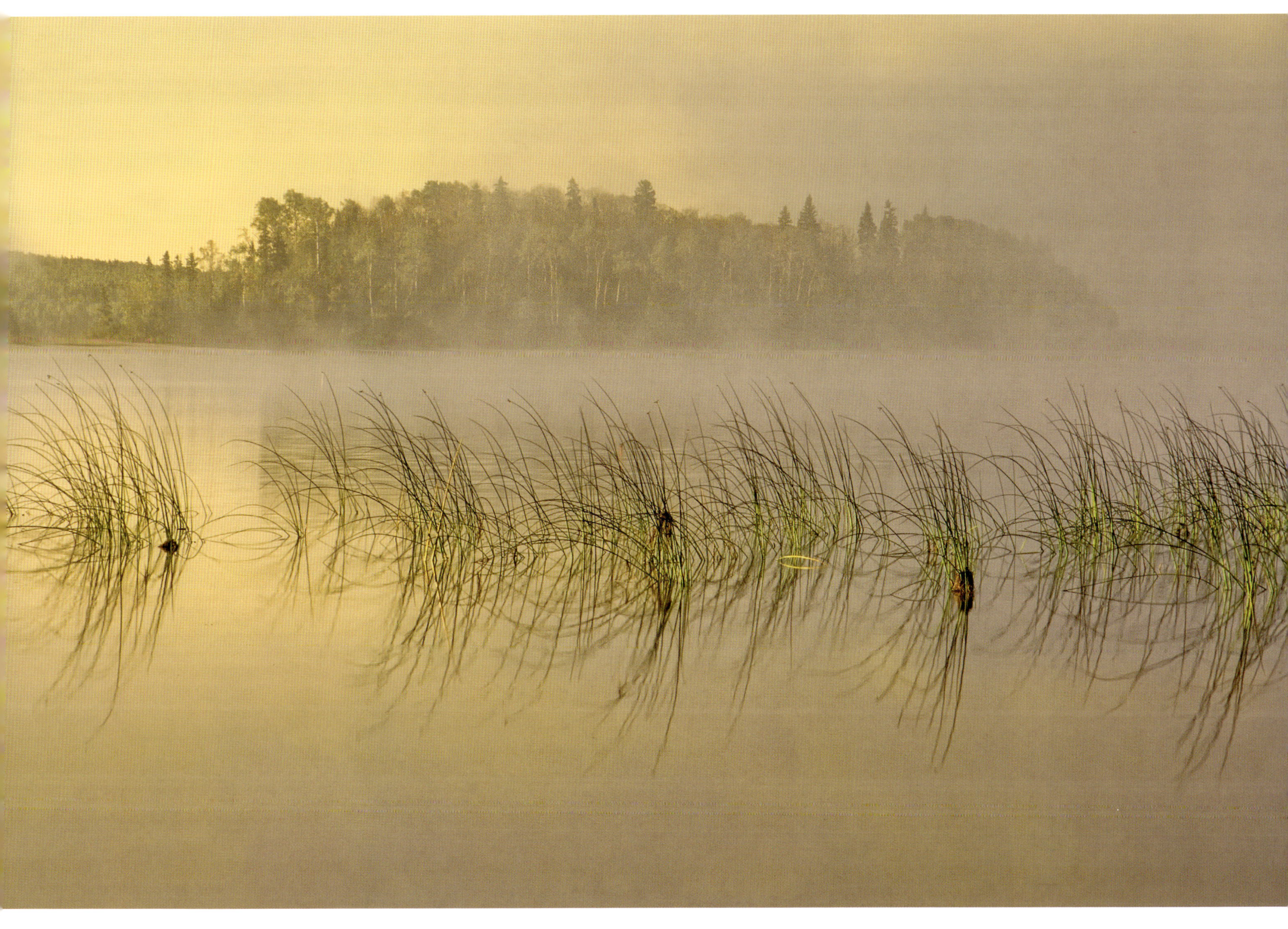

Reeds and mist early in the morning, White Lake
north of Lake Superior, Ontario.

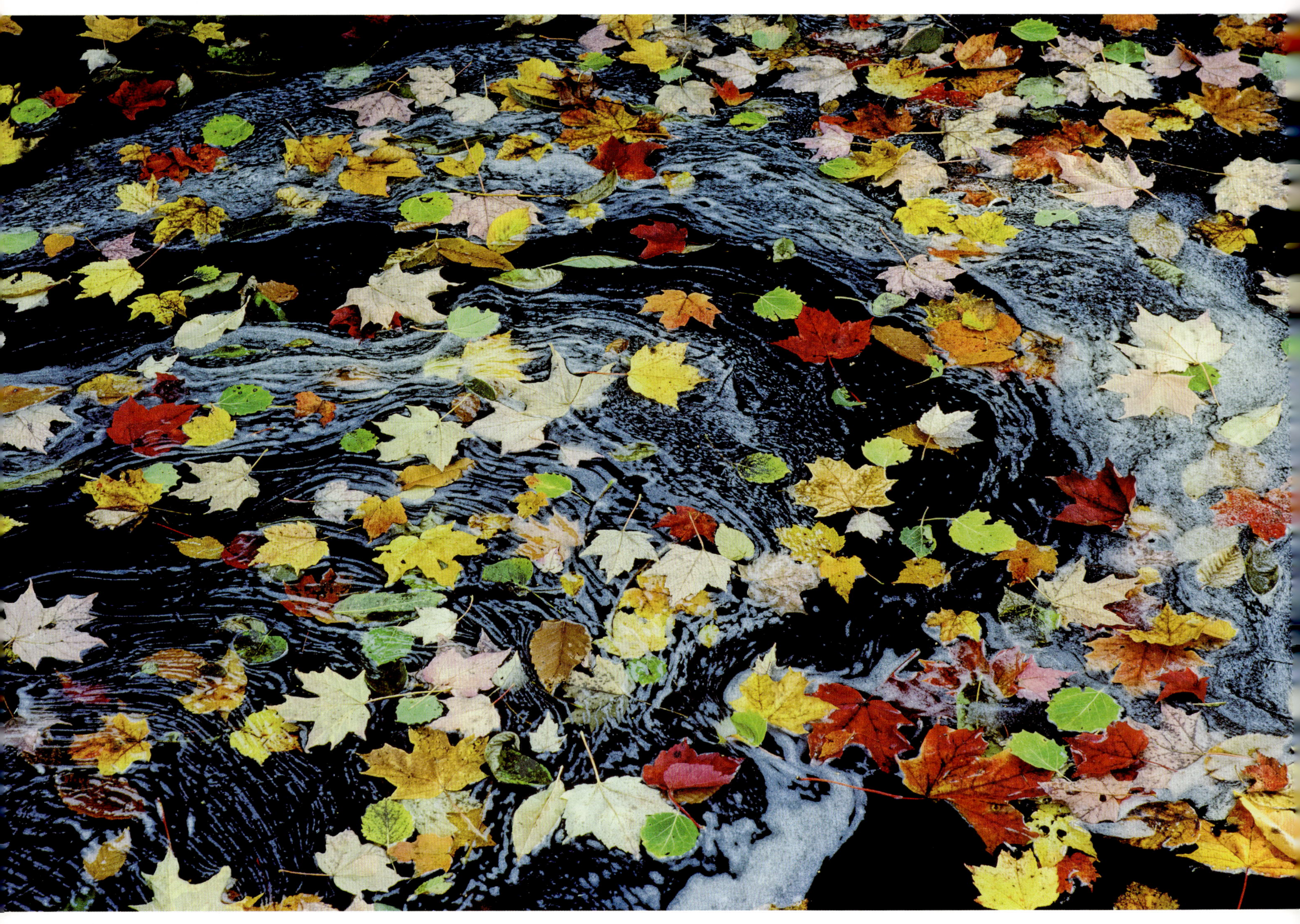

A swirl of autumn leaves, mostly maple, with
birch, aspen and beech, in a creek in Muskoka,
Ontario.

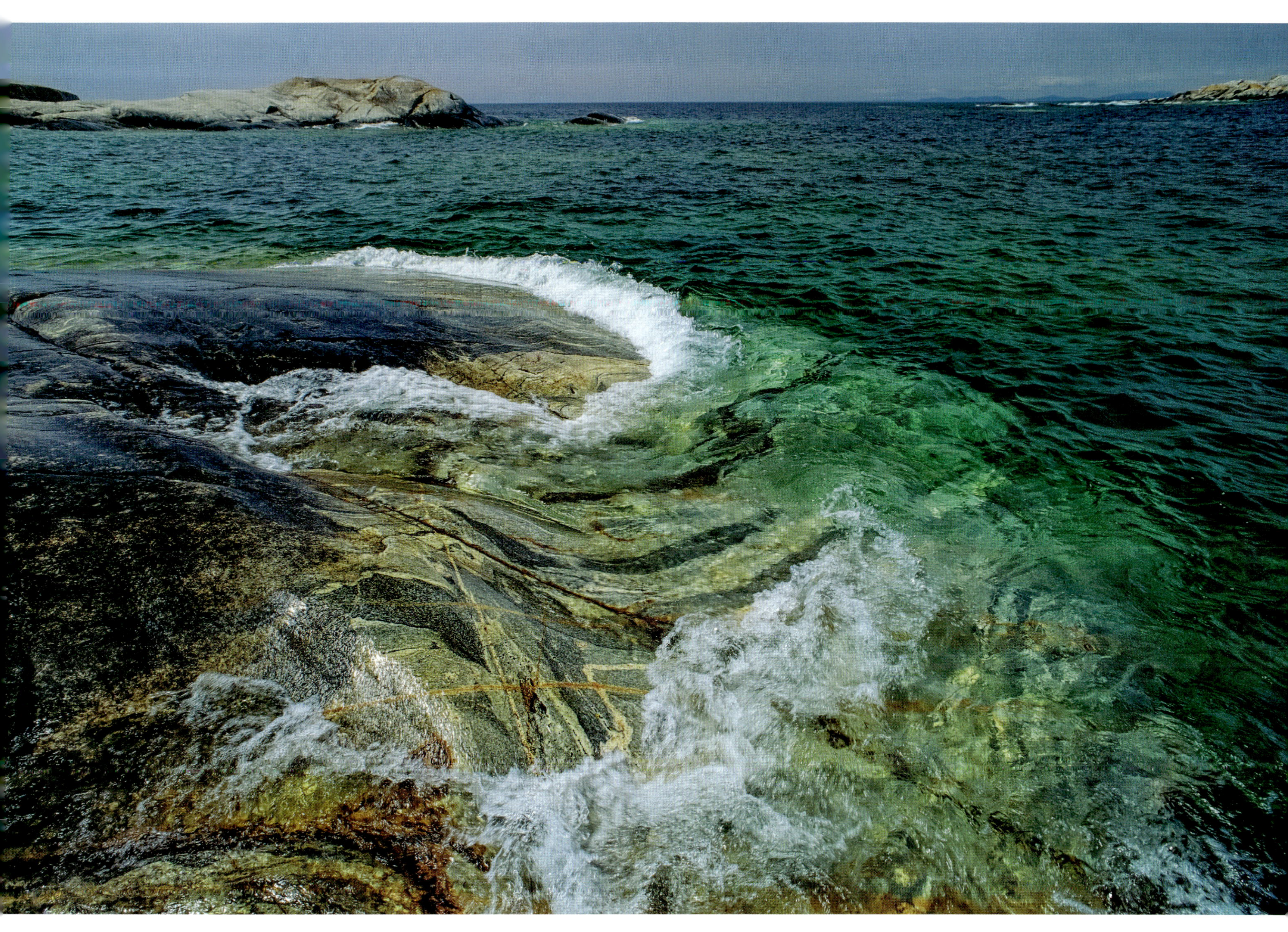

The strikingly clear emerald water of Lake Superior washes over the hard, smooth shoreline of banded gneiss in Pukaskwa National Park.

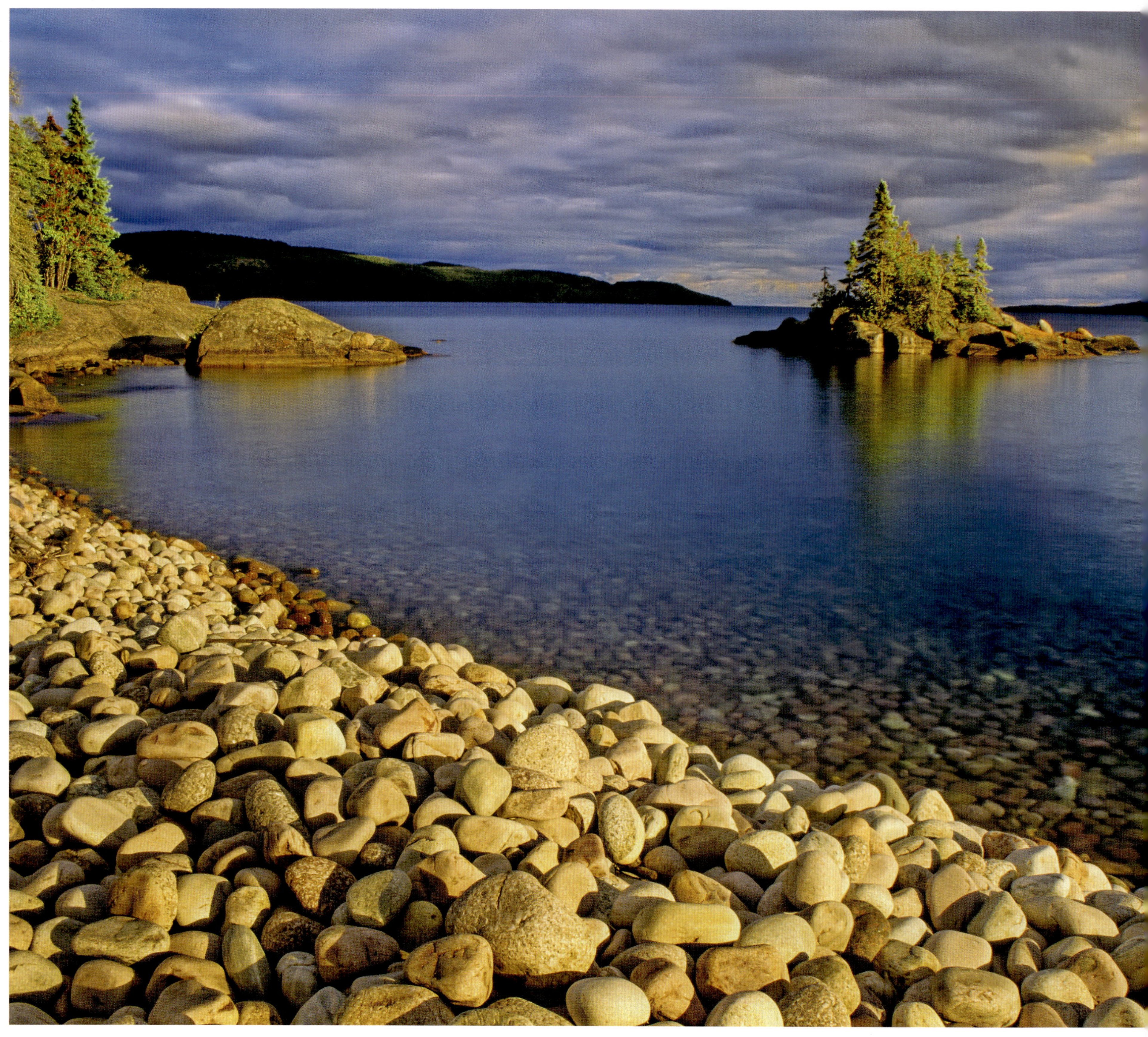

A lone island and cobble beach along the coast
of Lake Superior and beside the Trans-Canada
Highway east of Rossport, Ontario.

Ancient banded gneiss along the shore in Lake
Superior Provincial Park. Some of the rock in the
park is two-and-a-half billion years old.

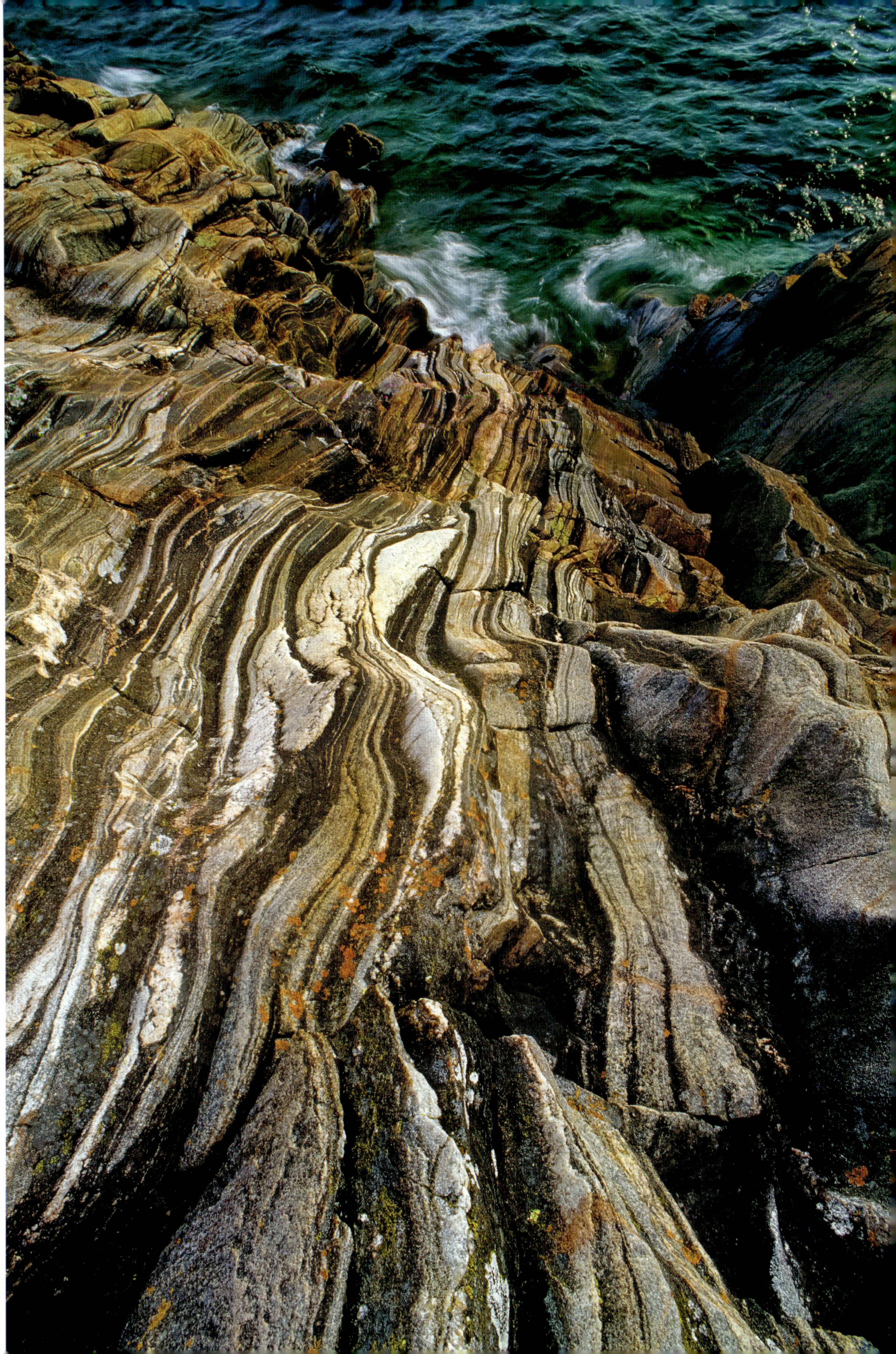

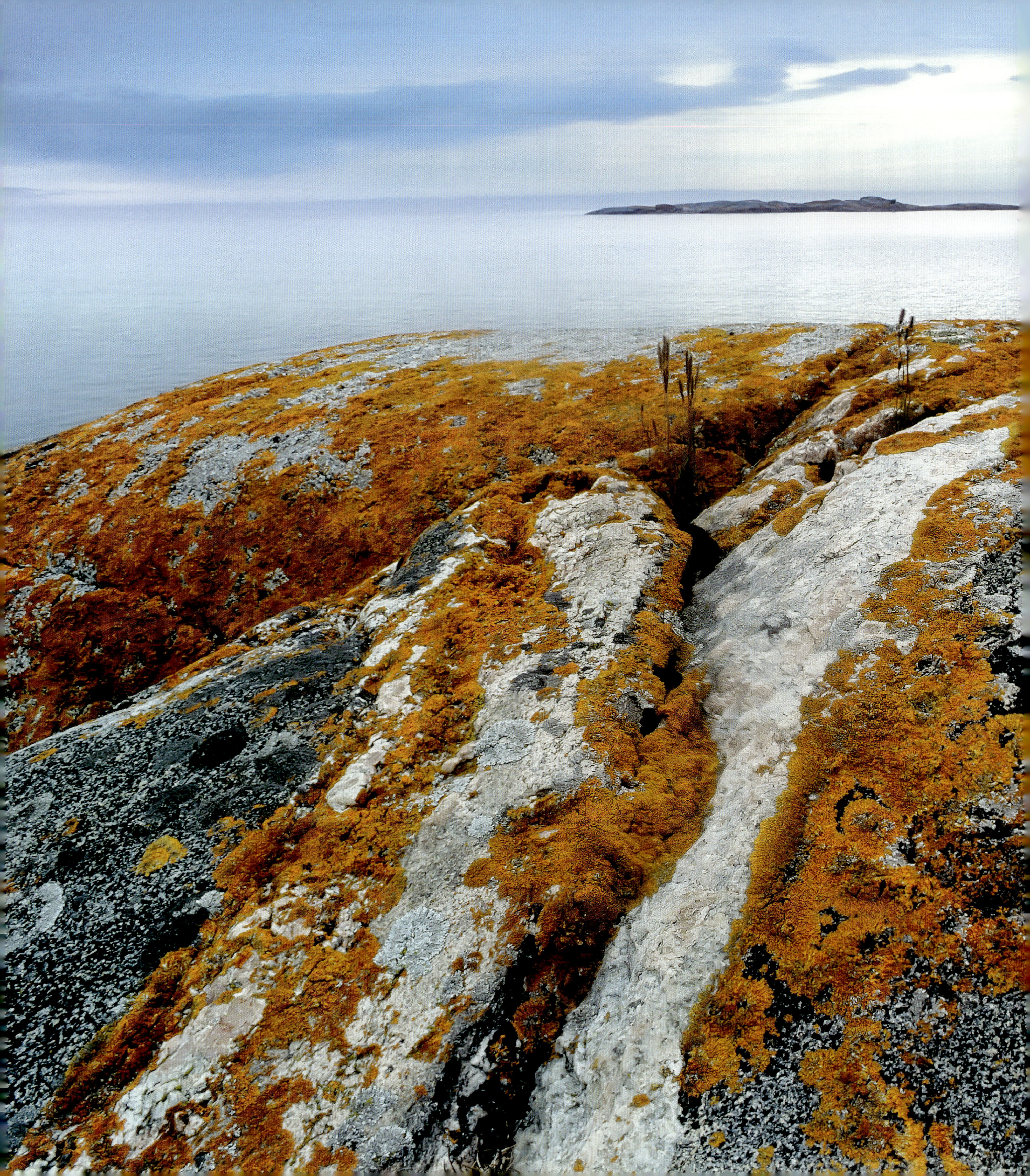

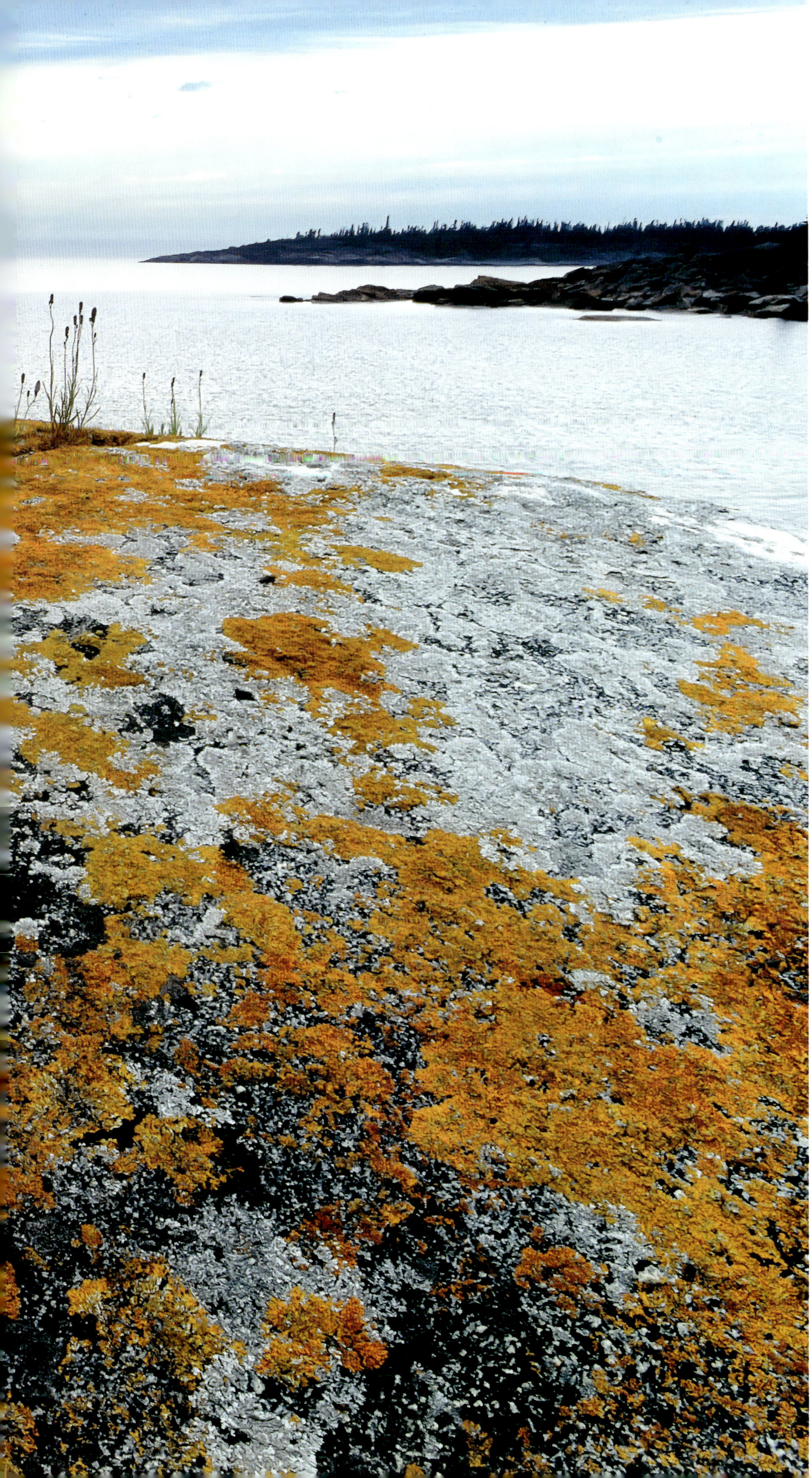

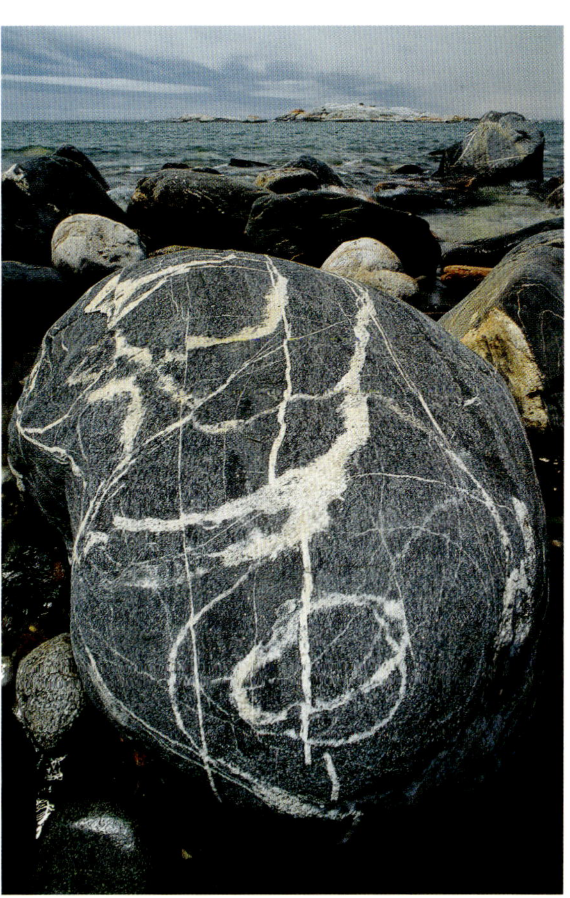

Outcrops and boulders of very ancient Precambrian stone are characteristic of the Lake Superior shoreline along the Coastal Hiking Trail in Pukaskwa National Park, Ontario.

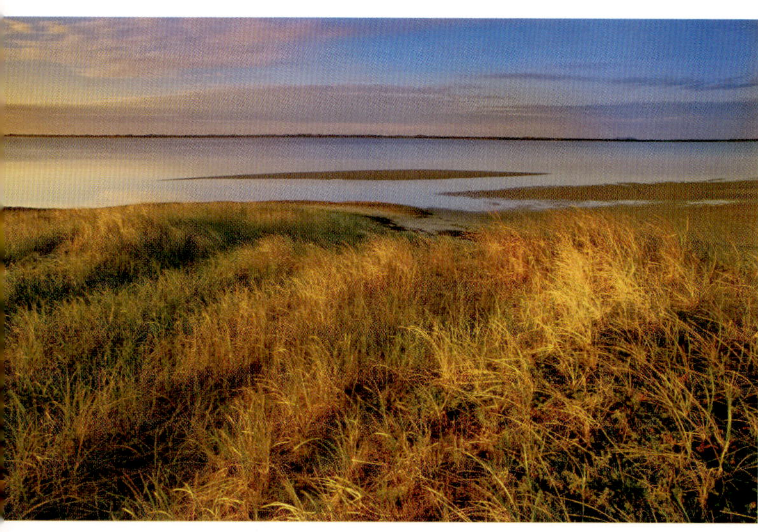

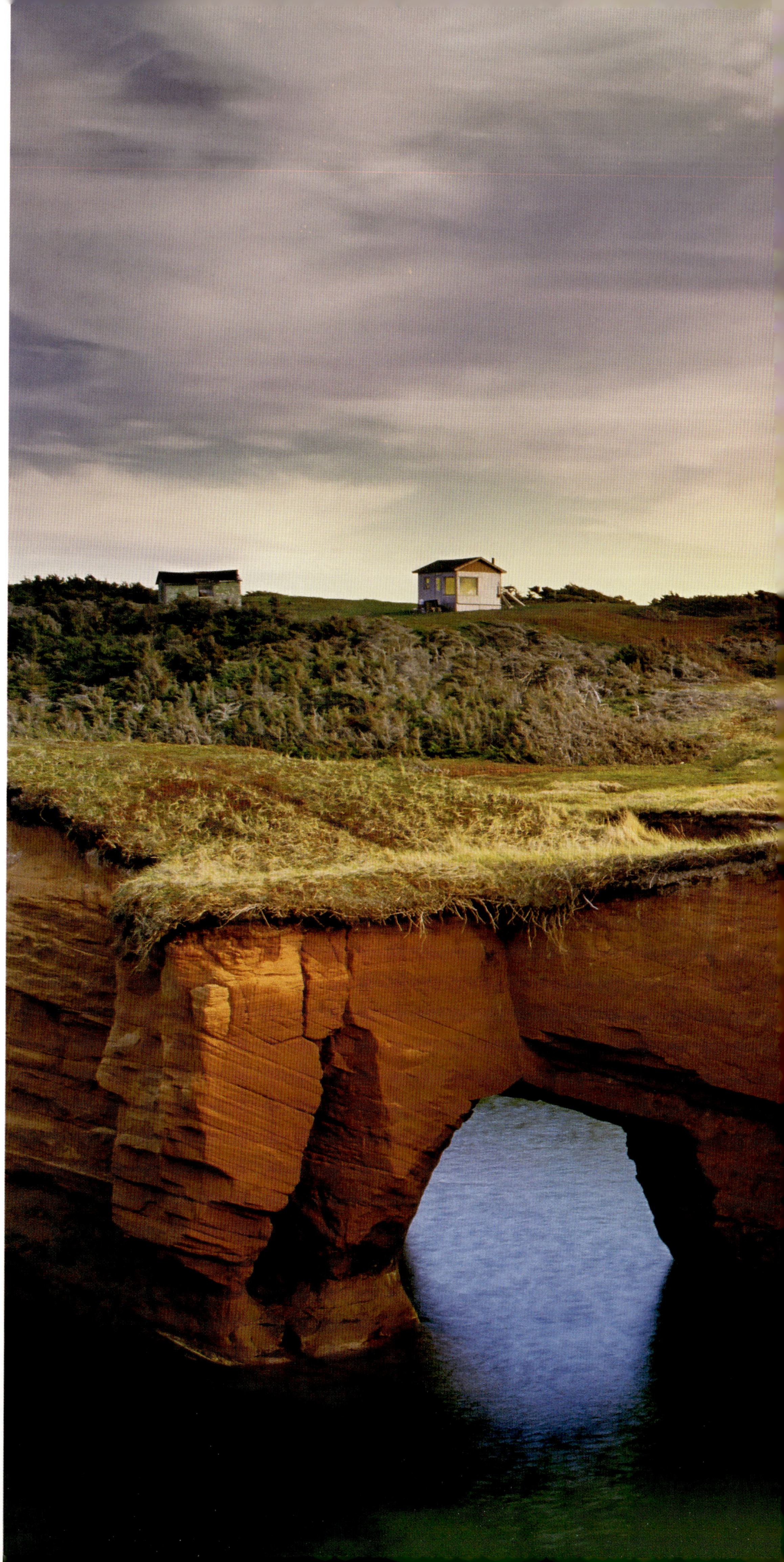

Along North Dune overlooking Grande-Entrée Lagoon
(above) and at Cap au Trou on the west coast of Île du
Cap-aux-Meules, Magdalen Islands, Quebec.

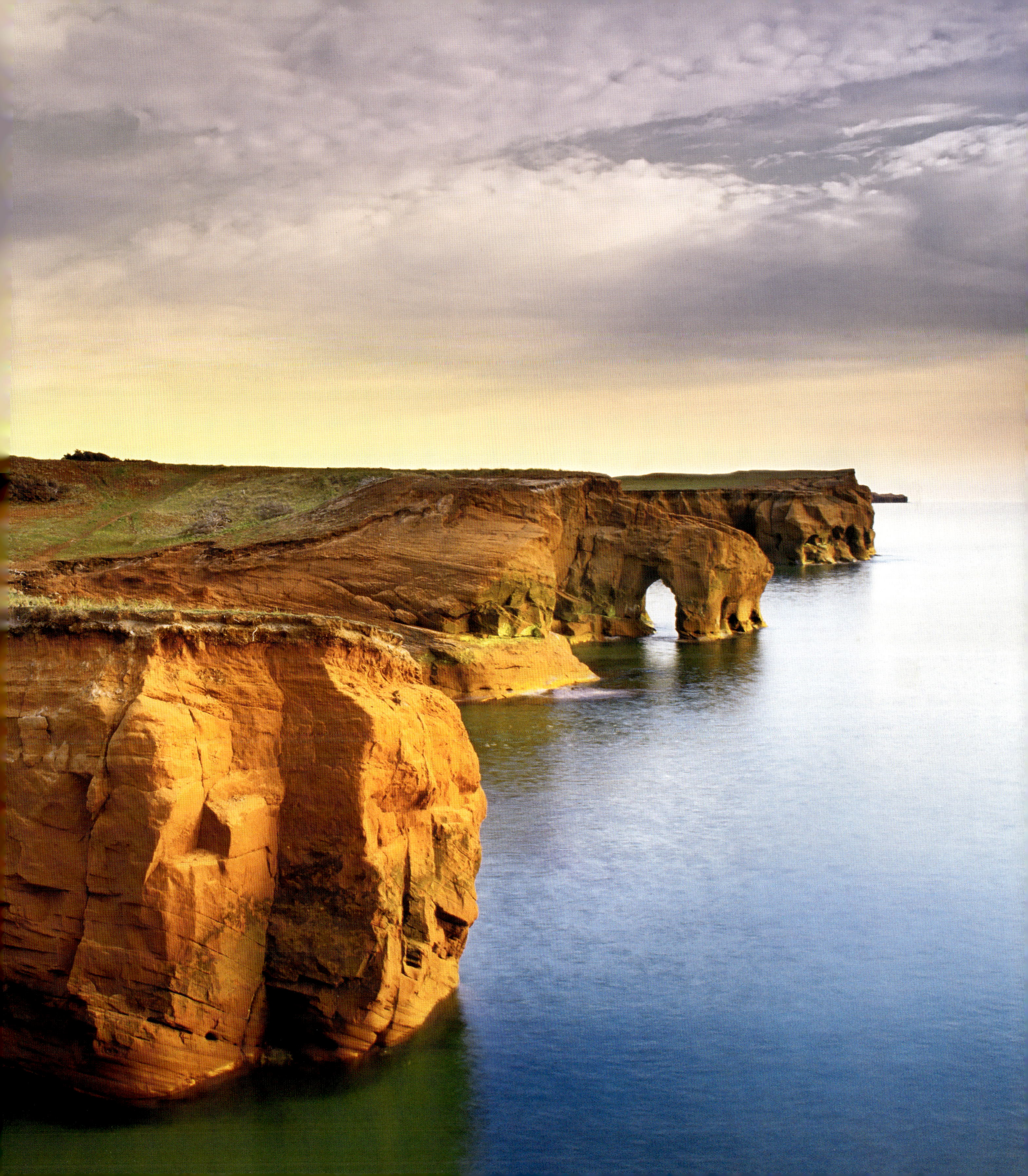

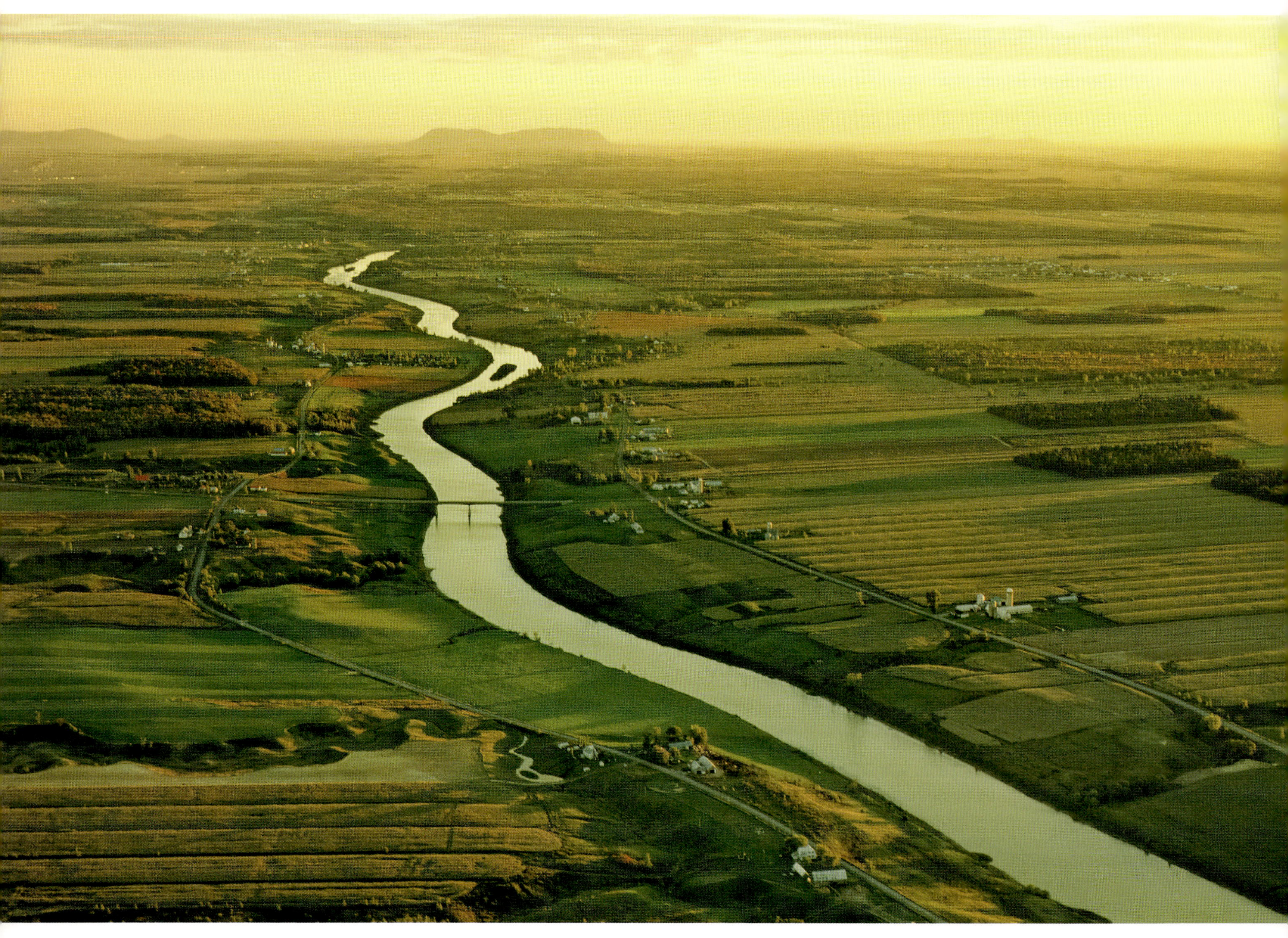

The Yamaska River winds through the long lots of
farmland common in the Saint Lawrence Lowlands
of Quebec.

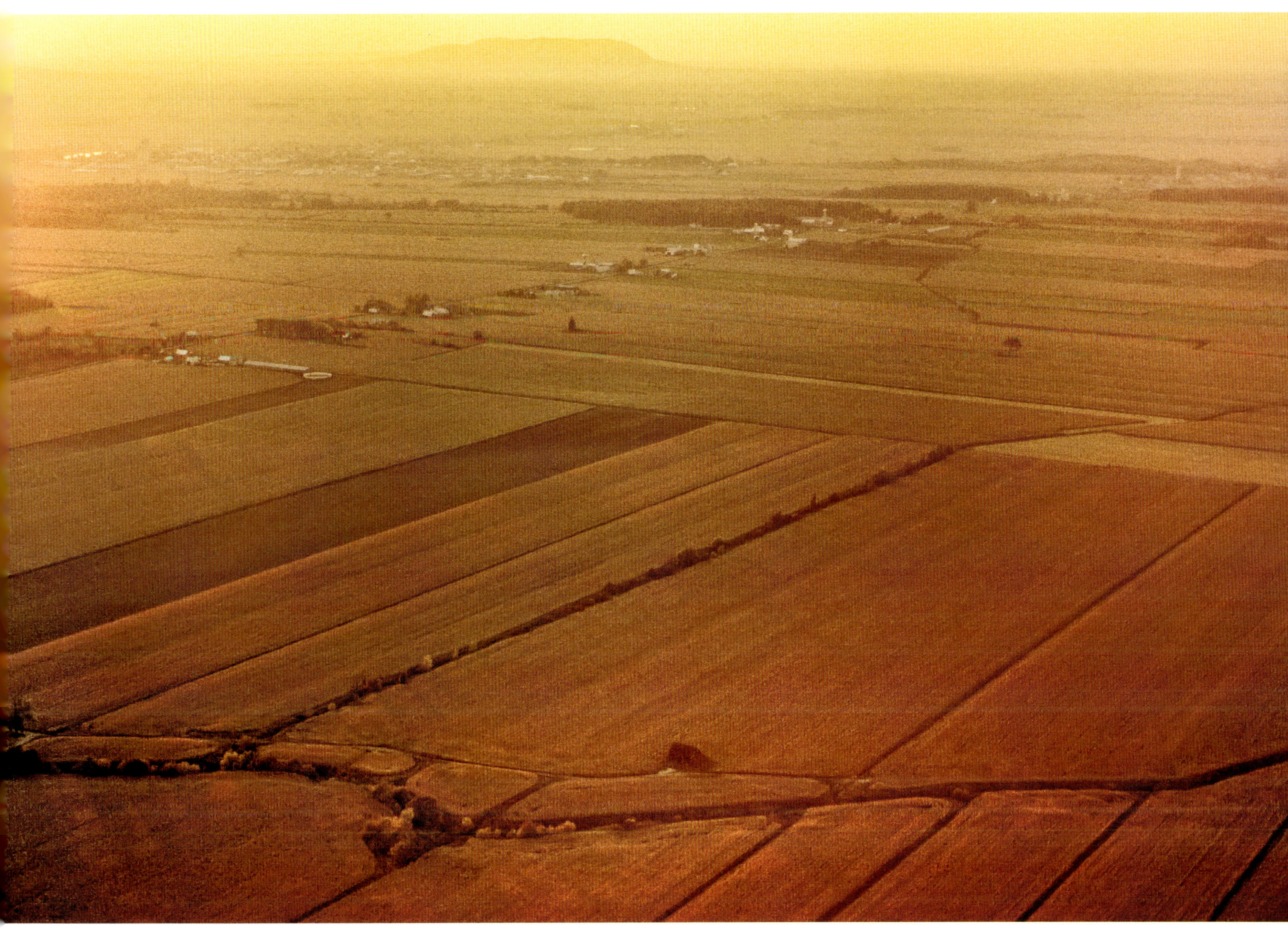

Above farmland at sunset in the Eastern Townships.
On the horizon in both aerial views are isolated
peaks of the Monteregian Hills.

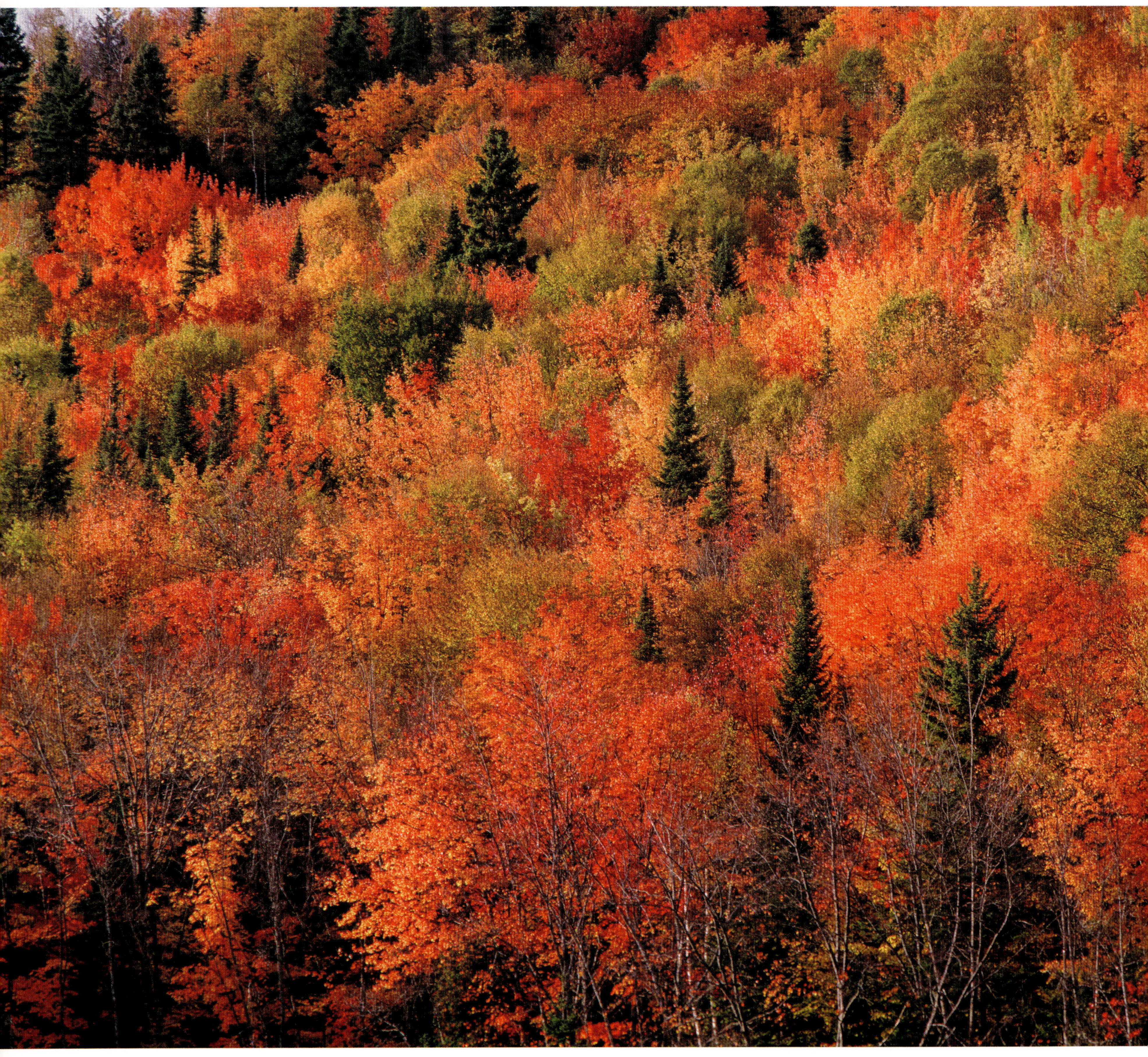

Fall colours at Mistagance in La Mauricie National Park
(above) and near Lost River in the Laurentians, Quebec.

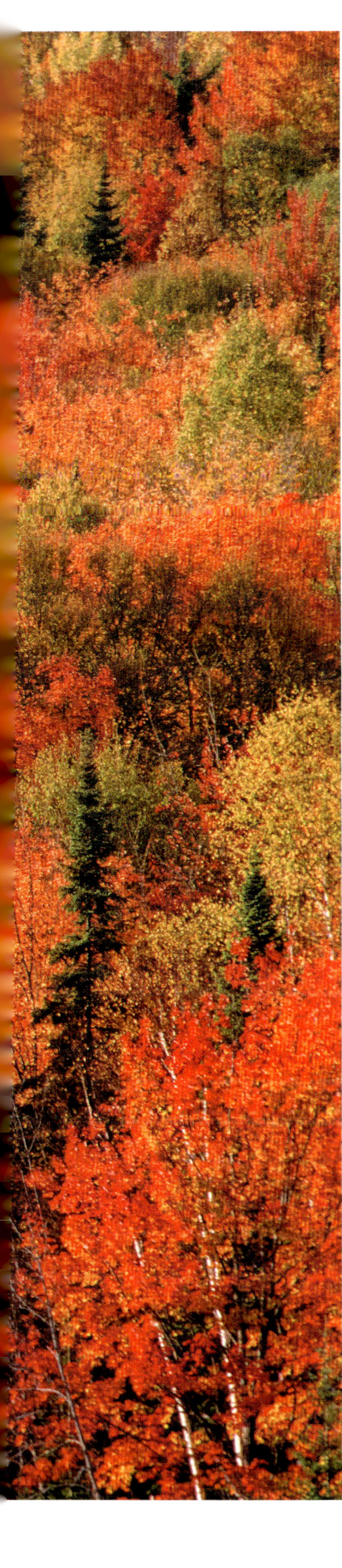

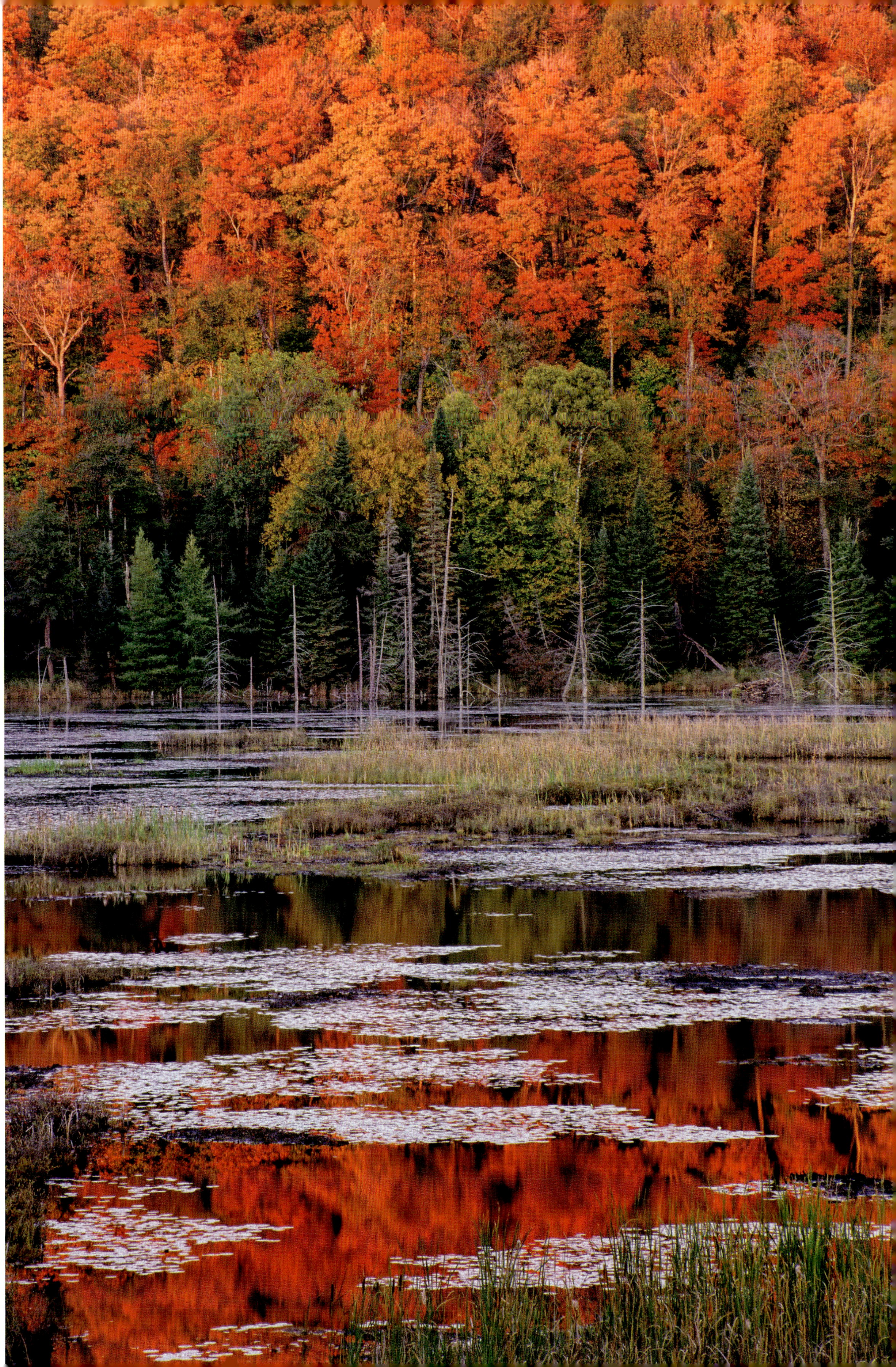

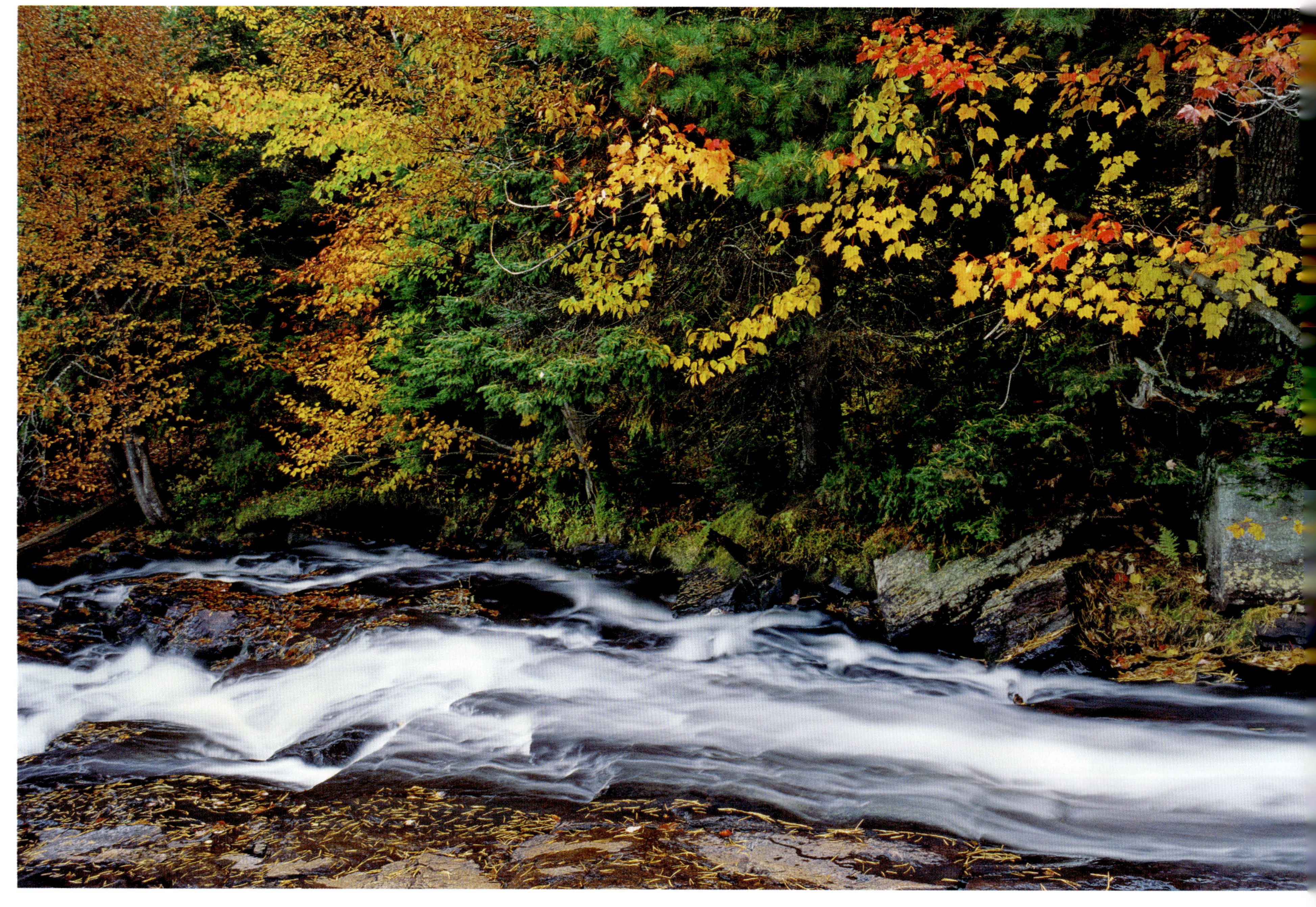

Les Cascades in the southwestern corner of La Mauricie National Park, Quebec (above), and maple trees at various stages of turning colour early in the fall in Gatineau Park, Quebec.

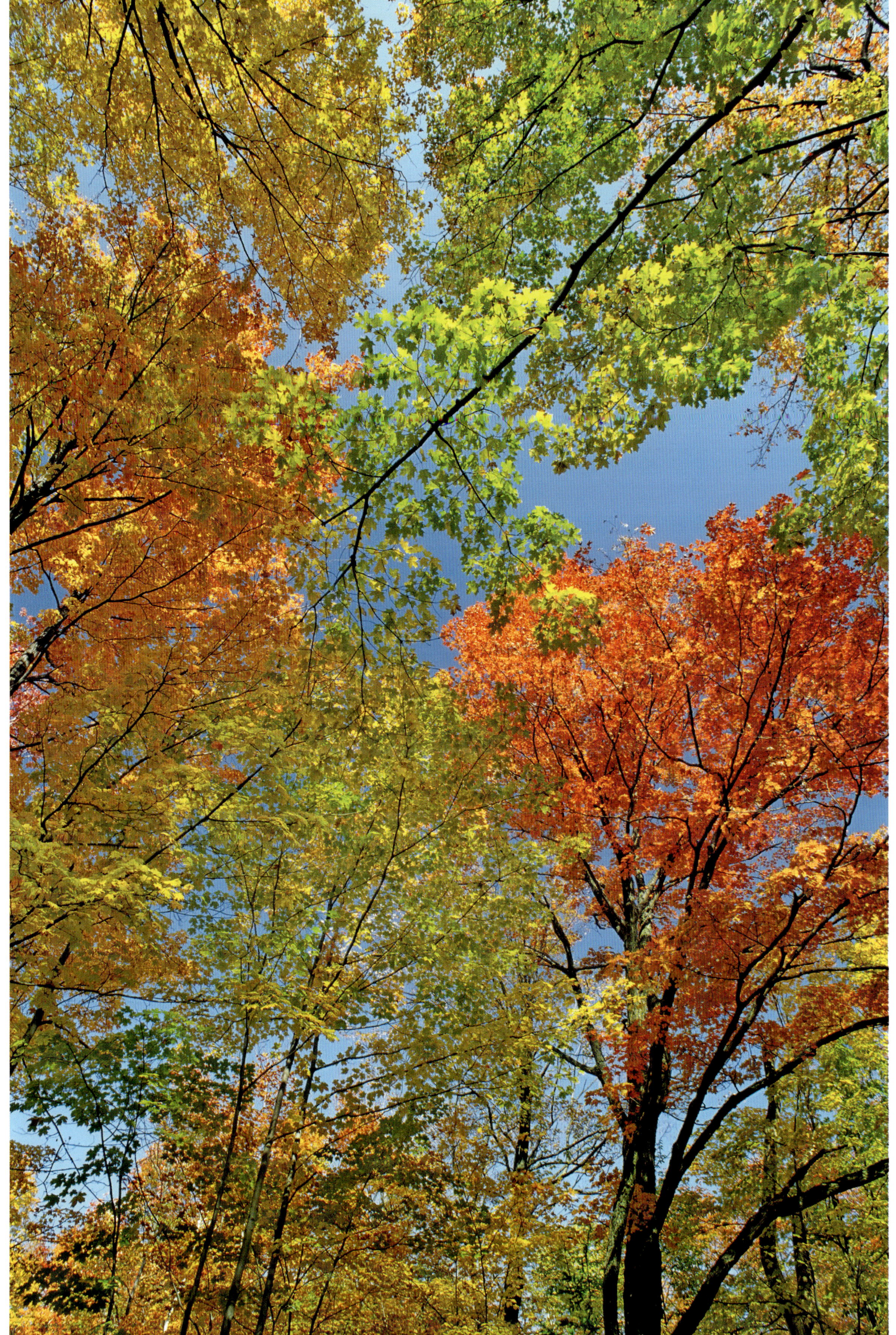

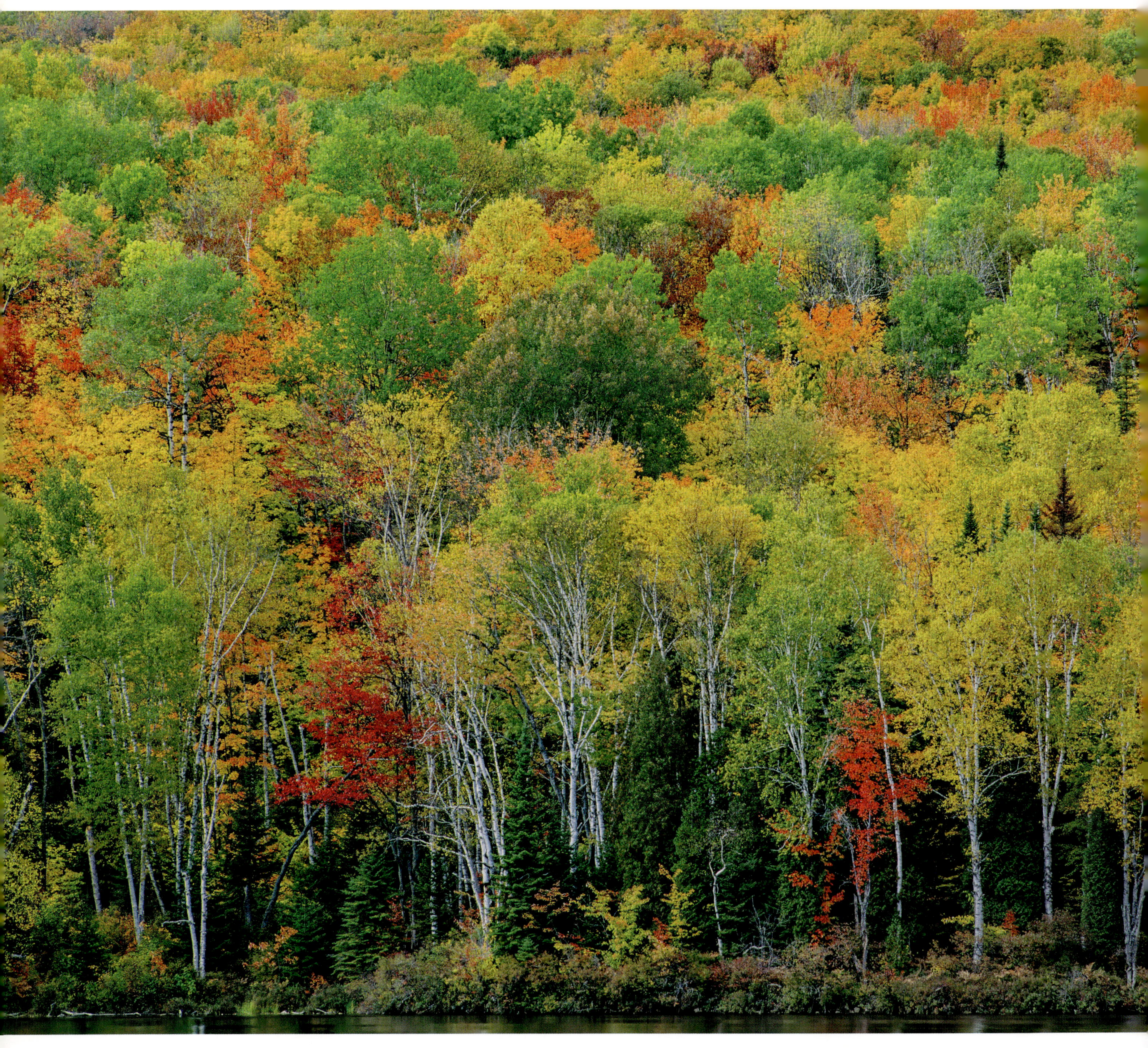

Autumn colours at Lac Bouchard, La Mauricie National Park (above)
and viewed from the air in the Eastern Townships, Quebec.

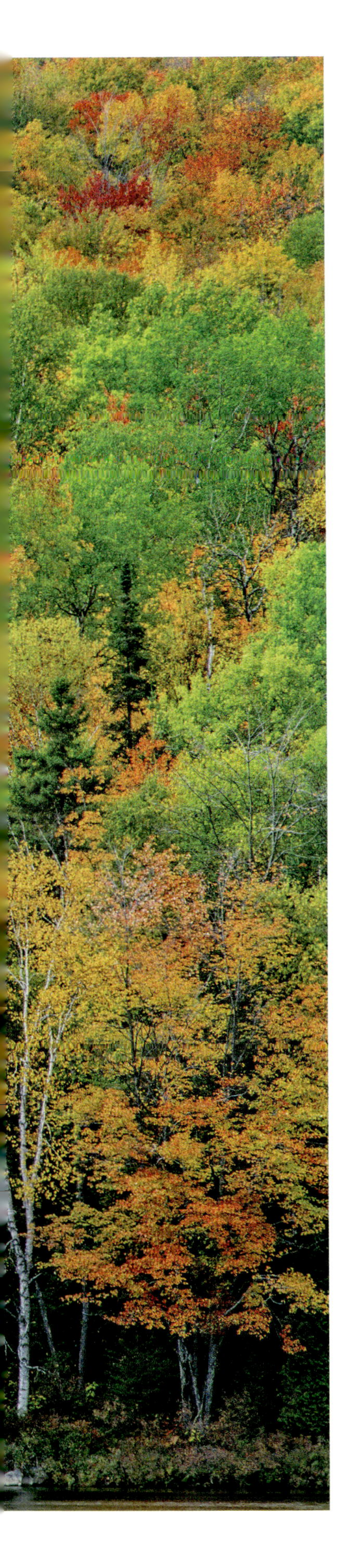

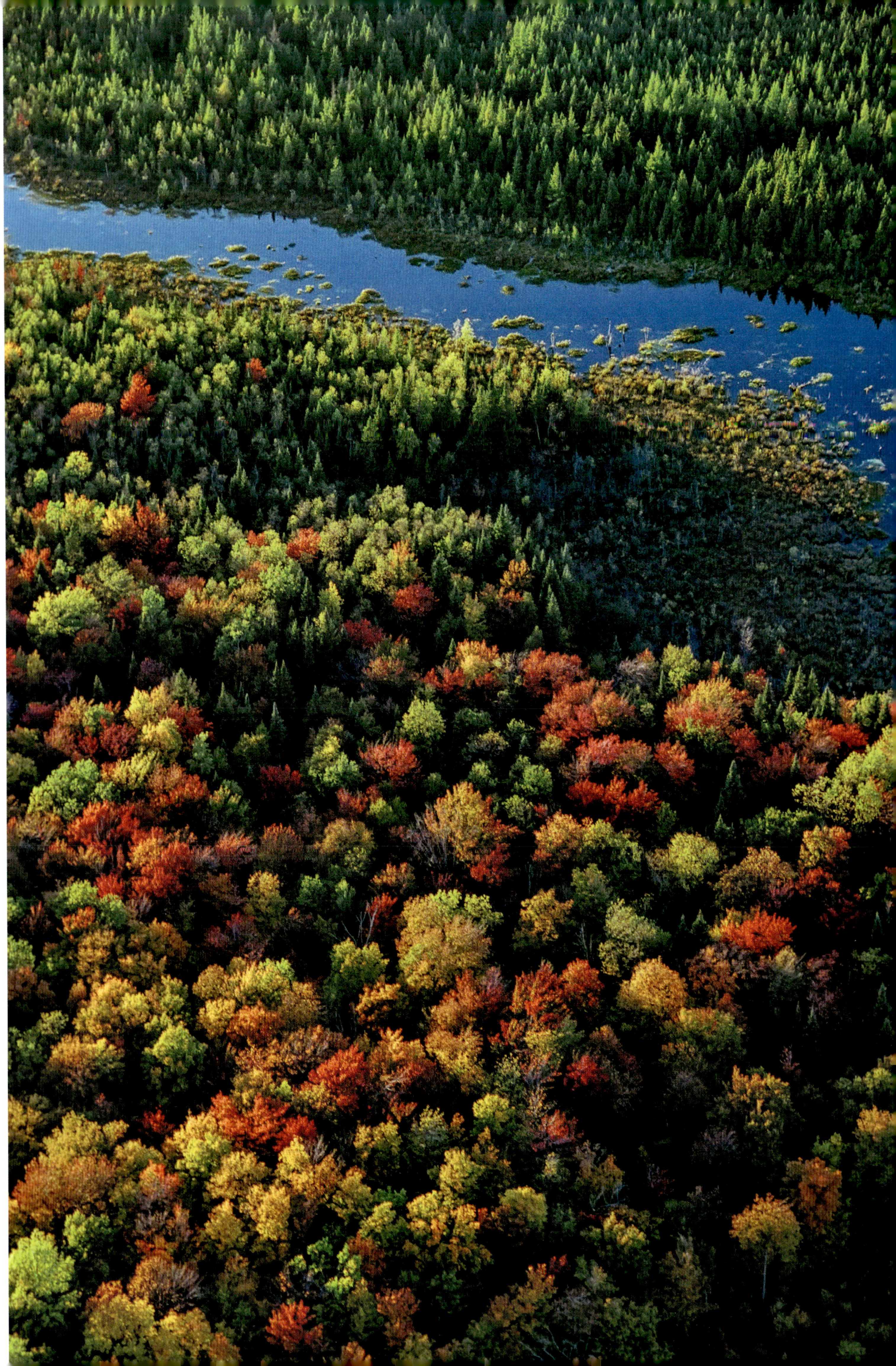

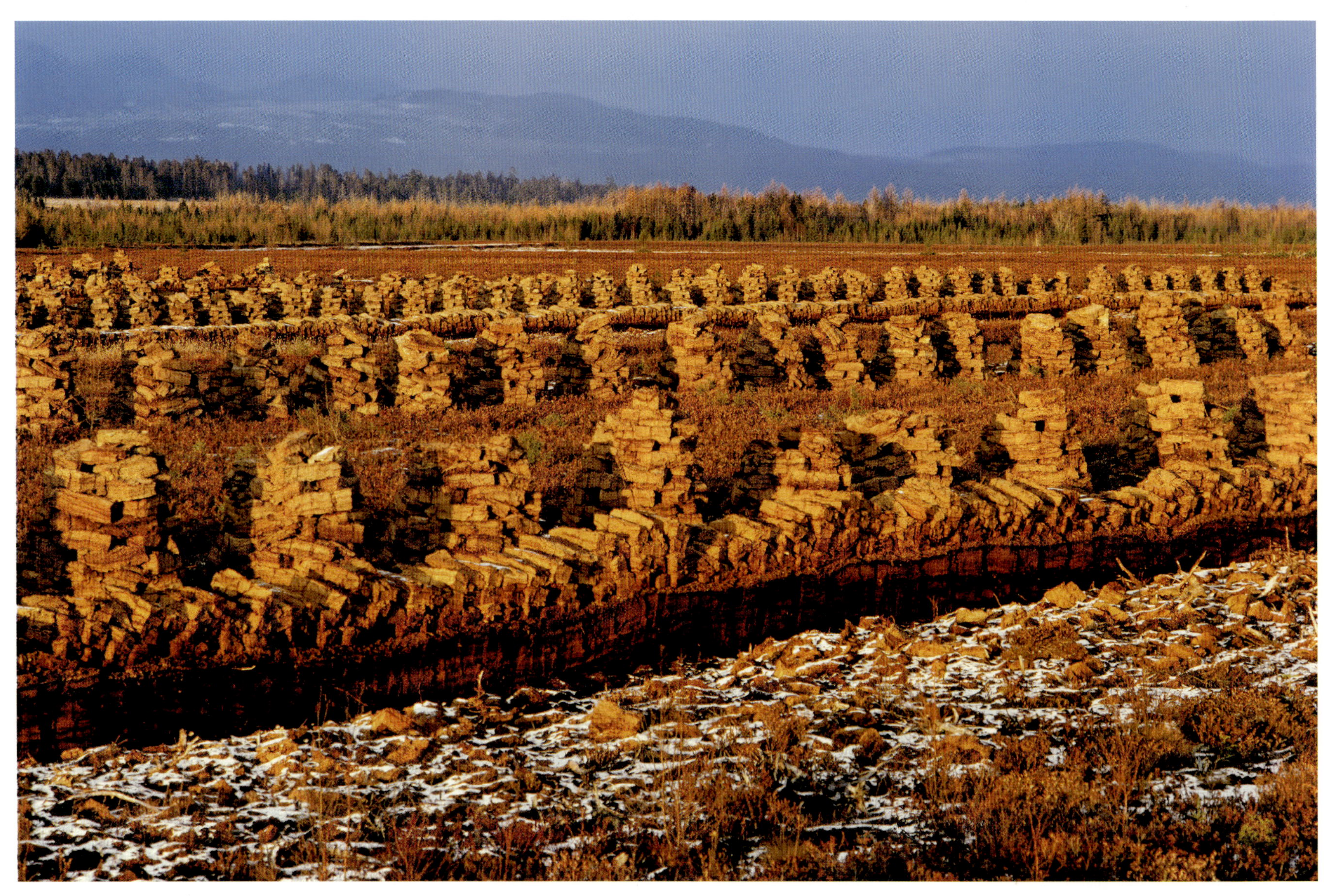

Rows of harvested peat on L'Isle-aux-Coudres in
the Saint Lawrence River, Quebec (above) and an
aerial of fields northeast of Montreal.

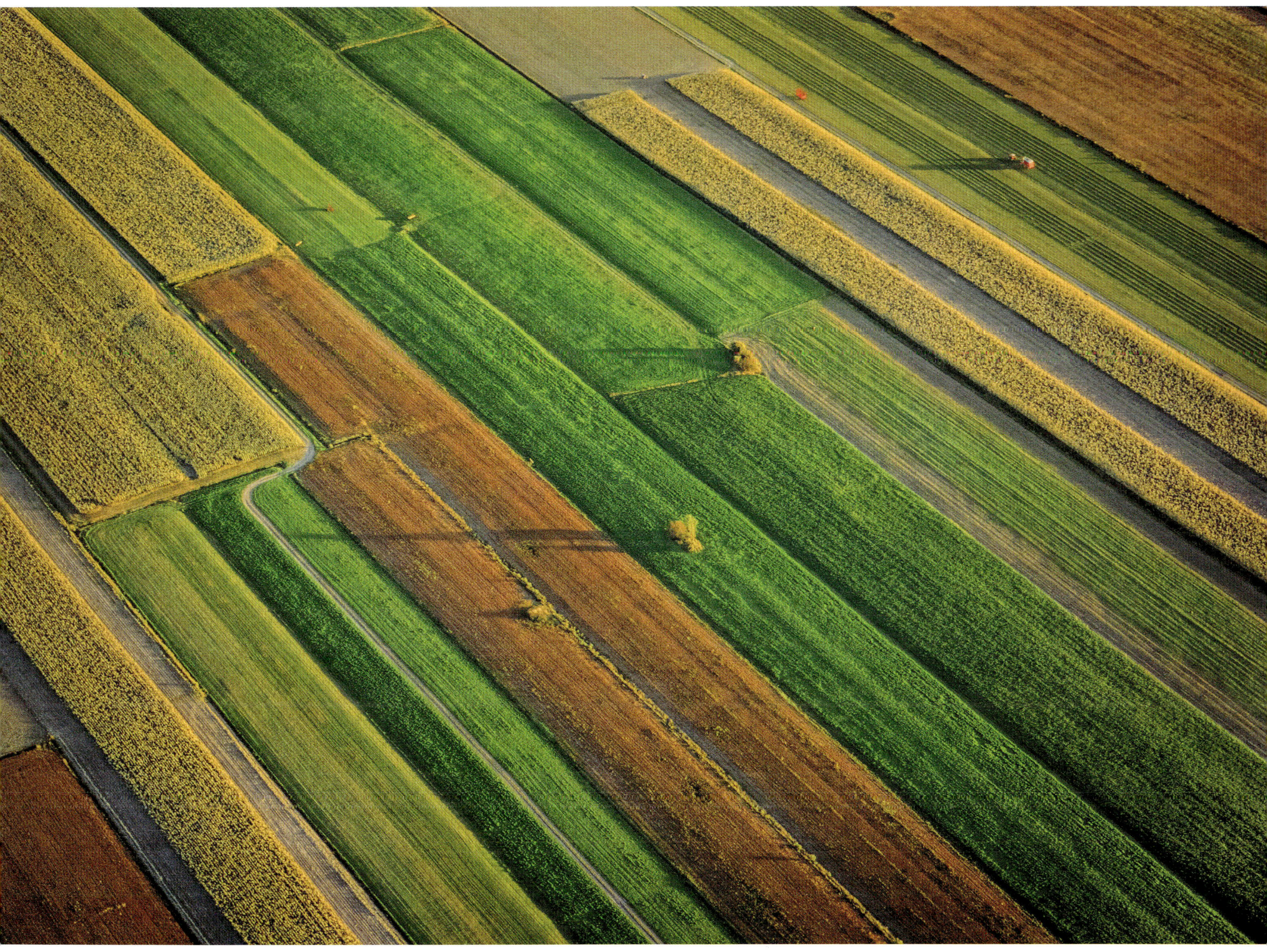

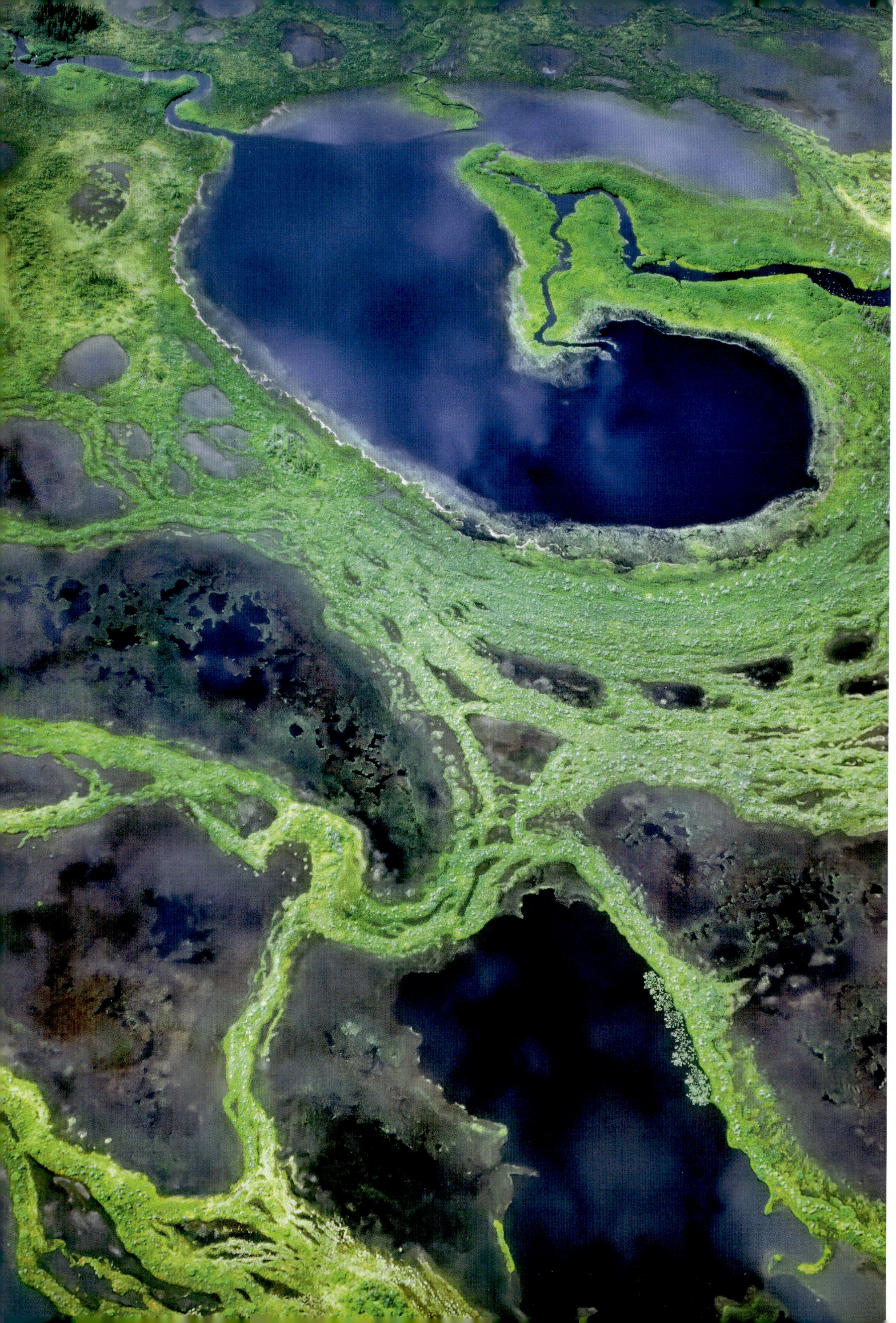

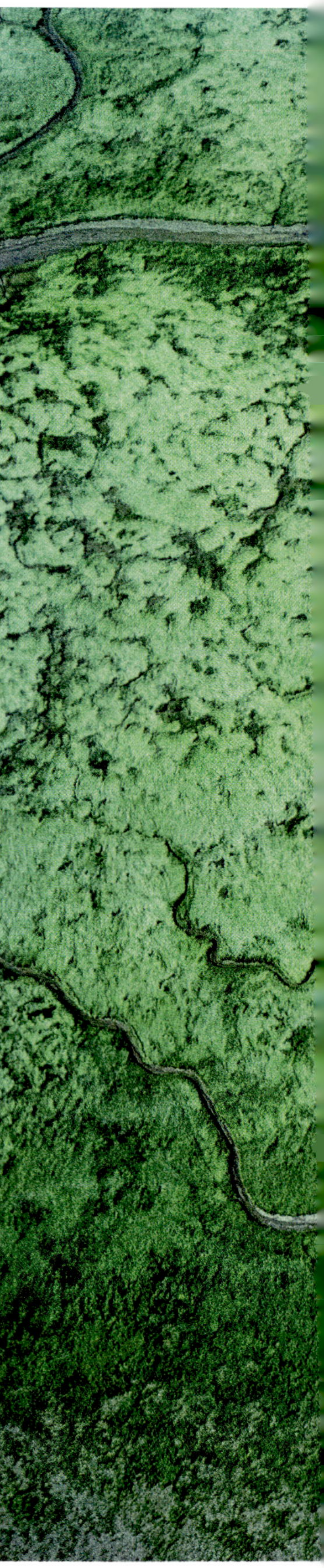

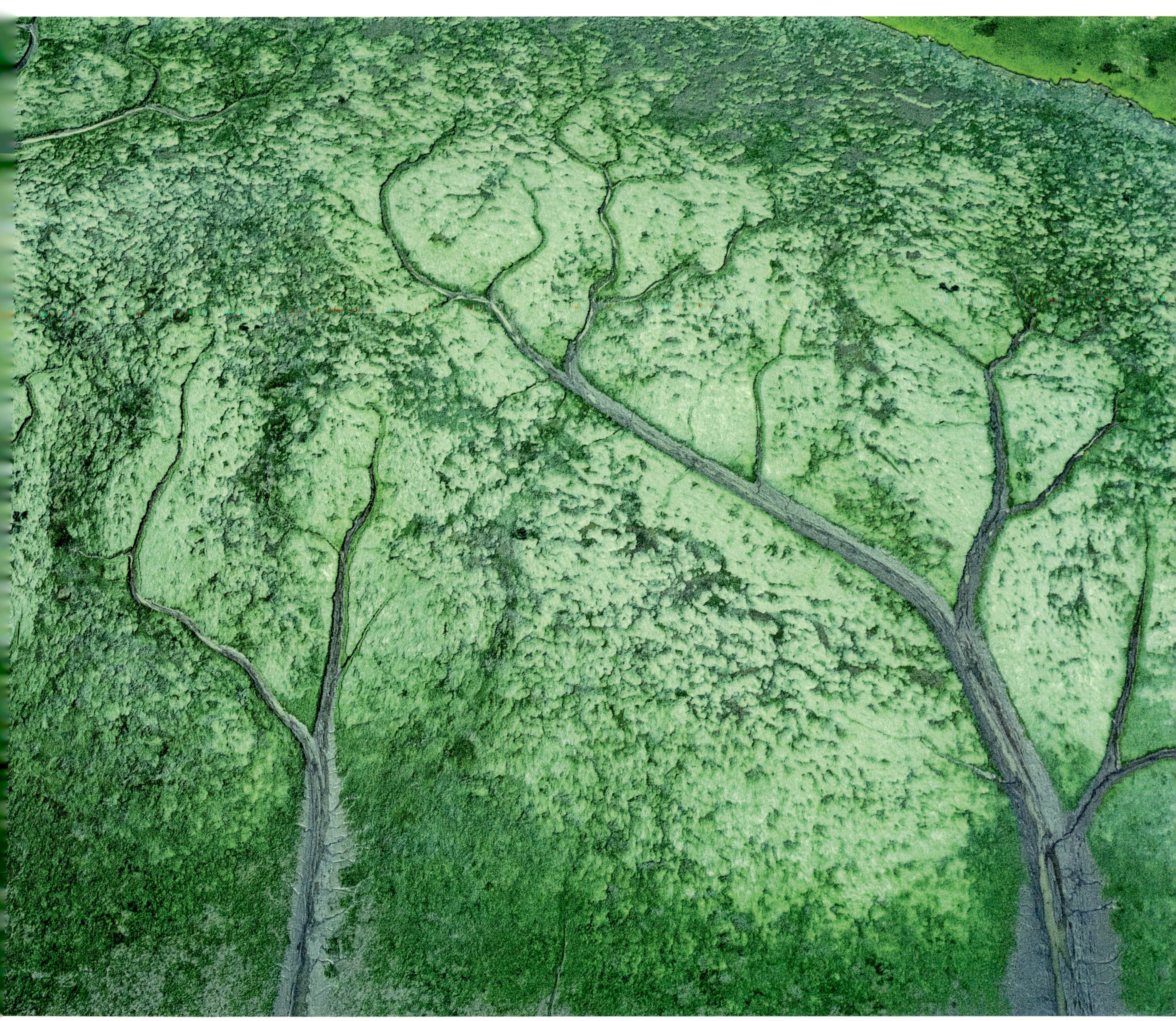

Aerial views of a small portion of the vast string bog in northern Quebec (left) and of drainage channels in seaweed-covered mudflats exposed at low tide north of Quebec City.

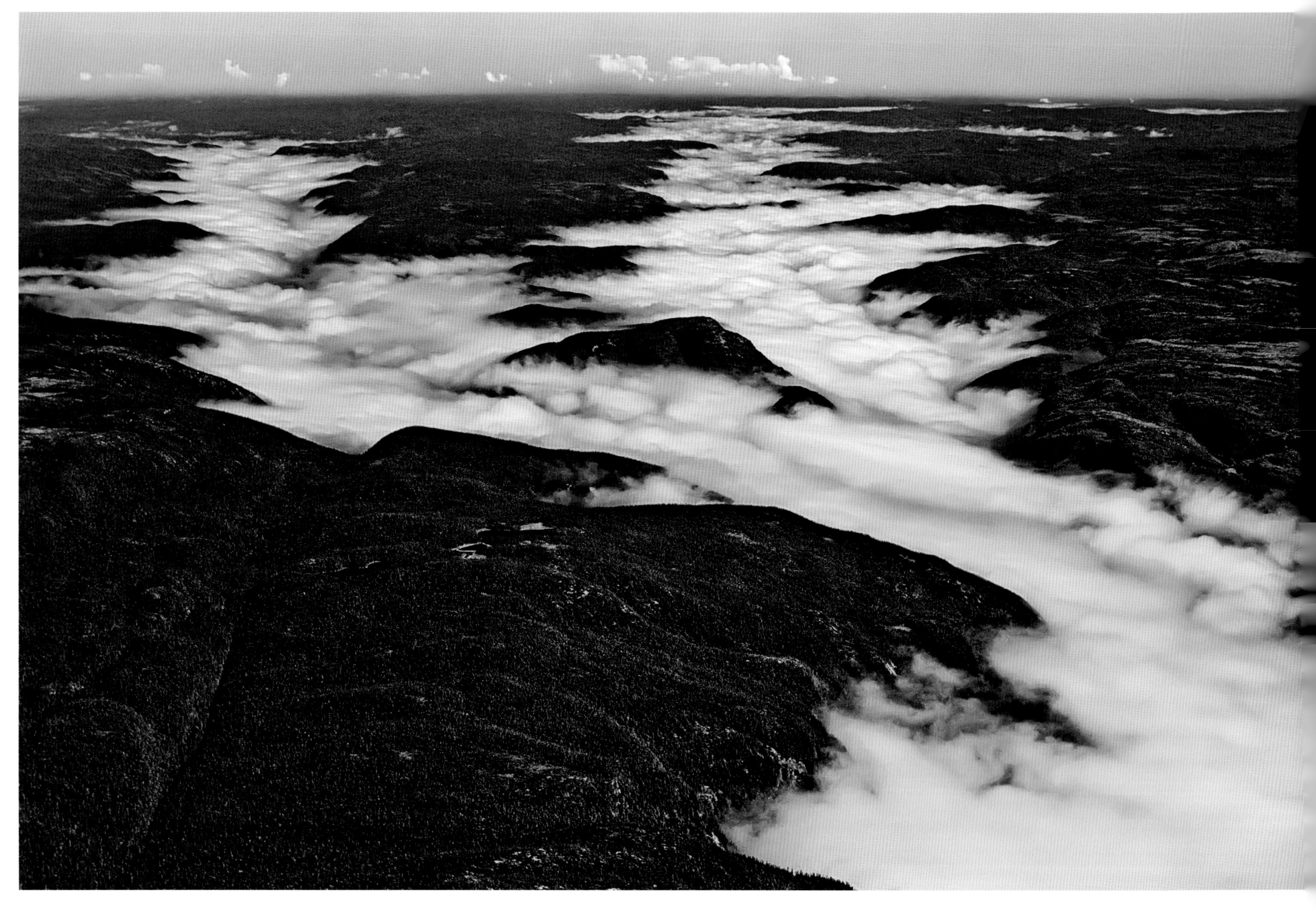

Aerial views of trackless wilderness north of Sept-Îles, Quebec. Morning fog lingers in two merging river valleys (above) while many parts of the Canadian Shield are a maze of land and water, of uncountable lakes and islands.

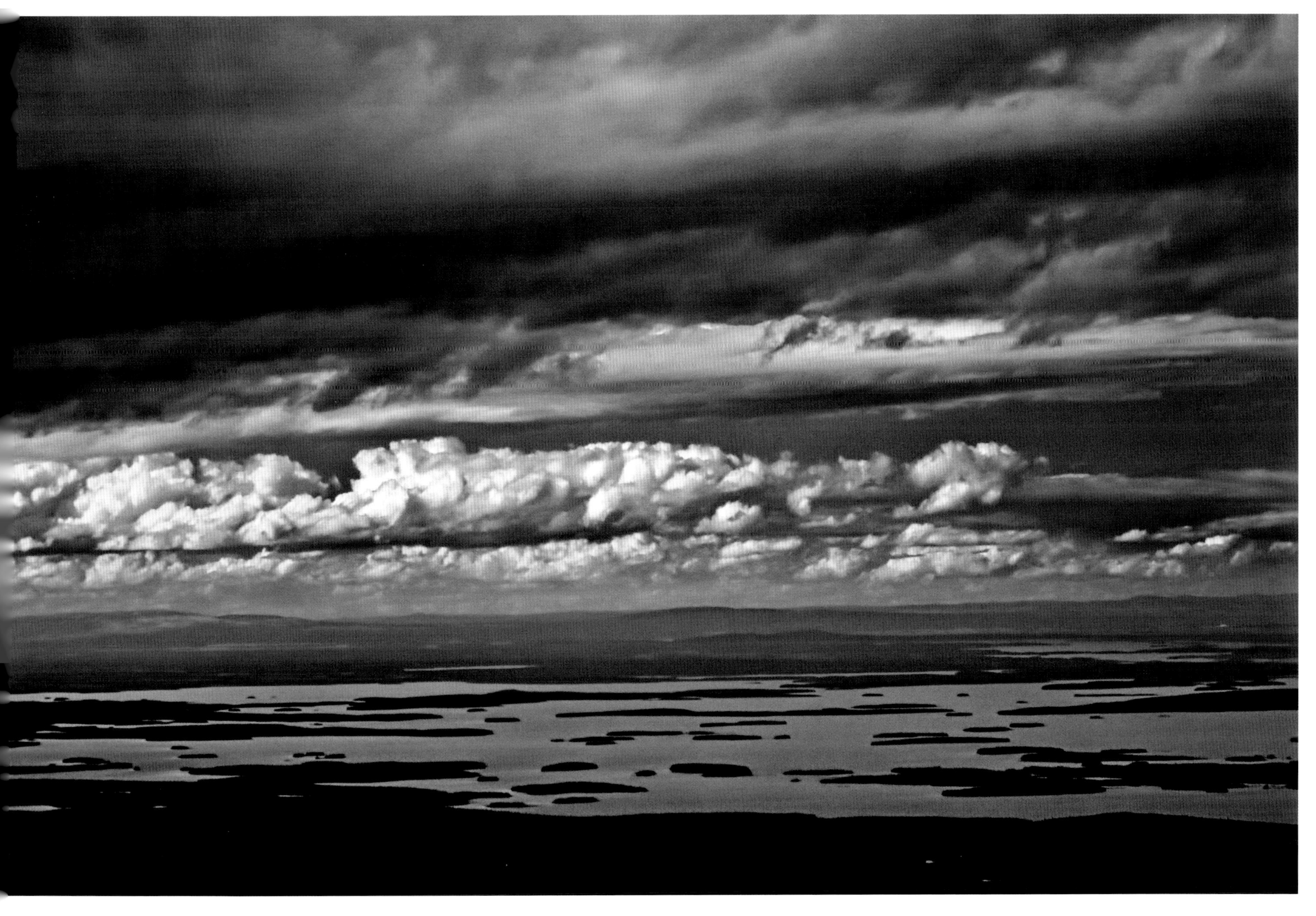

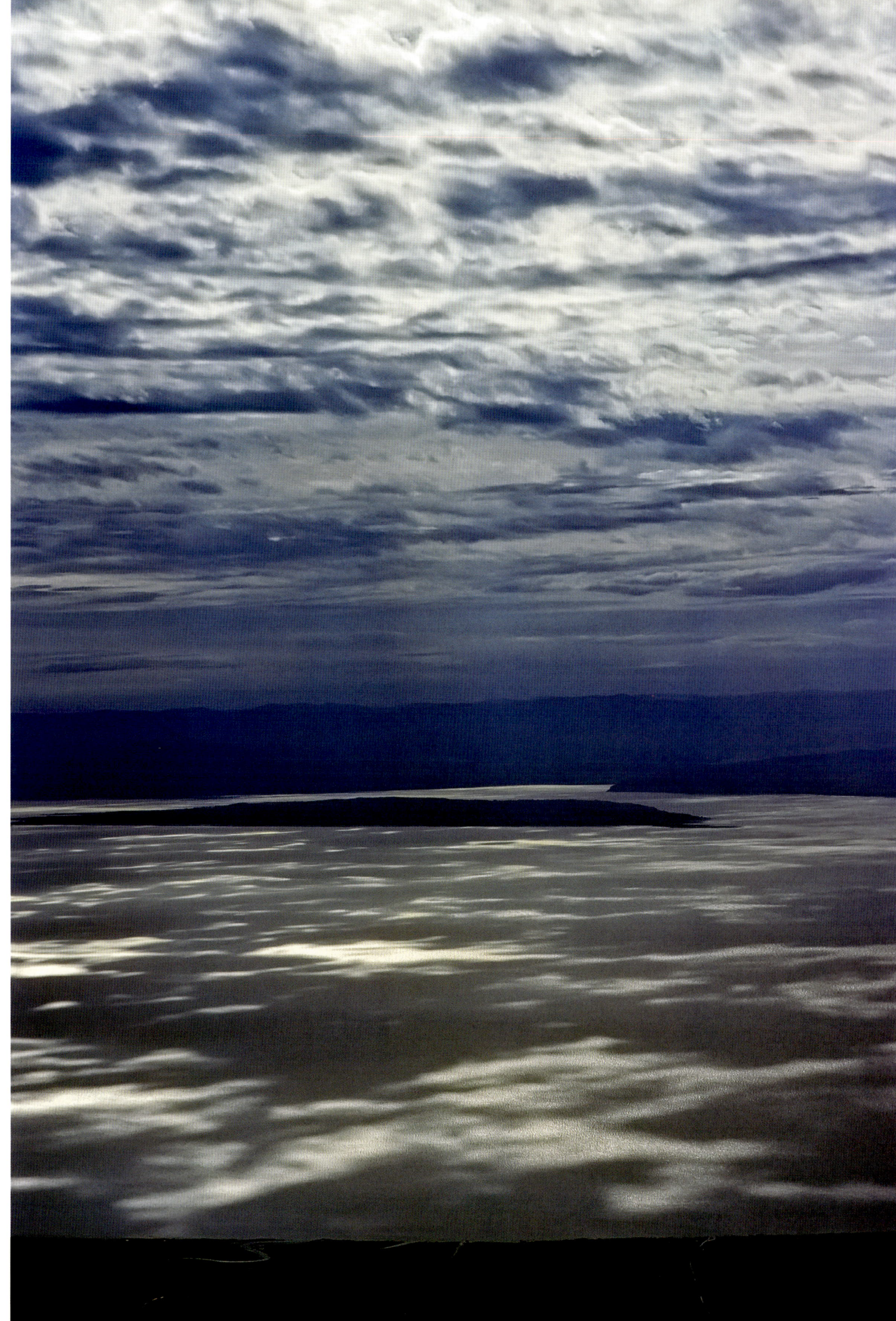

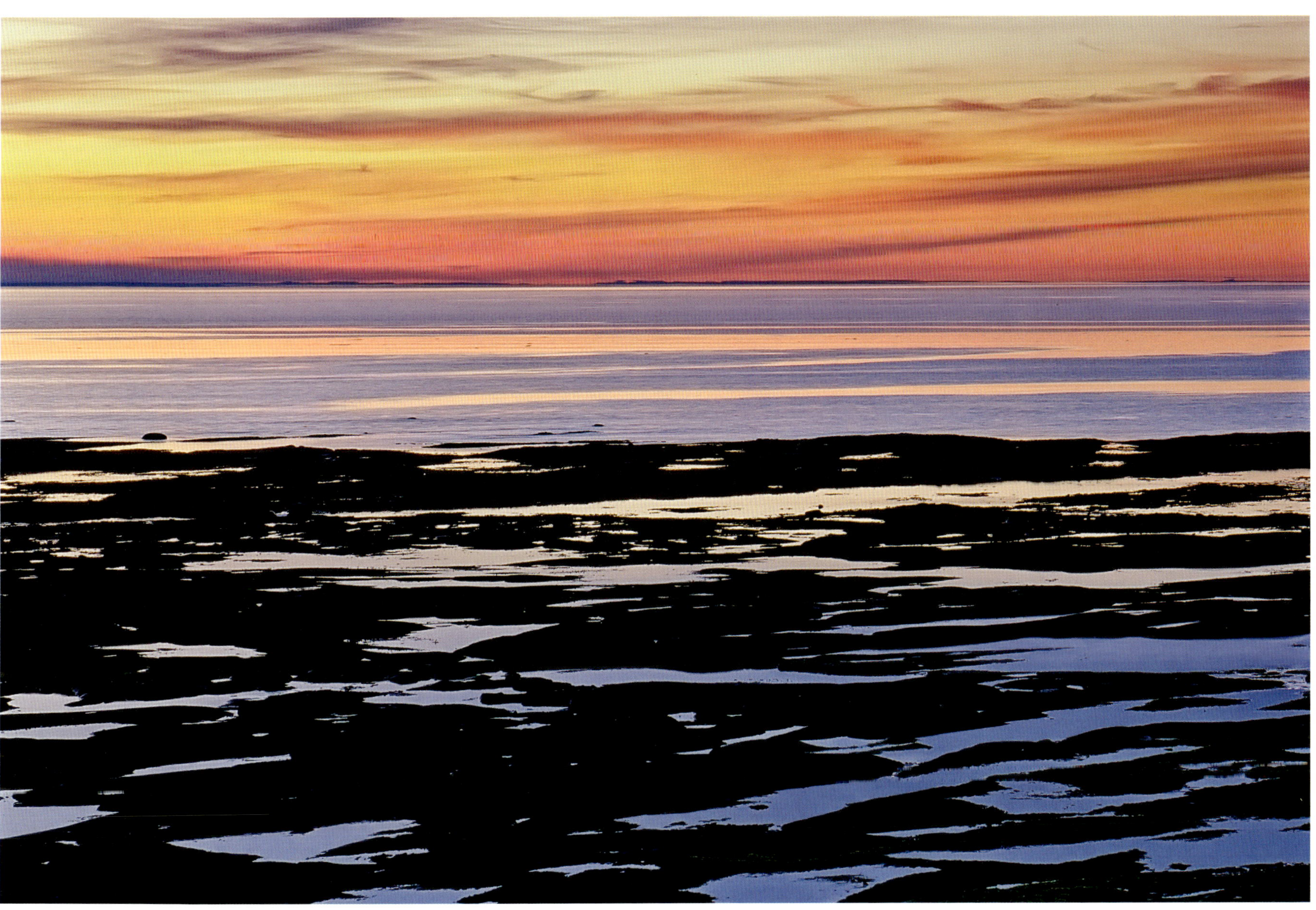

Splashes of sunlight speckle the Saint Lawrence
River in an aerial view from above Rivière-Ouelle on
the south shore looking towards L'Isle-aux-Coudres
and the Laurentian Mountains on the horizon (left).
Low tide at dusk exposes innumerable tide pools
along the rocky shore of the Saint Lawrence estuary
near Mont-Joli, Quebec.

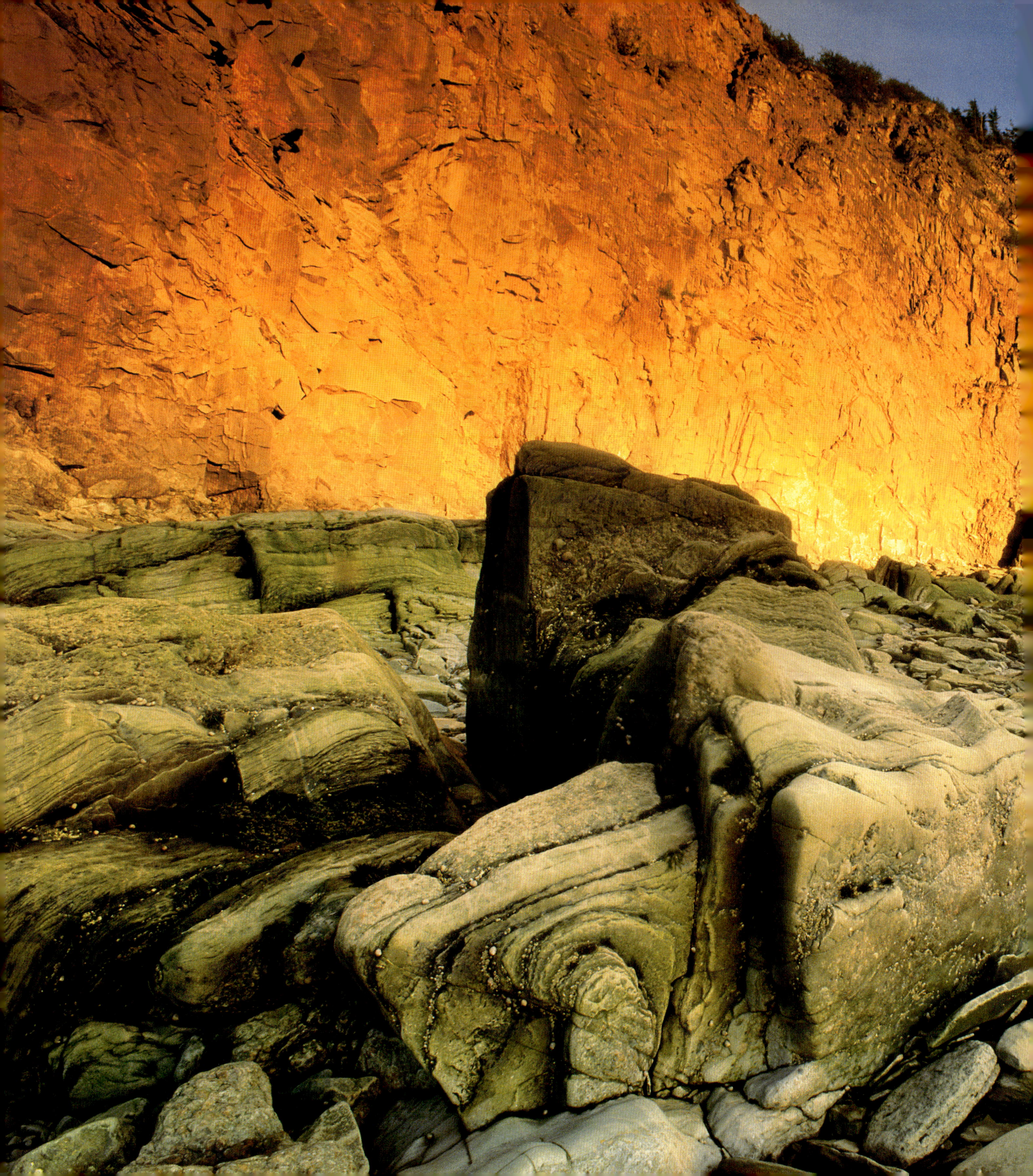

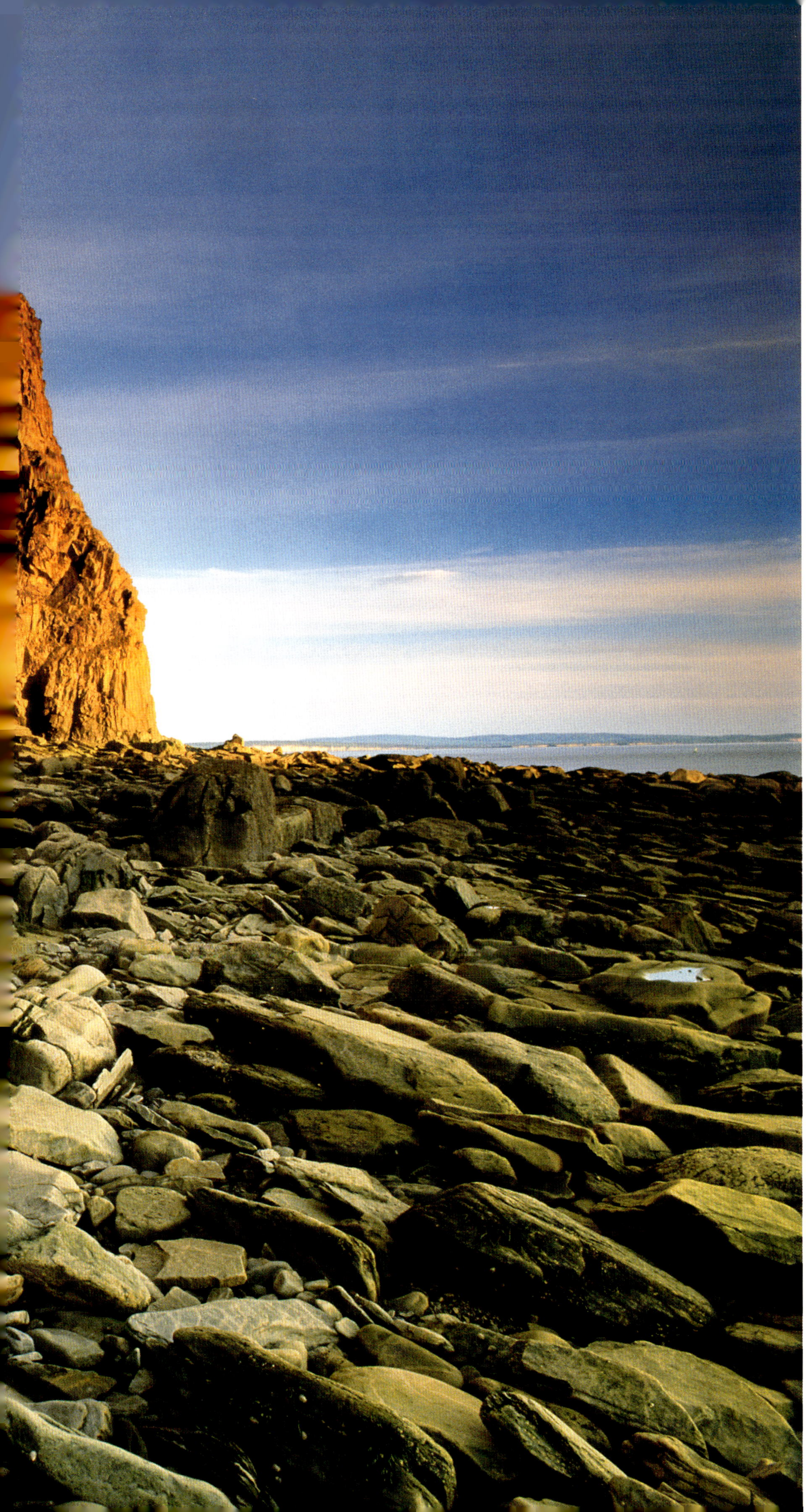

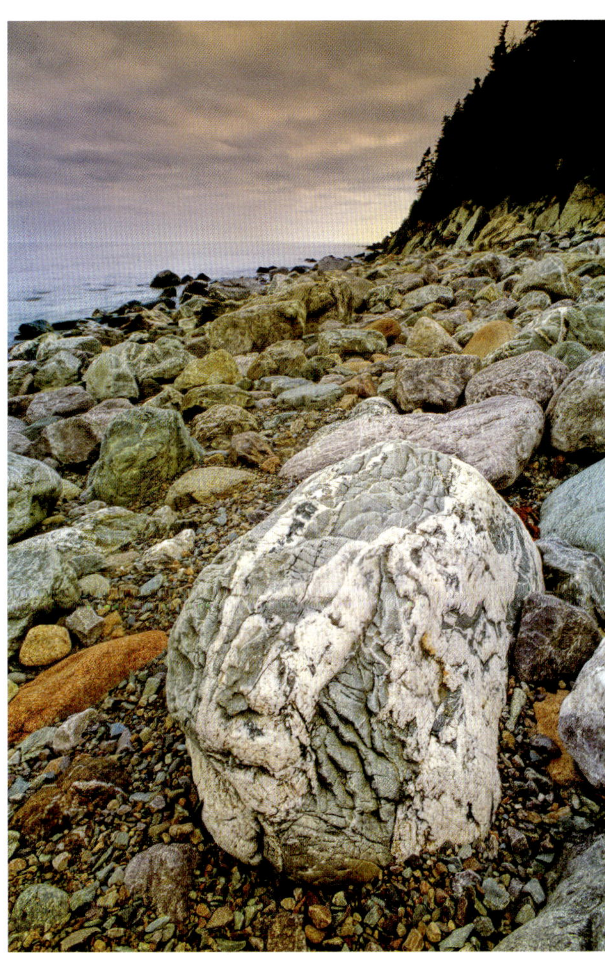

The evening sun illuminates a cliff at Cape Enrage
in Chignecto Bay (left) and boulders at Big Salmon
River, both along the coast of the Bay of Fundy,
New Brunswick.

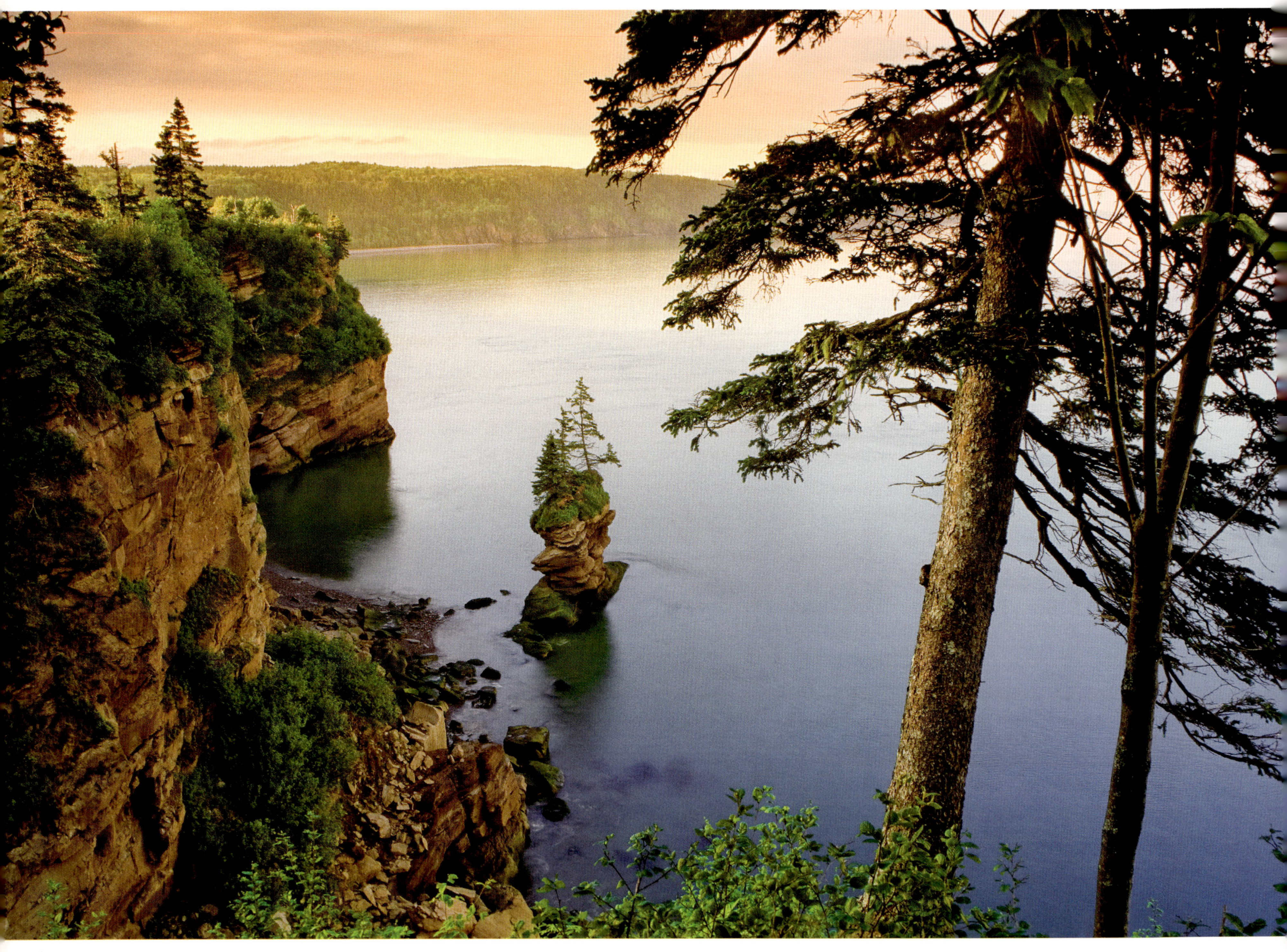

Flowerpot Rock in the Bay of Fundy along the
Fundy Trail, New Brunswick (above).

An aerial view of surf and the end of one of the
long barrier islands in Kouchibouguac National
Park on the east coast of New Brunswick.

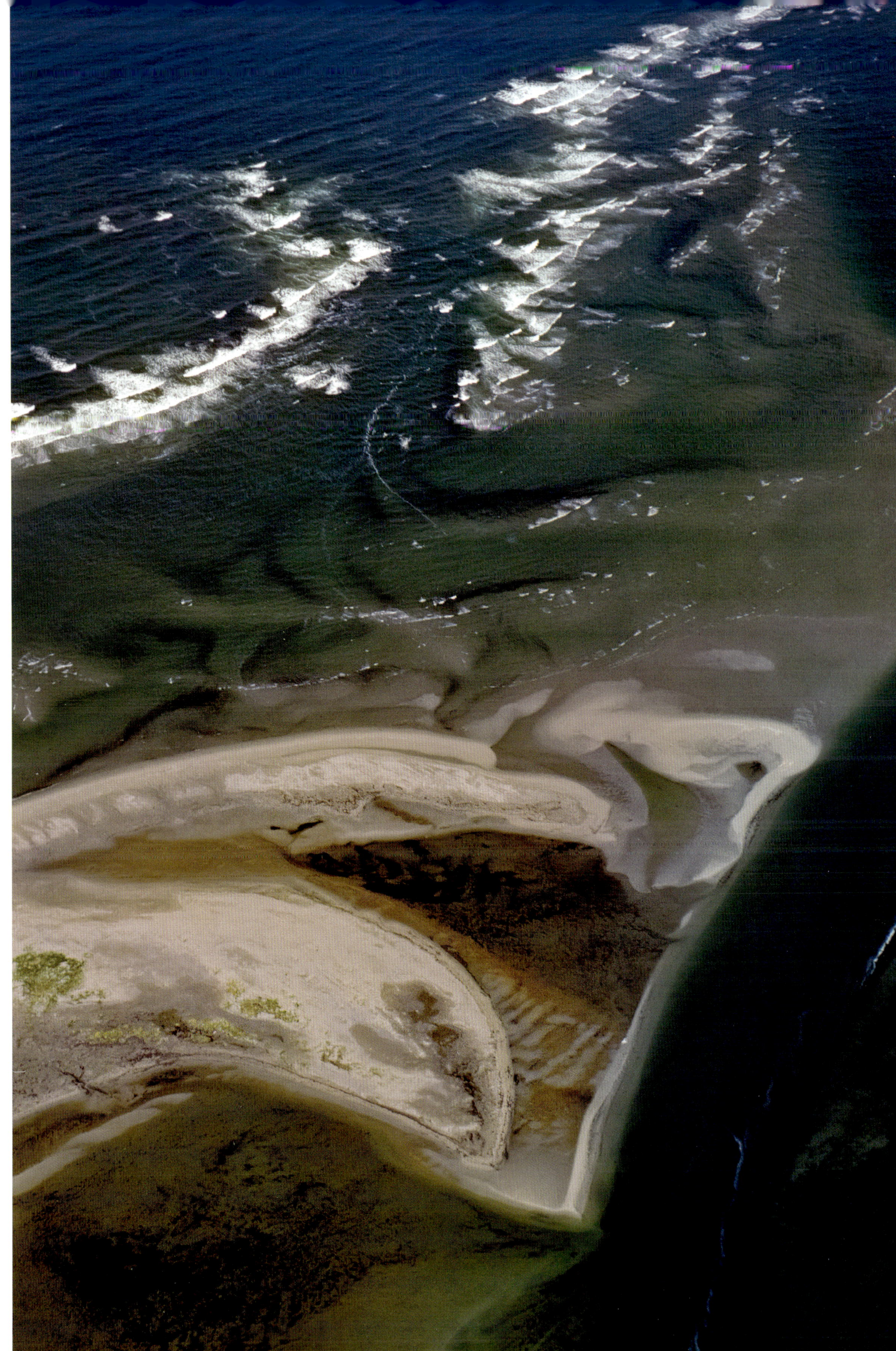

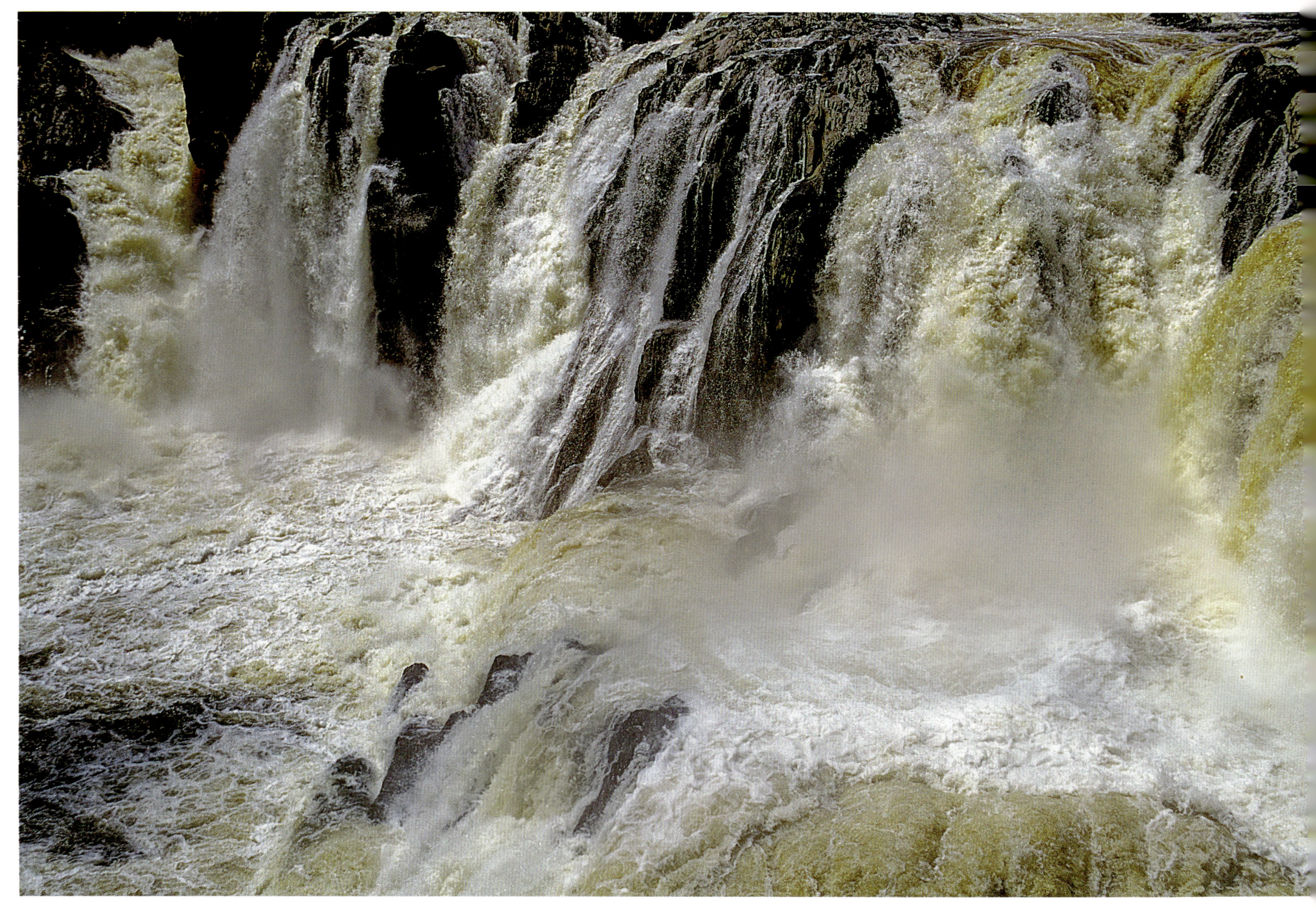

The Saint John River, here at Grand Falls,
New Brunswick, is the second longest waterway
on the eastern seaboard of North America between
the Saint Lawrence and Mississippi Rivers.

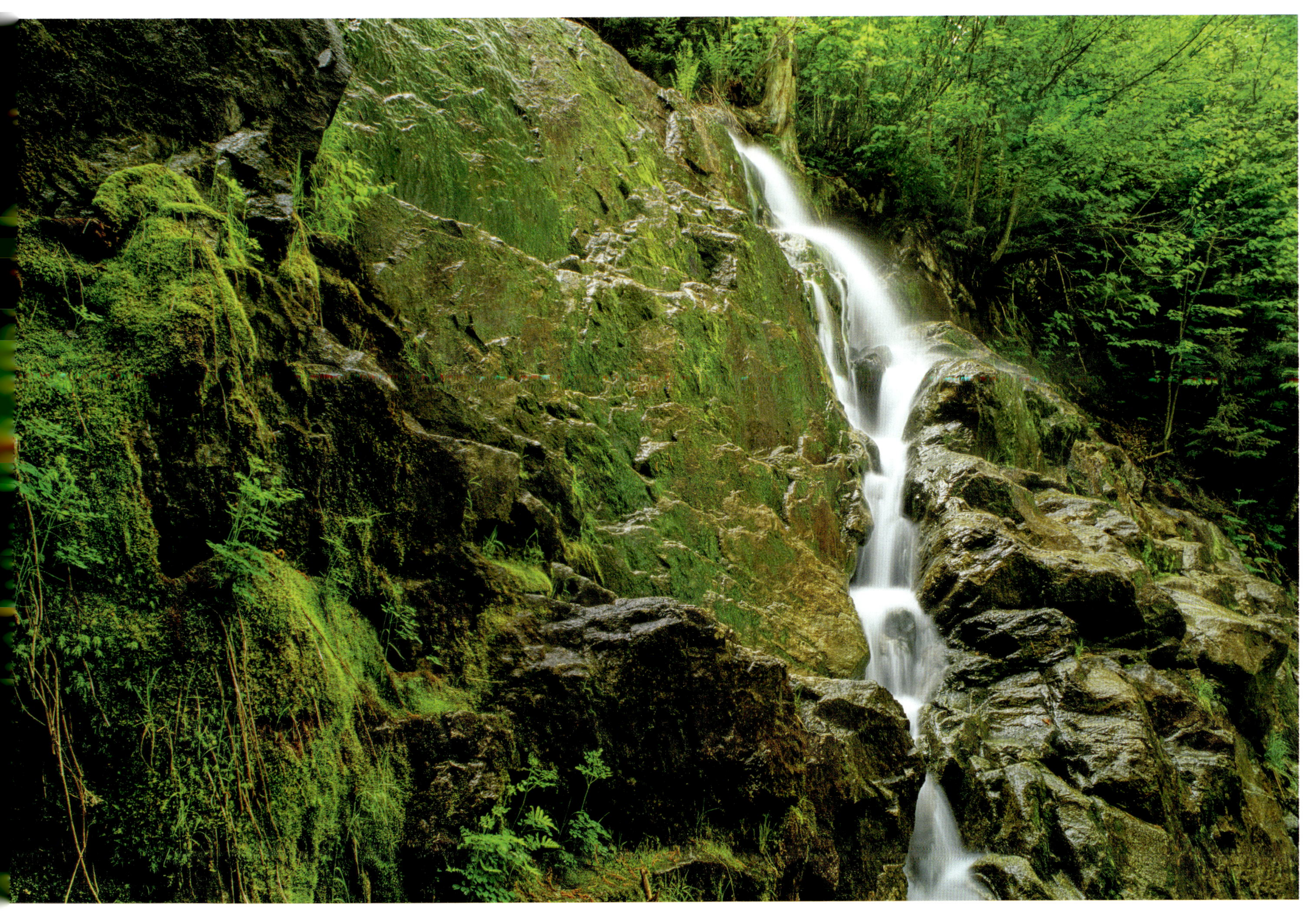

A small waterfall on the Moosehorn Trail,
Fundy National Park.

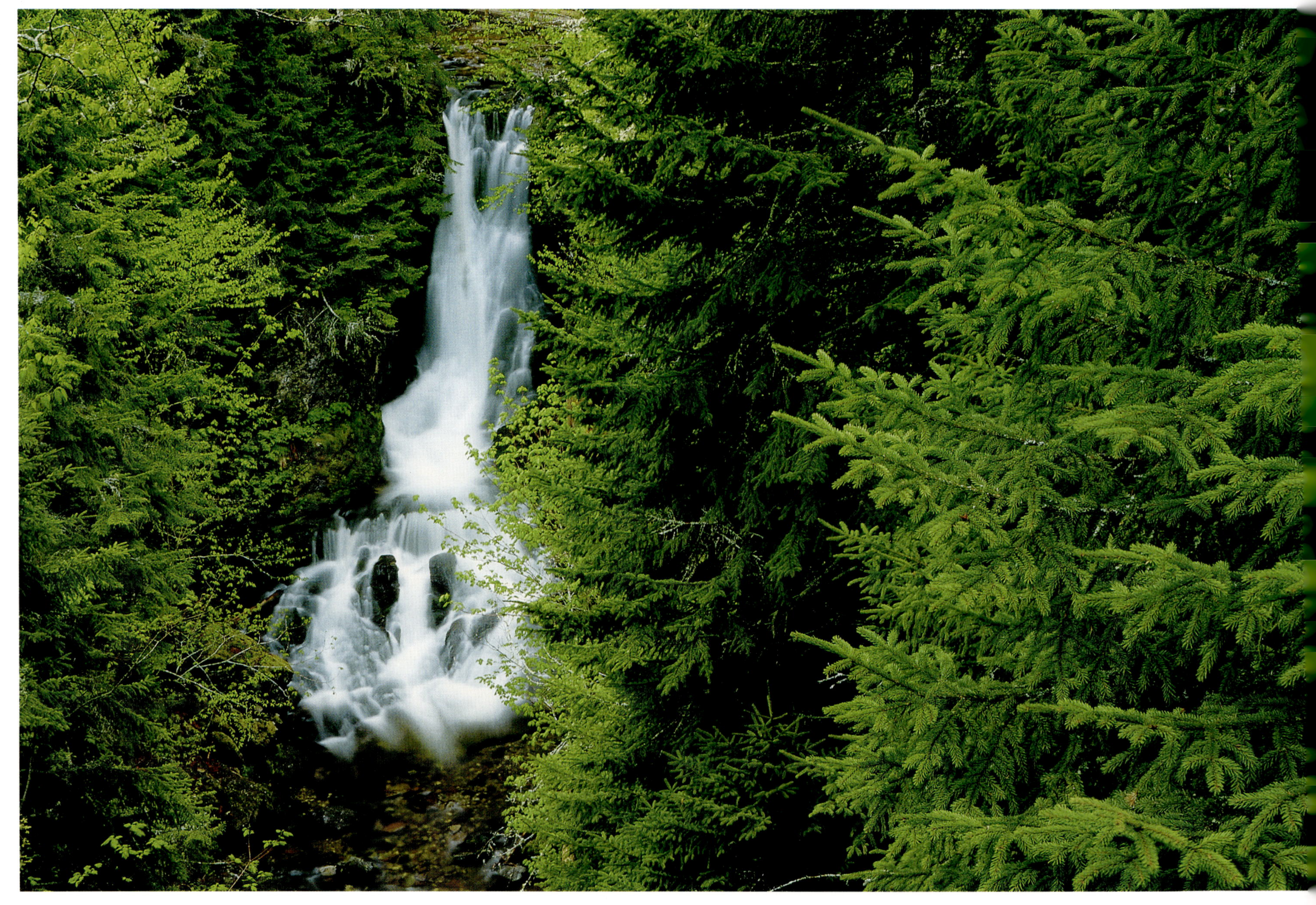

Dickson Falls, surrounded by trees in spring green,
is one of more than two dozen waterfalls and
cascades in Fundy National Park.

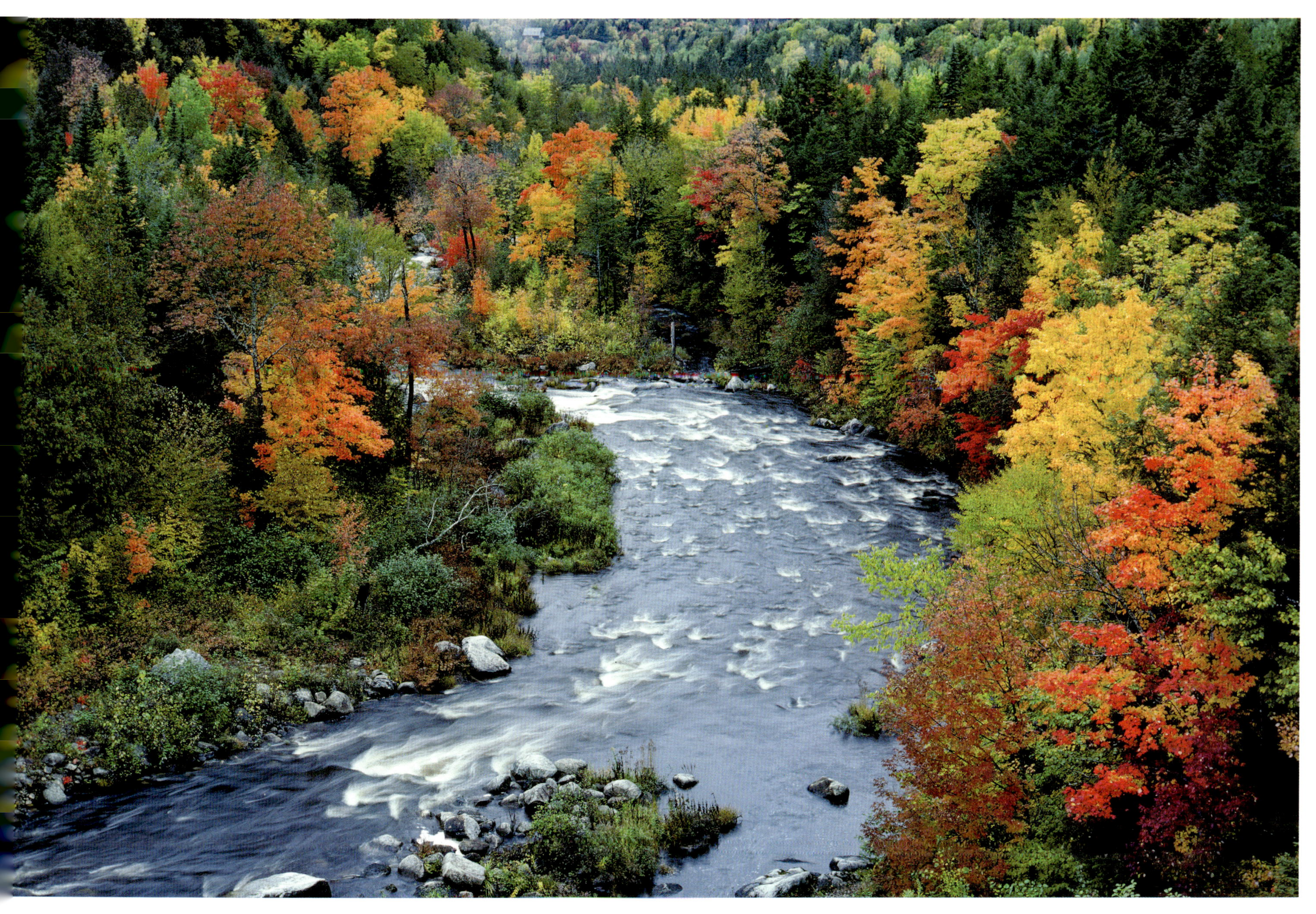

Shogomoc Stream flows through a mixed forest
of conifers and deciduous trees in autumn, one
kilometre above its junction with the Saint John
River, New Brunswick.

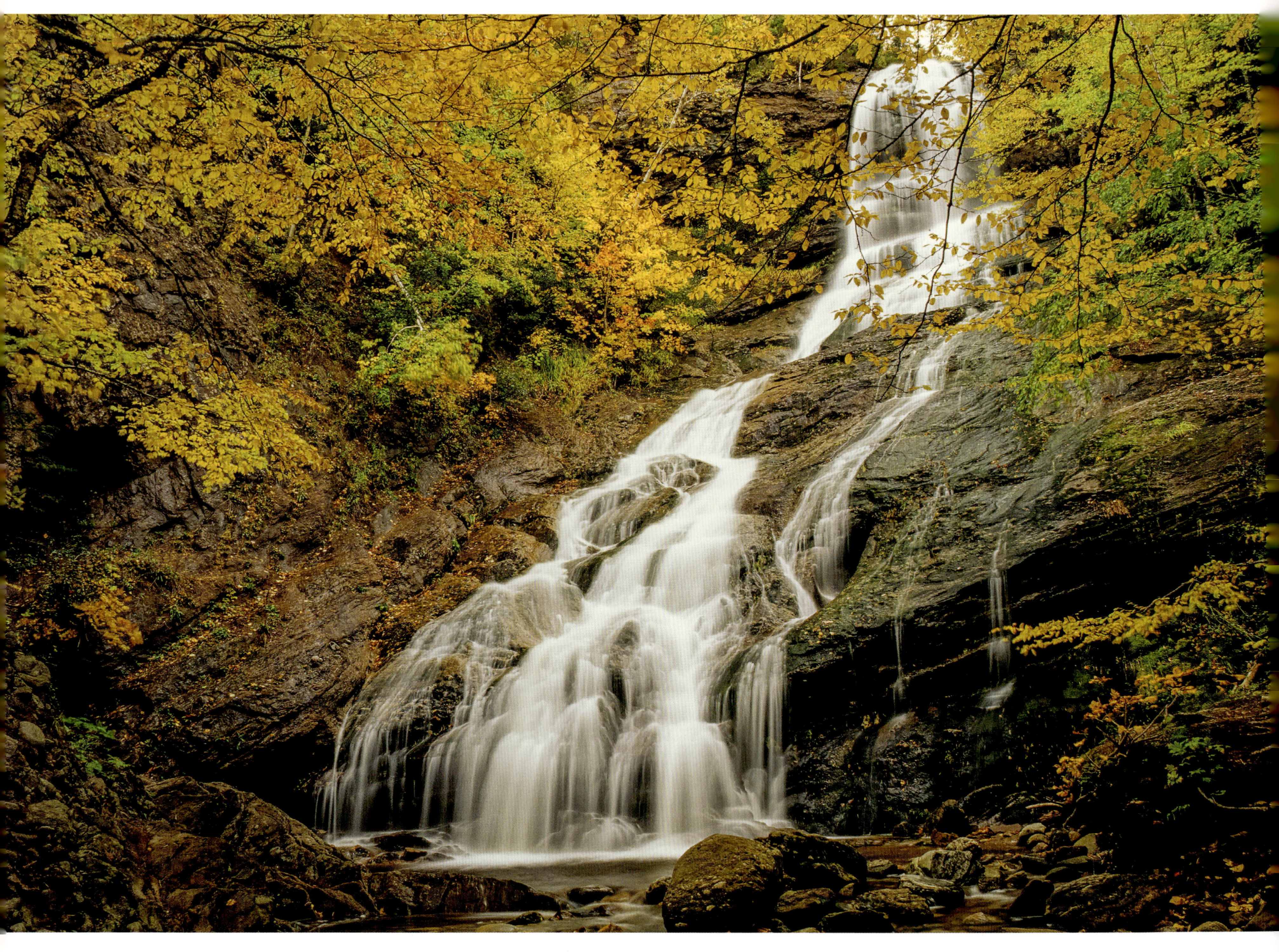

Golden foliage around Beulach Ban Falls in Cape Breton Highlands National Park (above) and a red maple with a spruce near Yarmouth, Nova Scotia, in autumn.

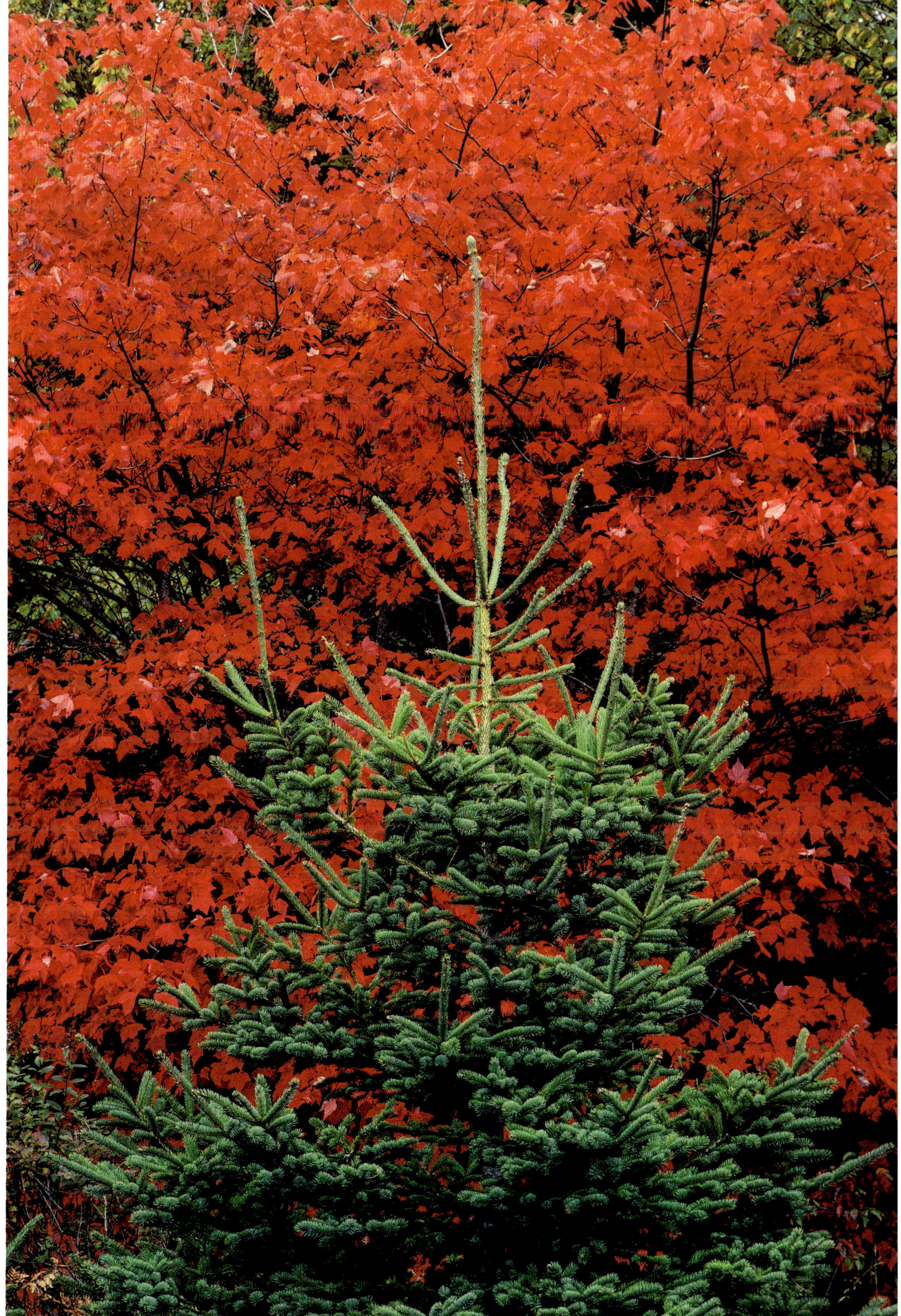

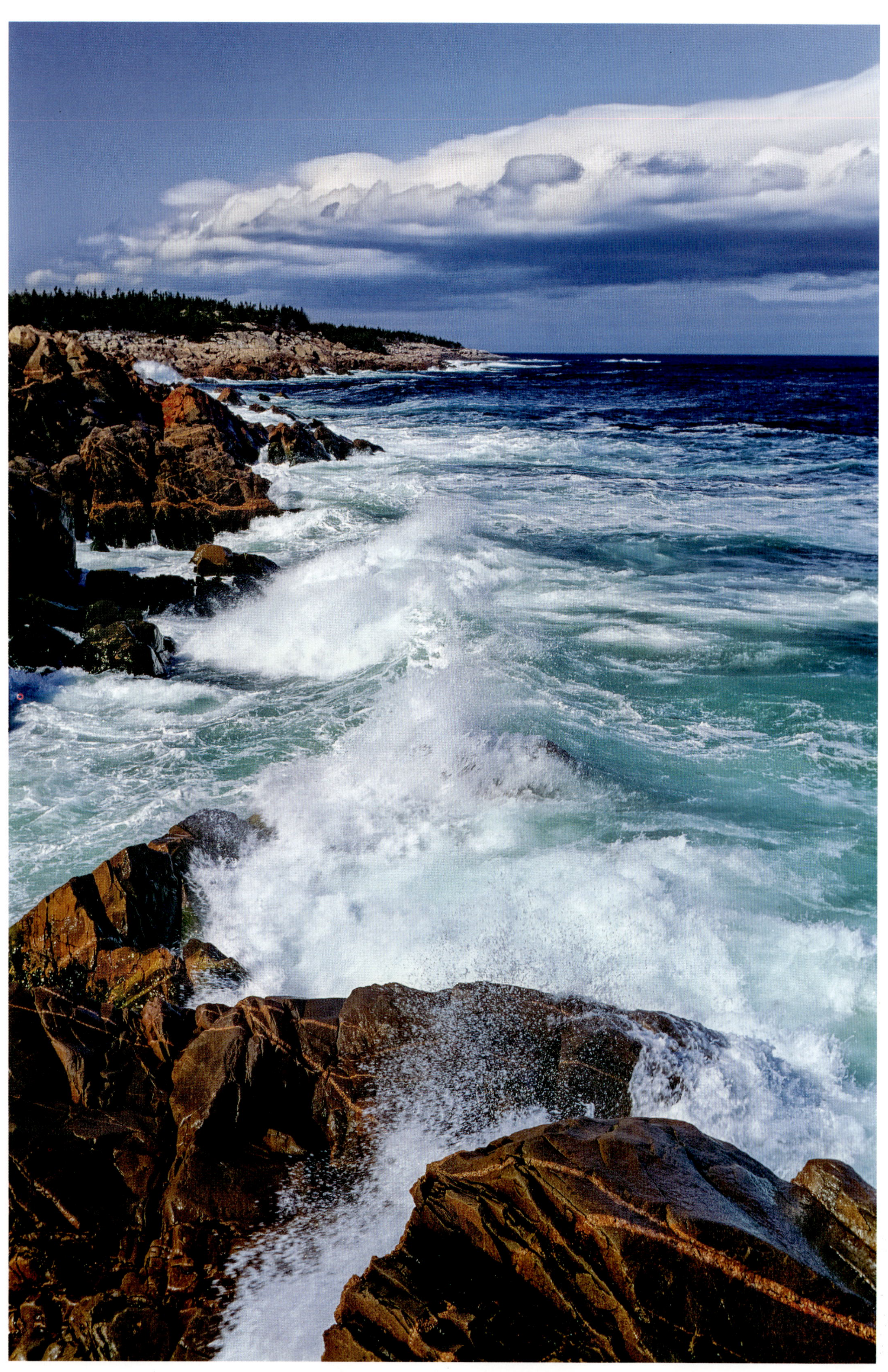

Heavy Atlantic surf rushes in at Green Cove (left) and explodes against a rocky pinnacle at Middle Head, both in Cape Breton Highlands National Park, Cape Breton, Nova Scotia.

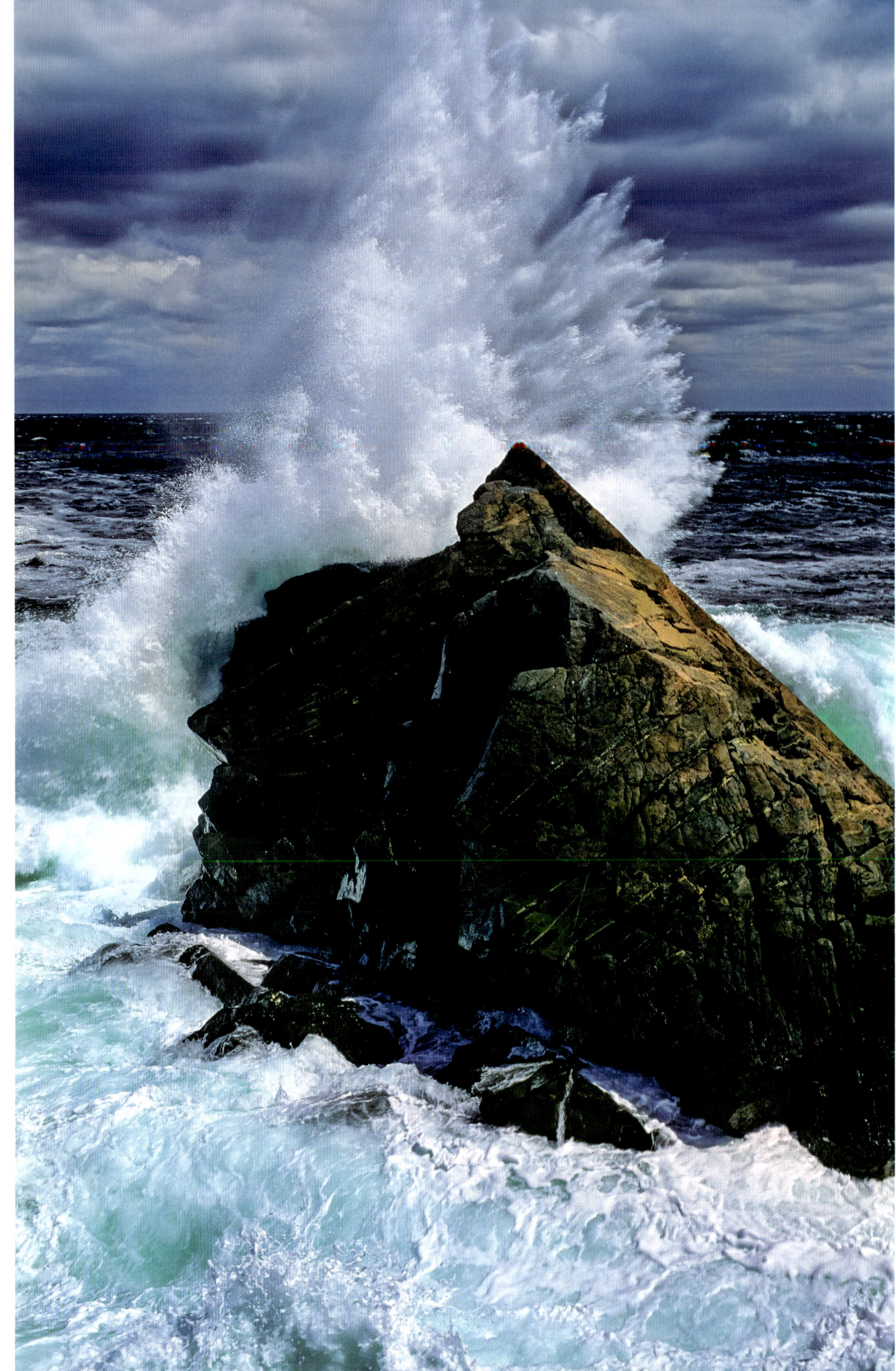

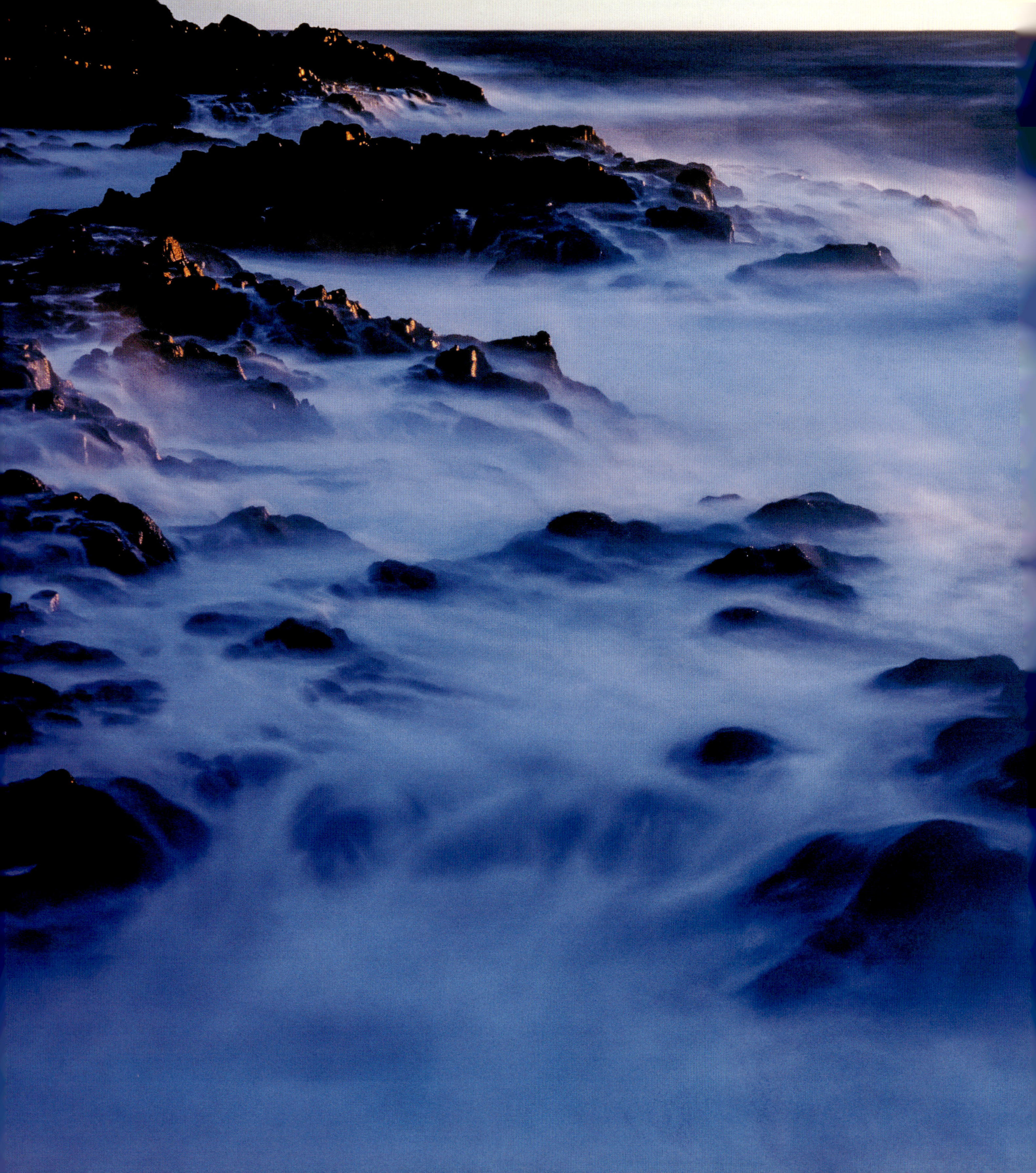

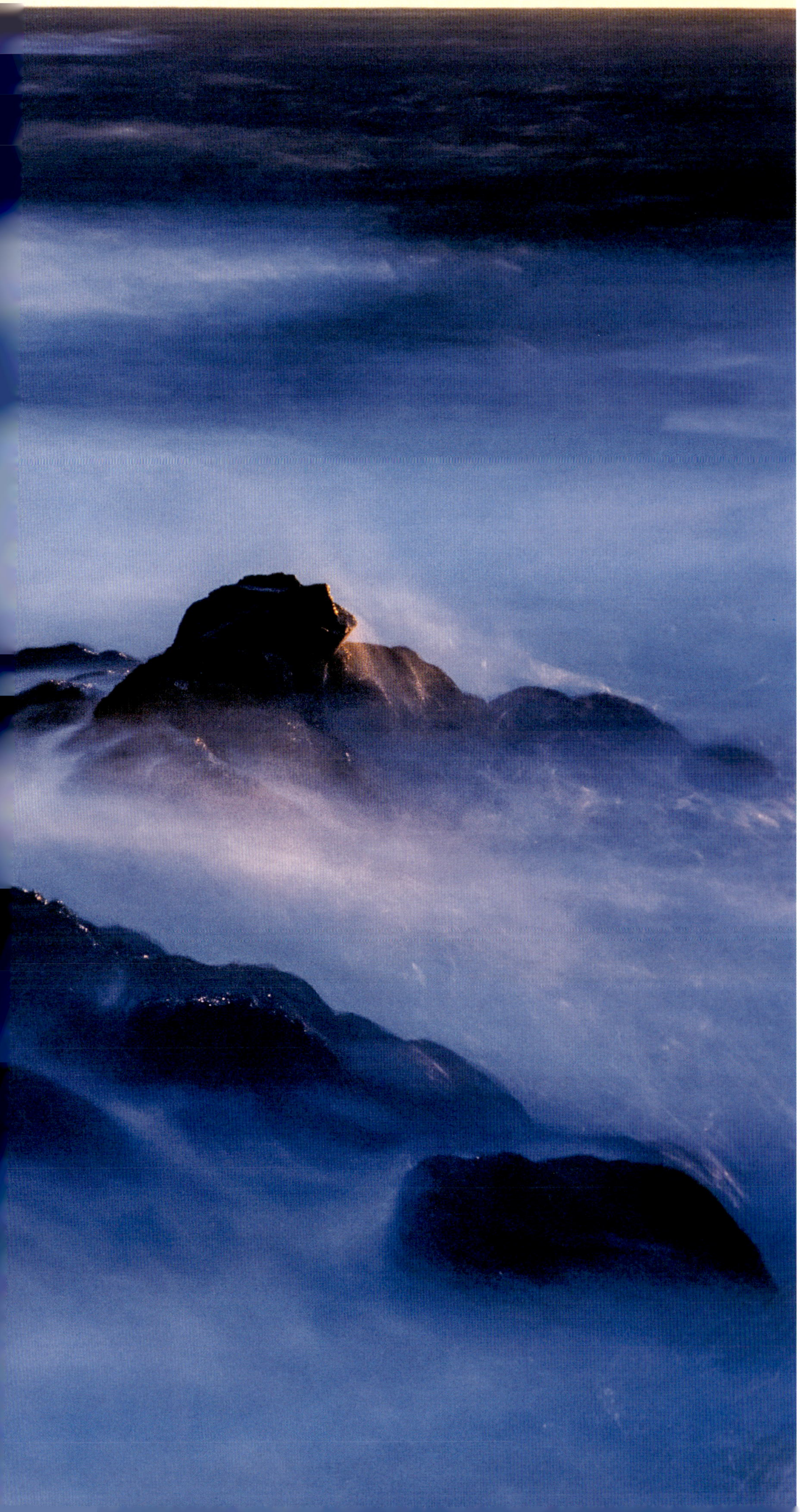

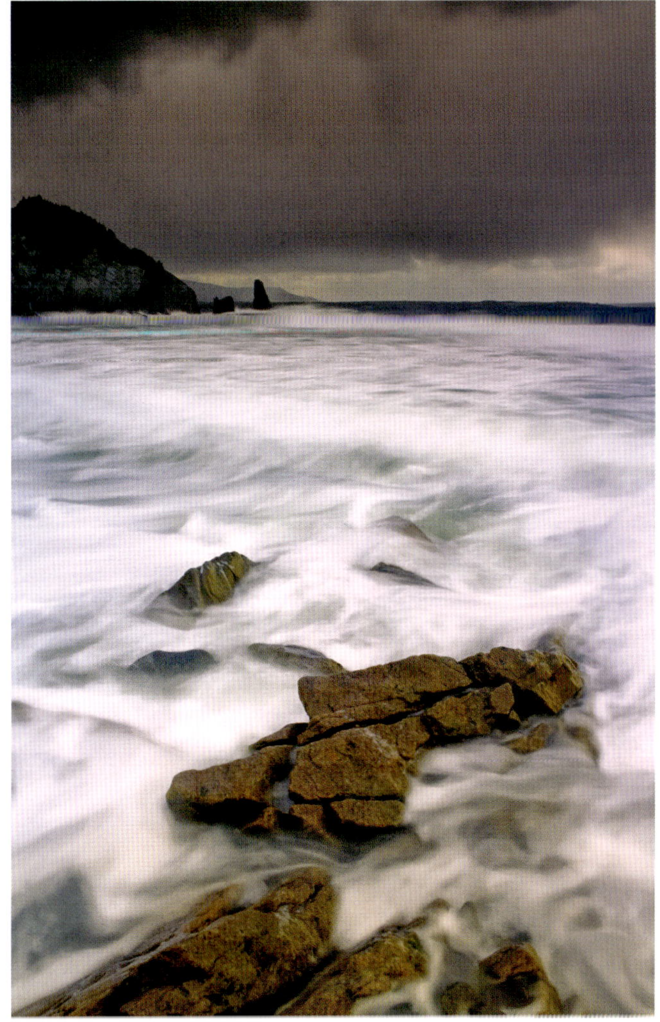

Long exposures of strong surf late in the evening at the entrance to the Bay of Fundy at the south tip of Brier Island, the westernmost point in Nova Scotia (left) and at Pillar Rock along the Cabot Trail on the west side of Cape Breton Highlands National Park.

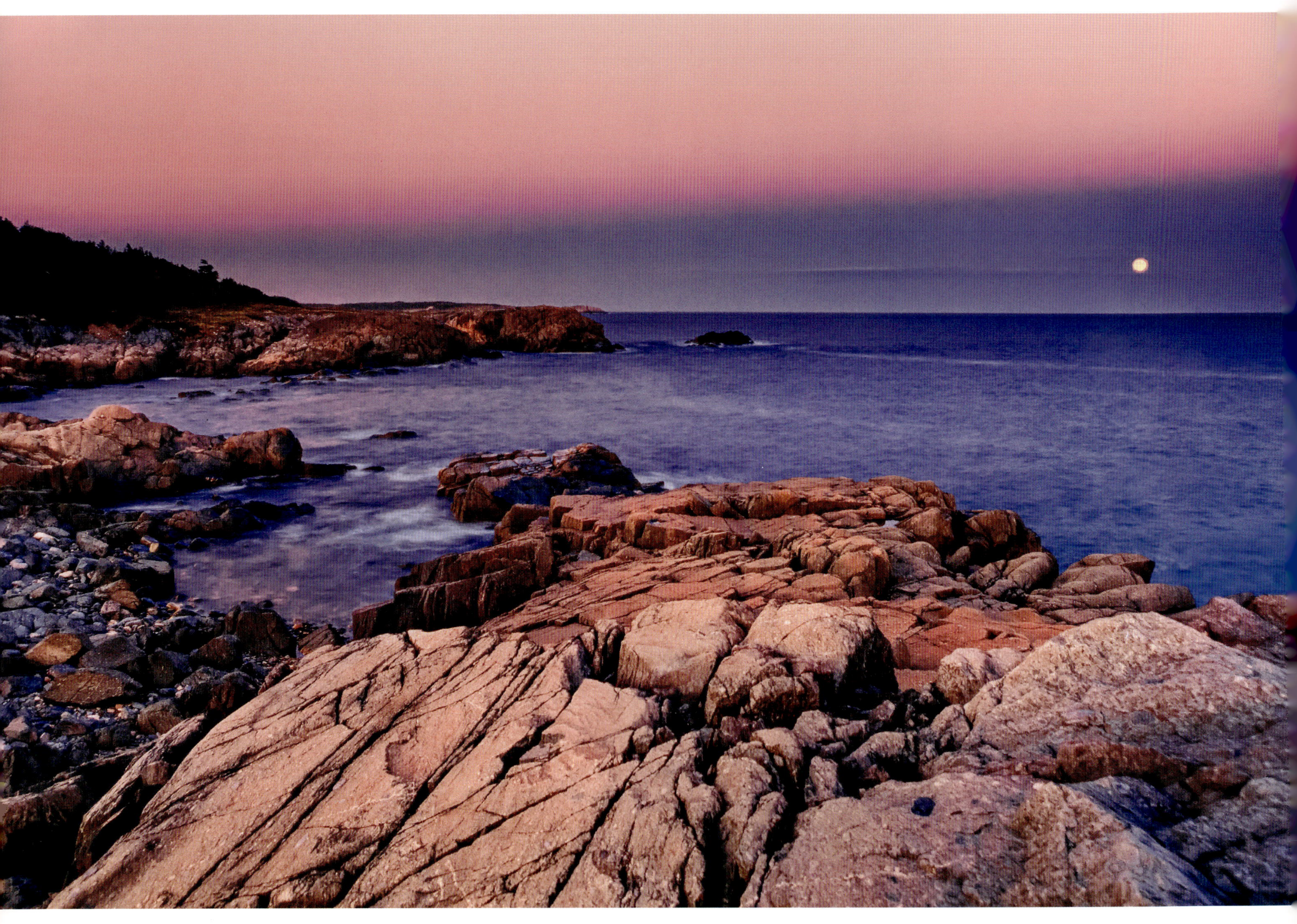

Moonrise at dusk over the Atlantic at Lighthouse Point near Louisbourg, Cape Breton, site of the first lighthouse in Canada (above) and dawn at Green Point along the east coast of Cape Breton Highlands National Park, Nova Scotia.

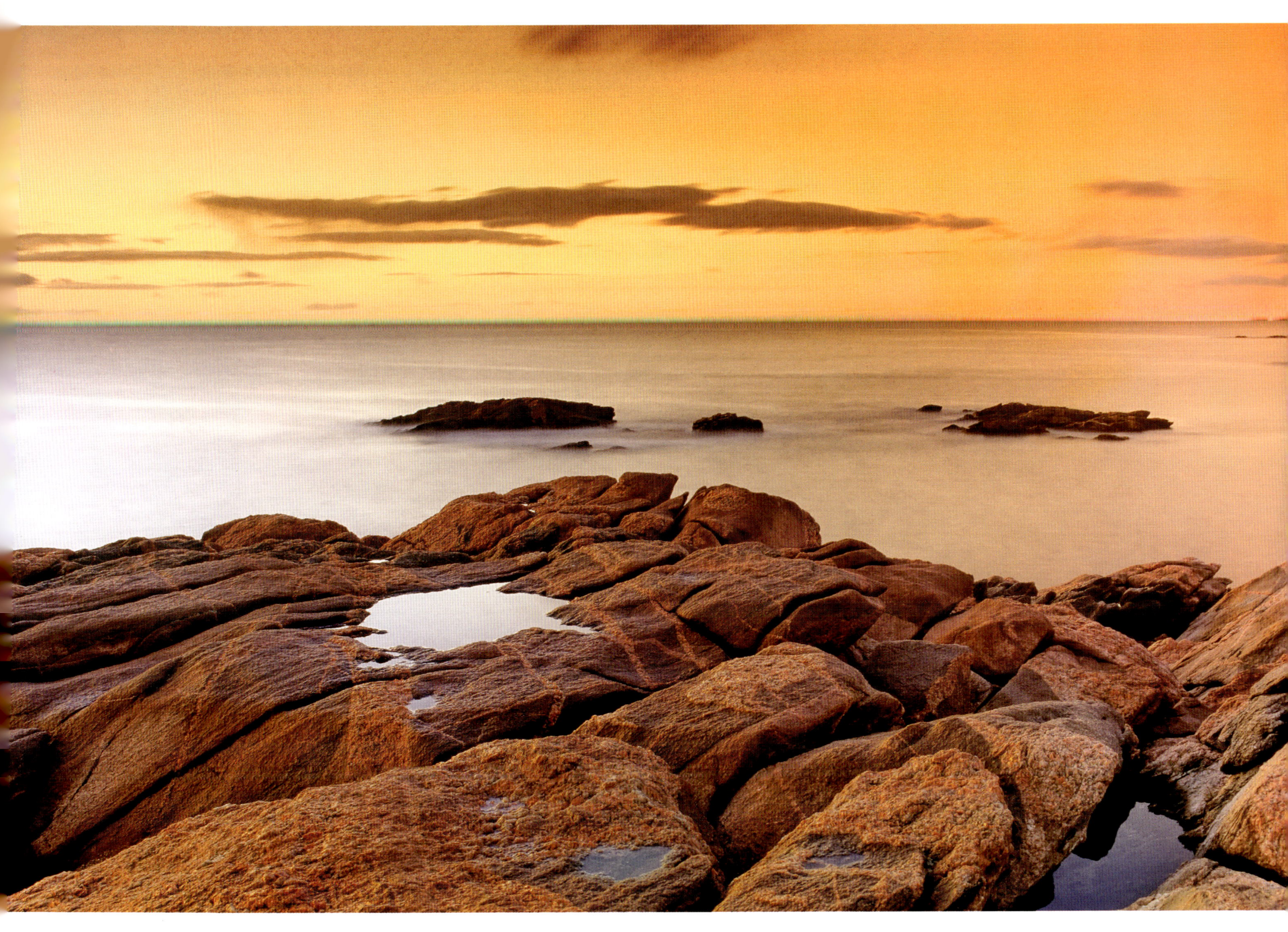

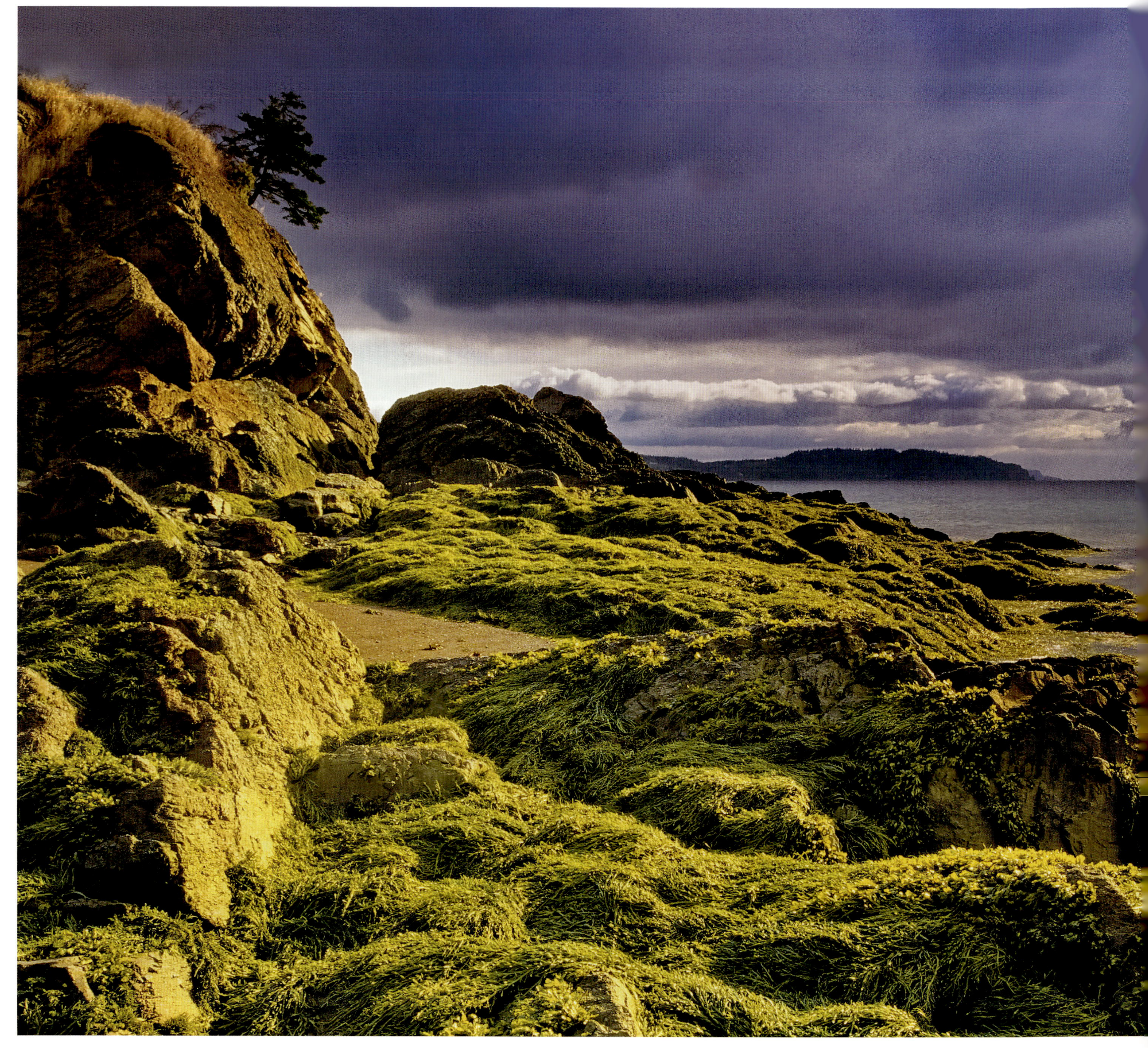

Low tide along the Bay of Fundy coast near Greenhill east of Parrsboro, Nova Scotia. Looking eastward across the Minas Basin (above) and westward towards Partridge Island.

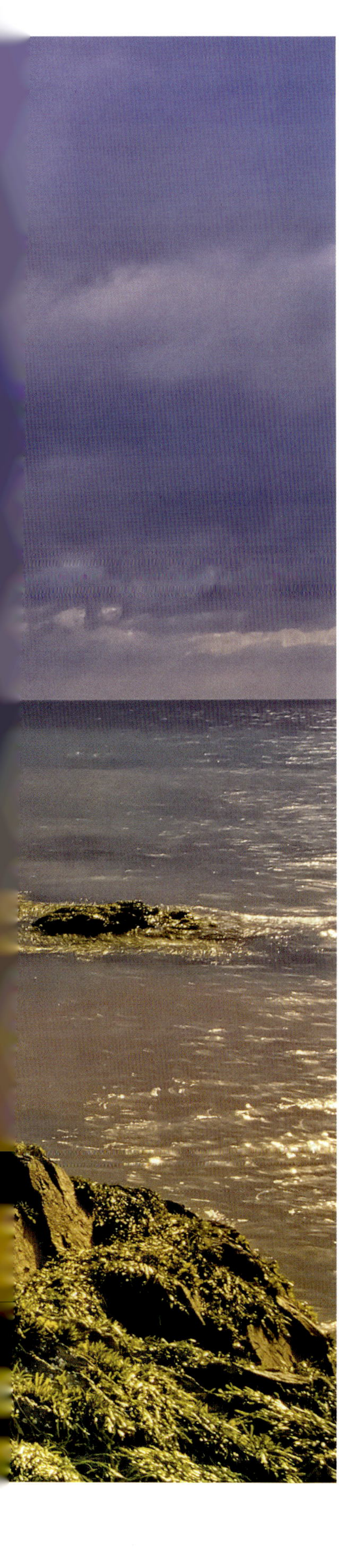

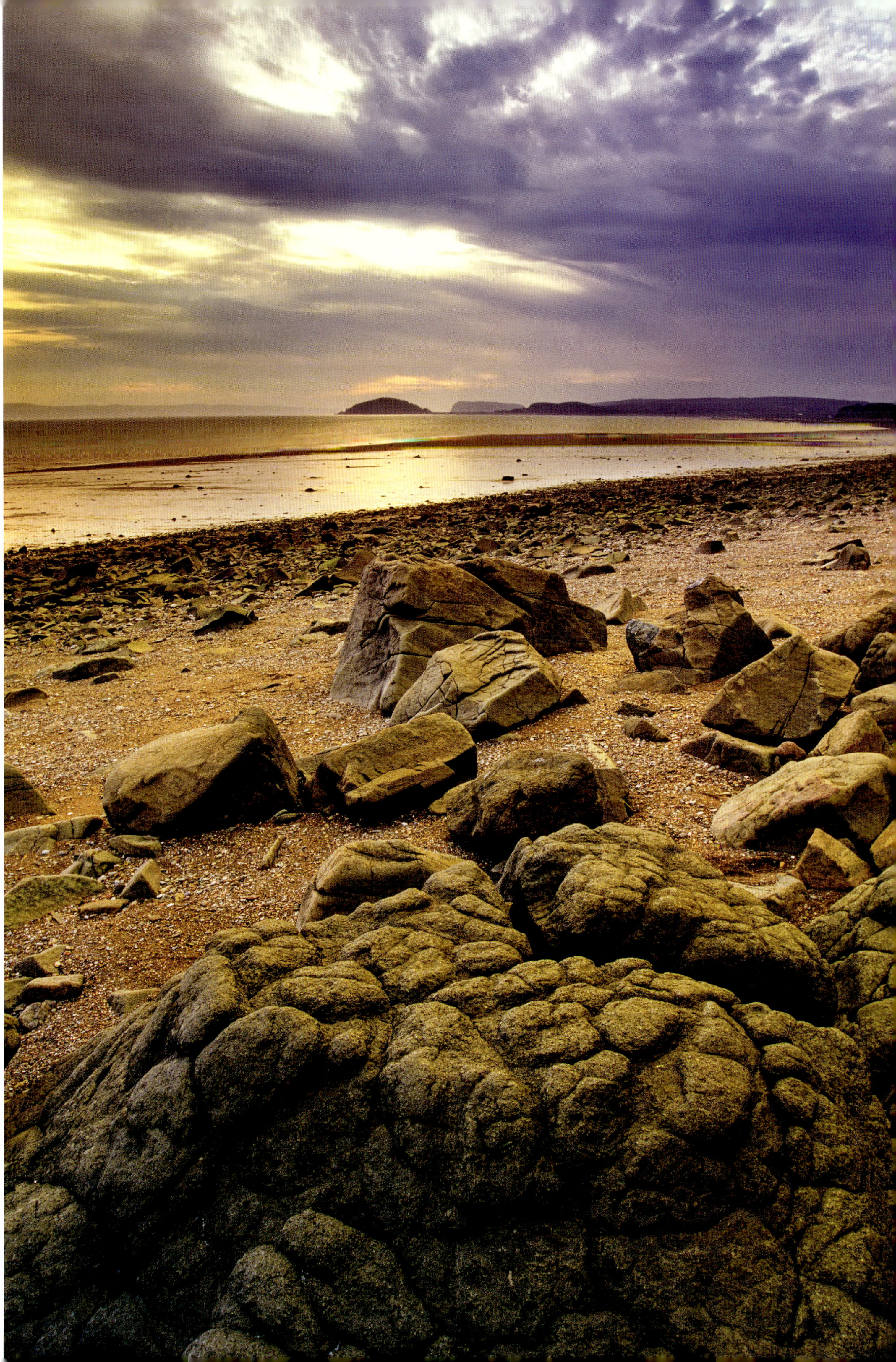

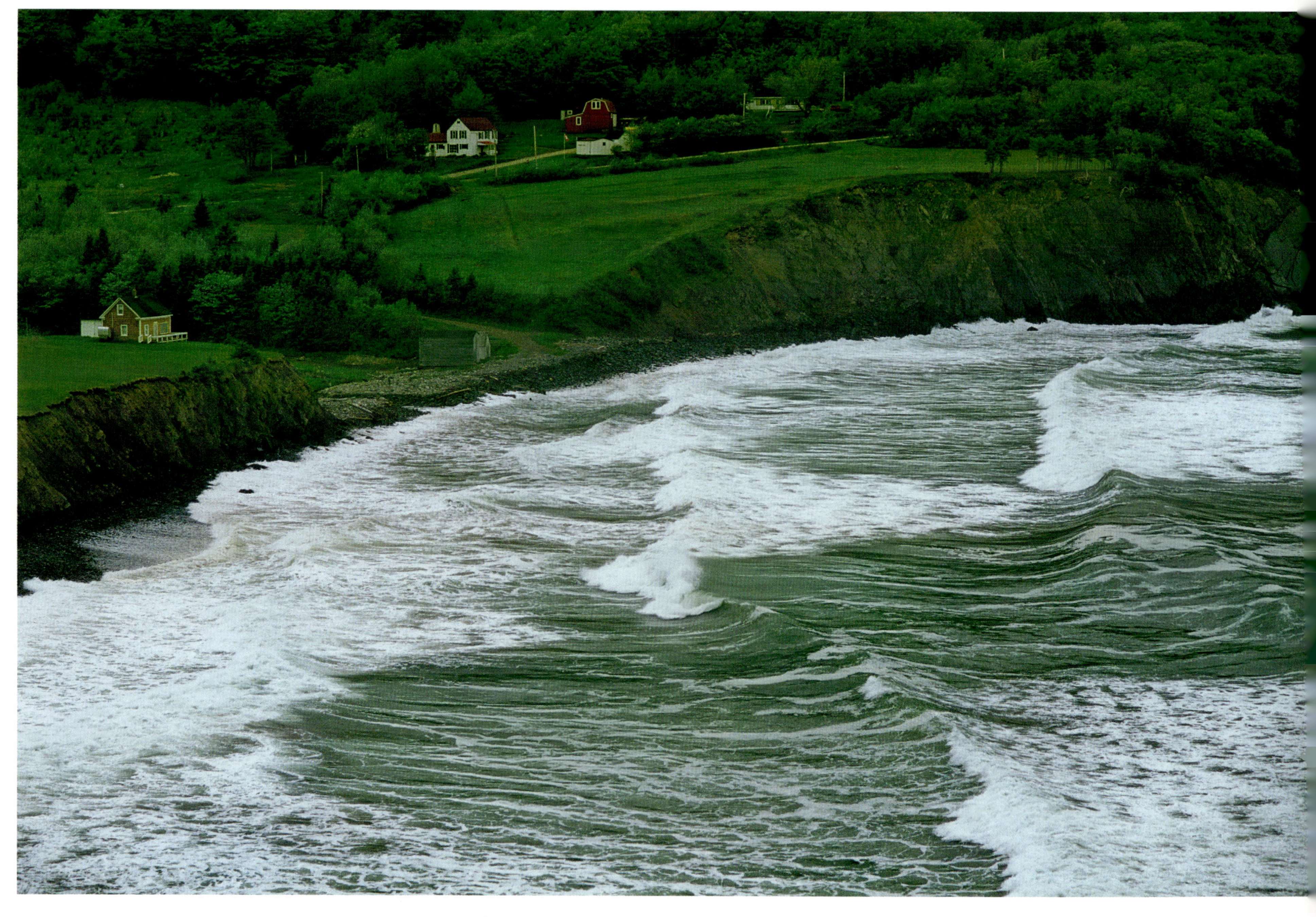

Surf rolls into Wreck Cove at Capstick at the north end of Cape Breton (above) and washes over the 400-million-year-old rocks of Devonian granite at Peggy's Cove, Nova Scotia.

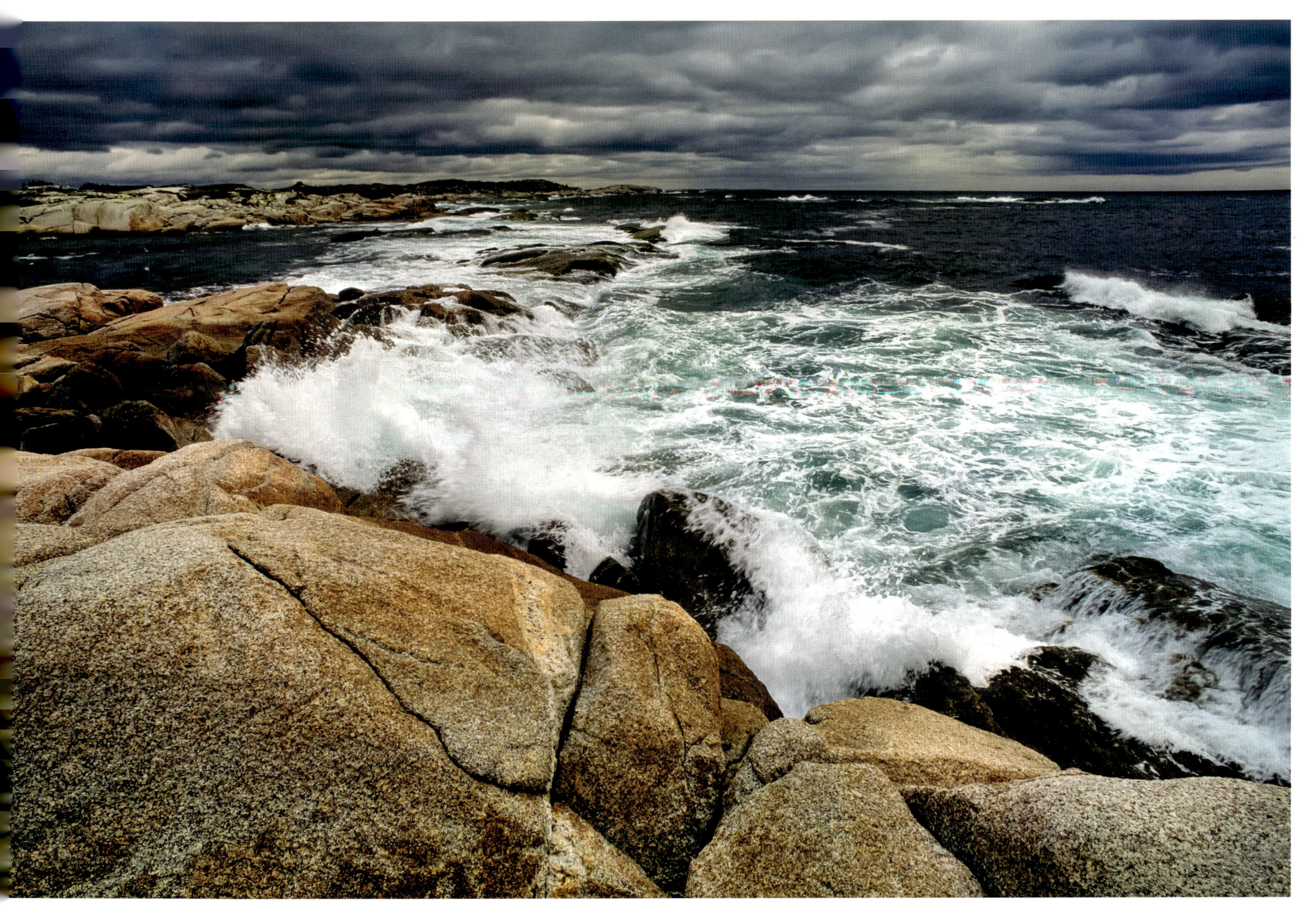

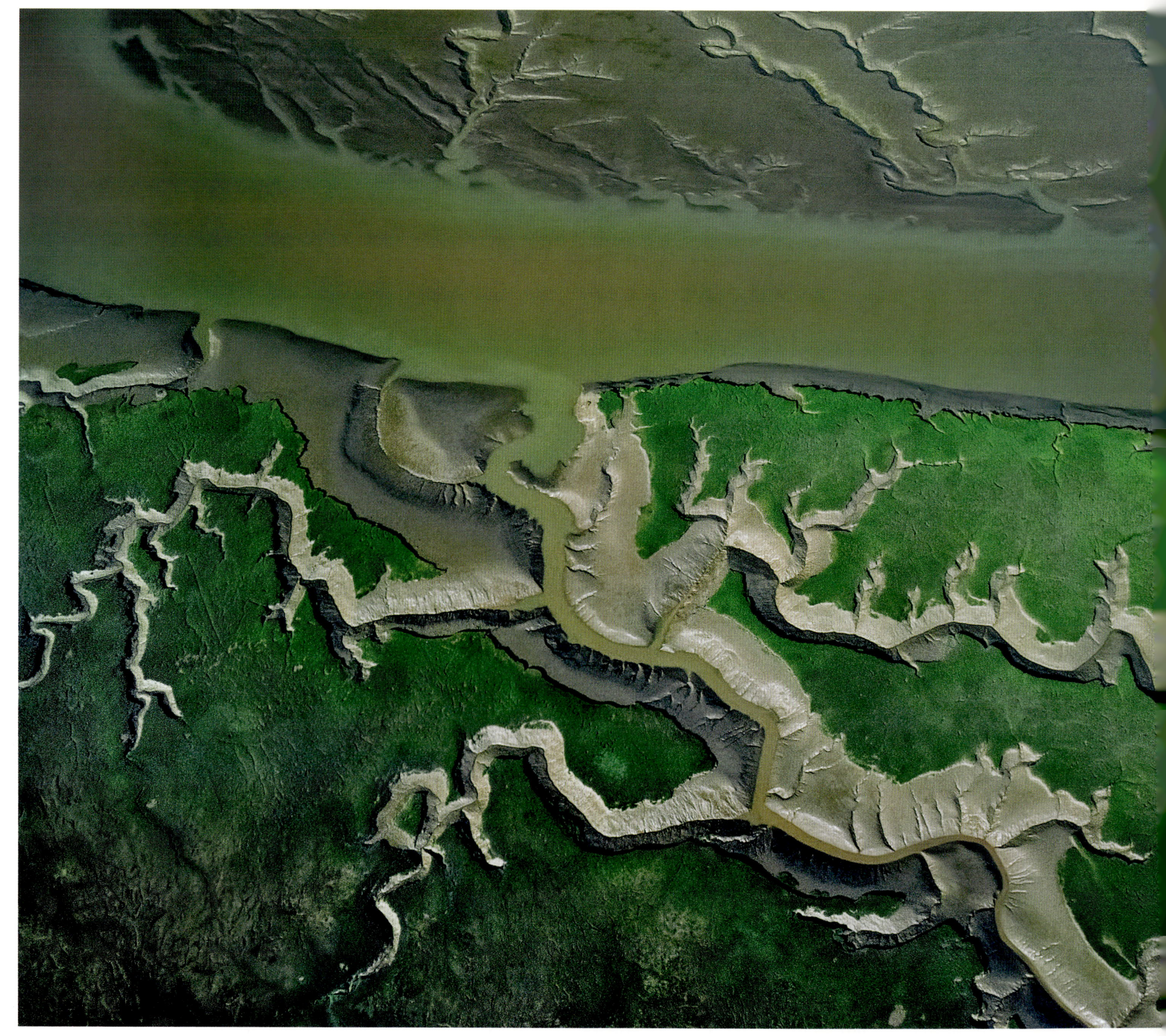

Two aerial views of the vast mudflats exposed at low tide in
Cobequid Bay, the site of the highest tides in the world at
the head of Minas Basin in the Bay of Fundy, Nova Scotia.

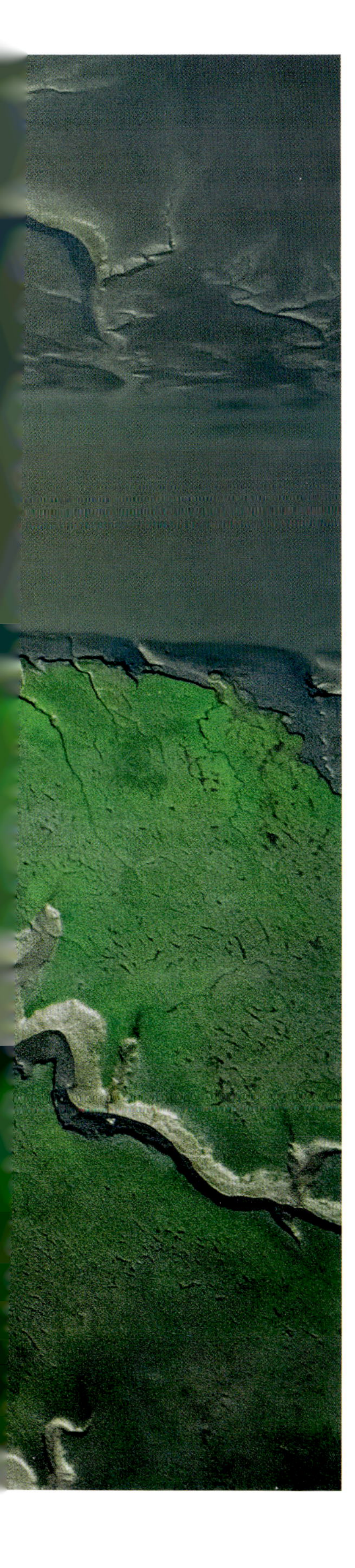

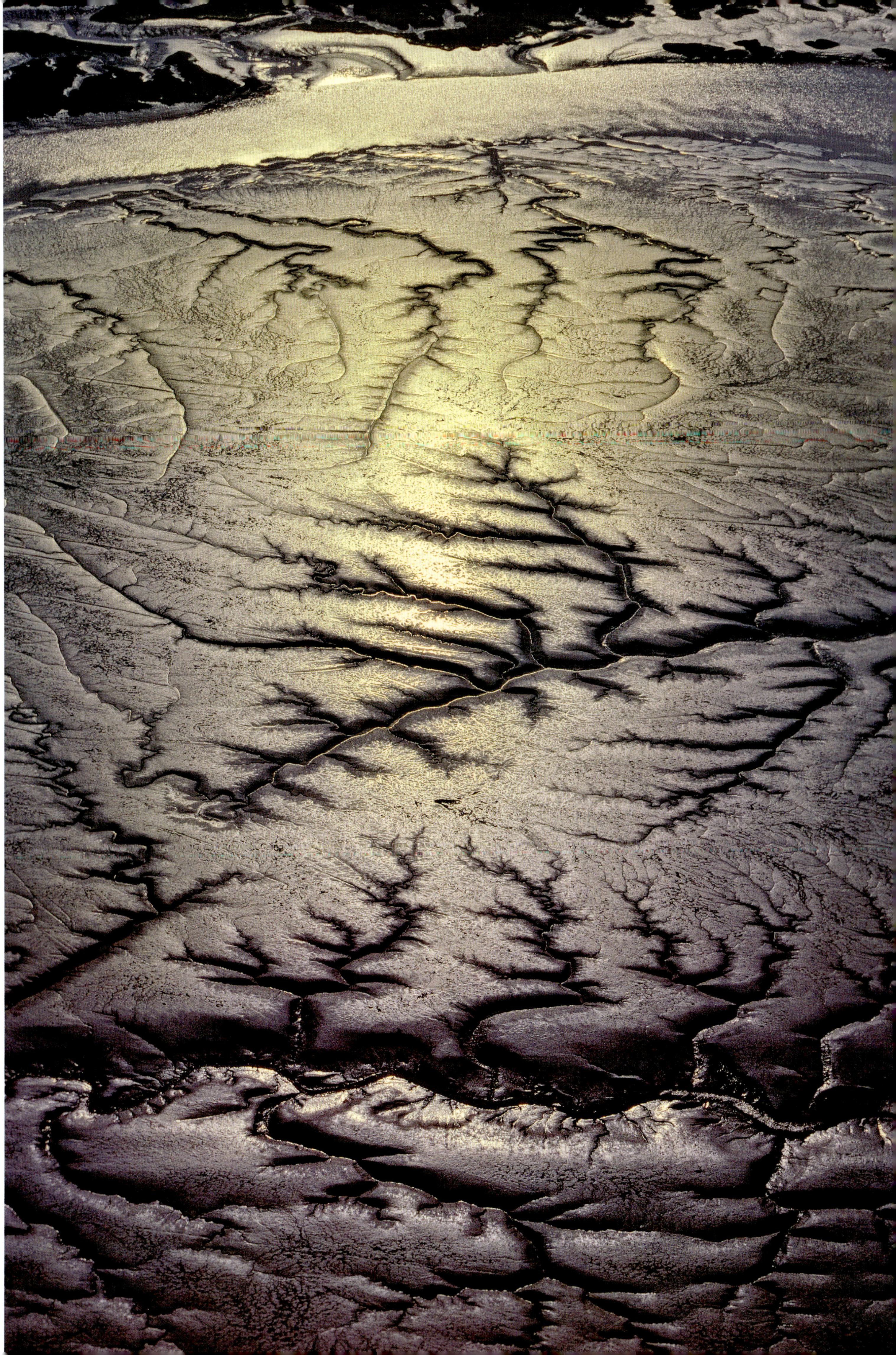

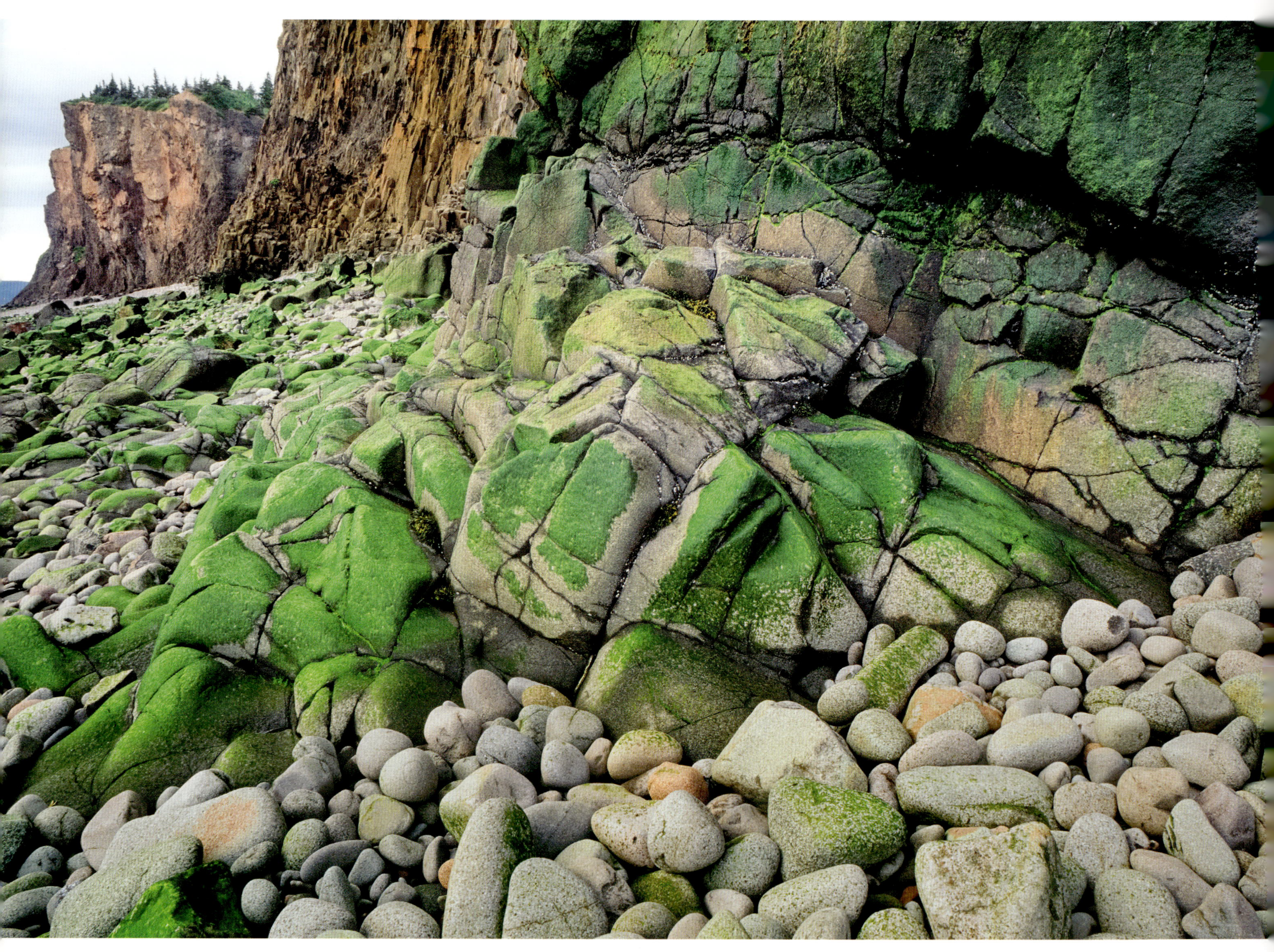

The great tides of the Bay of Fundy recede to expose a long
slope of cobbles and seaweed-covered stone at the base of
200-metre sea cliffs at Cape d'Or, Nova Scotia.

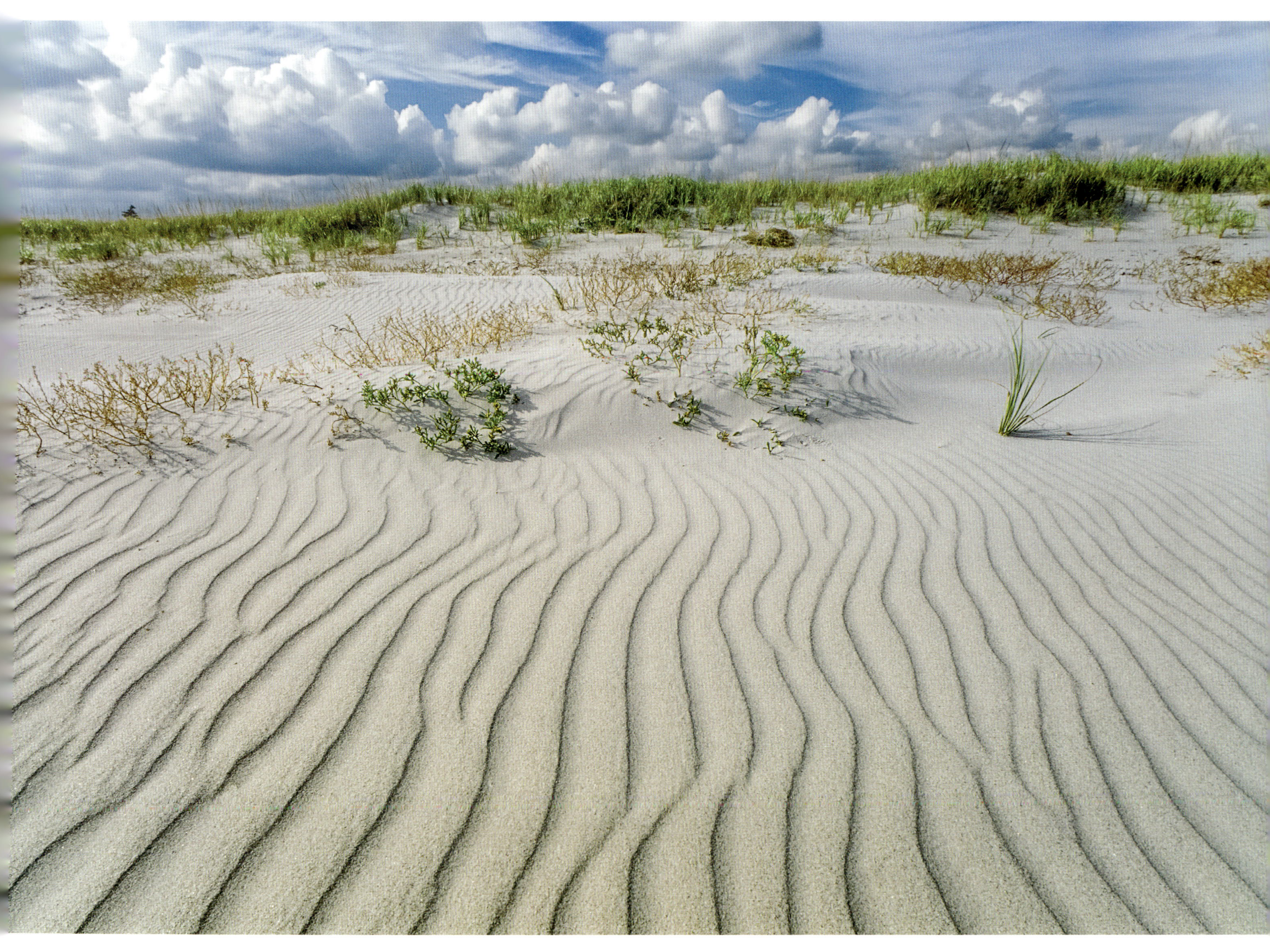

Wind-rippled white sand at Saint Catherines River
Beach in Kejimkujik Seaside, Kejimkujik National
Park, Nova Scotia.

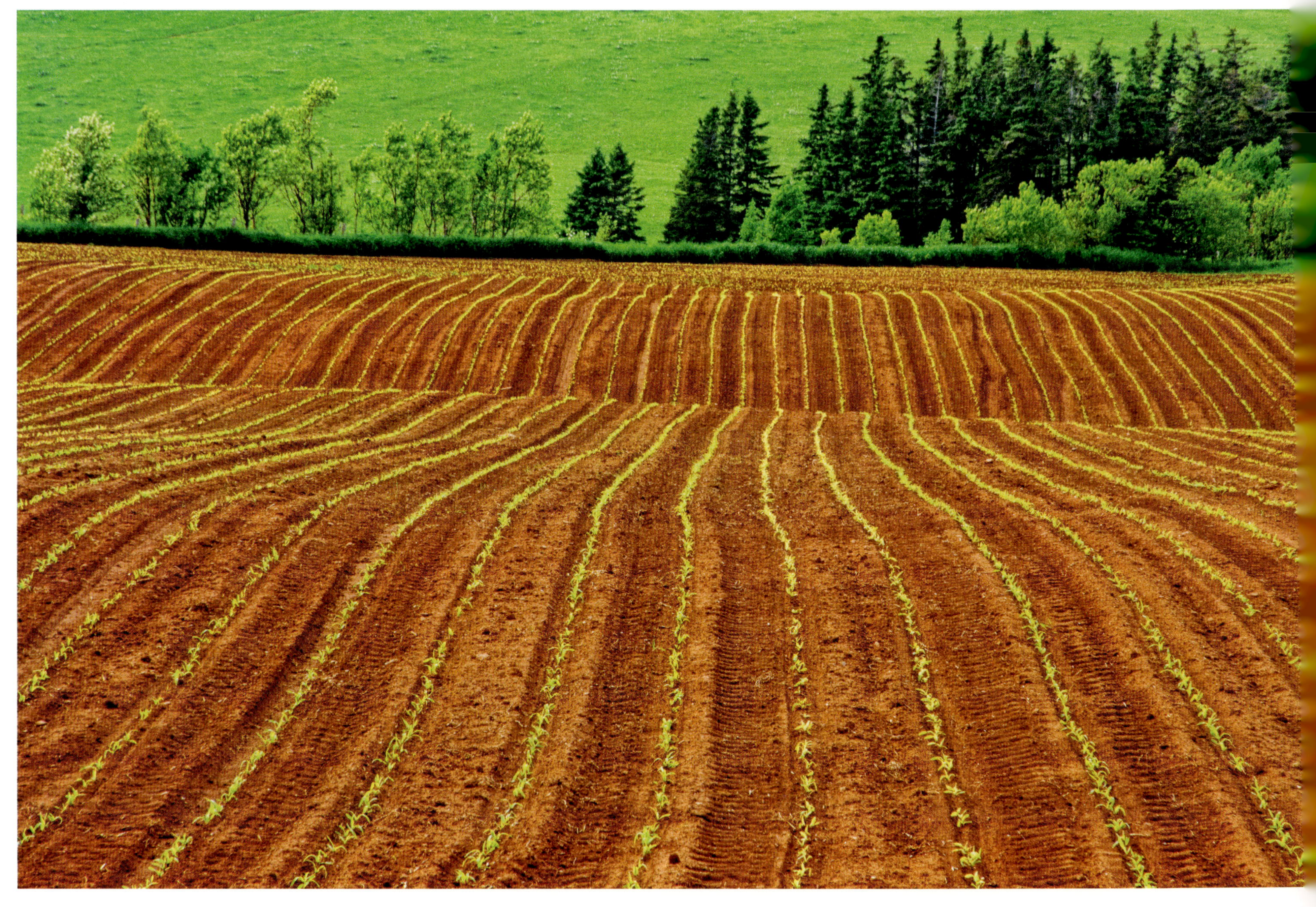

Sprouting fields in spring in the red soil of Prince
Edward Island south of Park Corner (above) and
north of Kensington, both in Queens County.

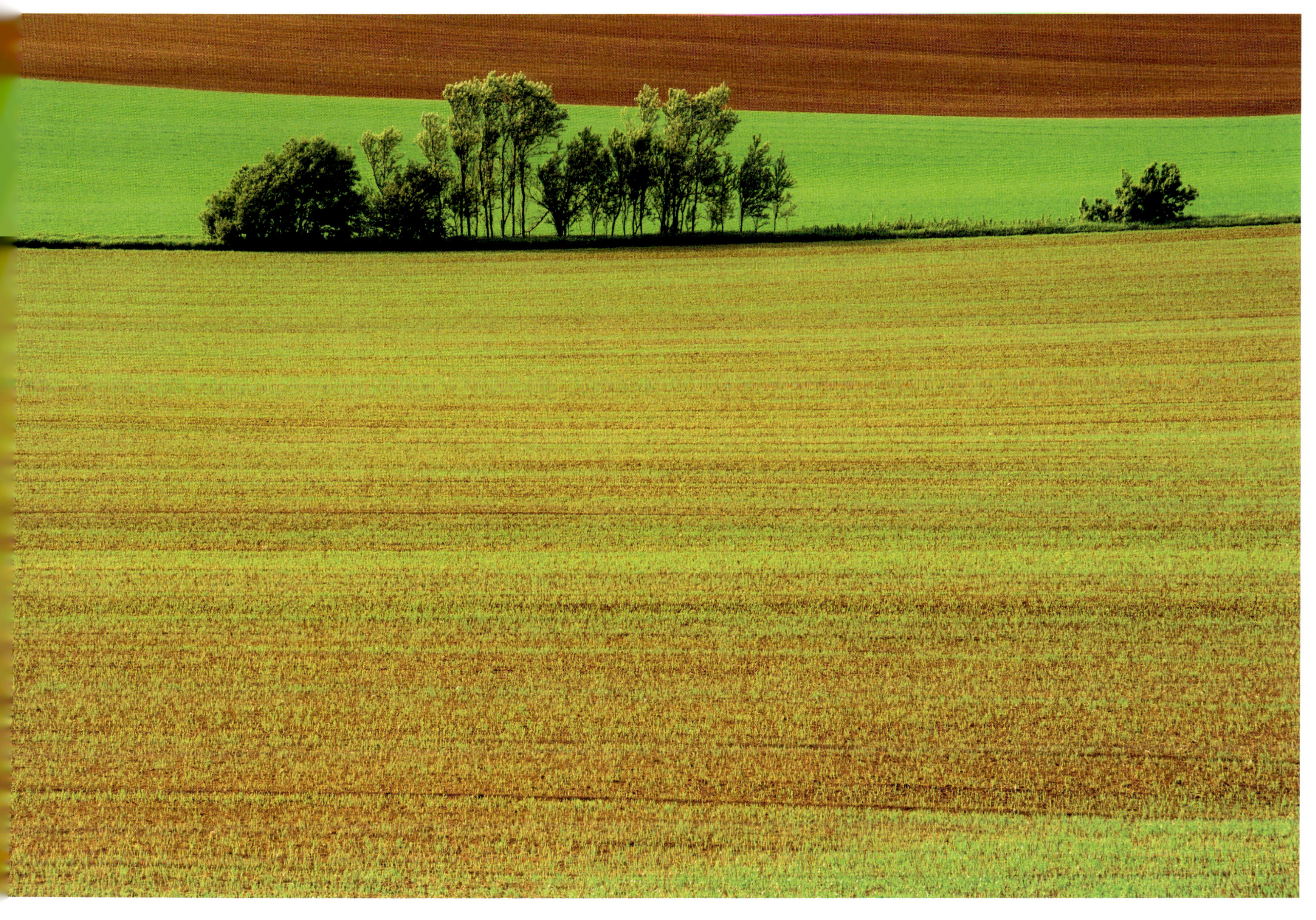

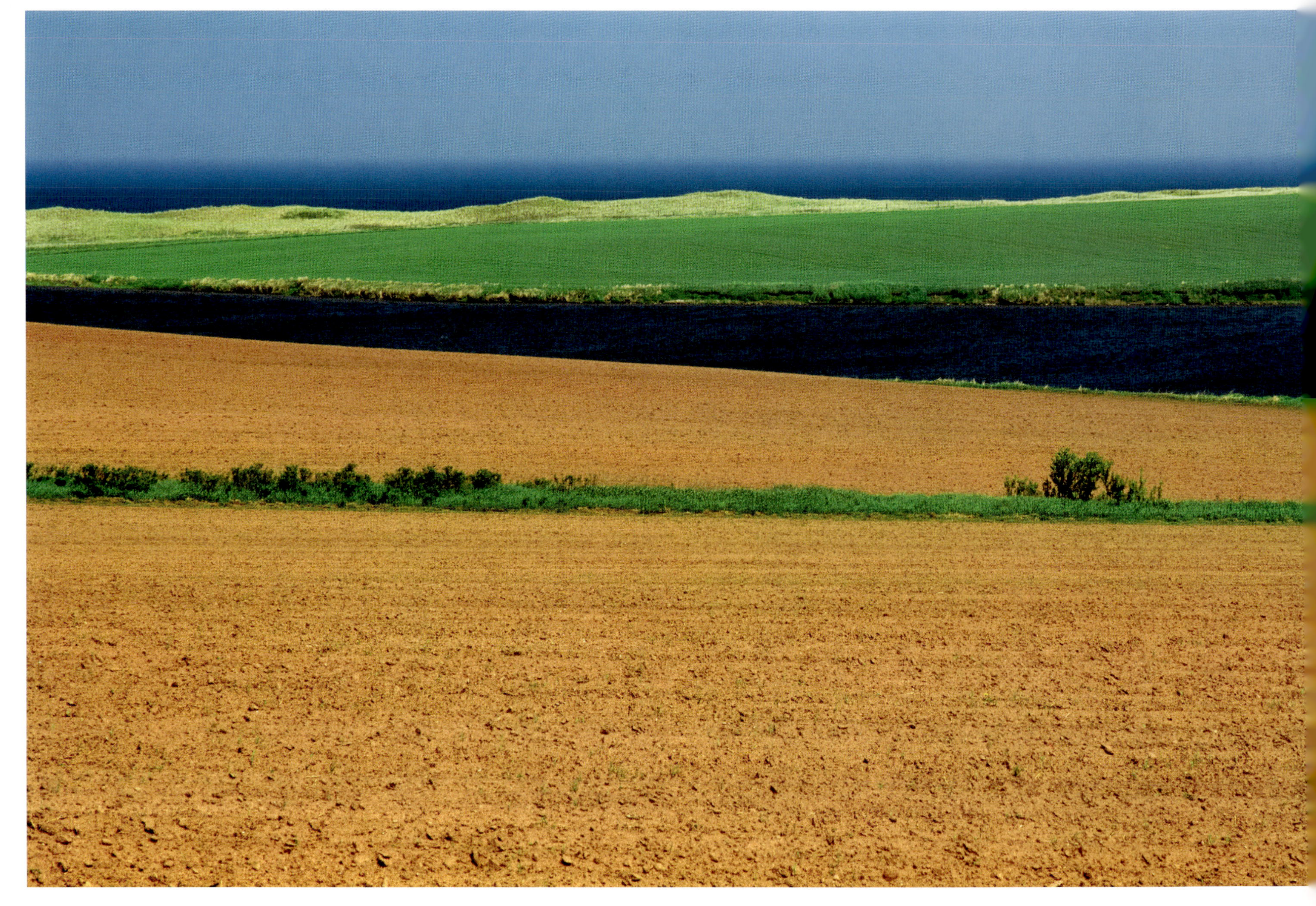

Farm fields along the north coast of Prince Edward Island. Grass-covered dunes with the Gulf of Saint Lawrence in the distance (above) and near Darnley in Prince County.

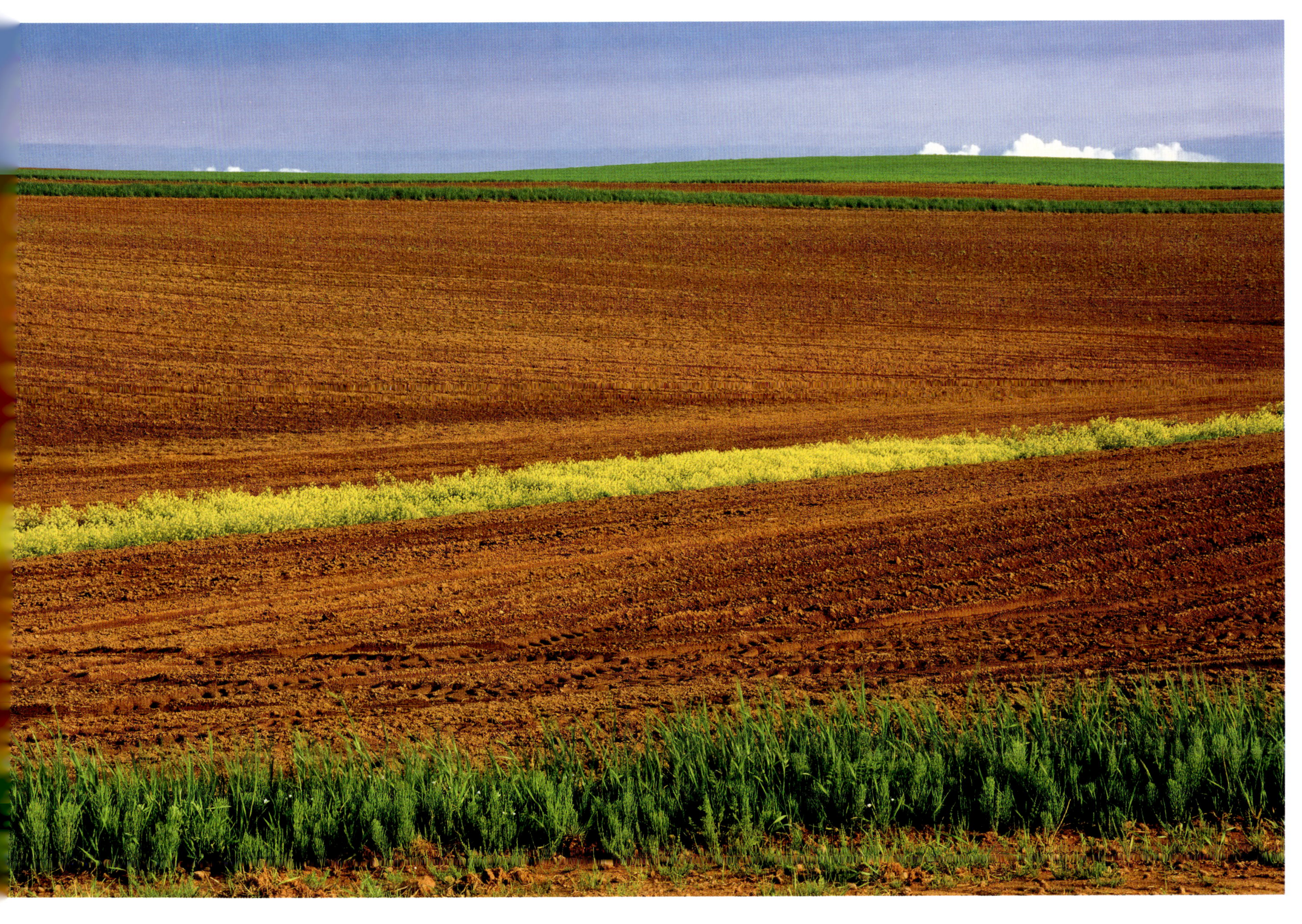

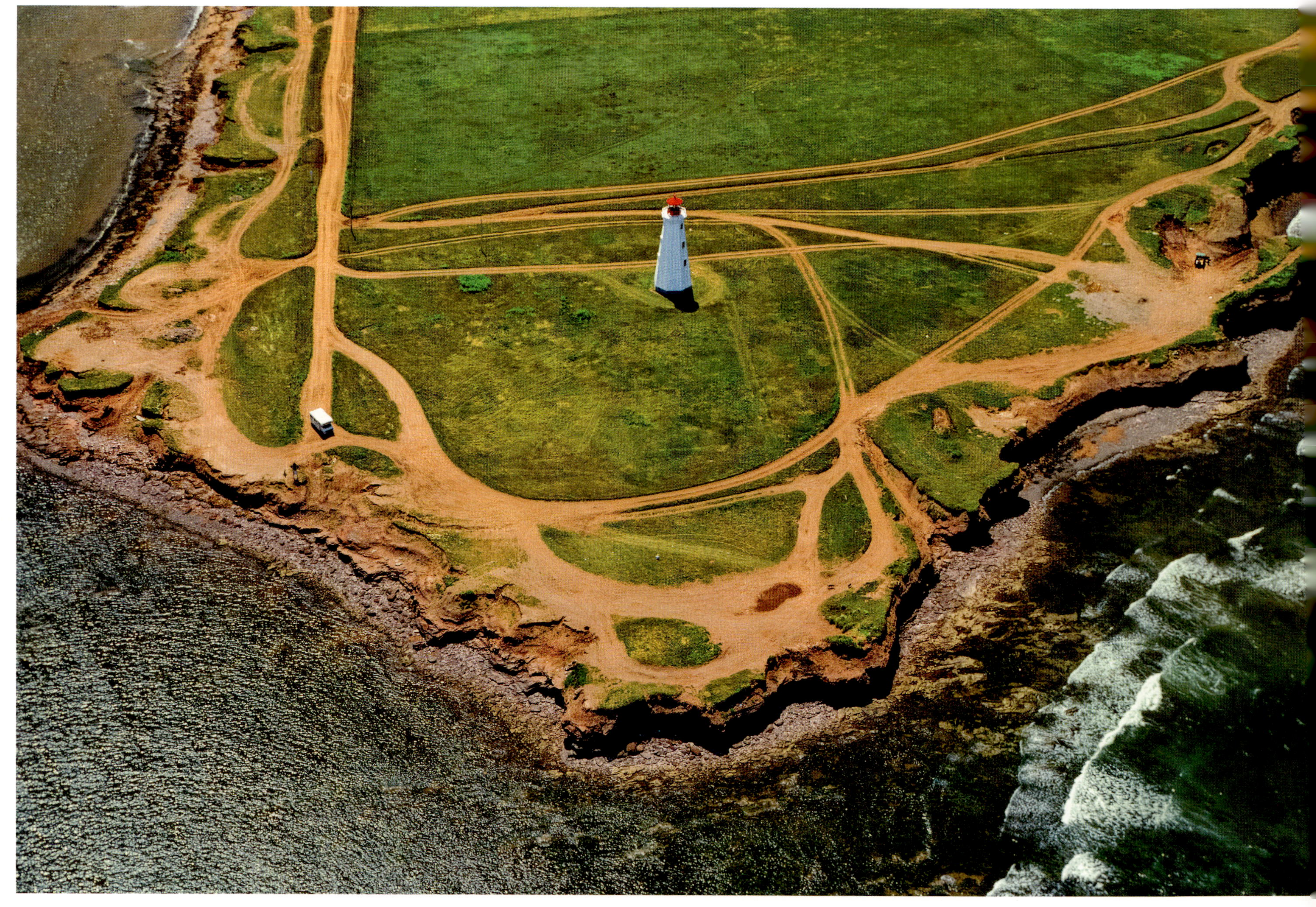

Cape North is the northwestern-most extremity of Prince Edward Island. It is not quite as pristine today as in this aerial view, with a new visitor centre and parking lot that would intrude into the top of the view and a tall radio mast beside the lighthouse.

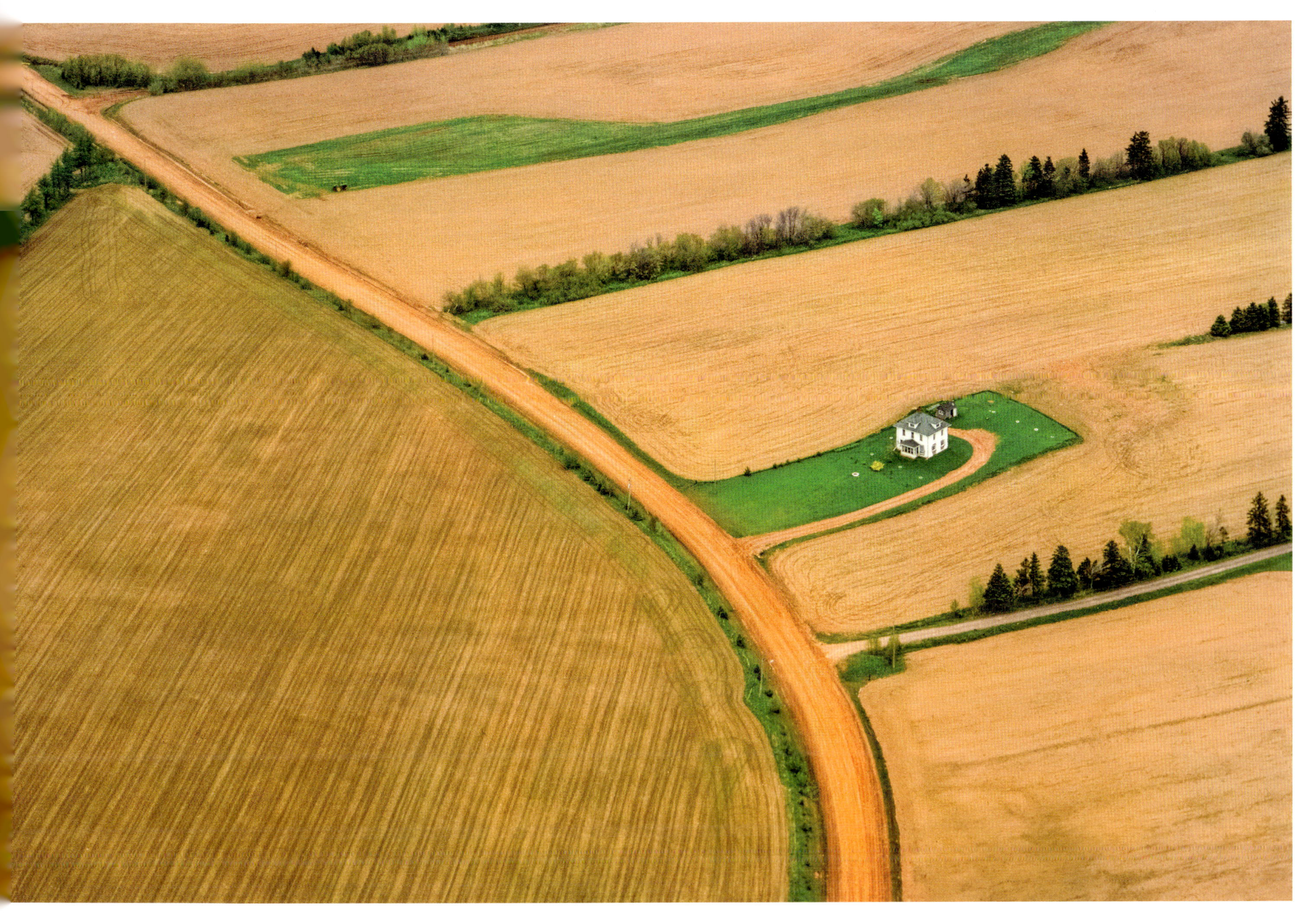

An aerial view of a two-story farmhouse amid the
famous red soil fields of Prince Edward Island.

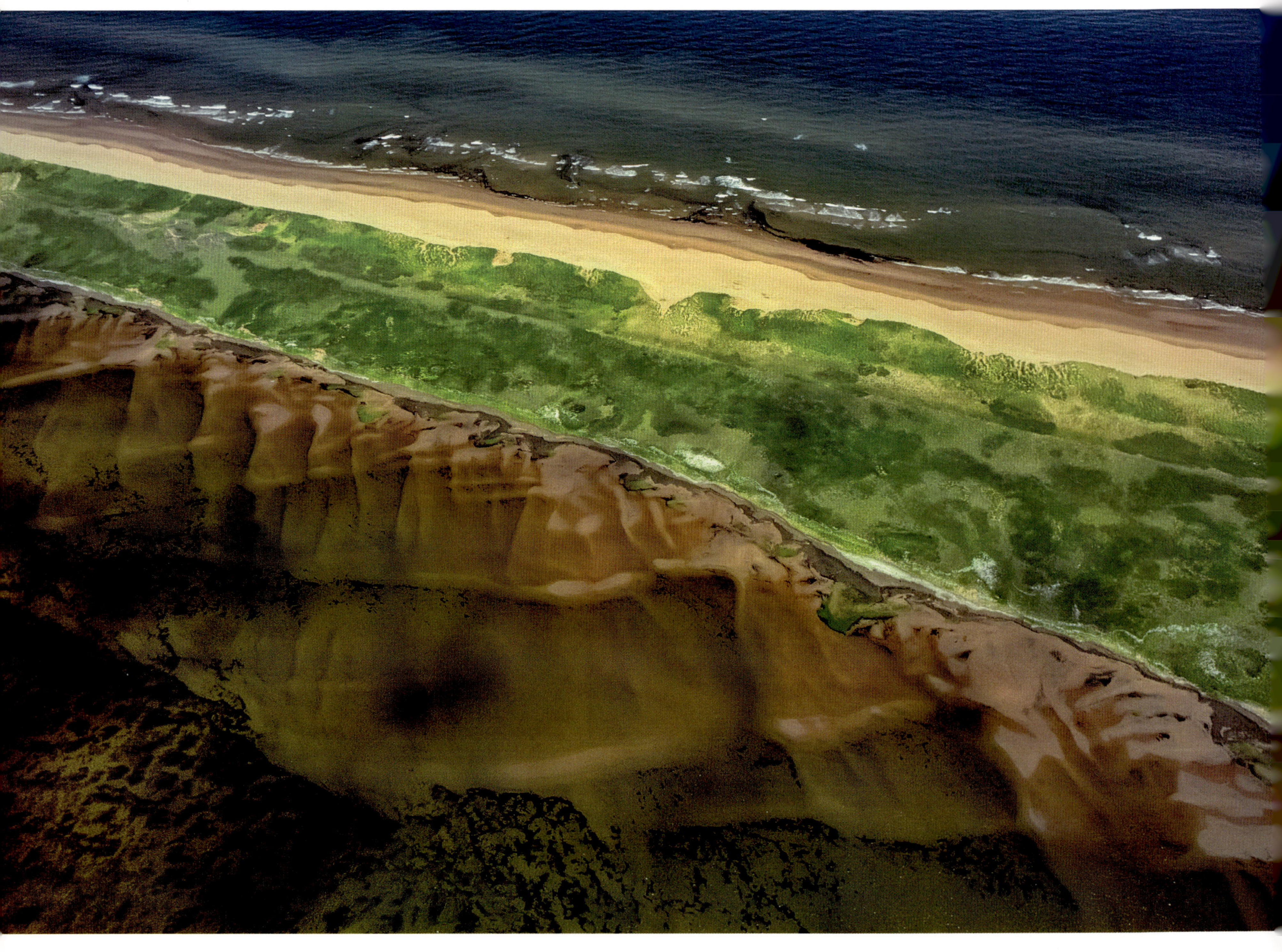

Aerial views of the north coast of Prince Edward Island in Prince County. The grass-covered Malpeque Sand Hills run along Hog Island, a barrier island at the entrance to Malpeque Bay (above). The Kildare River at Alberton is more a tidal inlet with marshy islands than it is a river.

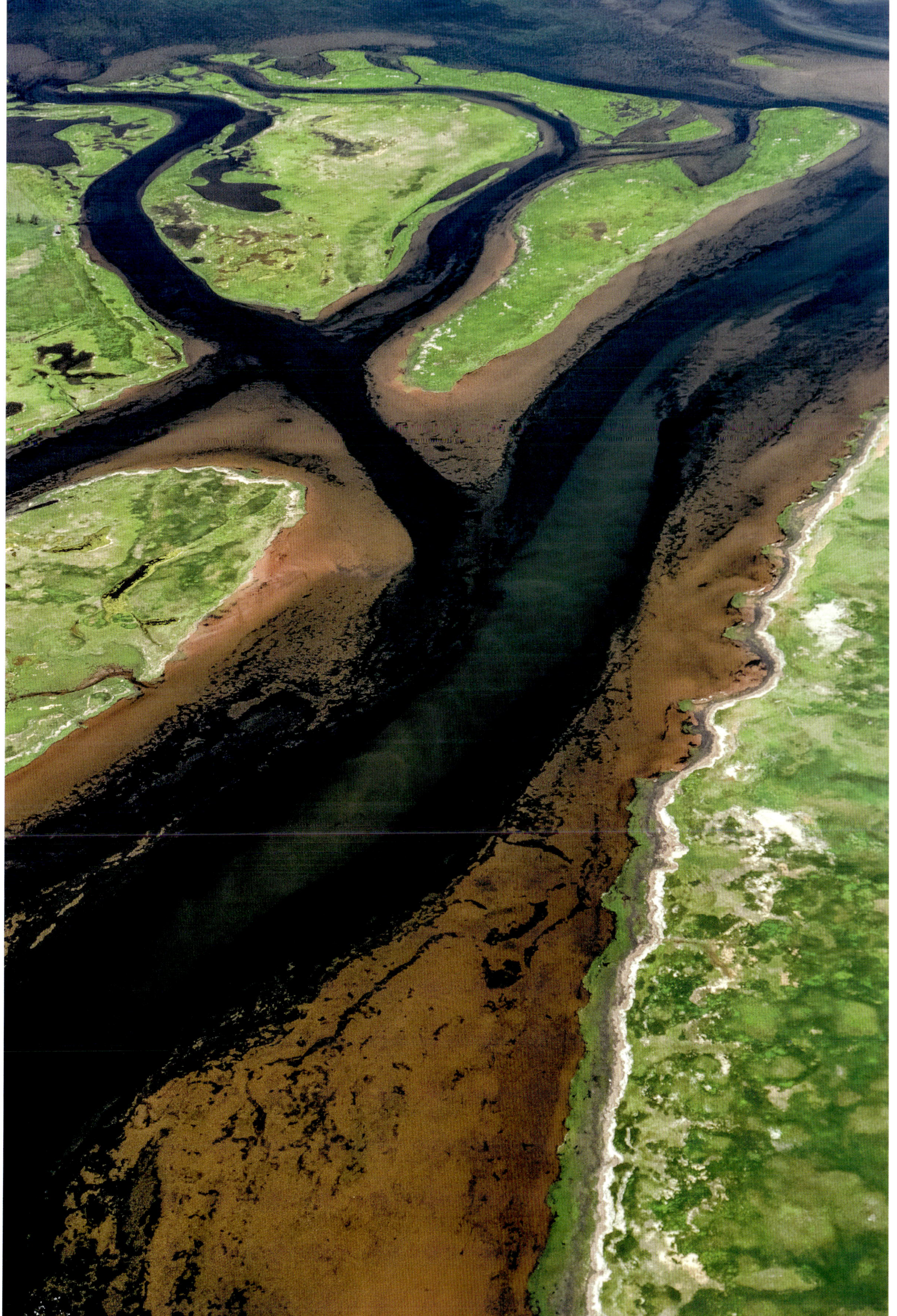

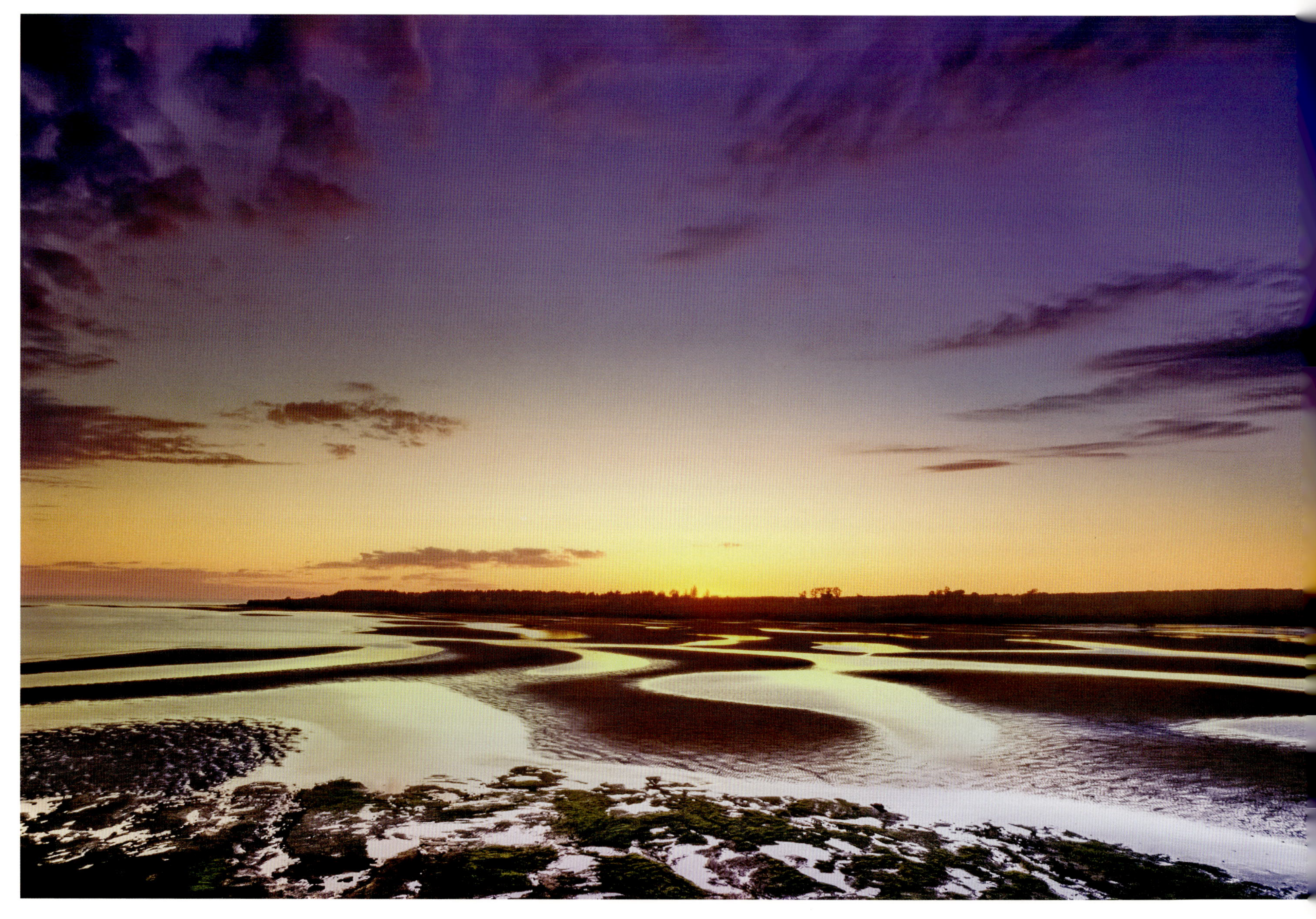

Two views of tidal flats at sunset at Canoe Cove,
Queens County, Prince Edward Island.

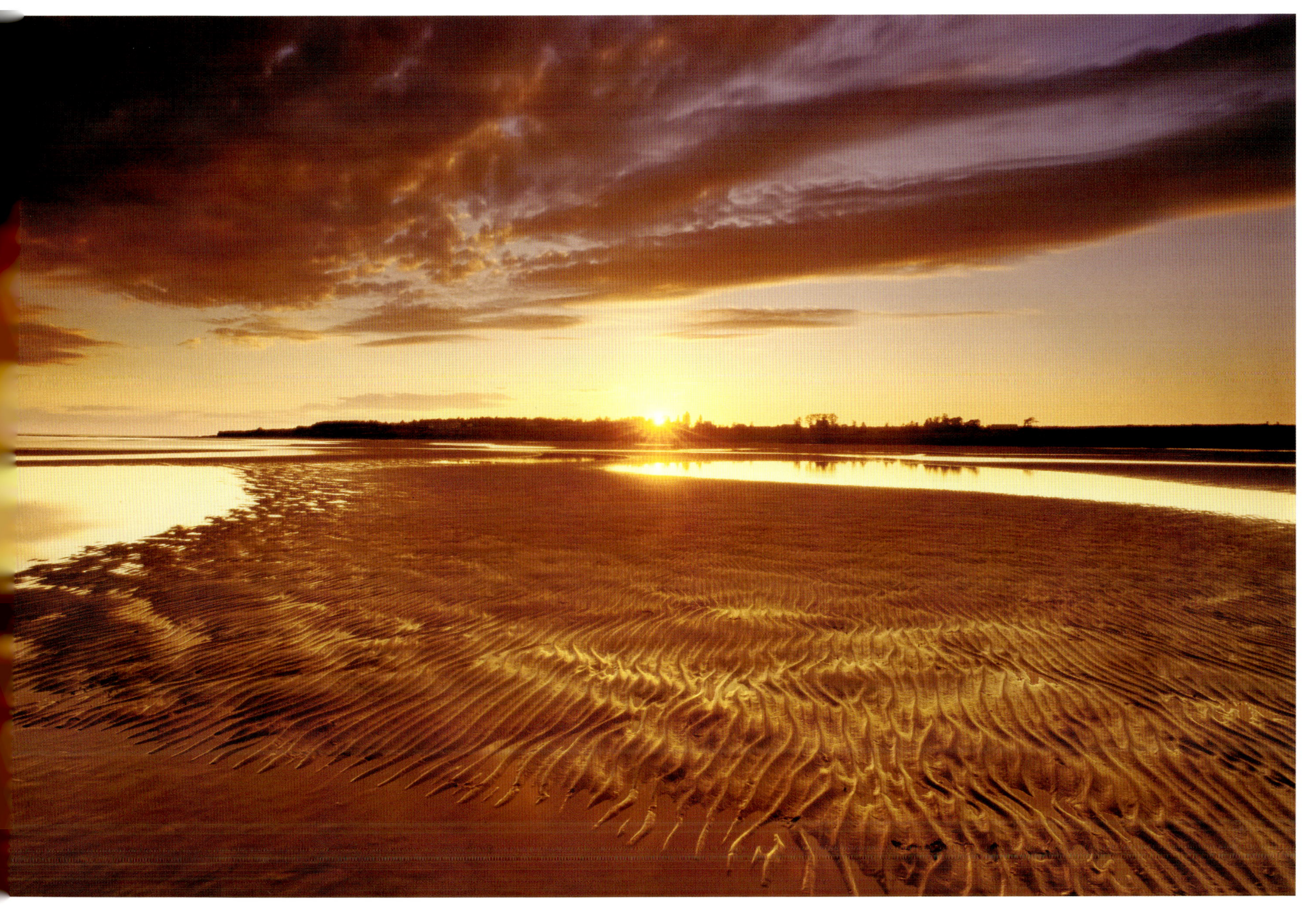

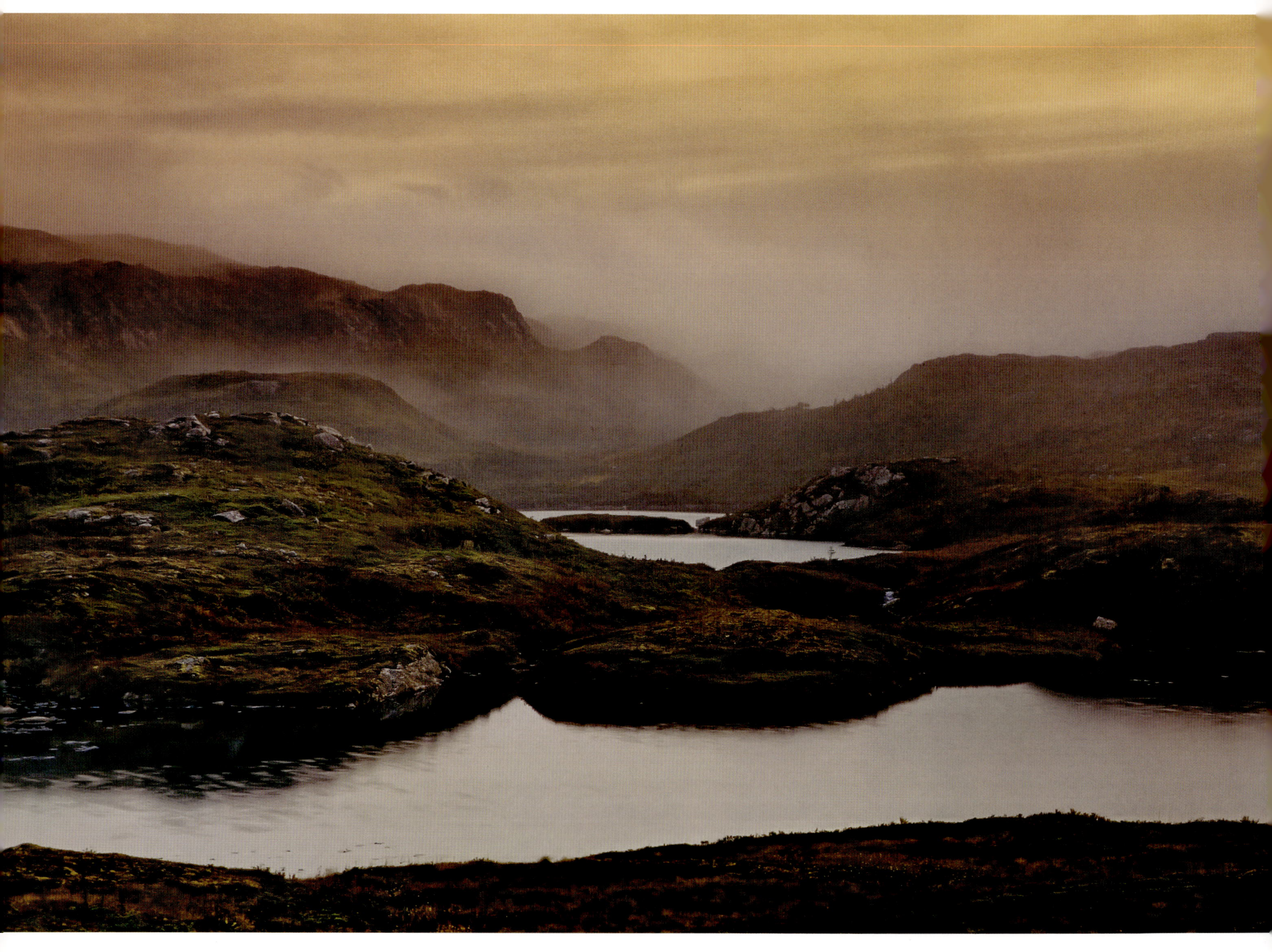

It is an understatement that fog is common along
the coasts of Newfoundland. Mists lift from the
pond-sprinkled landscape near Rose Blanche at
the southwestern corner of Newfoundland after
sunrise (above). The setting sun shines through
fog that has rolled in near Trout River on the
western coast.

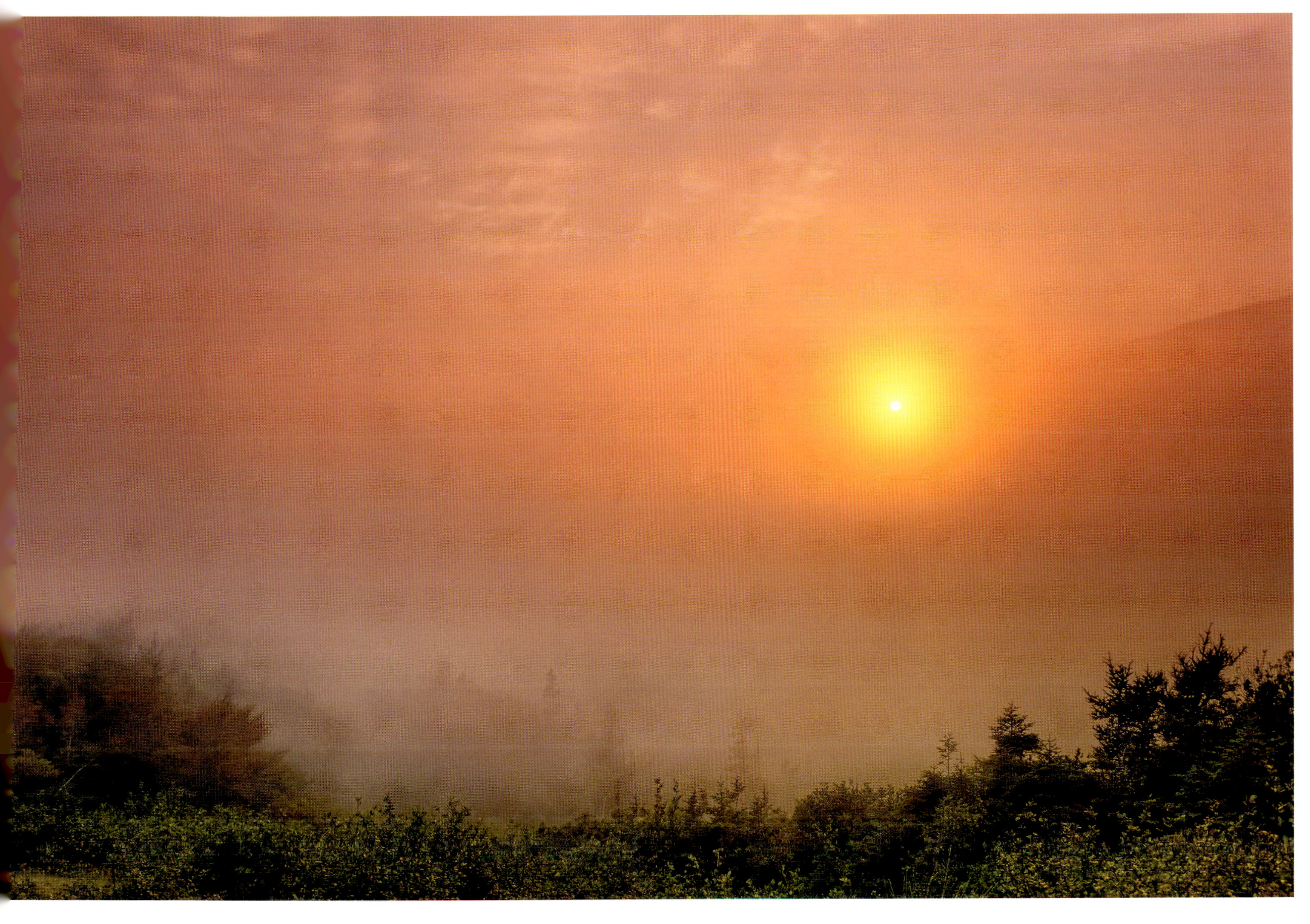

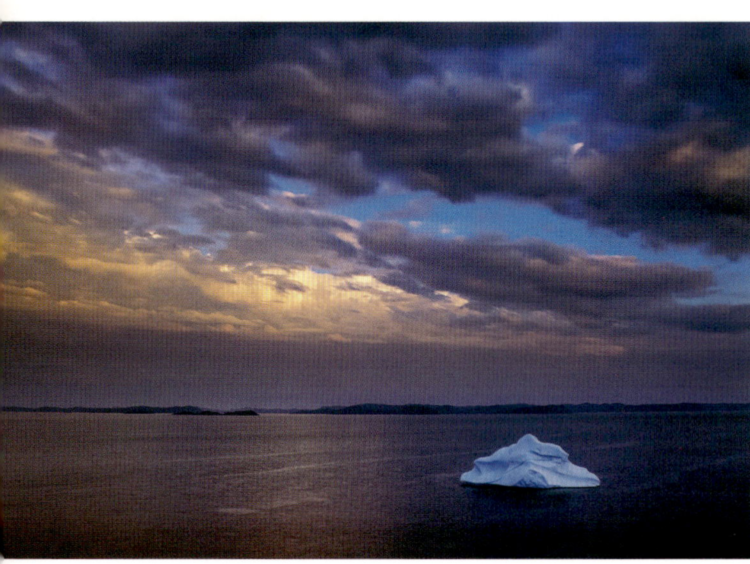

Evening views of the same iceberg off Twillingate, Newfoundland. With nine-tenths of it underwater and its proximity to shore it is likely grounded on the ocean floor.

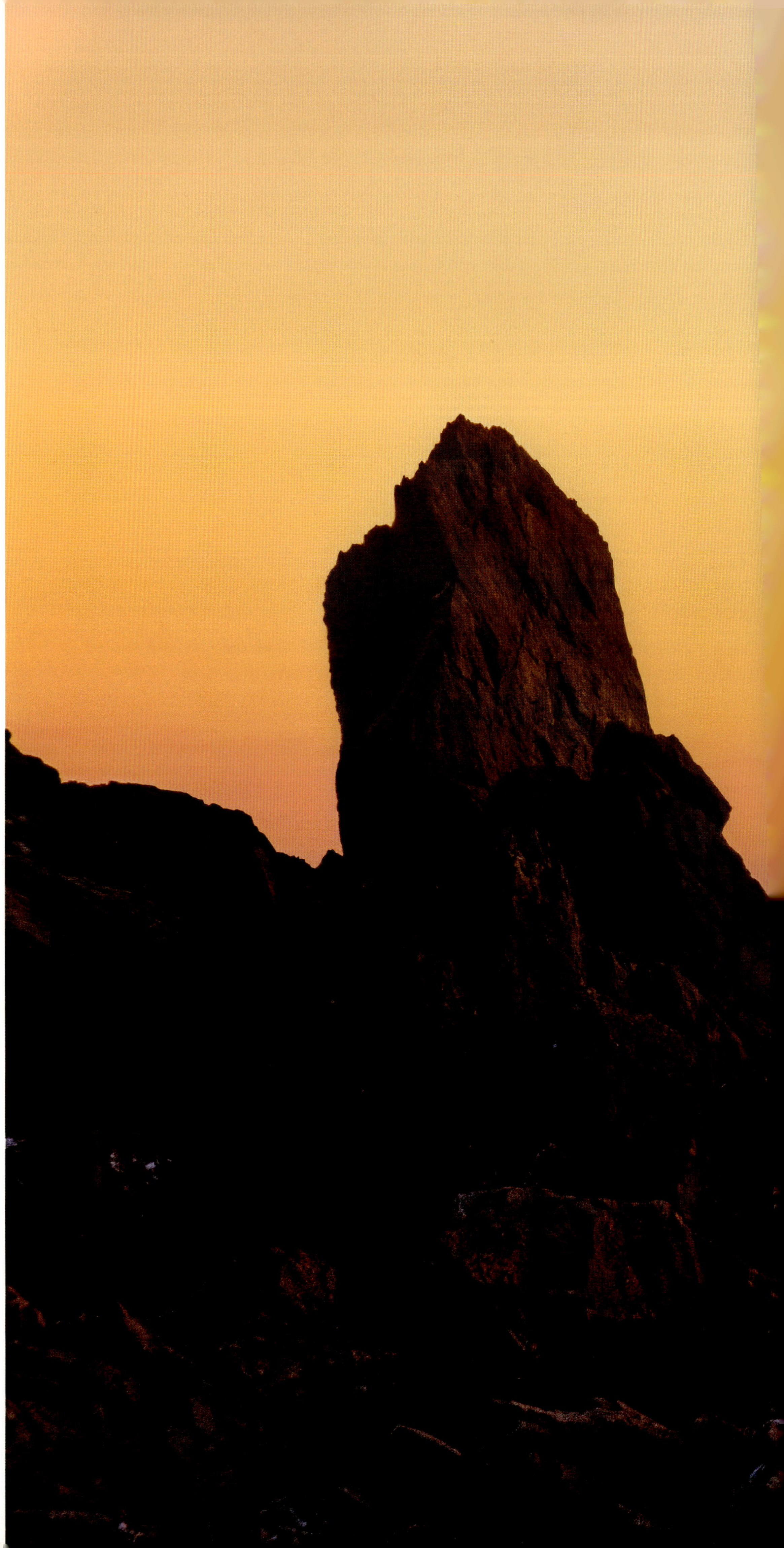

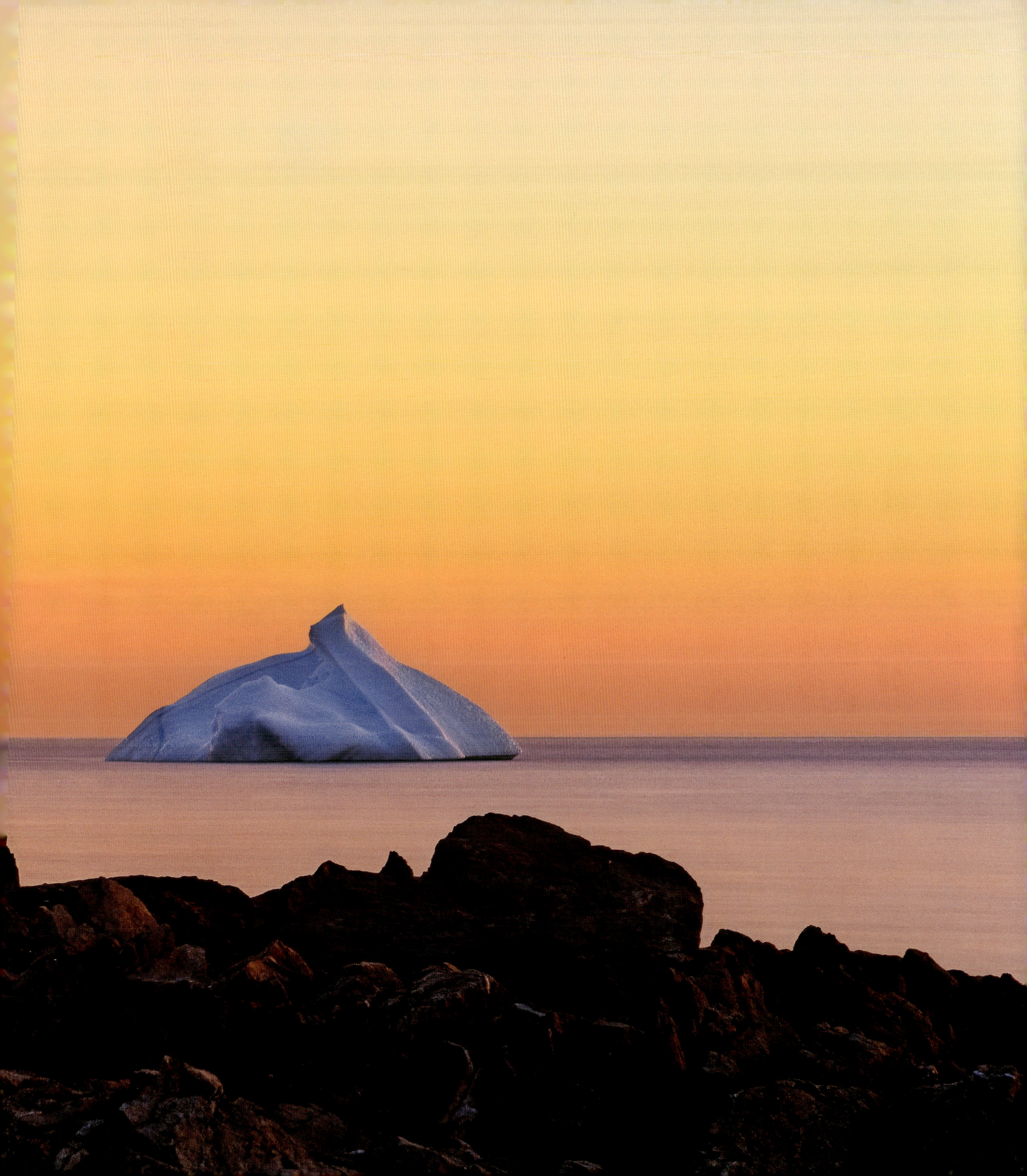

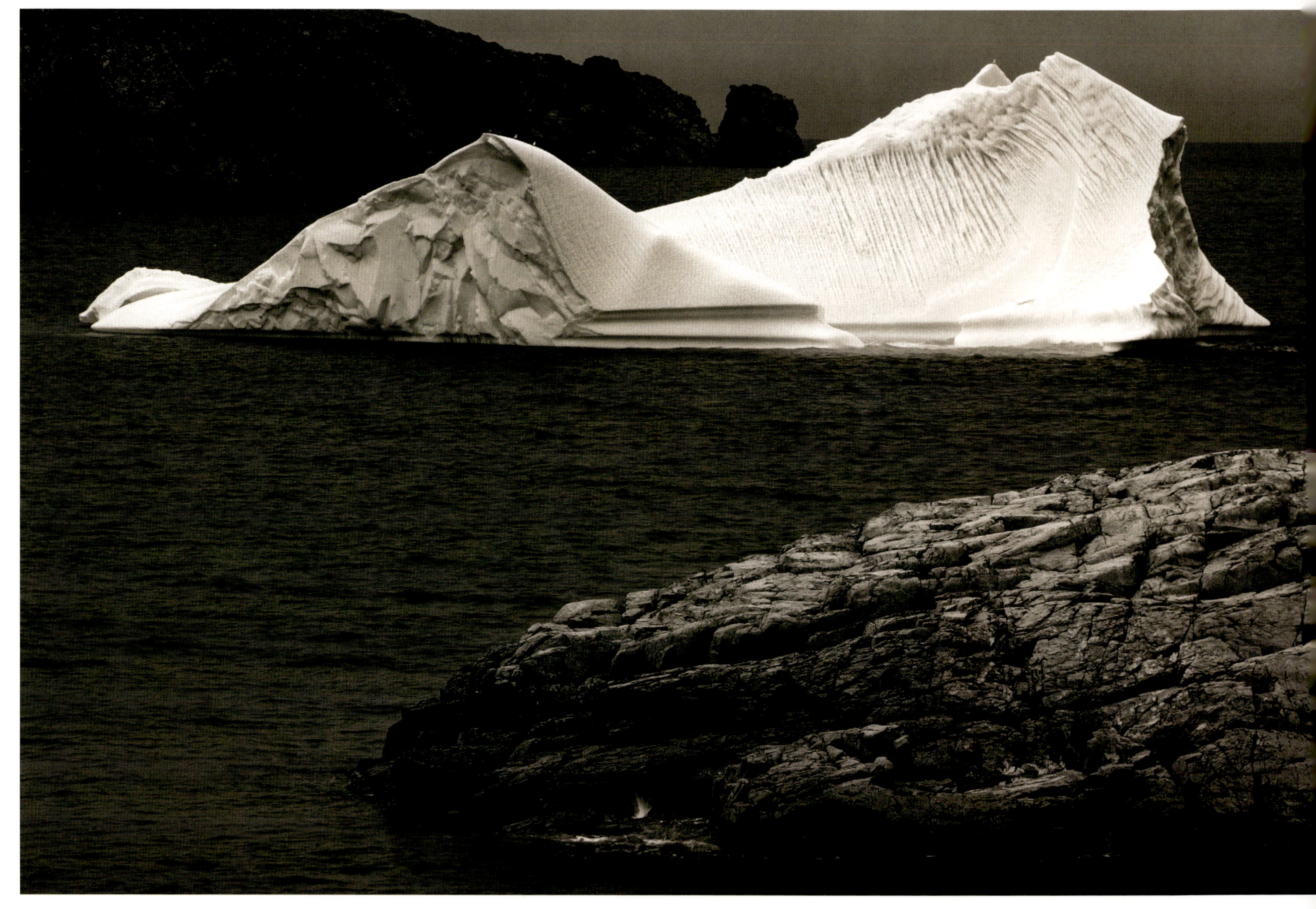

Icebergs in Little Harbour Bight, South Twillingate Island (above) and off Dumpling Point, North Twillingate Island. It takes three years for the giant blocks of ice to float on the Labrador Current from where they calve off glaciers on the west coast of Greenland until they reach the north coast of Newfoundland.

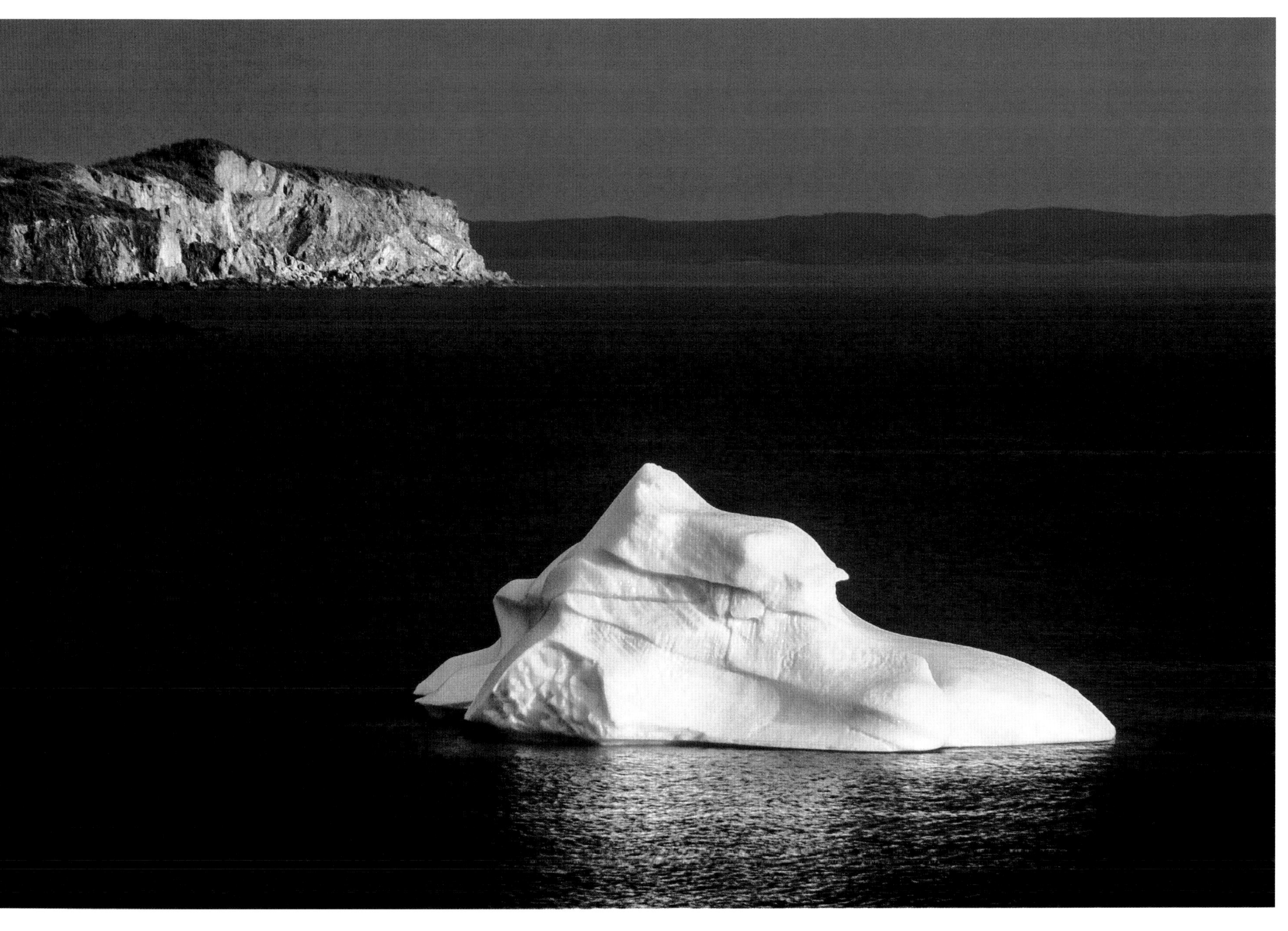

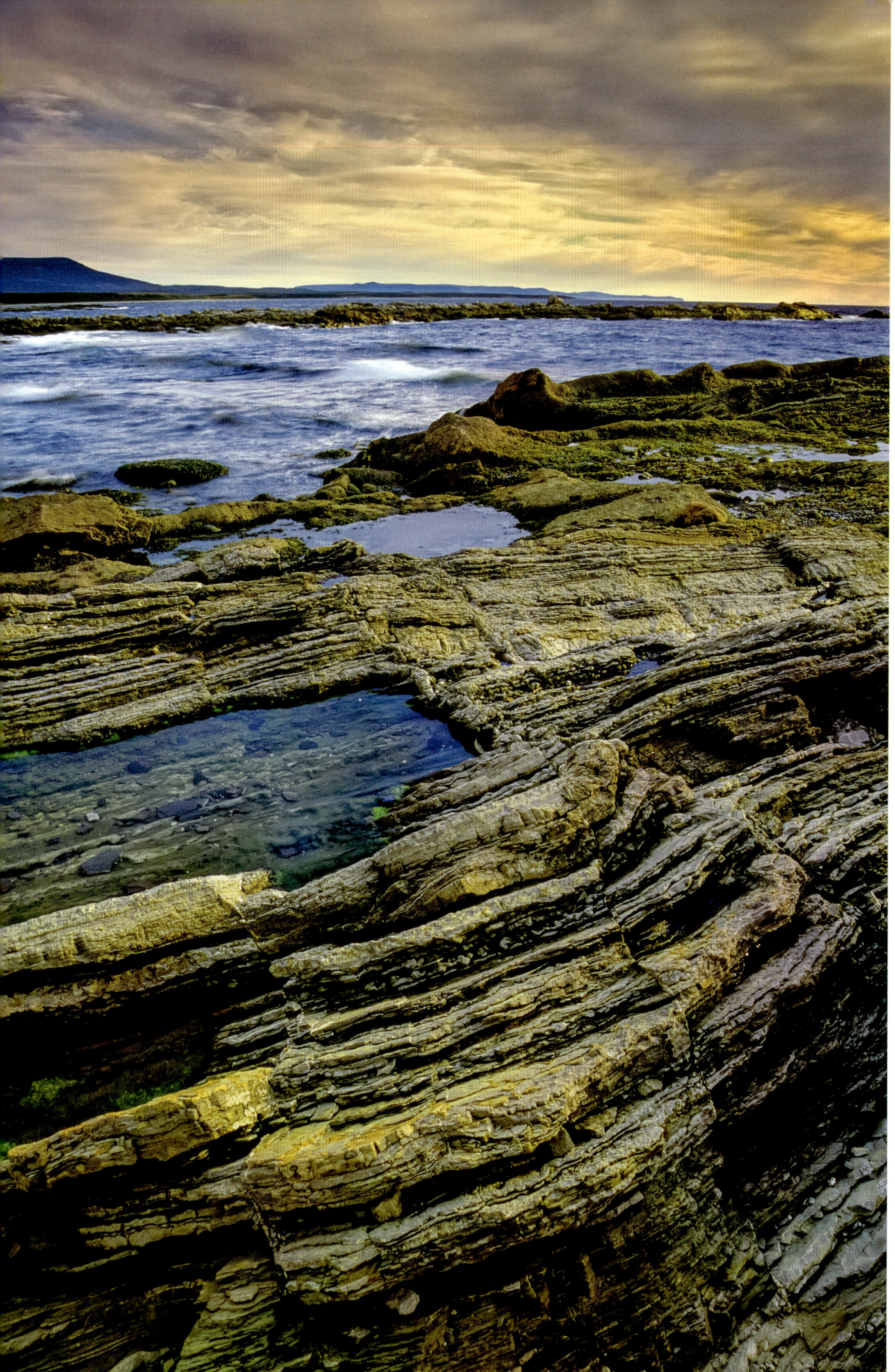

Shoreline rocks at Boom Point, Gros Morne National Park (left) and at Rose Blanche Point, east of Channel-Port aux Basques, Newfoundland.

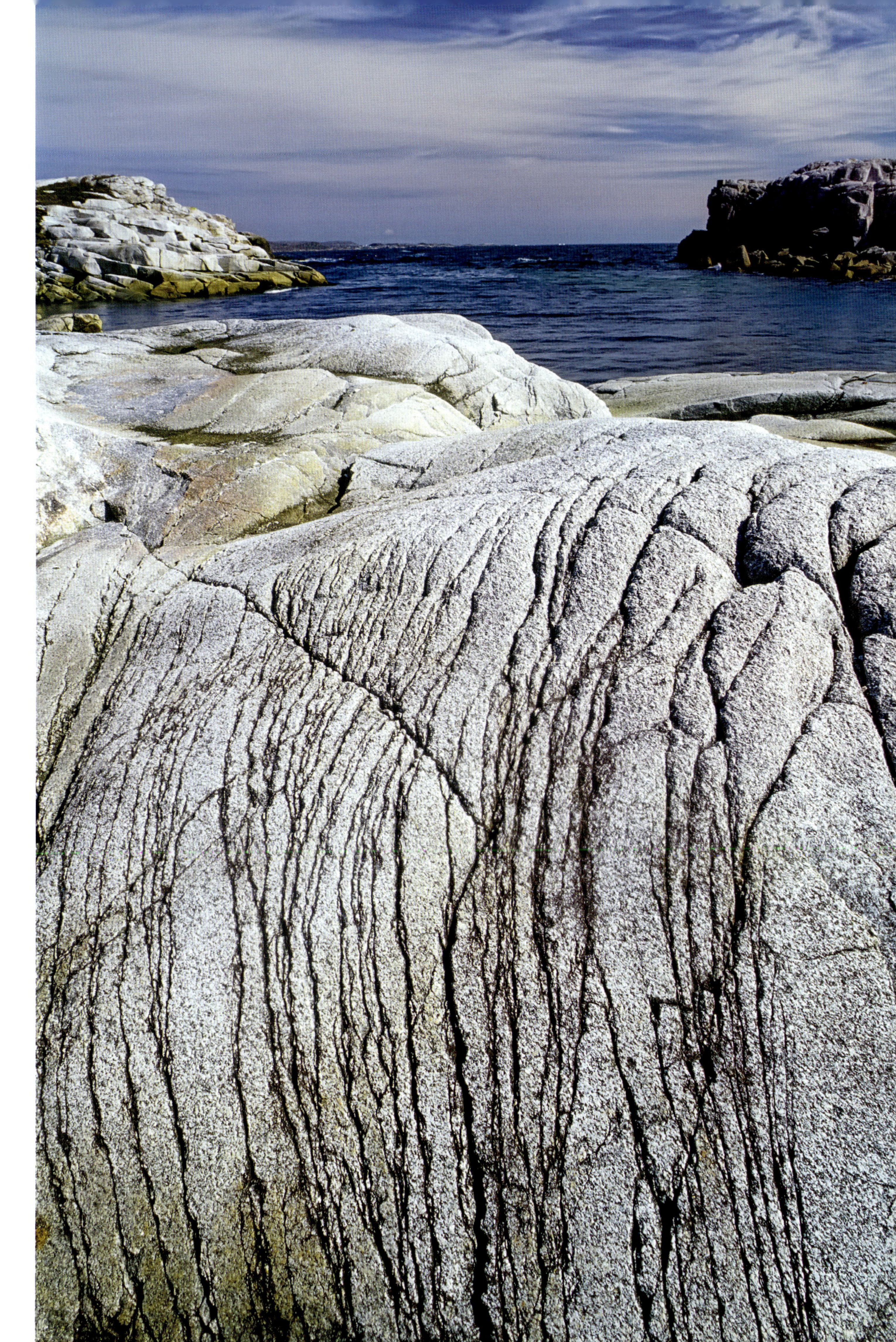

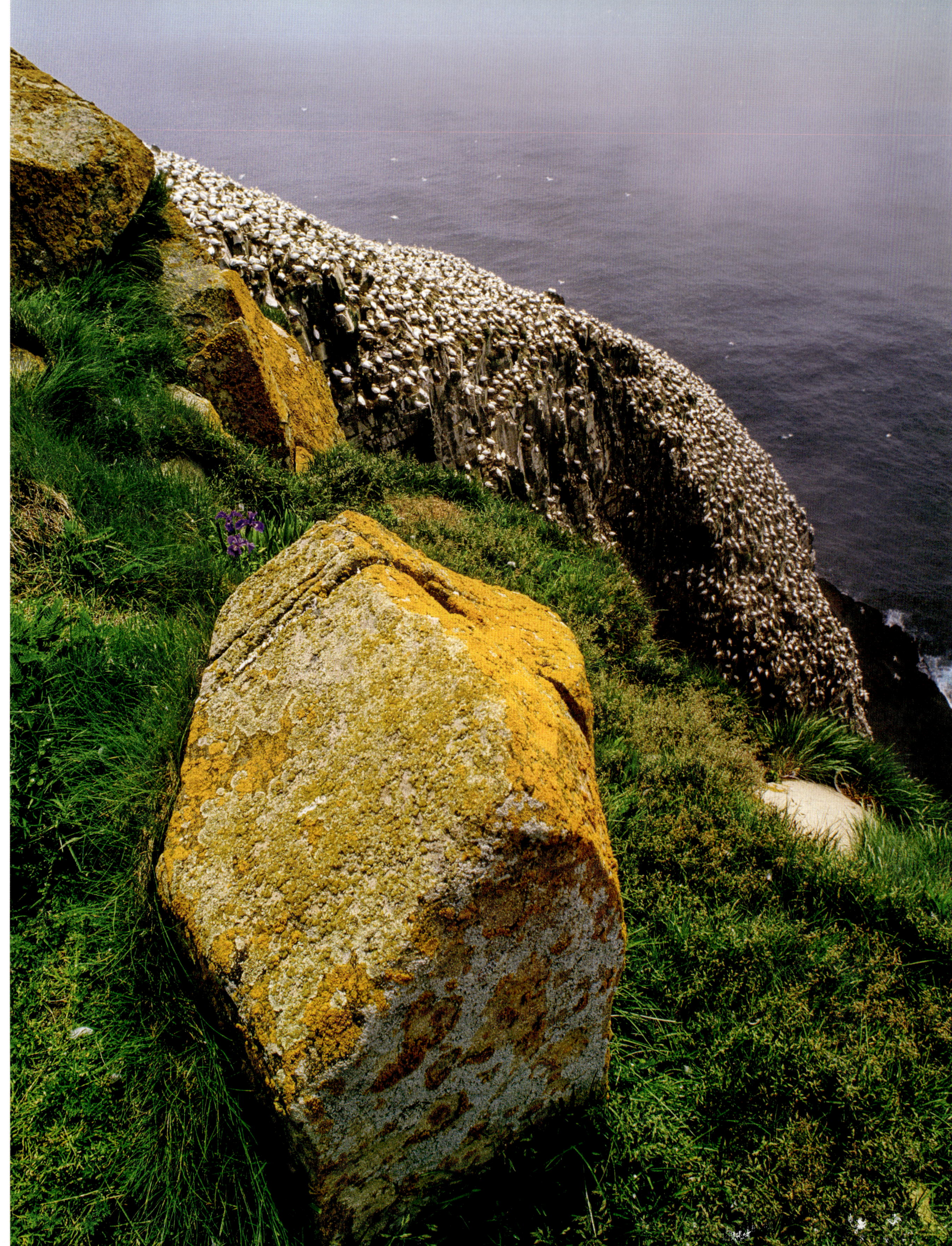

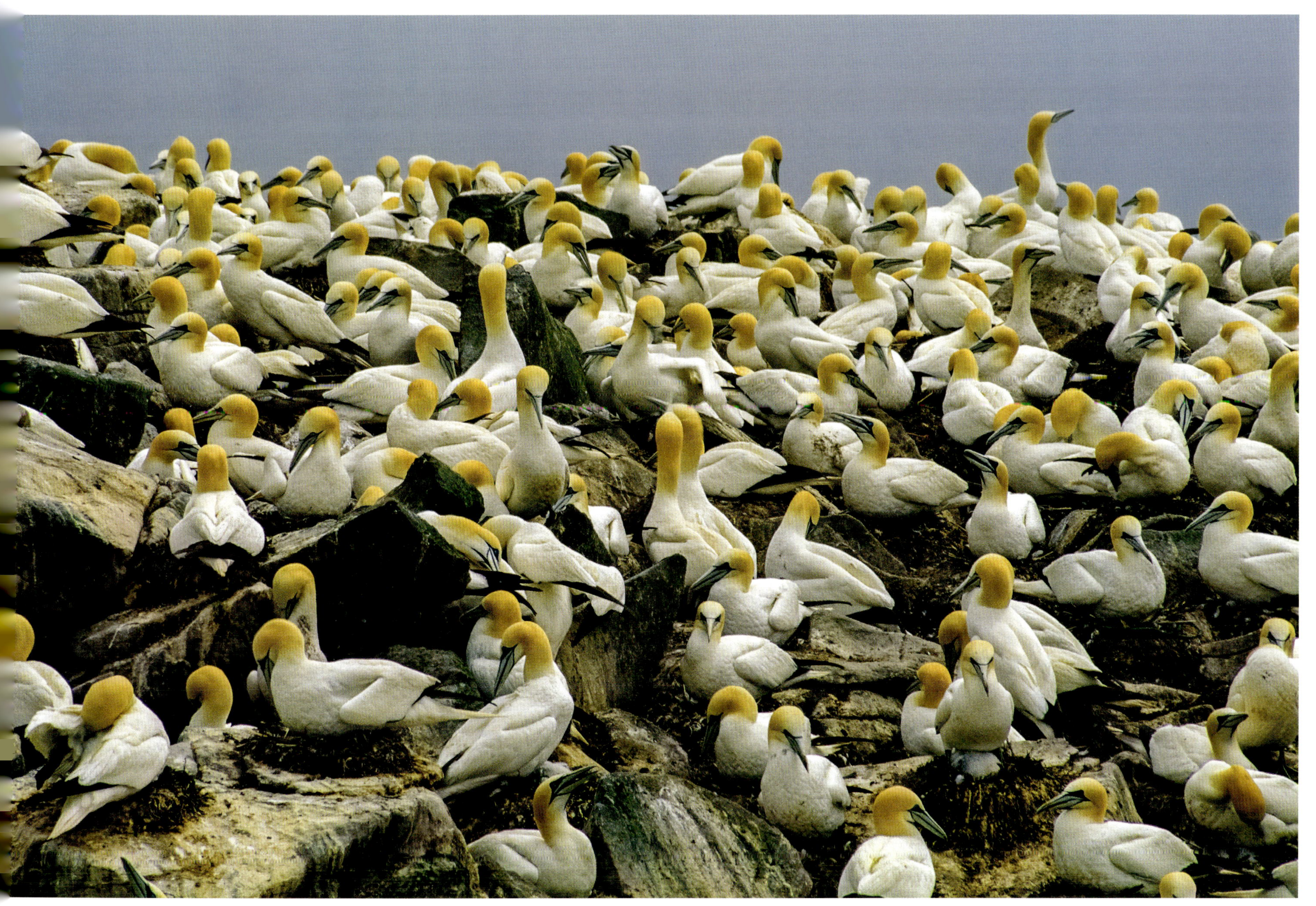

Cape St. Mary's Ecological Reserve at the tip of the
Avalon Peninsula is the nesting site of an estimated
24,000 northern gannets as well as some 40,000
seabirds of other kinds. Humpback whales can
occasionally be seen in the waters directly below
Bird Rock, a 120-metre pinnacle where the gannets
safely roost, mere metres from the mainland but
inaccessible across a sheer gap (left).

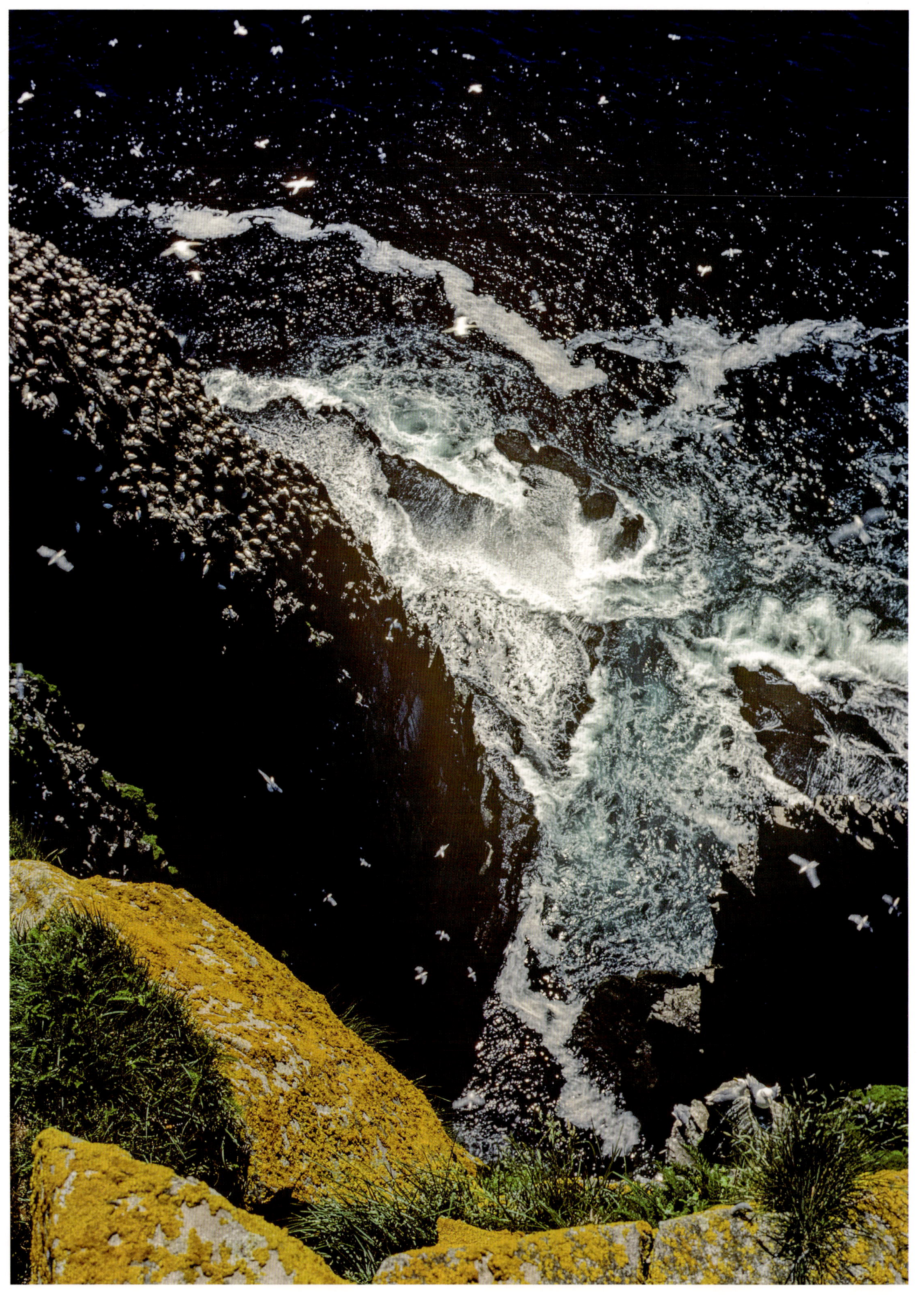

Surf breaks over a rock shelf at the base of Bird Rock, Cape St. Mary's, Newfoundland (left). A very rare aerial view of 75-metre-high Churchill Falls, Labrador in full flood. Since 1970 the waters of the Churchill River have been diverted for hydroelectric power and water flows over the falls less than once a decade, during spring thaw or periods of exceptional rains.

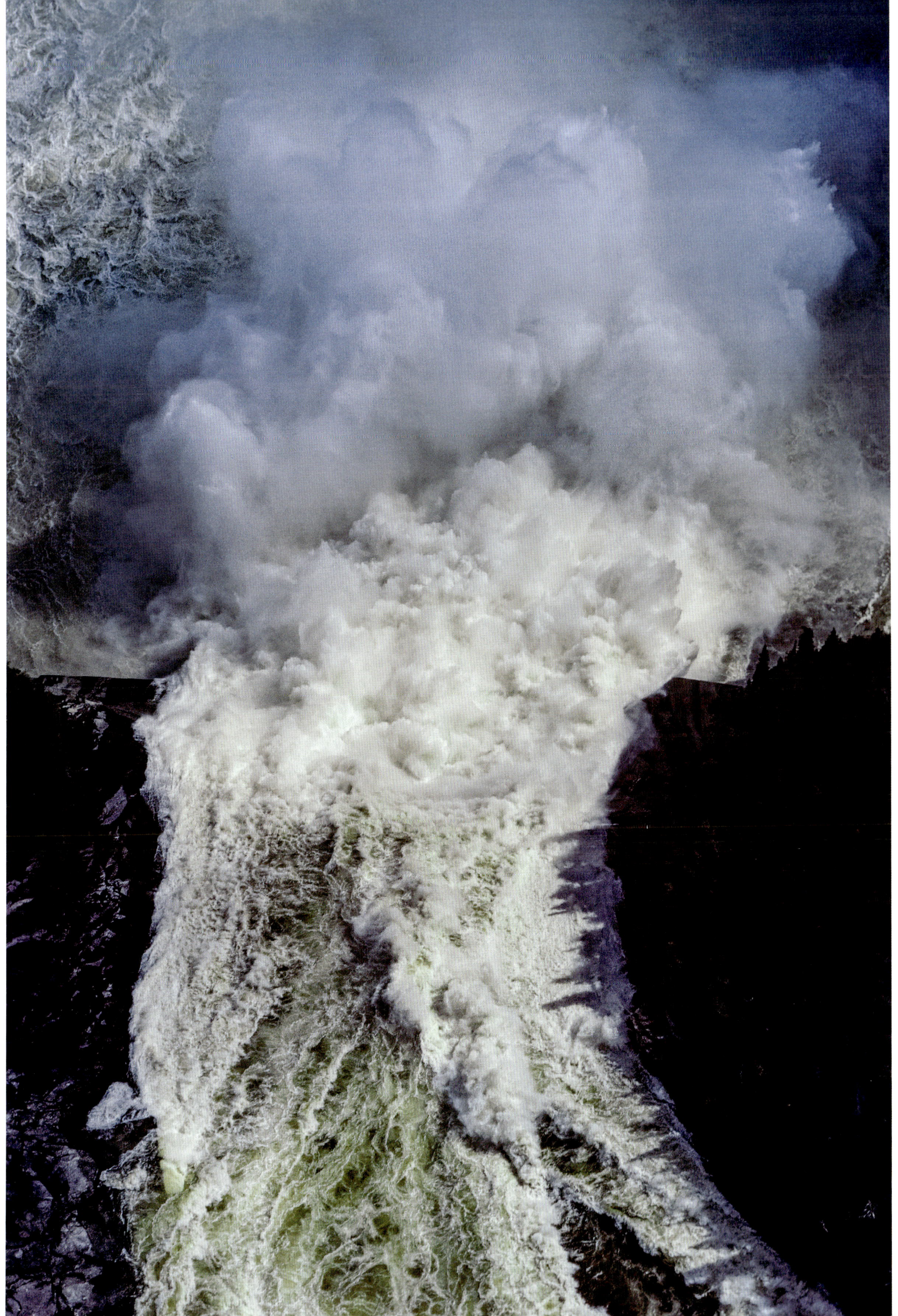

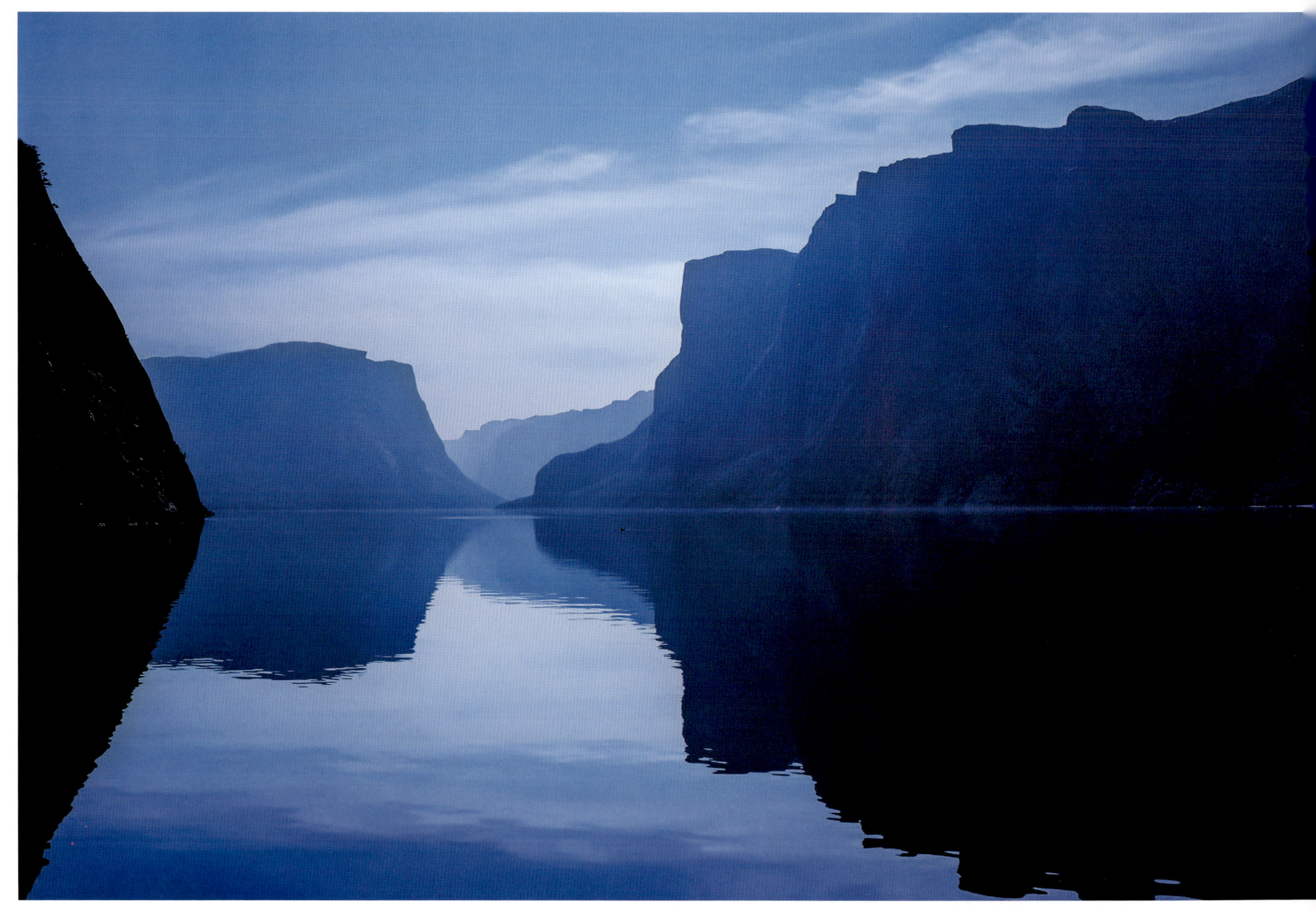

Grand cliffs, some sheer and more than 600
metres high, flank the glacier-carved fjord of
Western Brook Pond near its west end (above)
and at its east end in Gros Morne National Park,
Newfoundland.

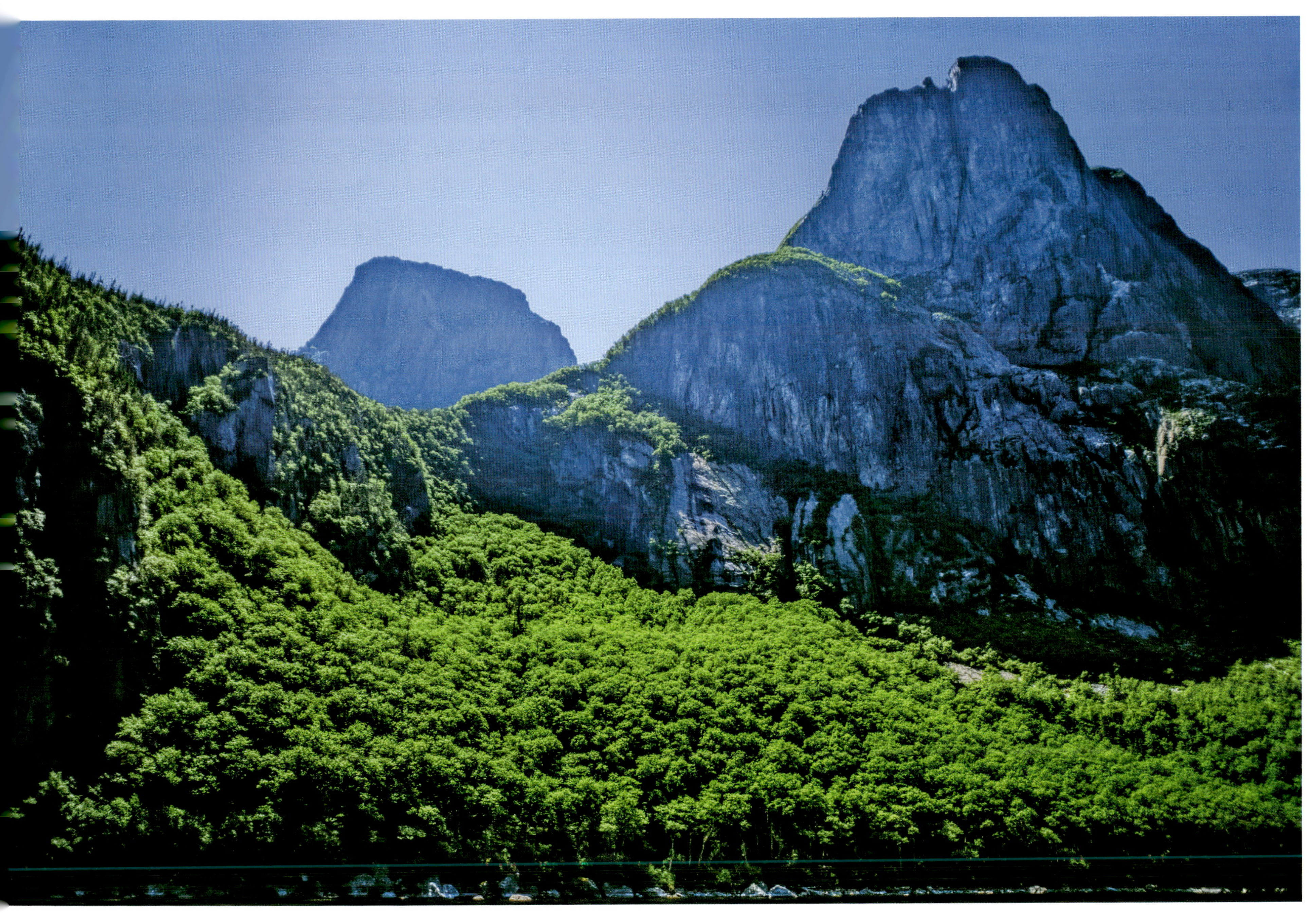

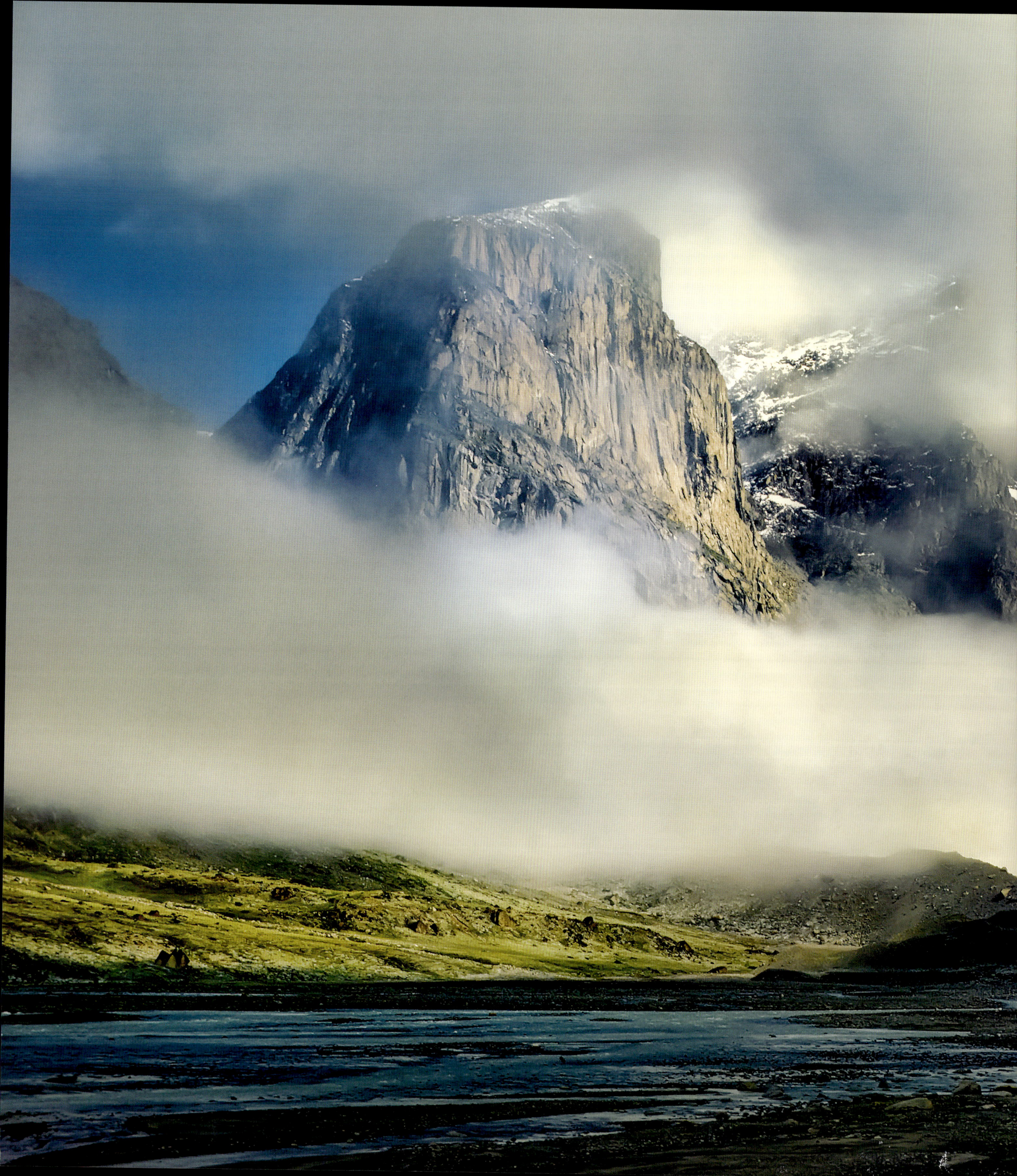

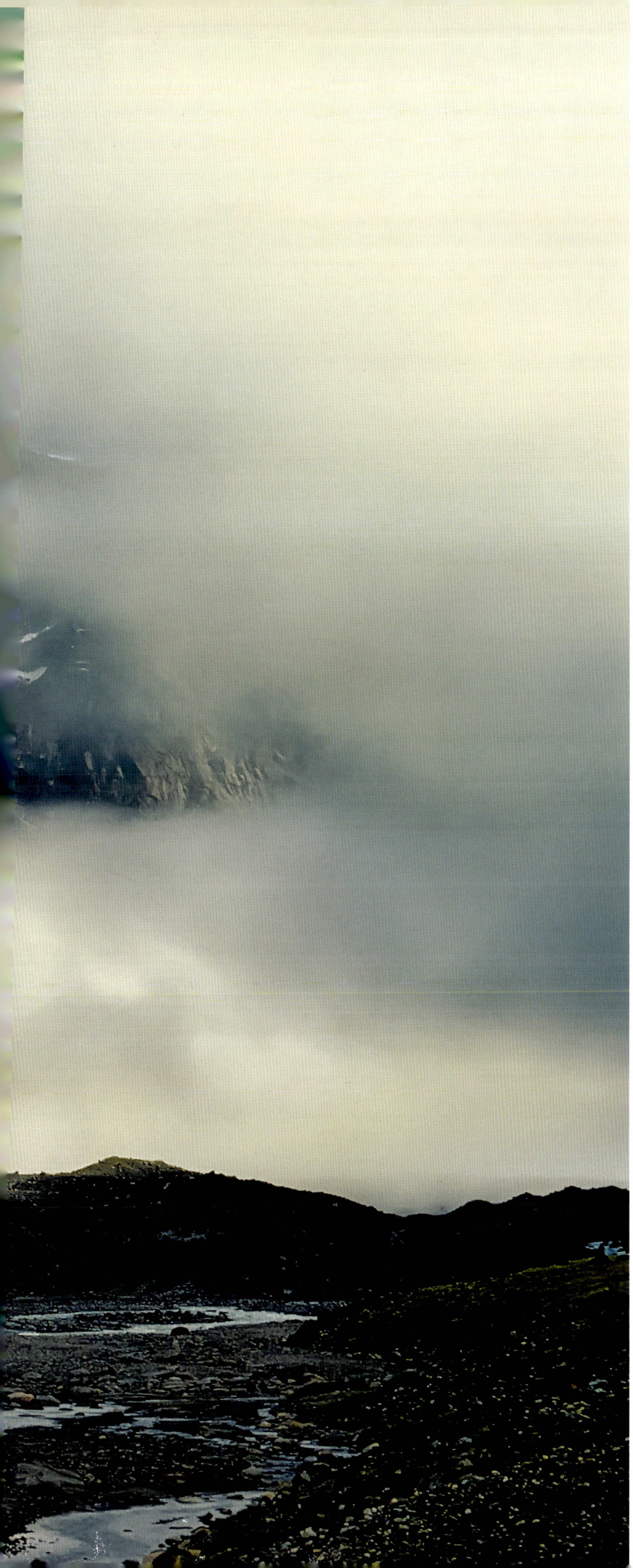

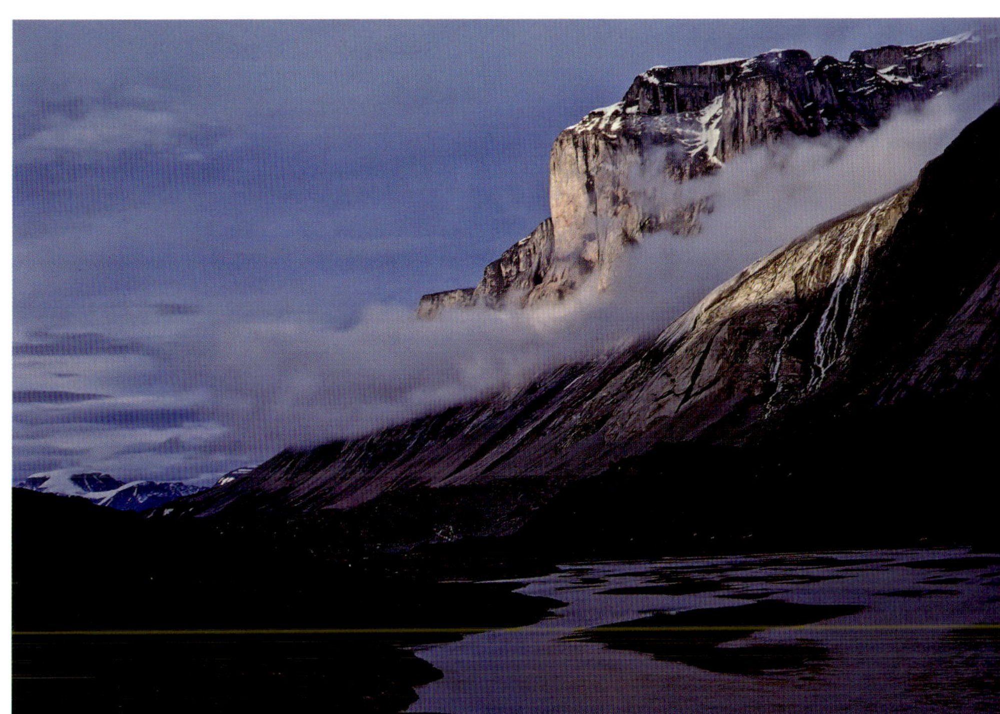

Mount Odin, the highest peak on Baffin Island,
emerges out of the clouds and mist (left) and
Mount Breidablik-Baldr catches late-evening light,
both above flats along the braided Weasel River in
Auyuittuq National Park, Baffin Island, Nunavut.

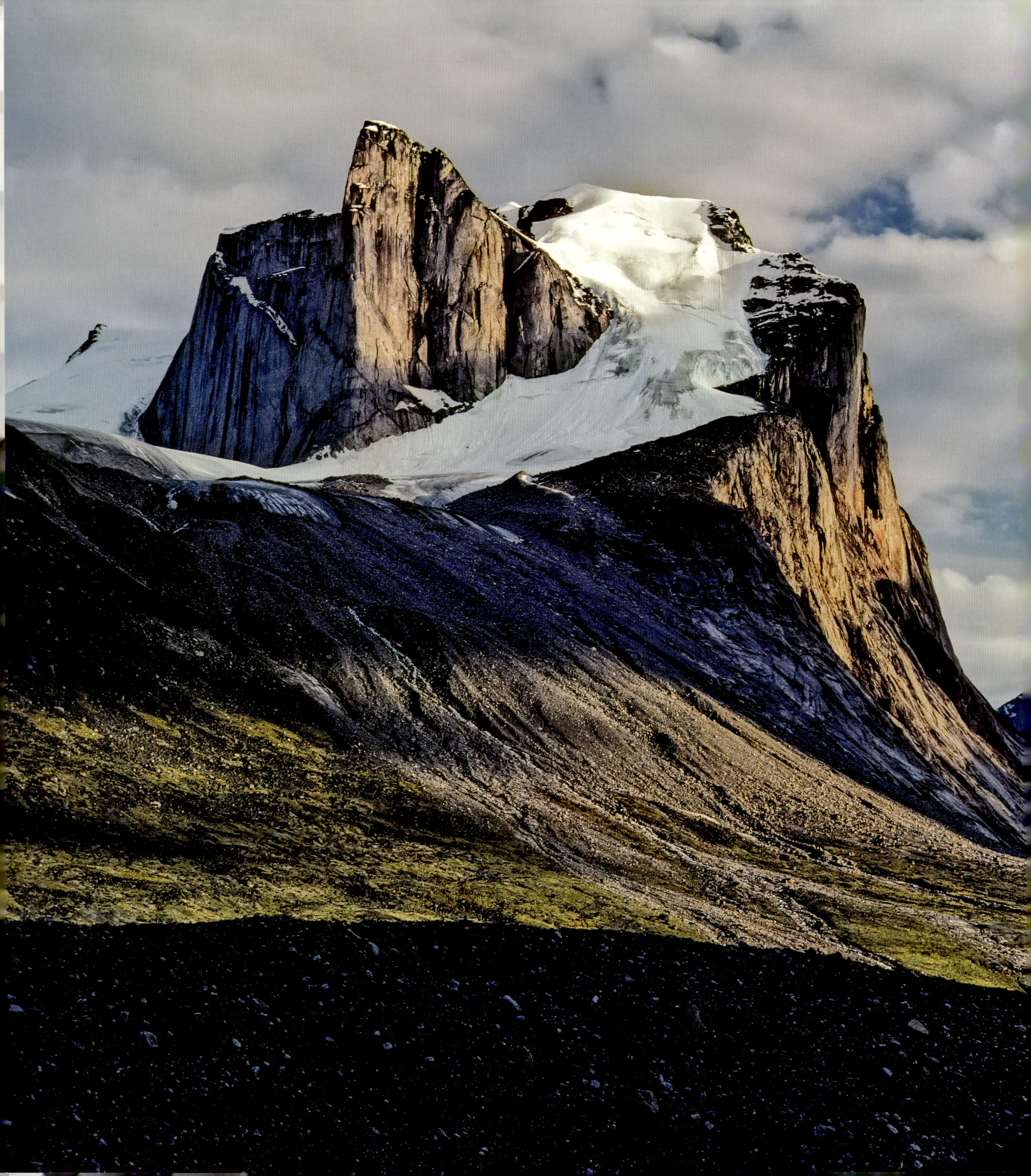

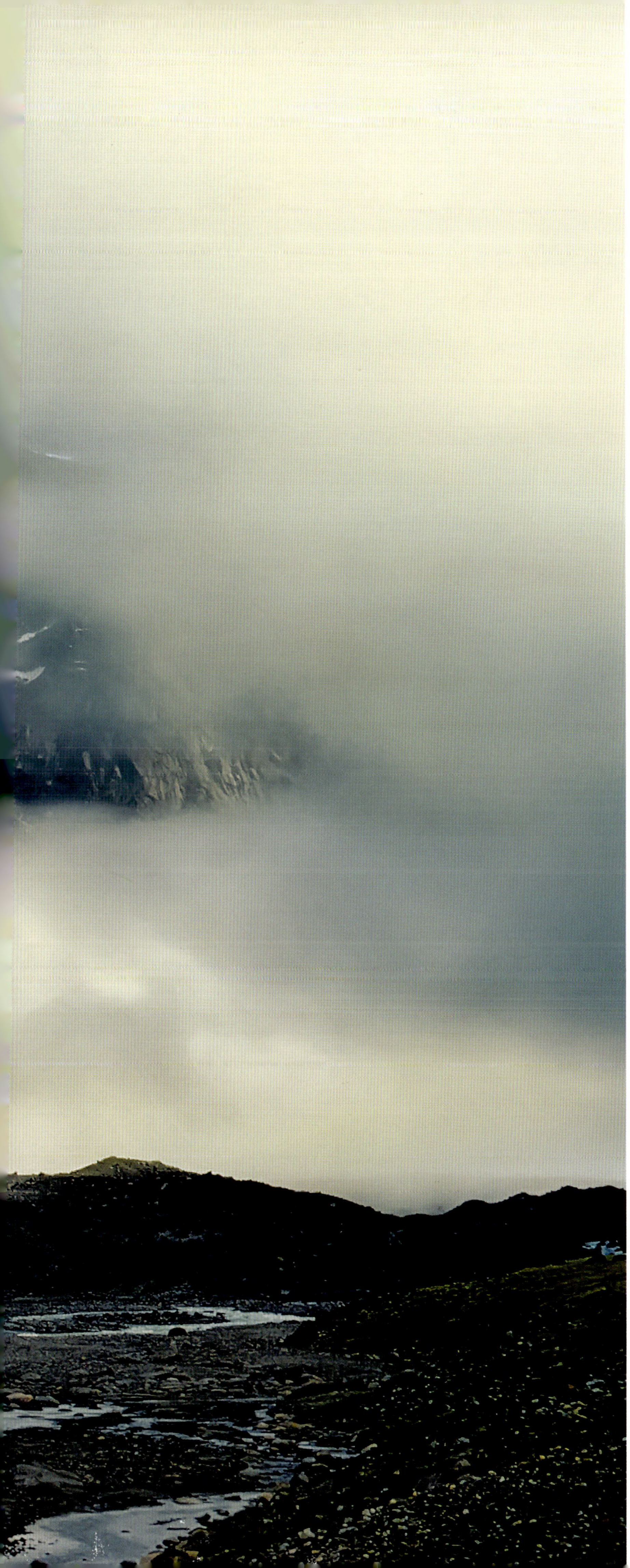

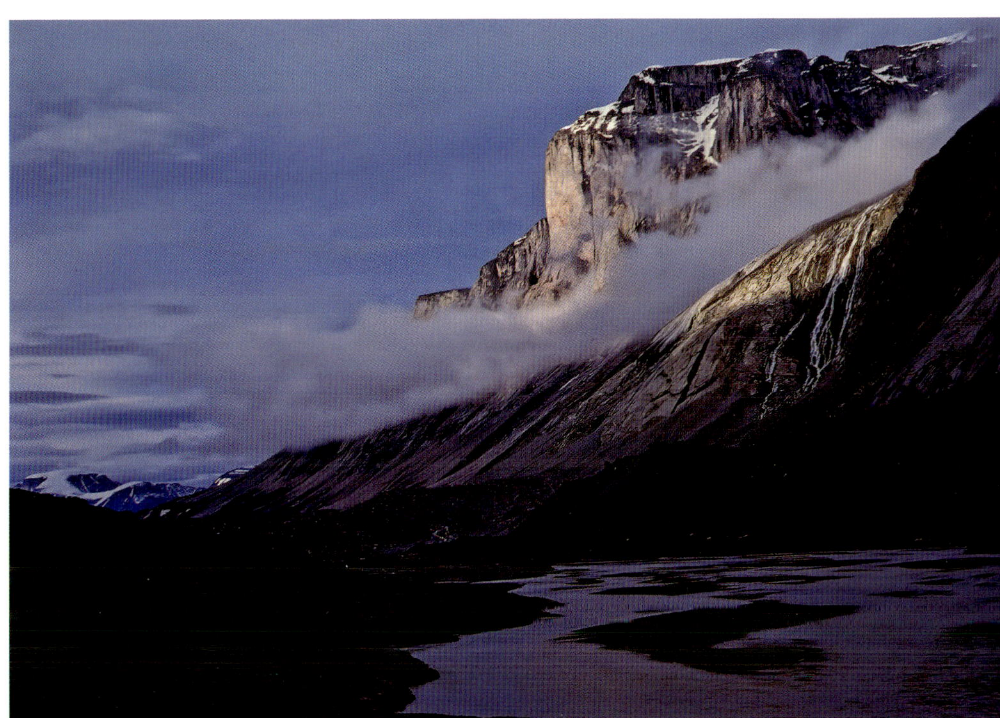

Mount Odin, the highest peak on Baffin Island,
emerges out of the clouds and mist (left) and
Mount Breidablik-Baldr catches late-evening light,
both above flats along the braided Weasel River in
Auyuittuq National Park, Baffin Island, Nunavut.

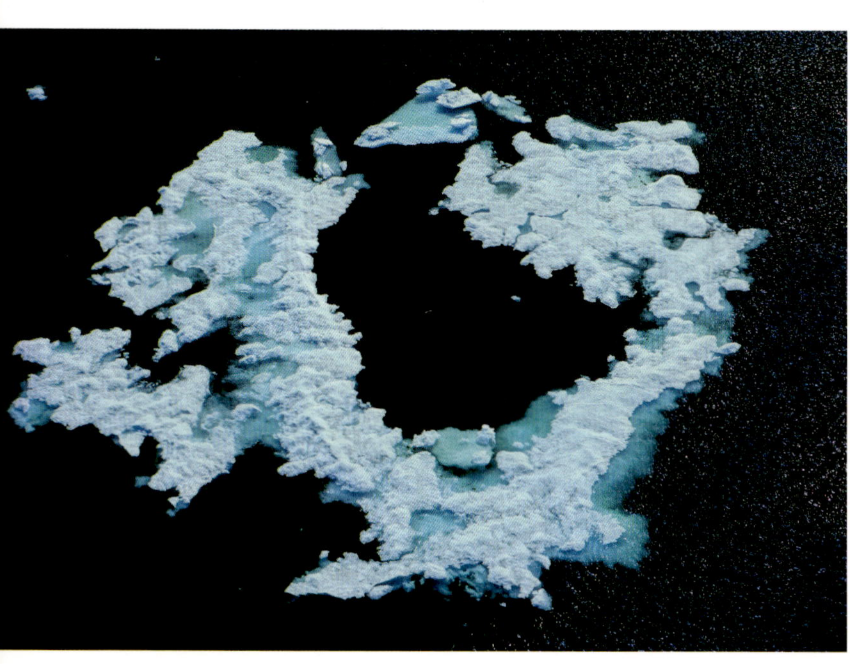

An aerial view (above), and one from shore through
a melting floe, of ice floes in August adrift in
Pangnirtung Fjord near Pangnirtung on the
Cumberland Peninsula, Baffin Island, Nunavut.

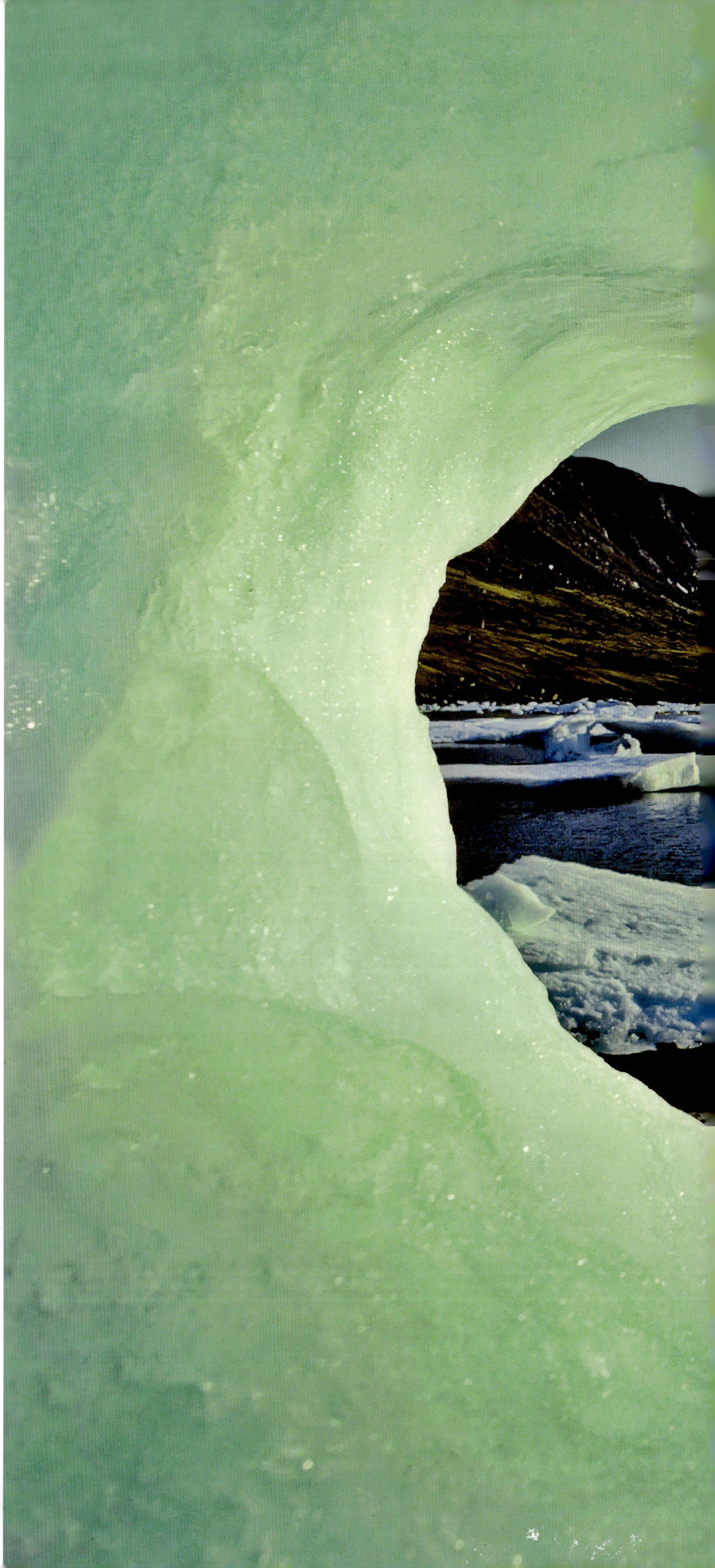

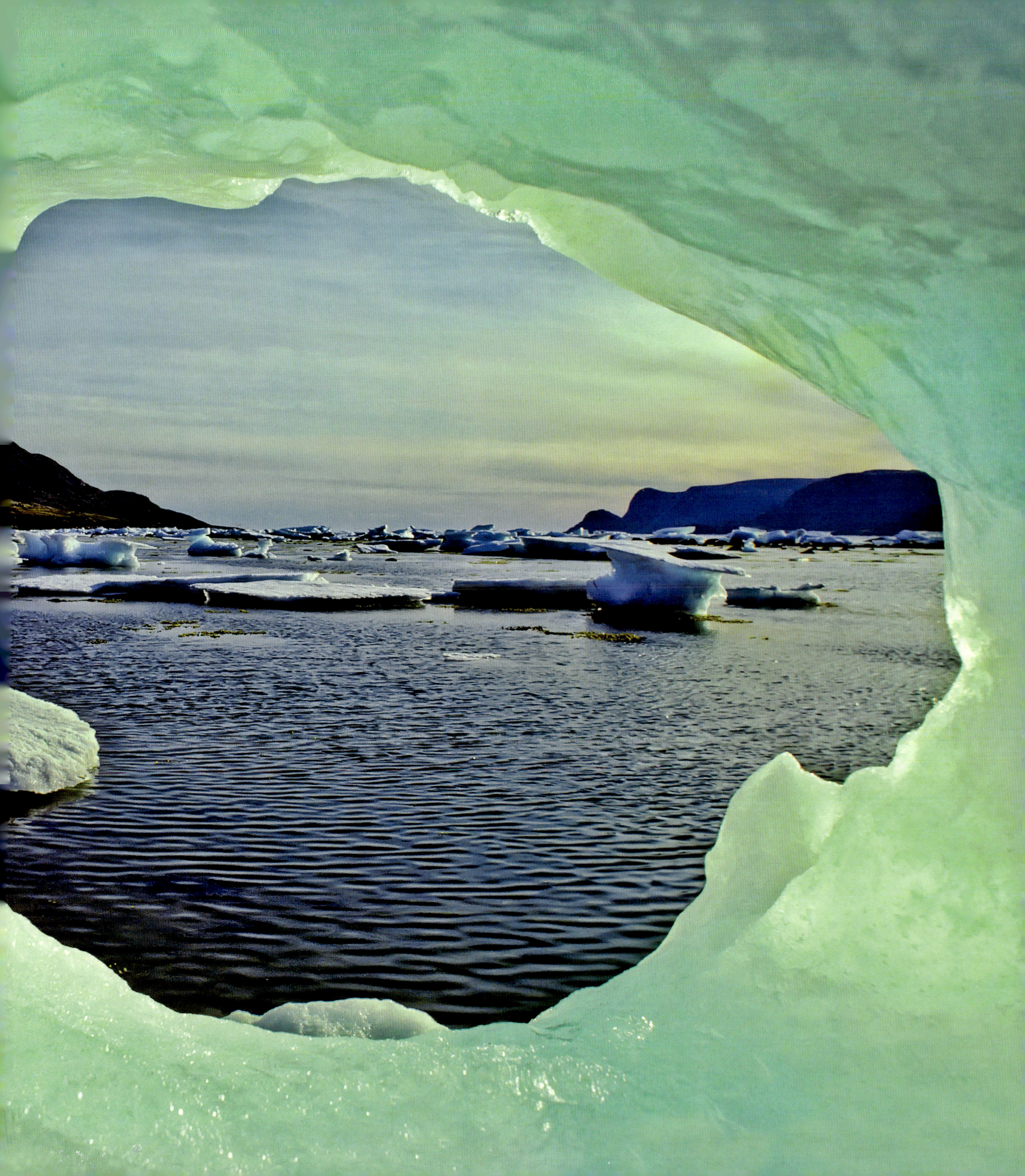

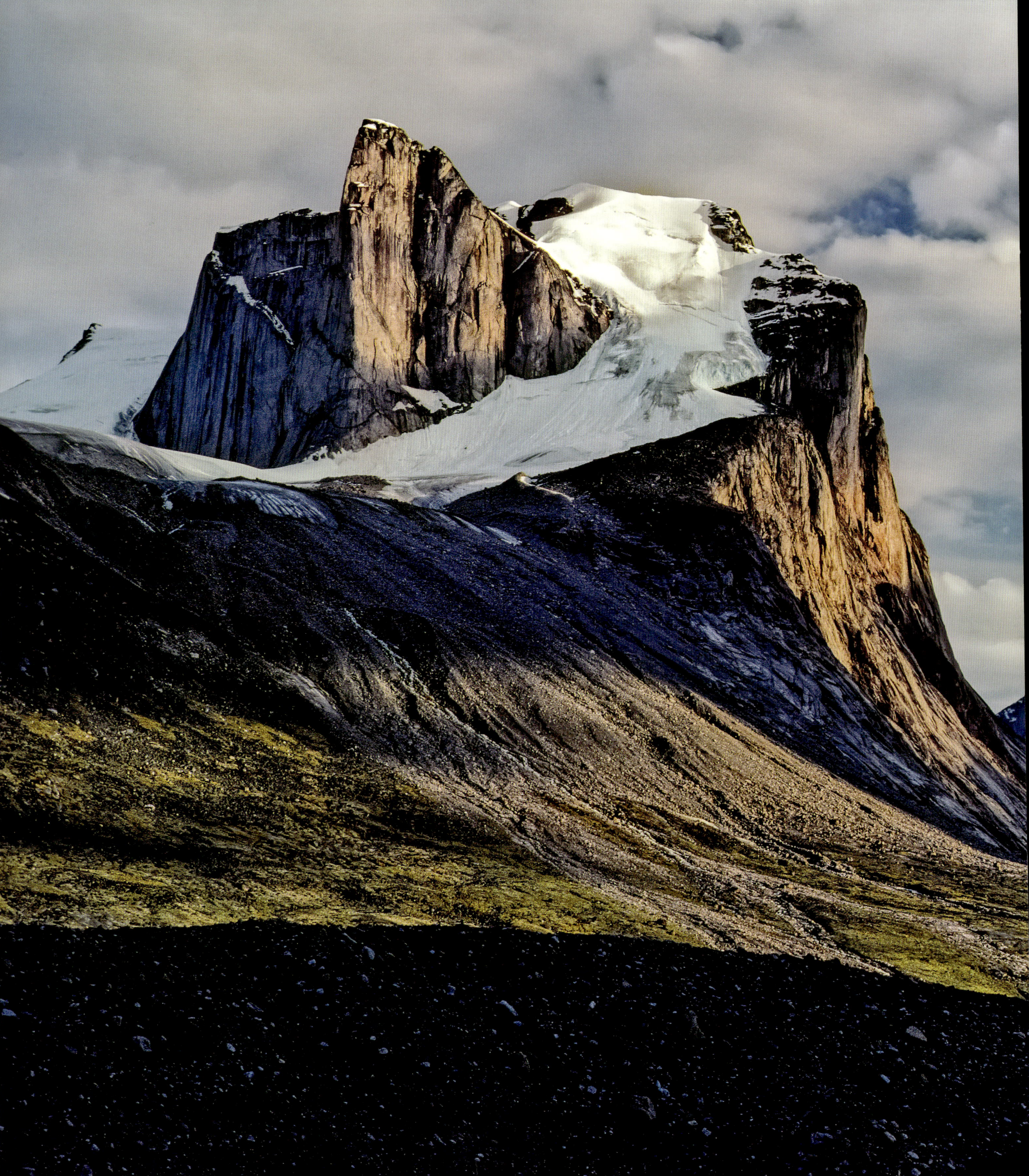

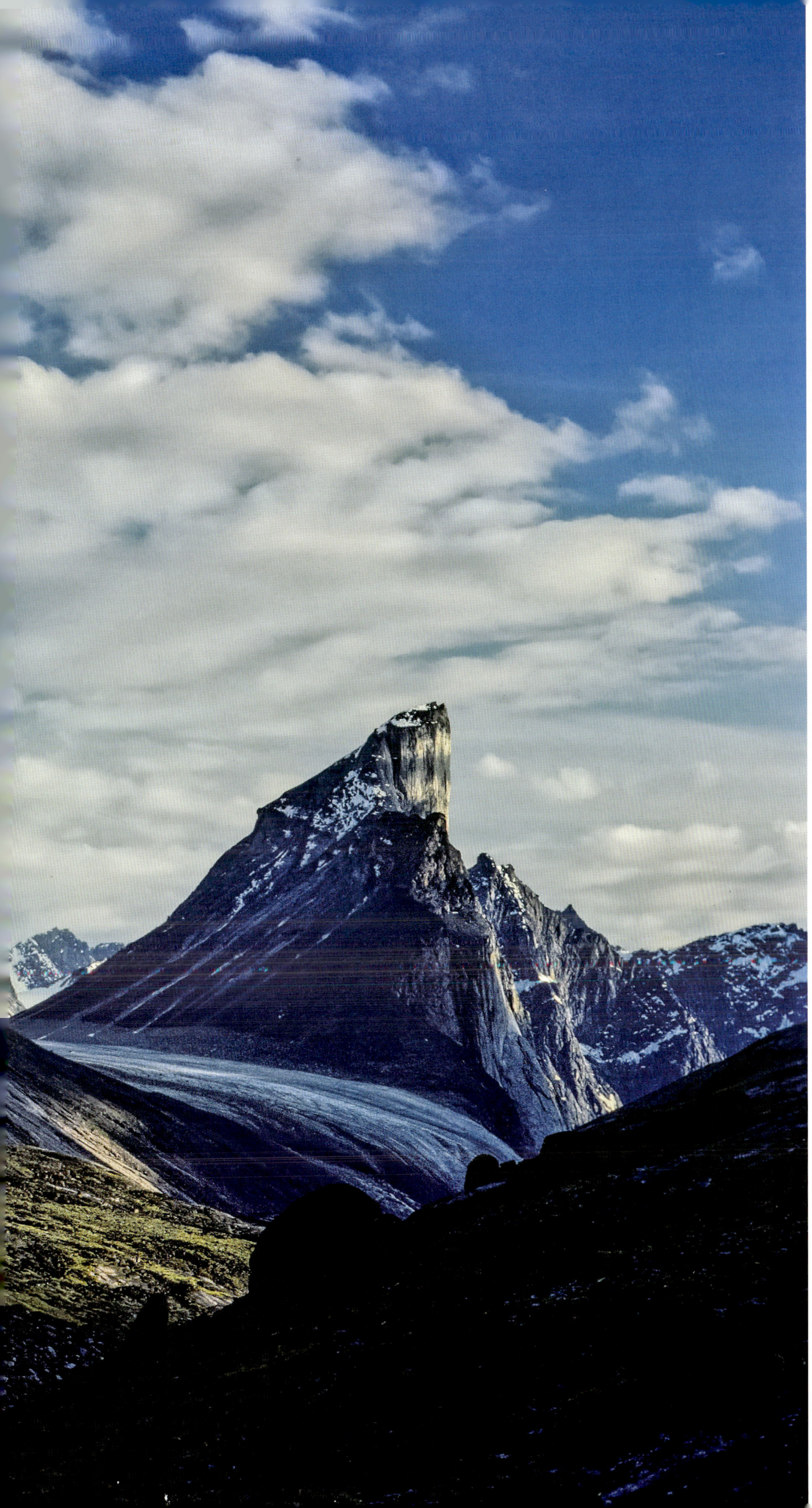

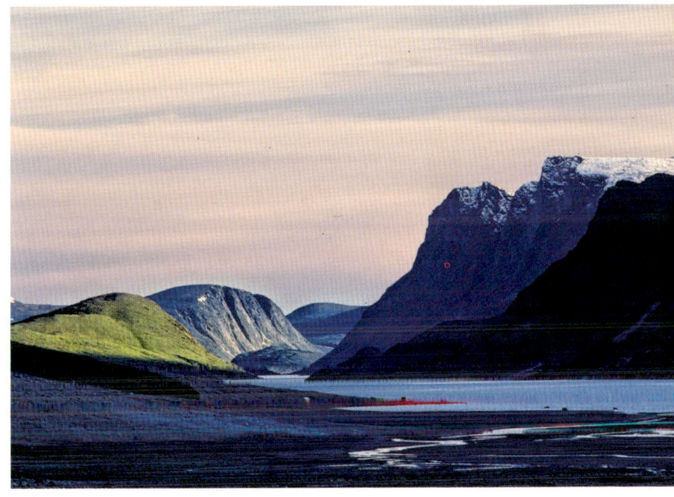

A number of peaks in the southern Baffin
Mountains take their names from Norse mythology,
including Mount Breidablik-Baldr and Mount
Thor, seen from the south end of Summit Lake at
Akshayuk Pass (left). The head of Pangnirtung Fjord
on an August evening, Baffin Island, Nunavut.

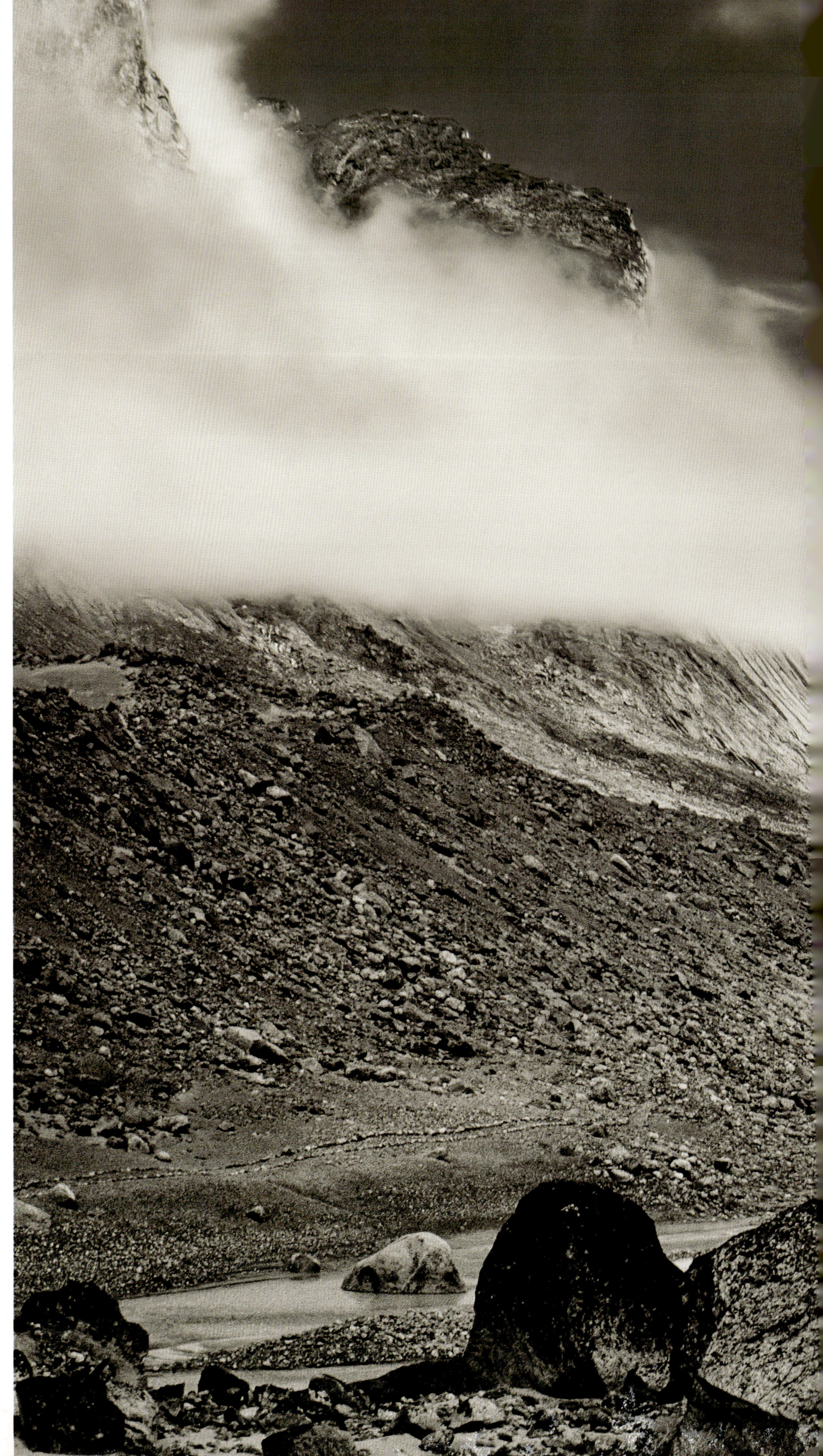

Although relatively low in elevation, many of the mountains on Baffin Island are among the most precipitous and impressive on the continent. The tremendous northwest face of Mount Thor, its upper portion actually overhanging for several hundred metres, has the greatest purely vertical drop (1,250 metres) of any cliff on Earth, yet its summit is below the altitude of Lake Louise in Alberta.

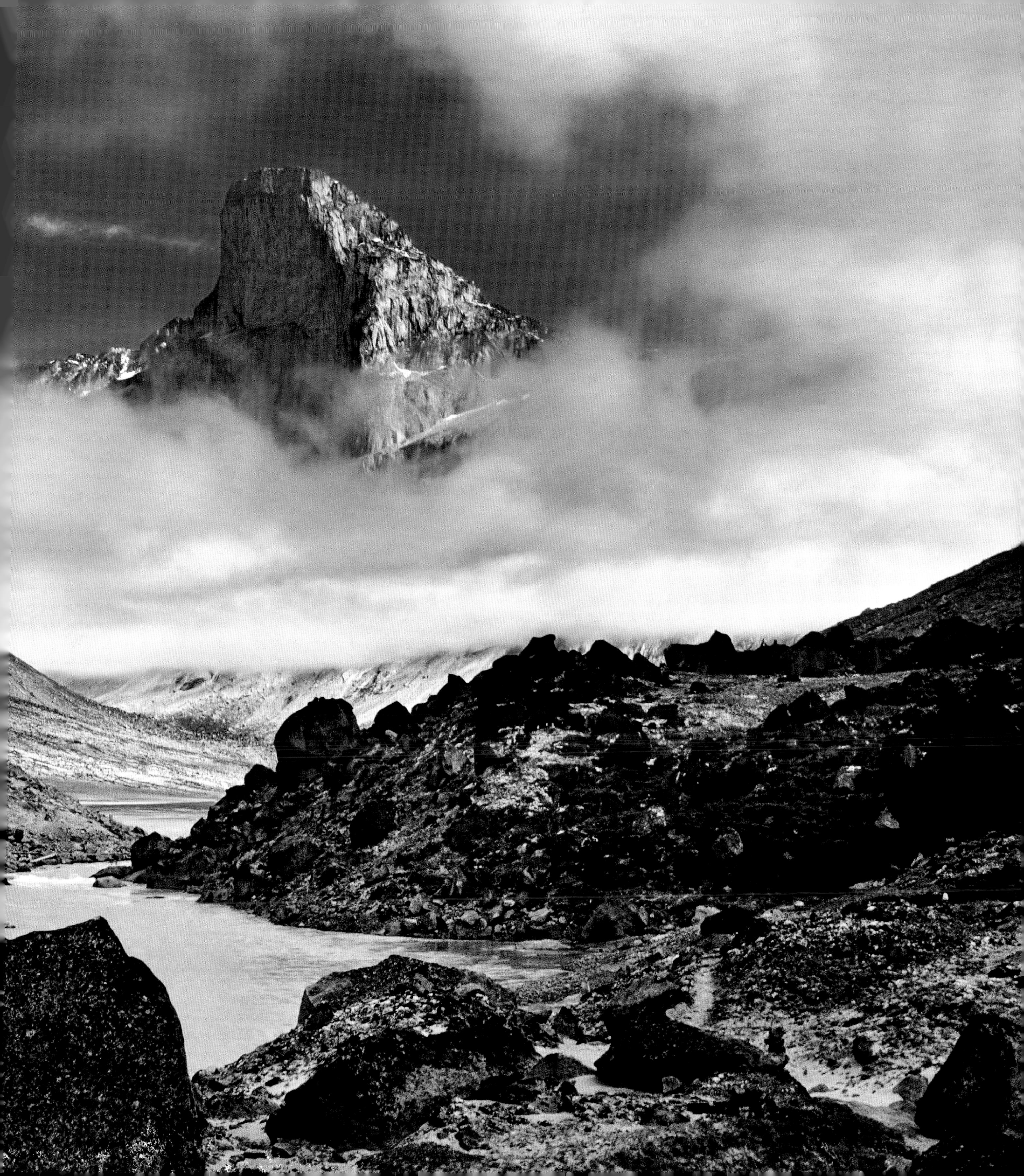

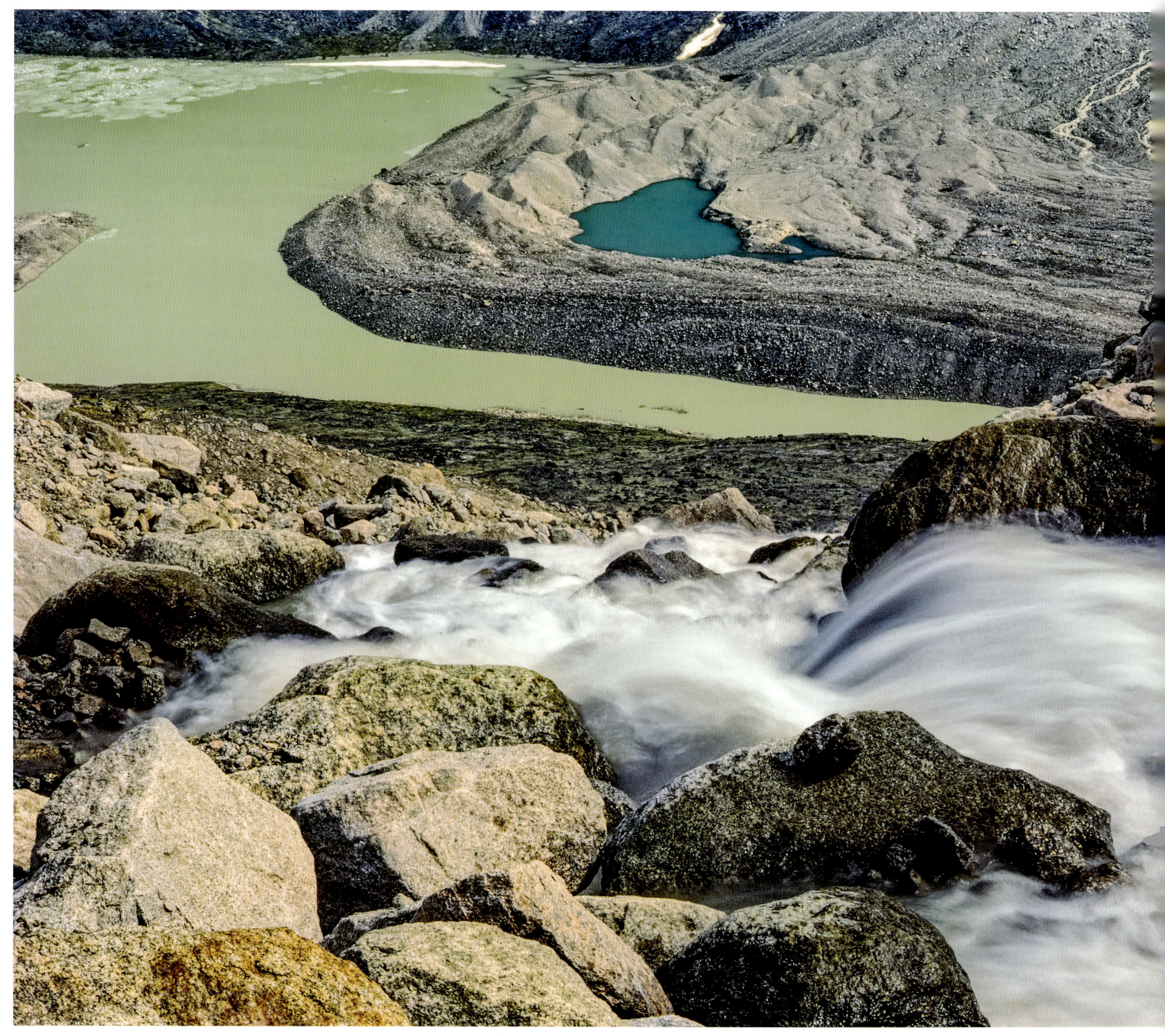

A creek tumbles down a talus slope on Tyr Peak towards Summit Lake (above) and a meltwater channel snakes down the Caribou Glacier towards the distant Nerutusoq Glacier on the opposed side of Akshayuk Pass, both In Auyuittuq National Park, Nunavut.

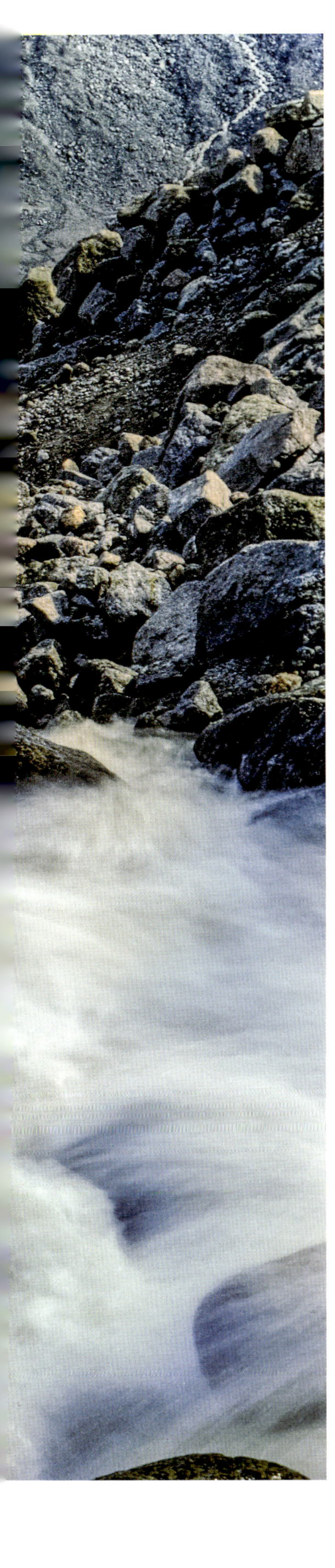

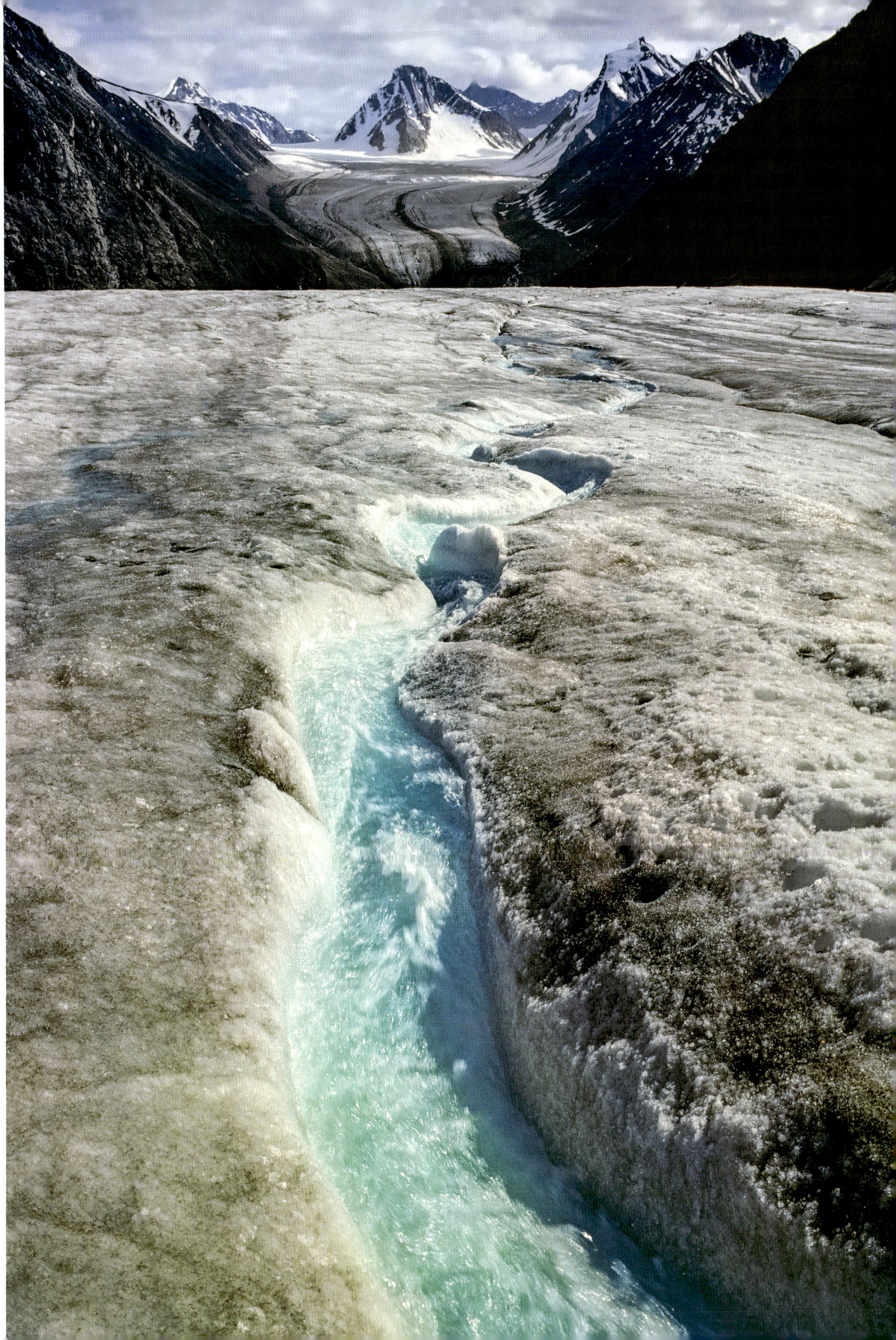

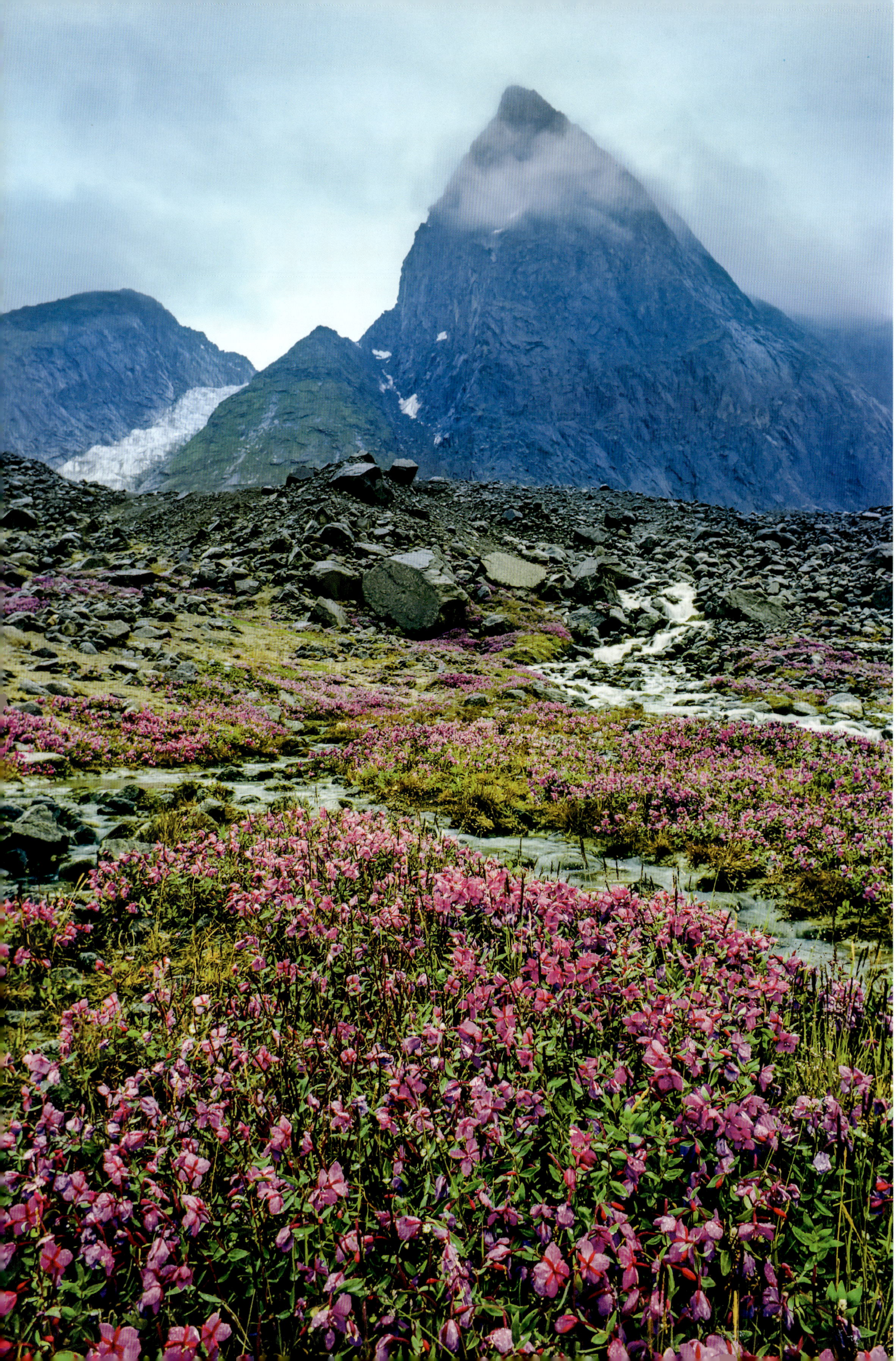

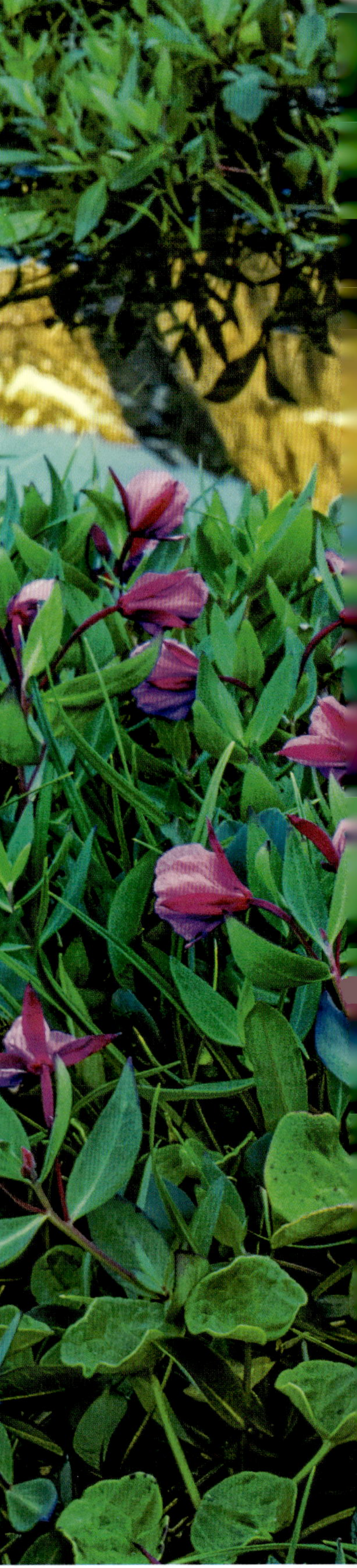

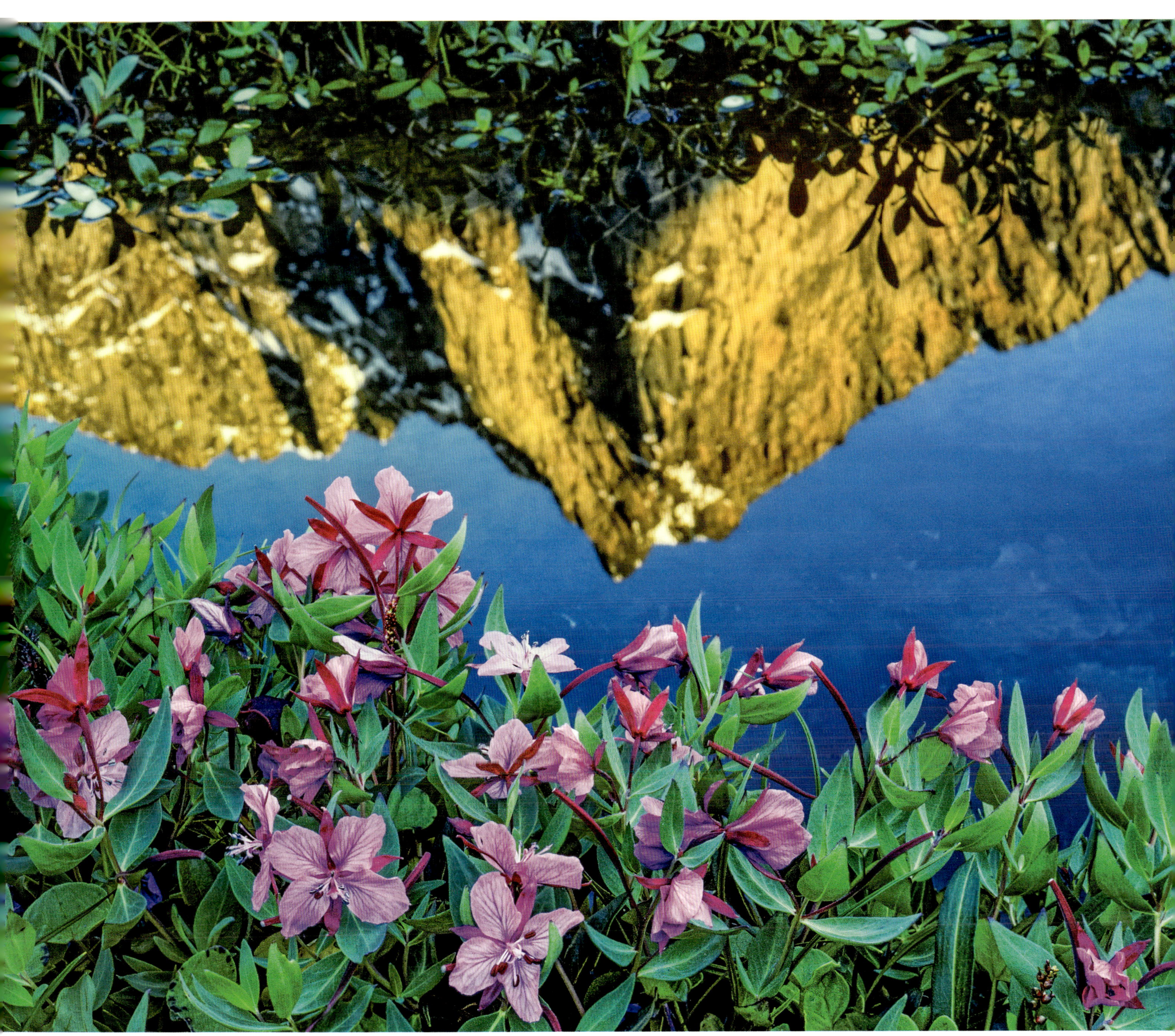

Broad-leaved willow herb in the Weasel River valley
below Sandcastle Peak (left) and reflected Mount Sif in
Auyuittuq National Park on treeless Baffin Island.

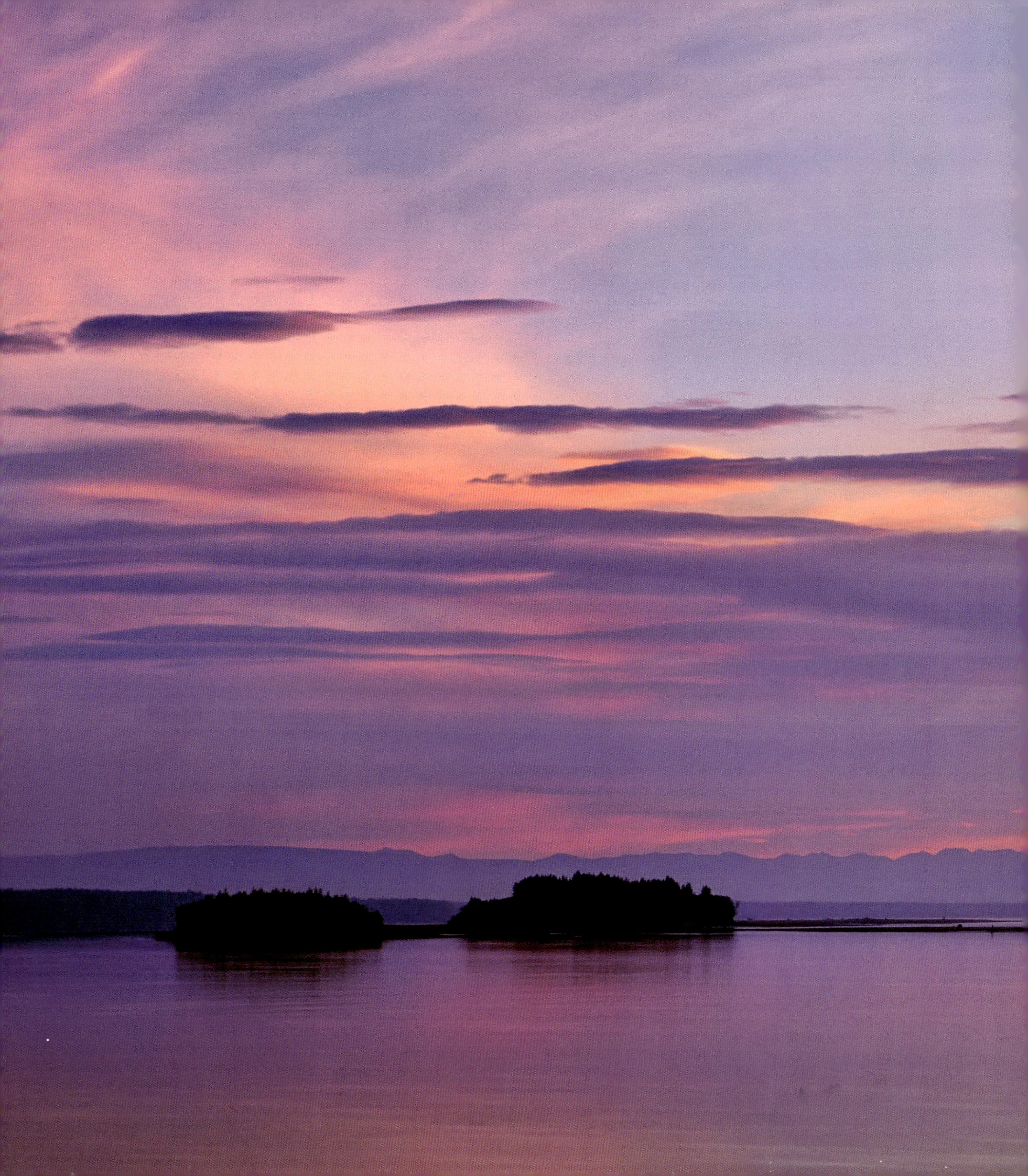

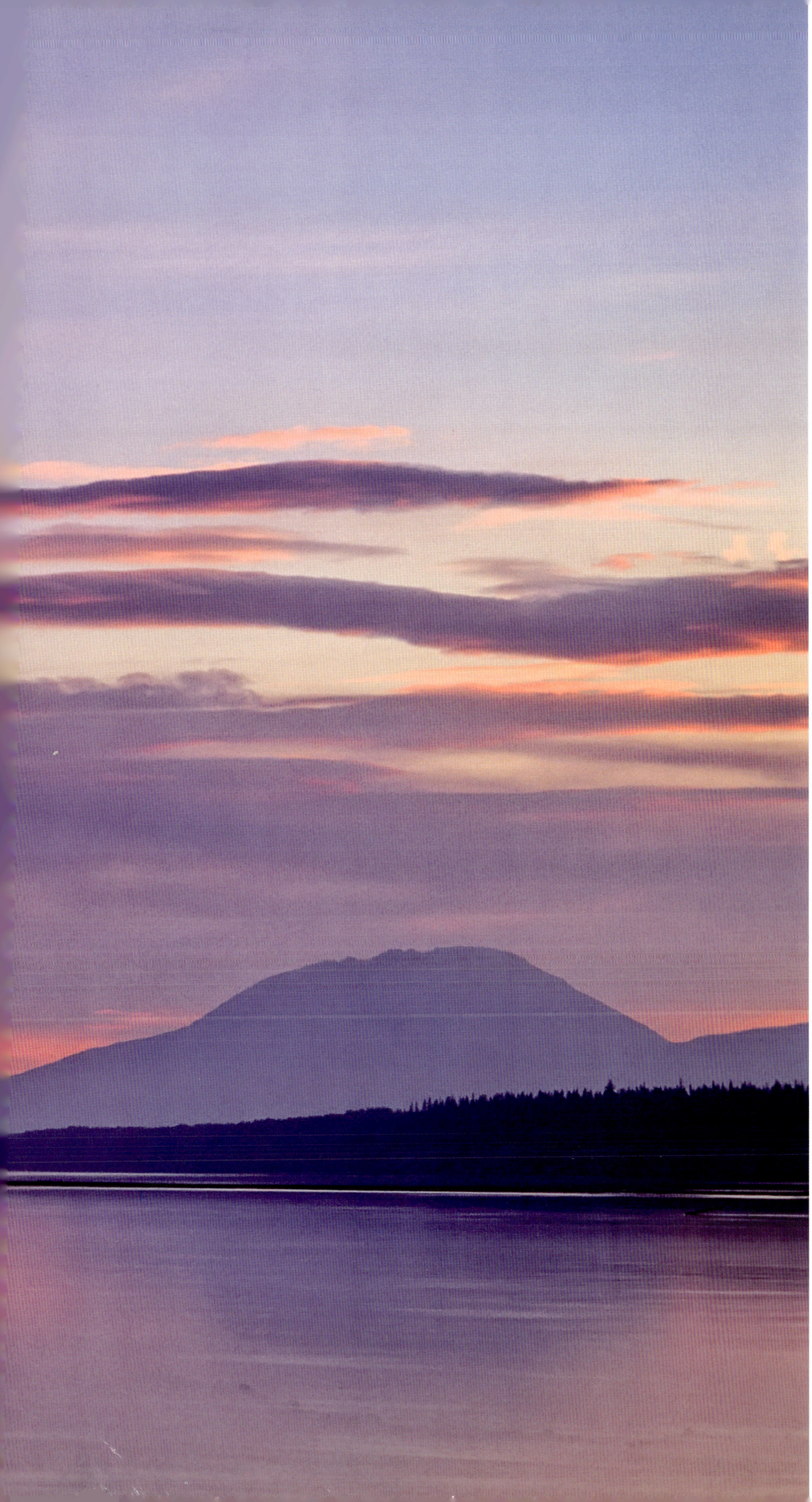

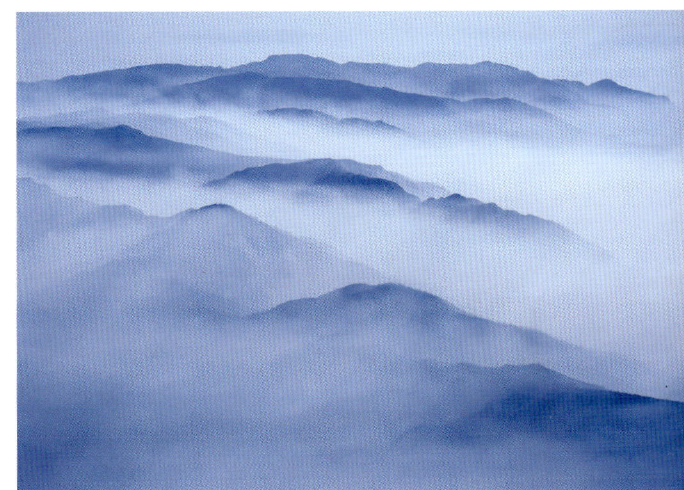

Nahanni Butte at sunset looking upstream from
the Liard River from Blackstone Territorial Park
(left). Smoke from forest fires swathes the Franklin
Mountains south of Great Bear Lake and east of the
Mackenzie River, Northwest Territories.

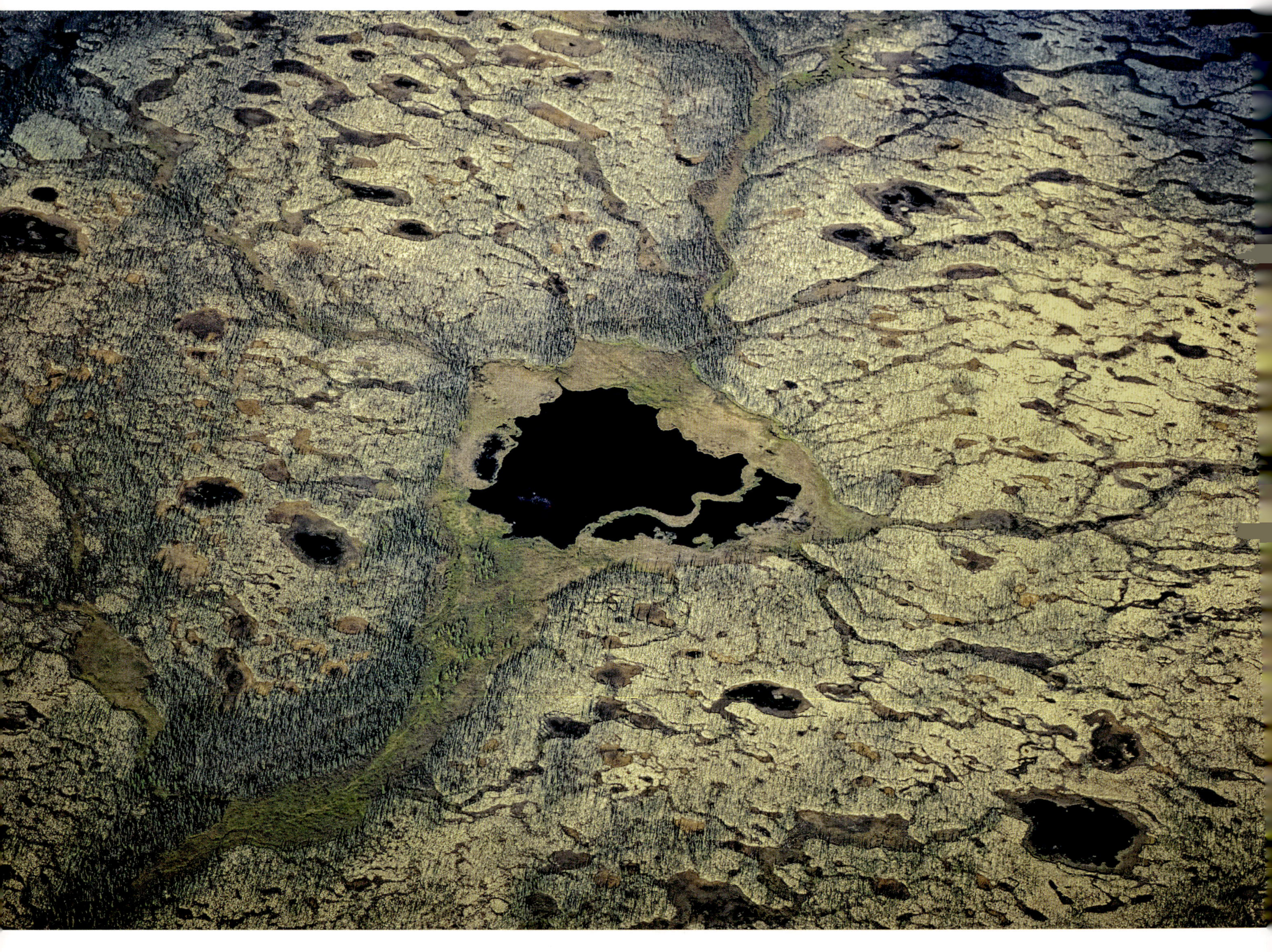

Aerial views of ponds and marsh-filled channels (above) and a sinuous stream channel near the continental tree line in the high subarctic taiga east of Inuvik, Northwest Territories.

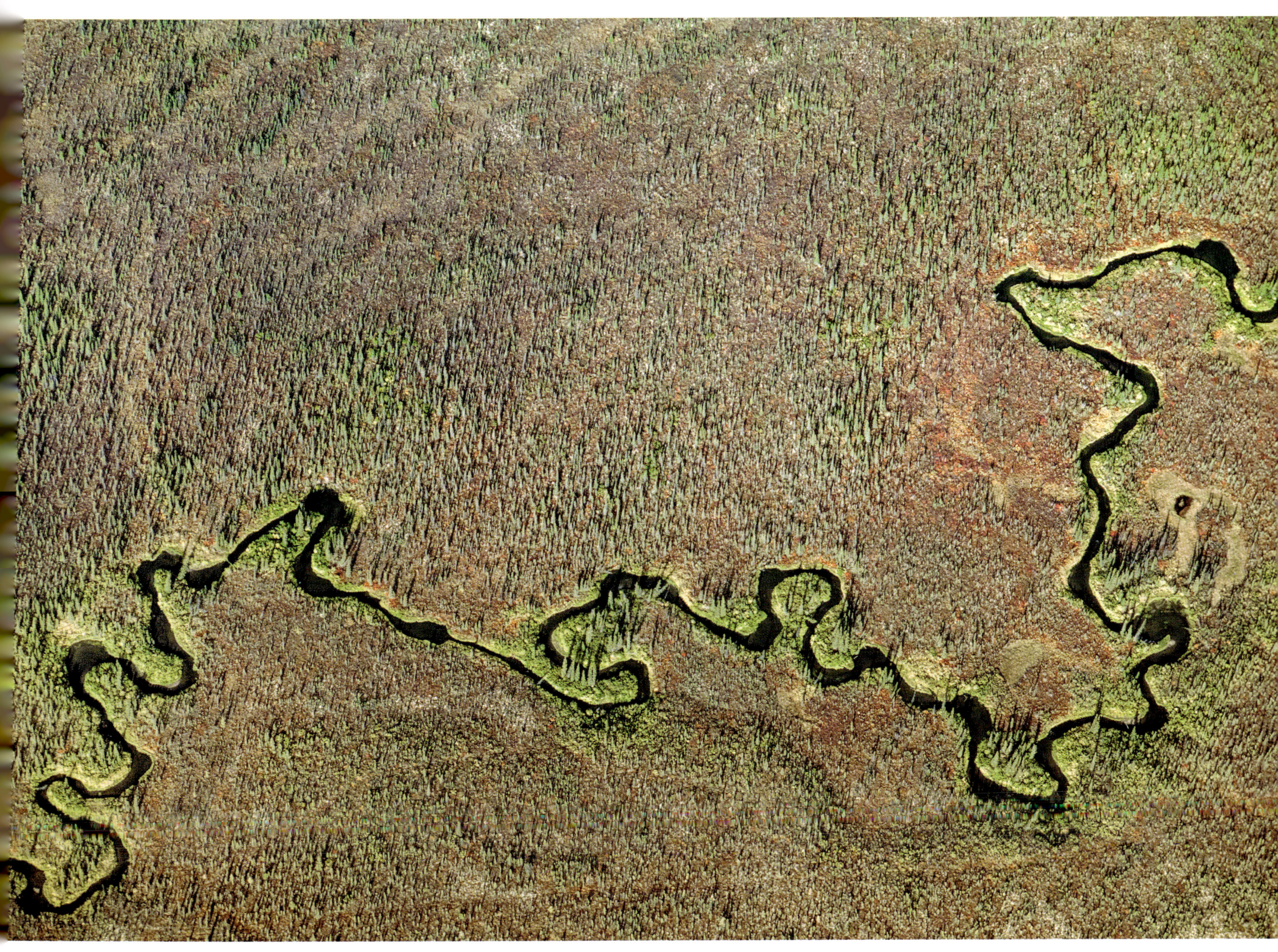

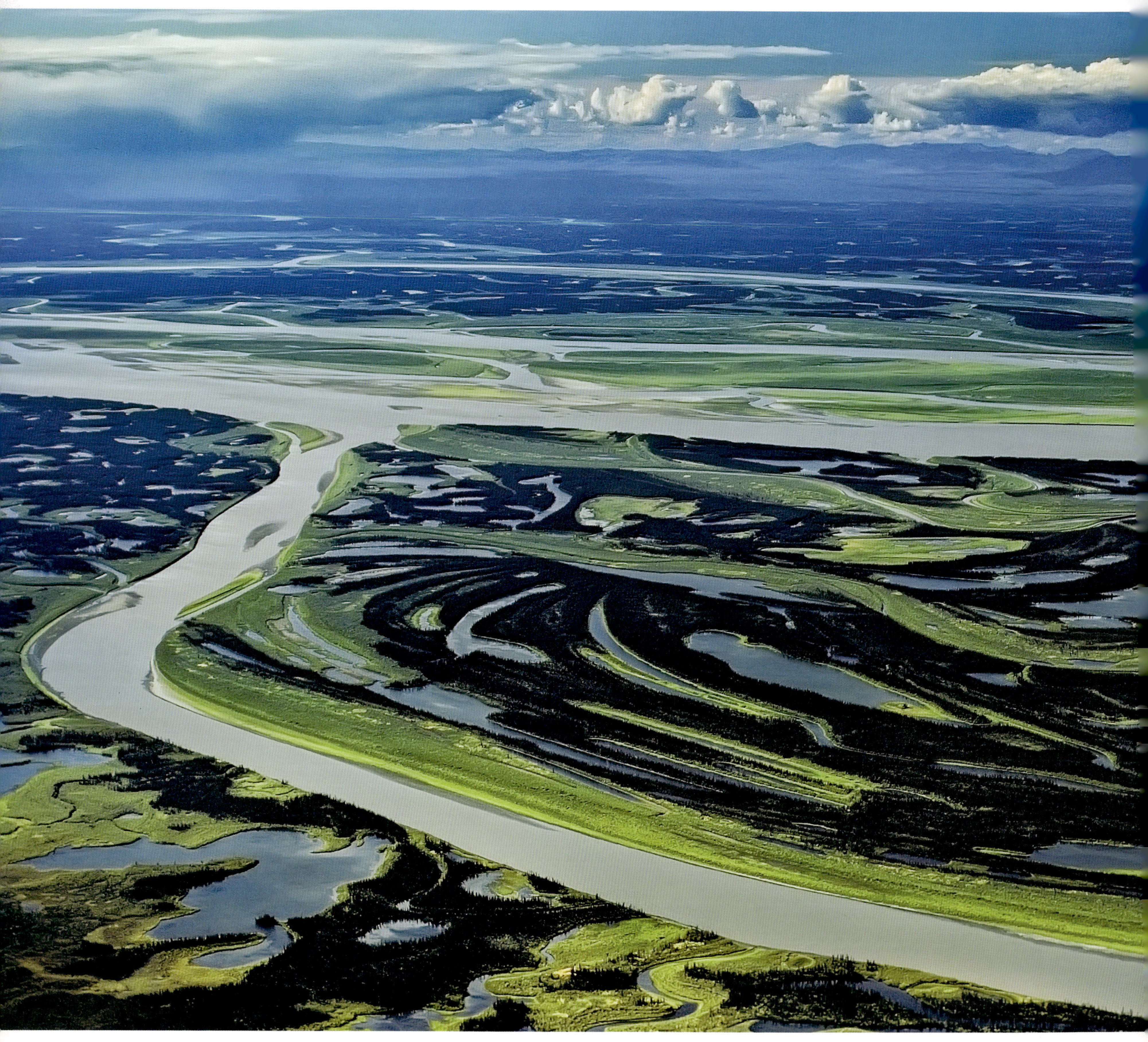

Aerial panoramas of relatively small parts of the great Mackenzie Delta,
Northwest Territories: looking west across the beginning of the delta at
its south end towards the Richardson Mountains on the horizon (above)
and southwest from a point 25 kilometres south of Inuvik.

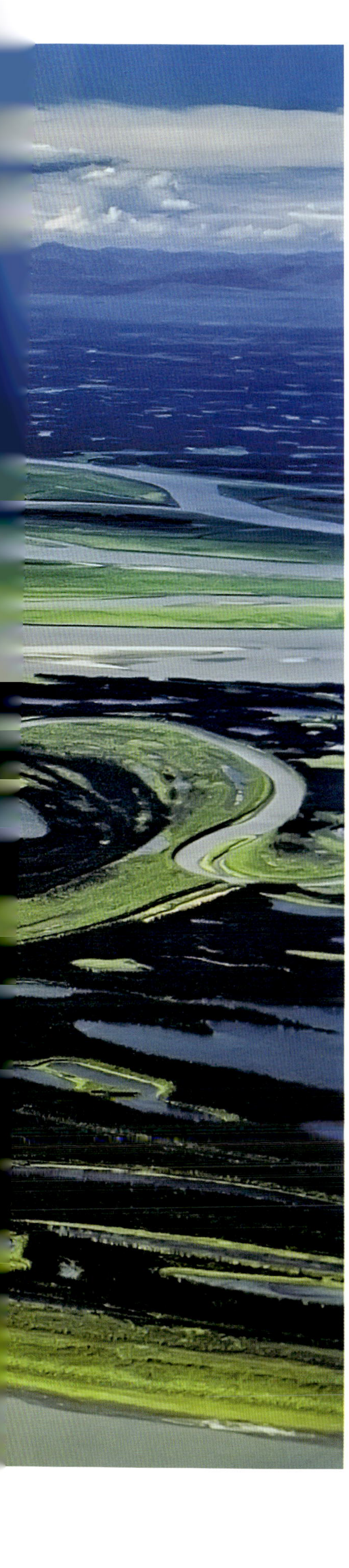

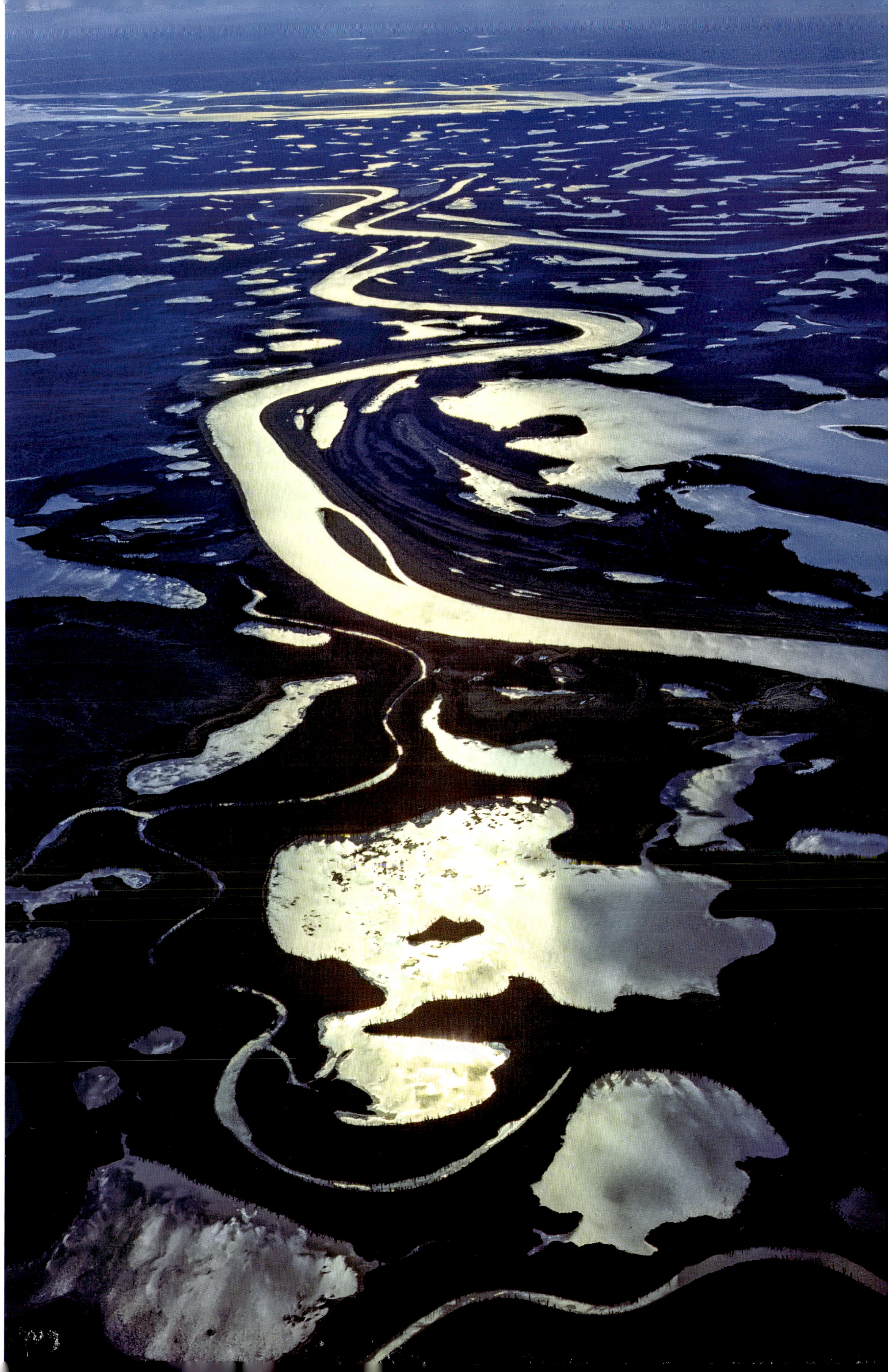

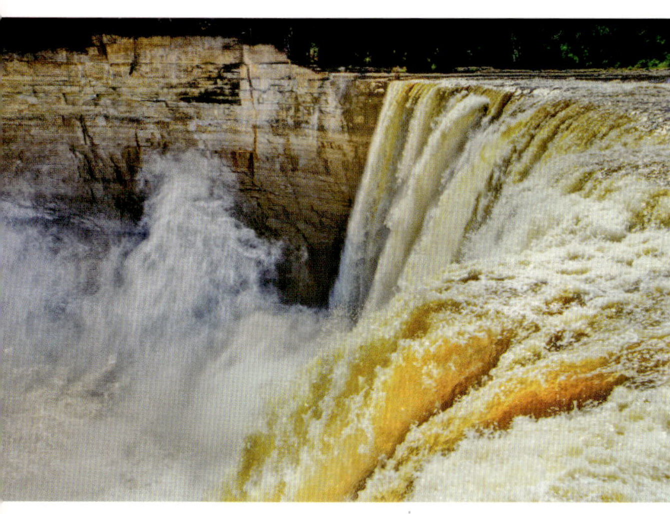

Thirty-metre high Alexandra Falls on the Hay River in Twin Falls Gorge Territorial Park (above) and Coral Falls on the Trout River in Sambaa Deh Falls Territorial Park, Northwest Territories.

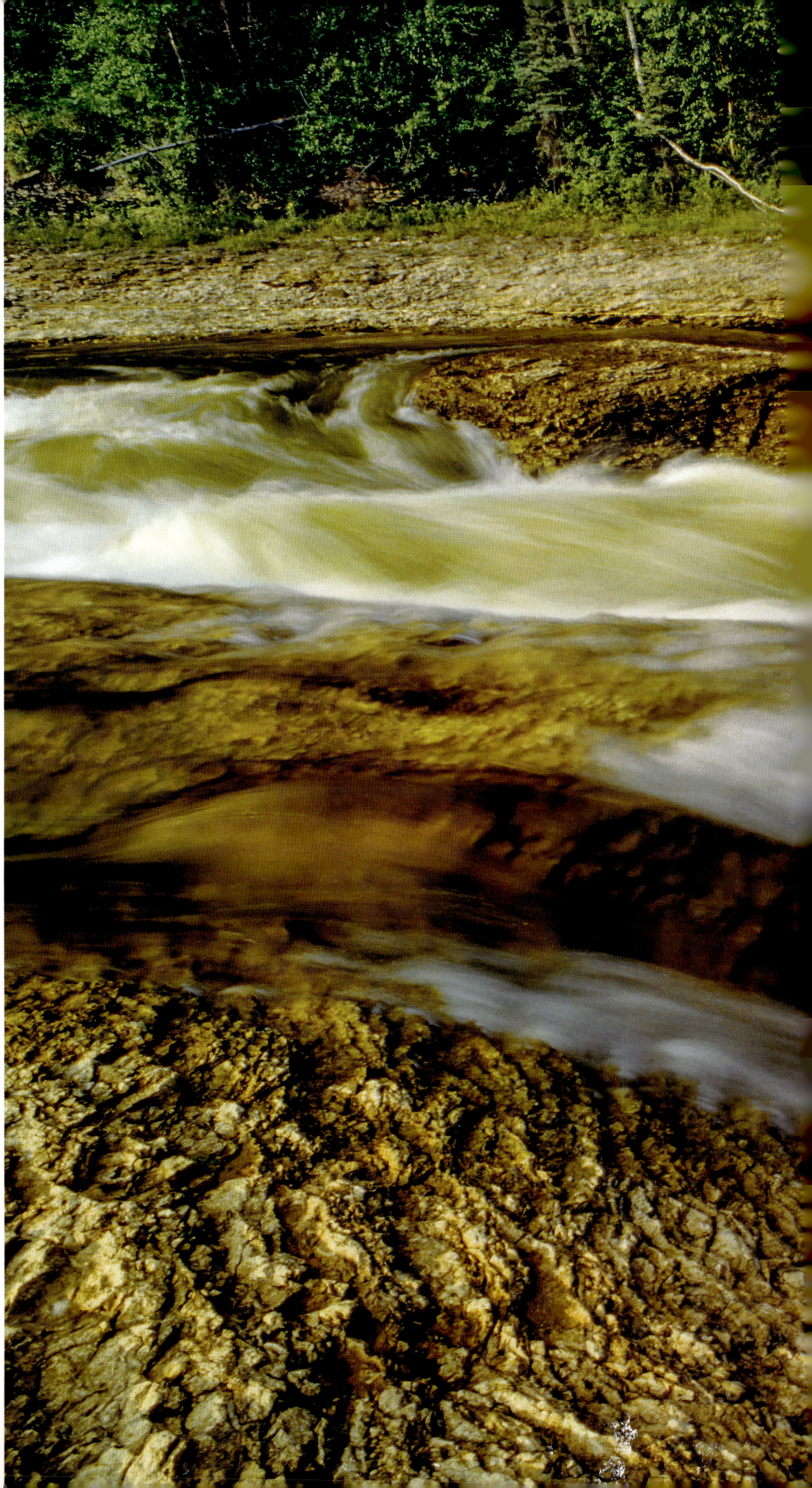

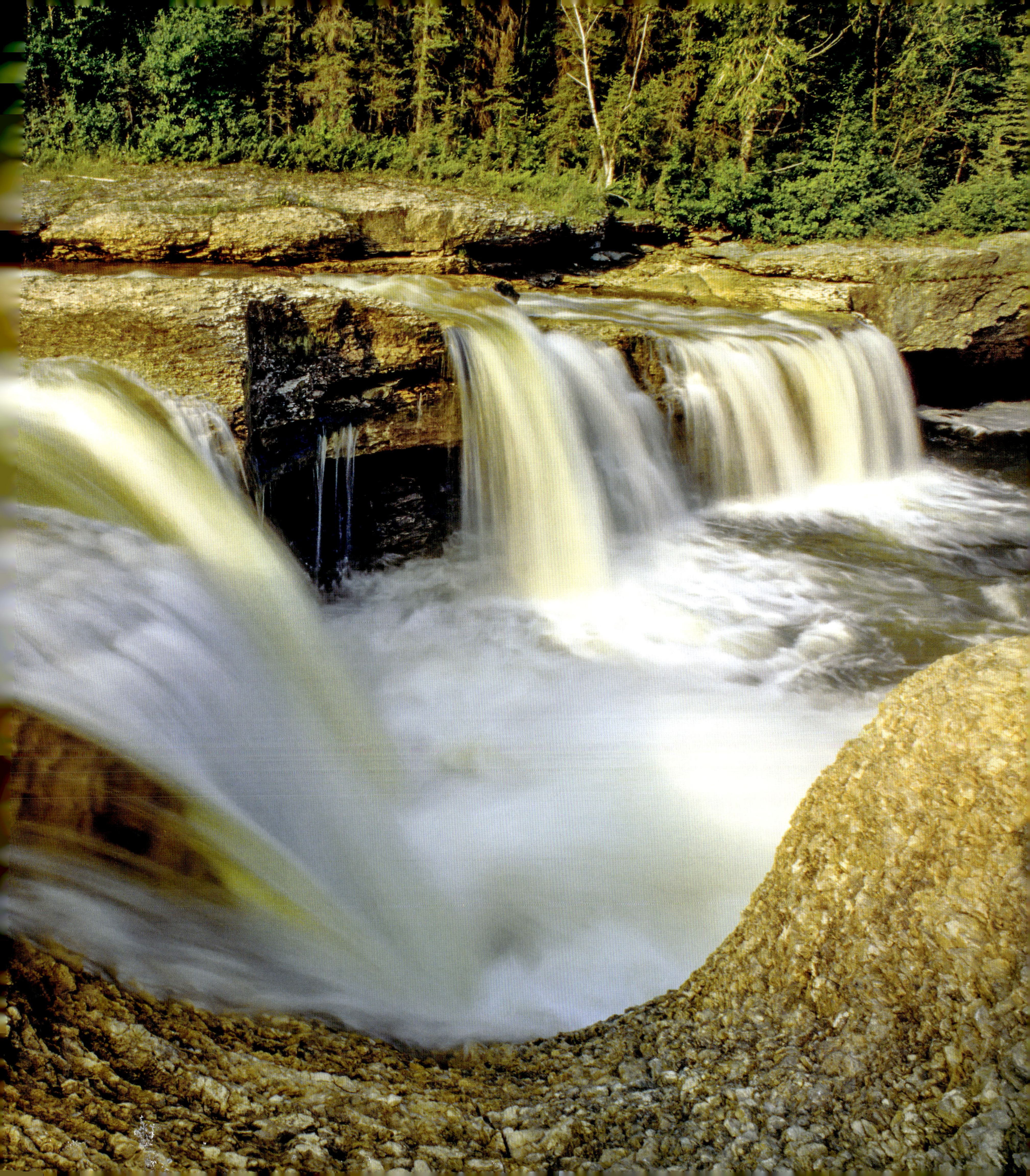

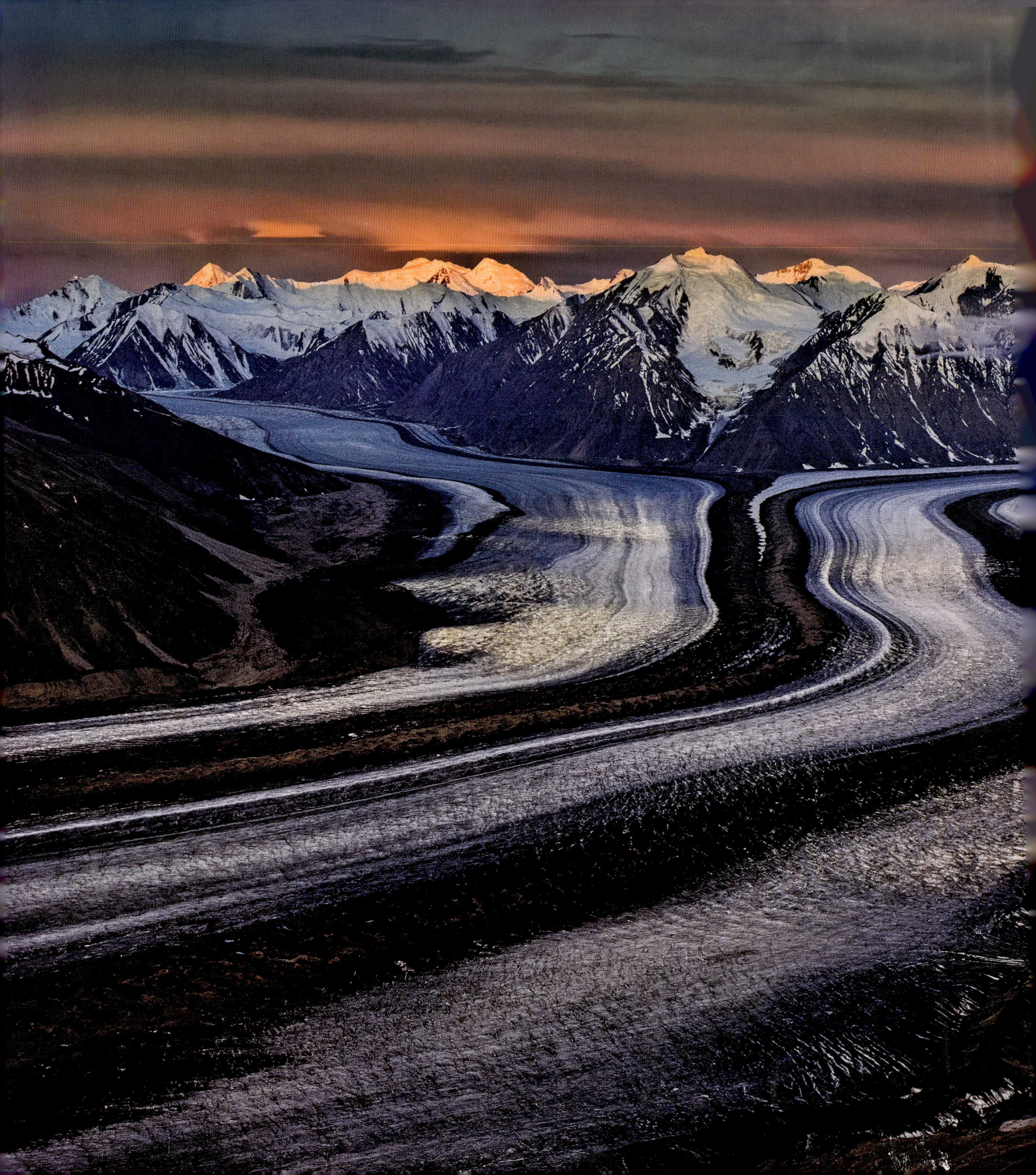

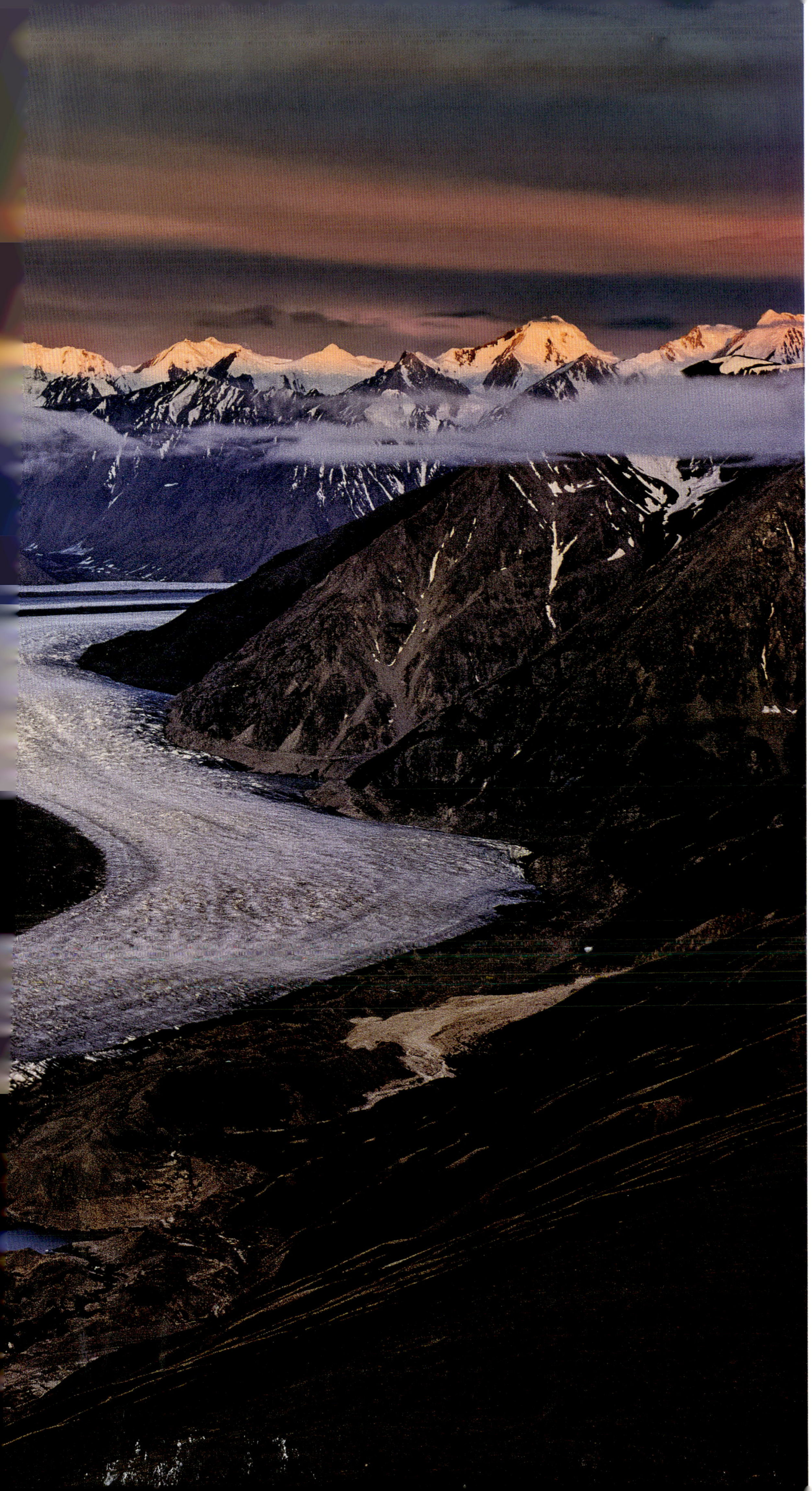

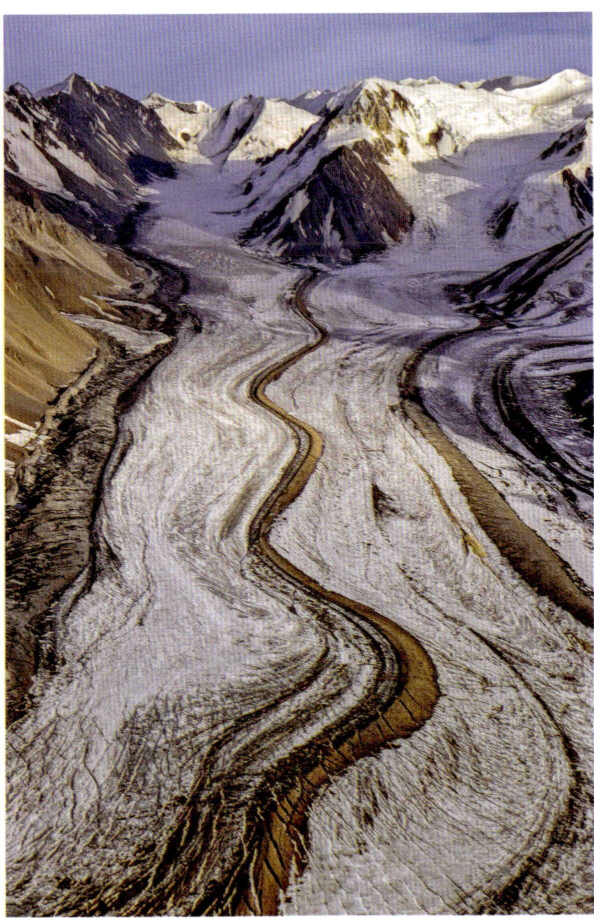

The Kaskawulsh Glacier, more than three kilometres wide after the merging of its north and south branches, viewed from Observation Mountain, Kluane National Park, Yukon. Sunrise lights the summits of the Icefield Ranges spanning the horizon (left). Periodic surges of a tributary glacier of the North Kaskawulsh have caused its central moraine to snake.

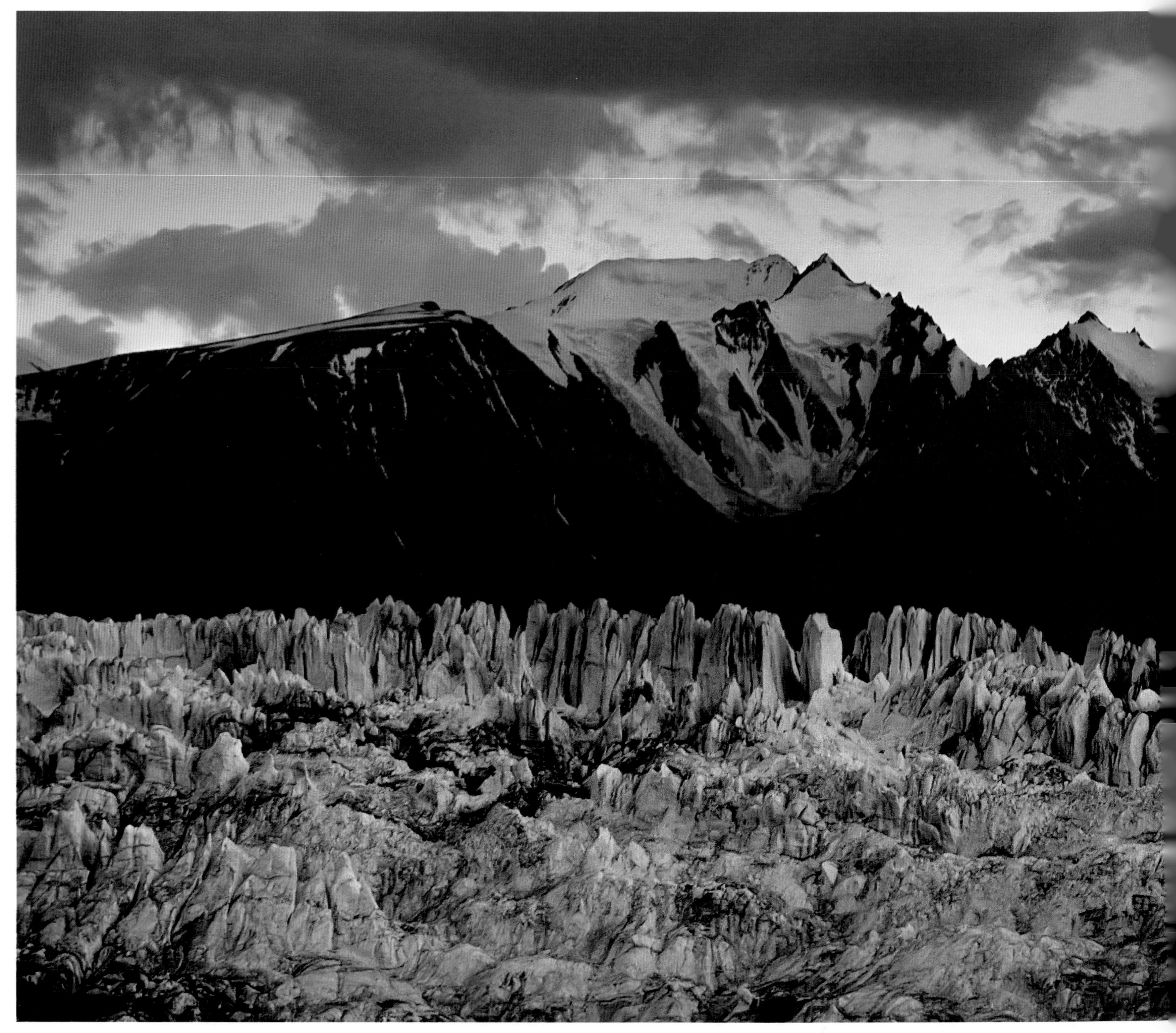

Ranks of seracs, towers of ice dozens of metres tall along the terminus
of the periodically surging Donjek Glacier (above) and a pool of
meltwater, intense blue in its basin of ice in the Icefield Ranges, both in
the Saint Elias Mountains, Kluane National Park, Yukon.

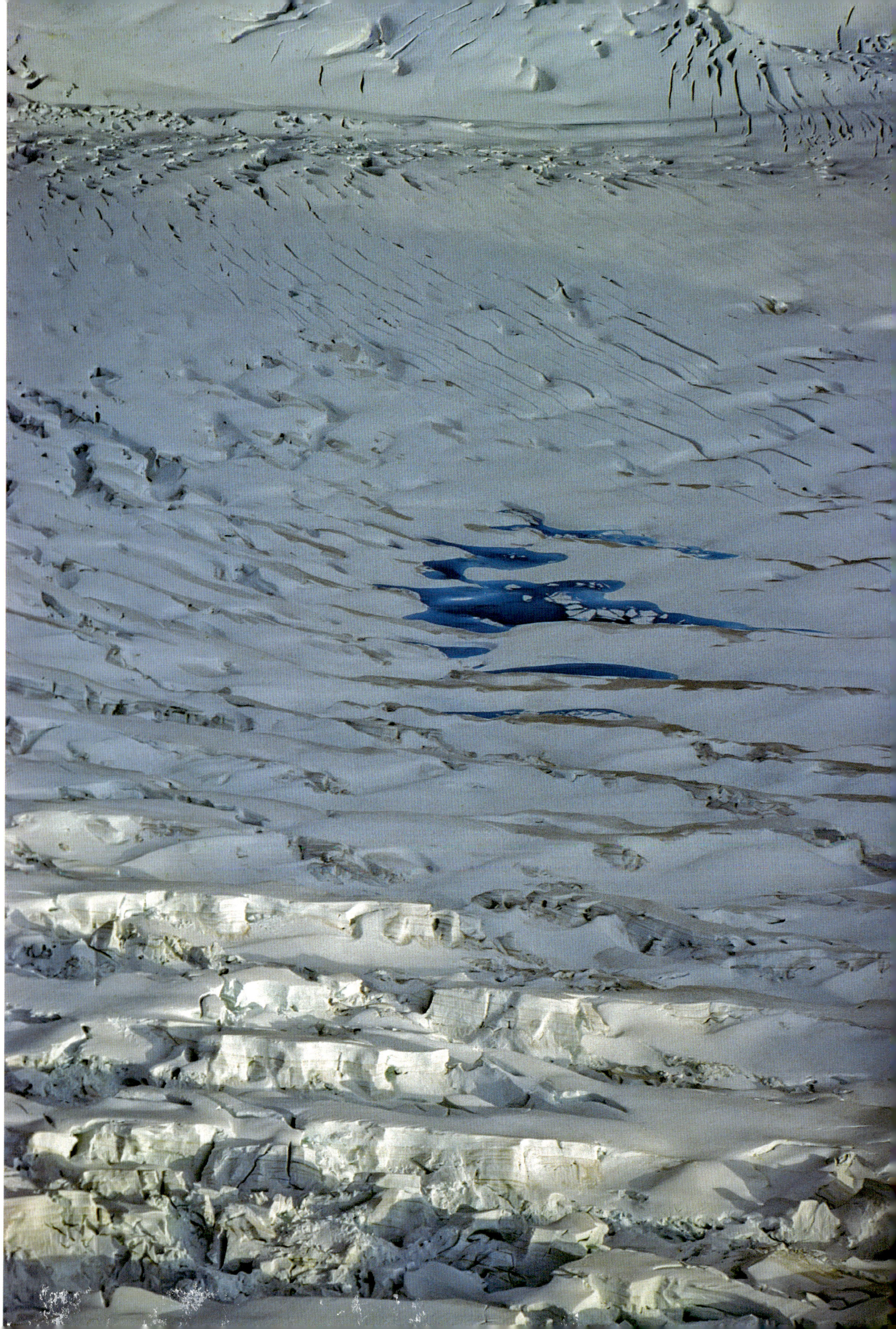

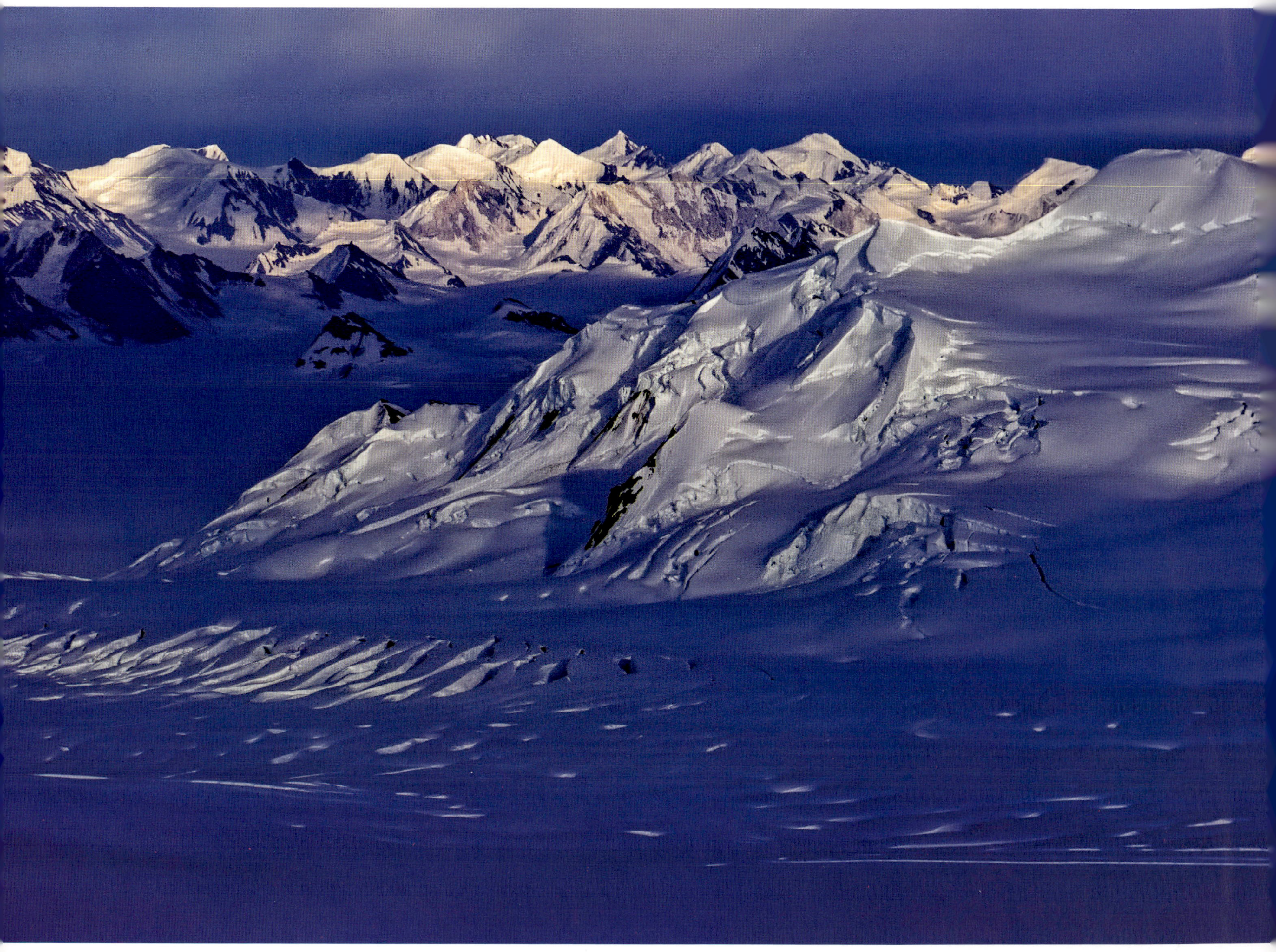

The Icefield Ranges of the Saint Elias Mountains in
Kluane National Park, Yukon, constitute one of the most
spectacular landscapes on the planet. Though not as high
or as extensive as the Himalayas or the Andes, nowhere
else do summits reach the same altitude surrounded by
ice fields as vast and glaciers as large.

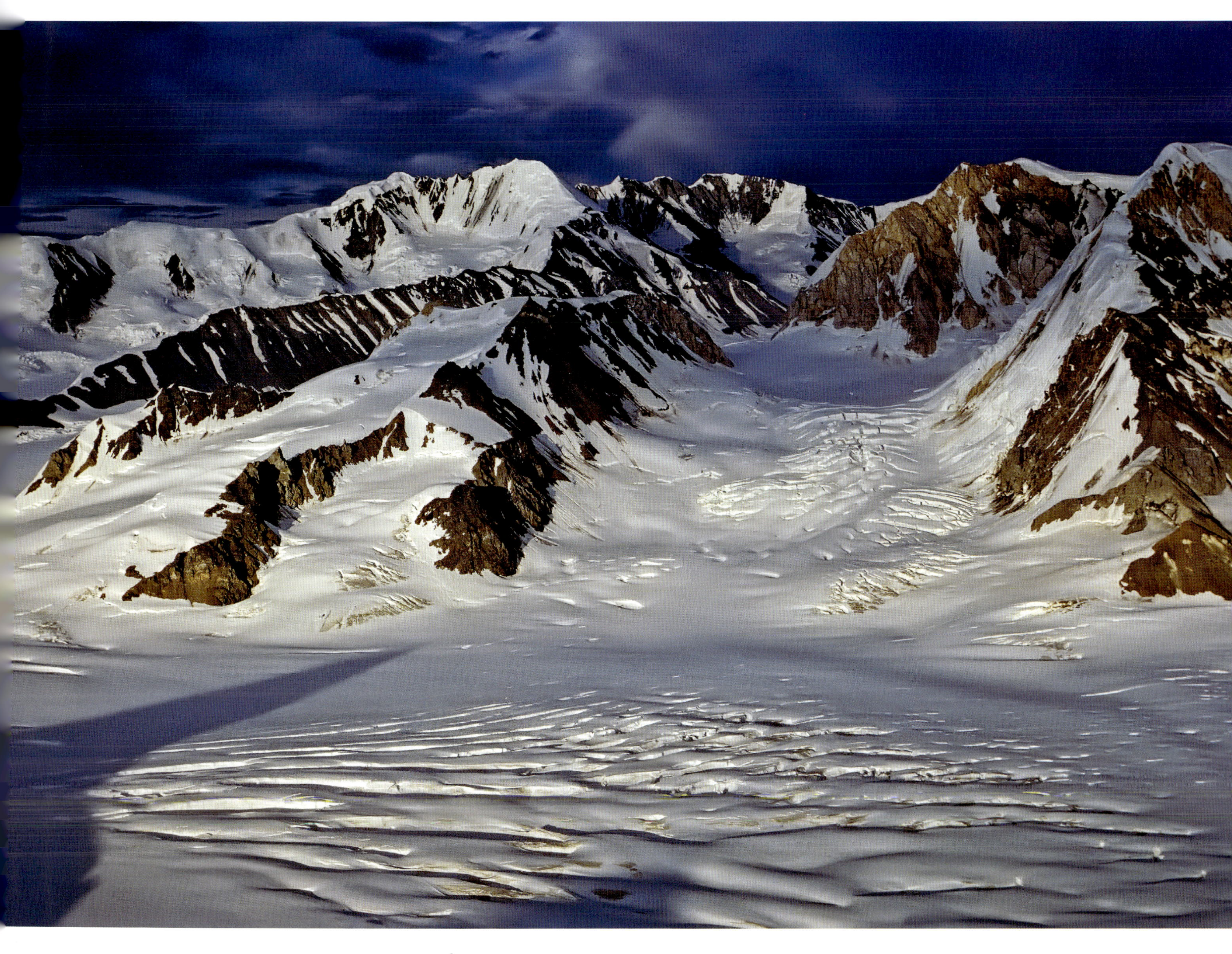

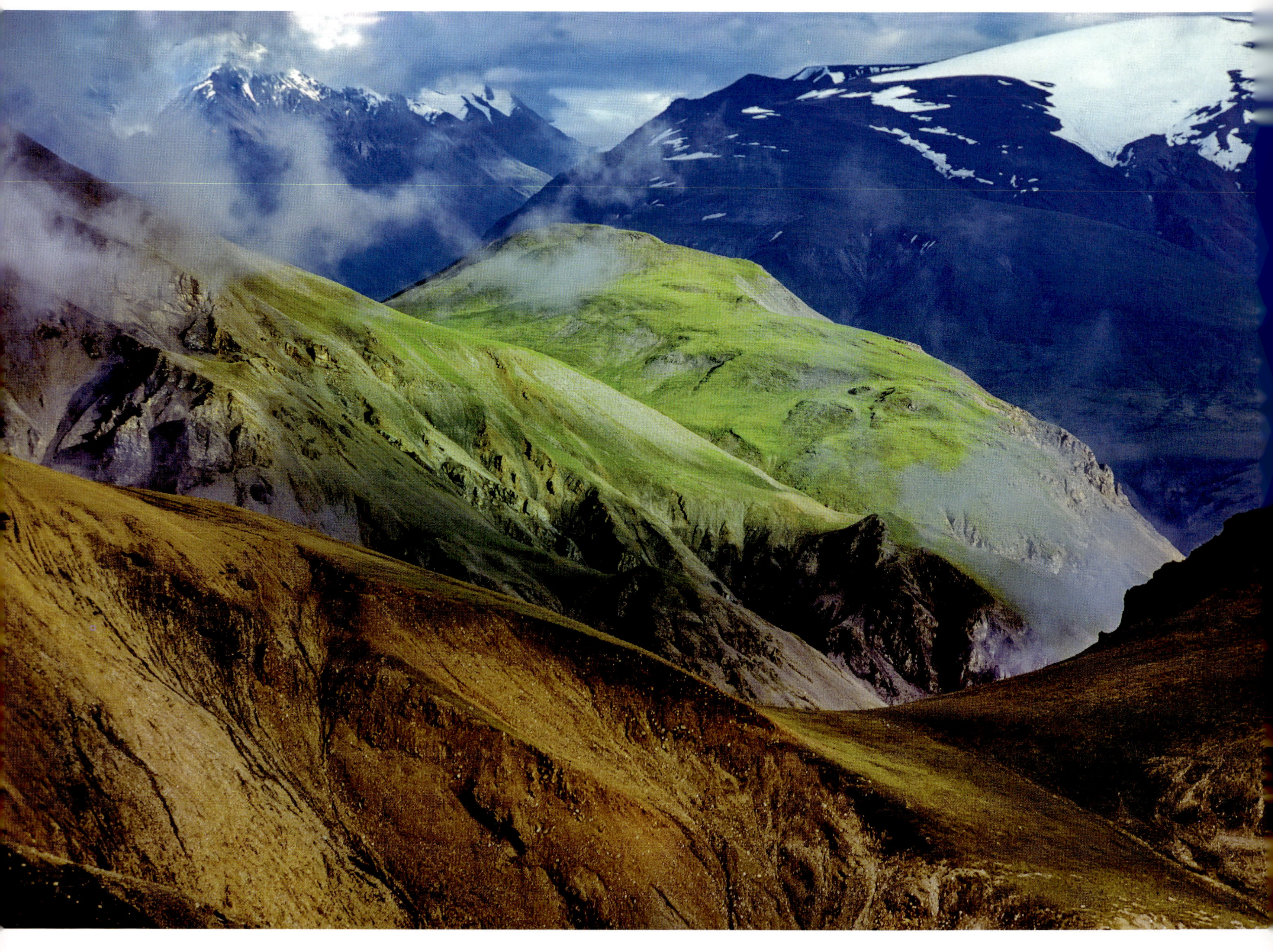

Looking south from high up on Mount Hoge in the
Donjek Range, Kluane National Park.

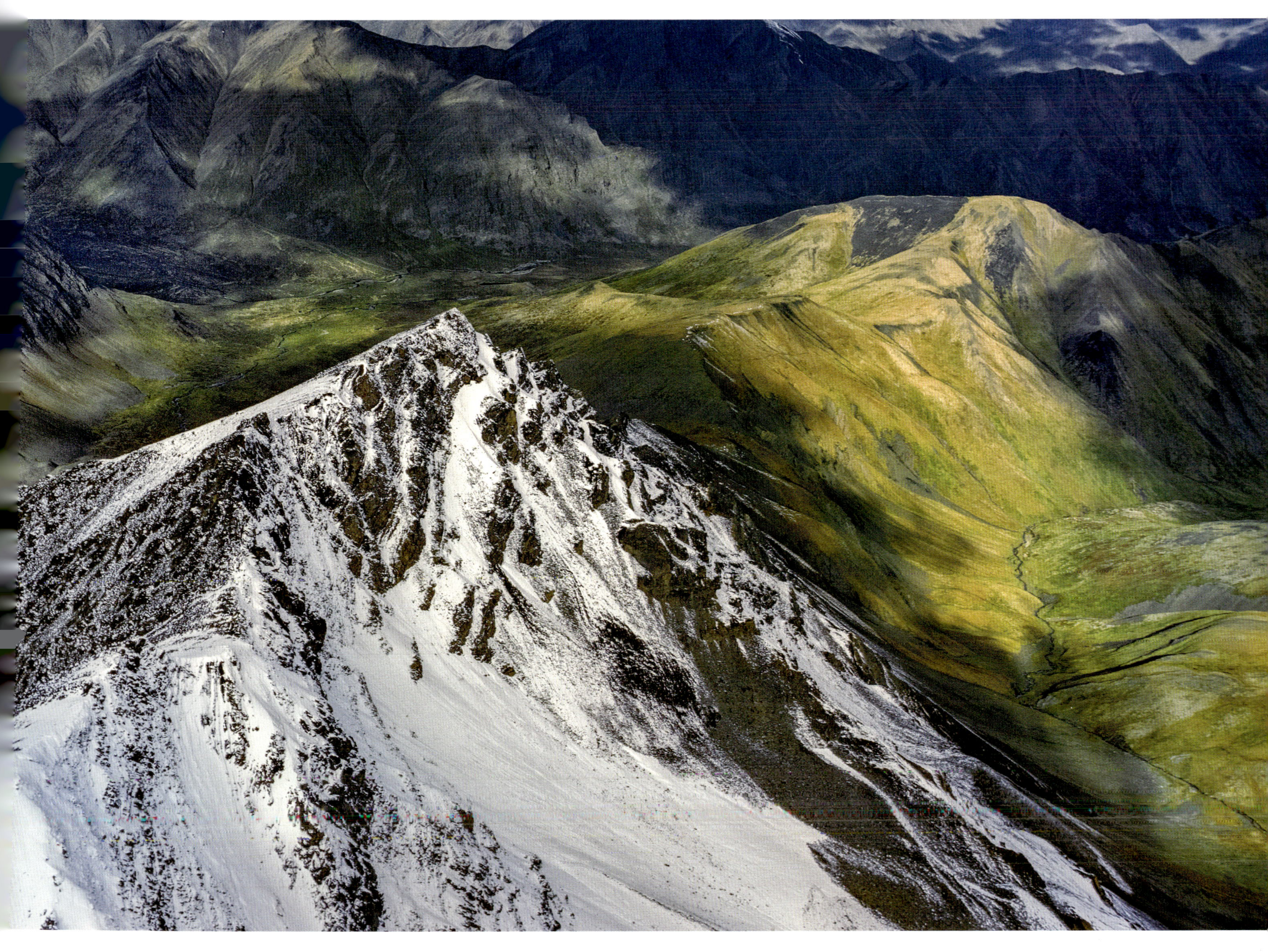

A peak higher than those that surround it shows the
difference altitude makes in capturing an August snowfall
in the Cloudy Range, Ogilvie Mountains, Yukon.

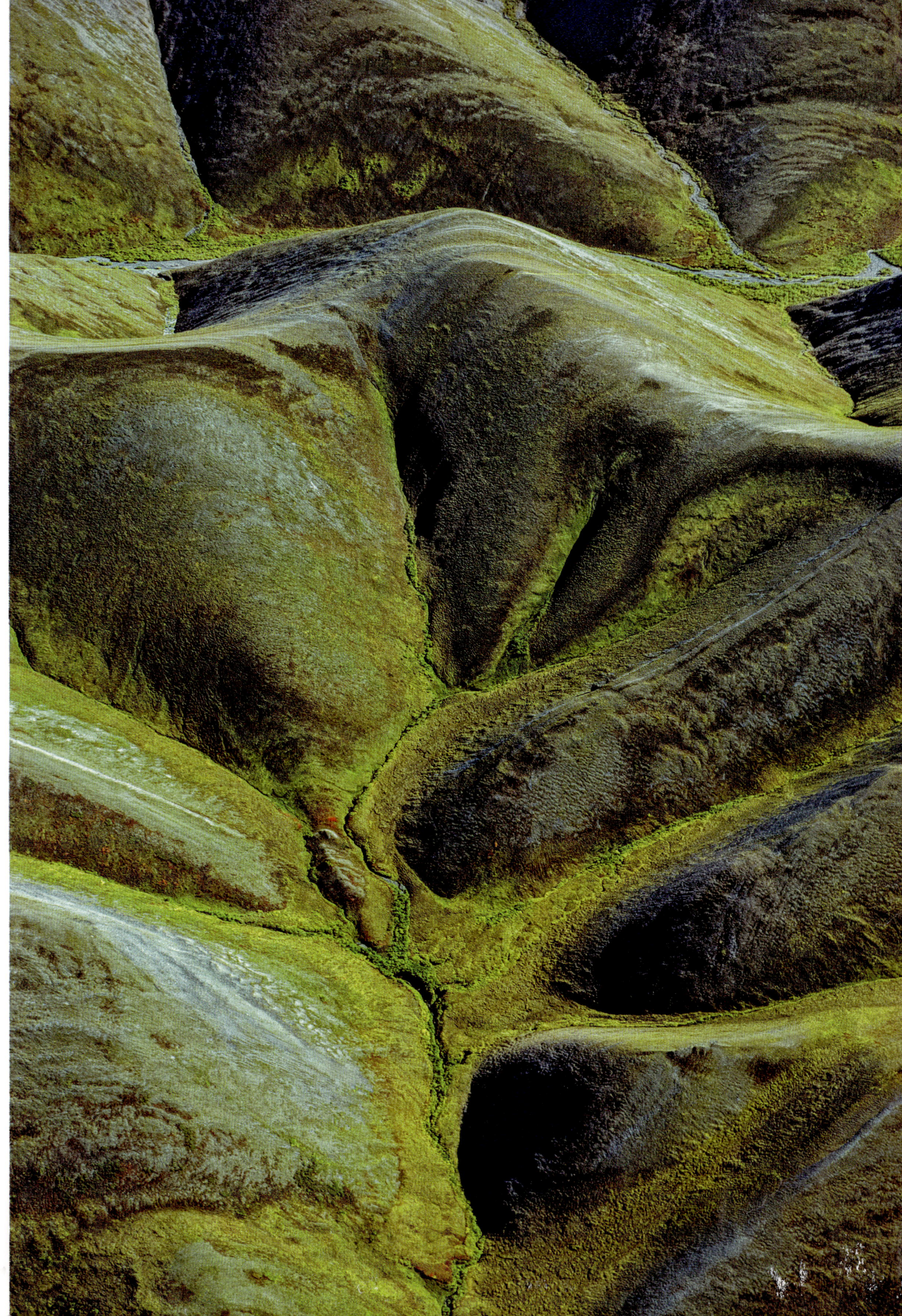

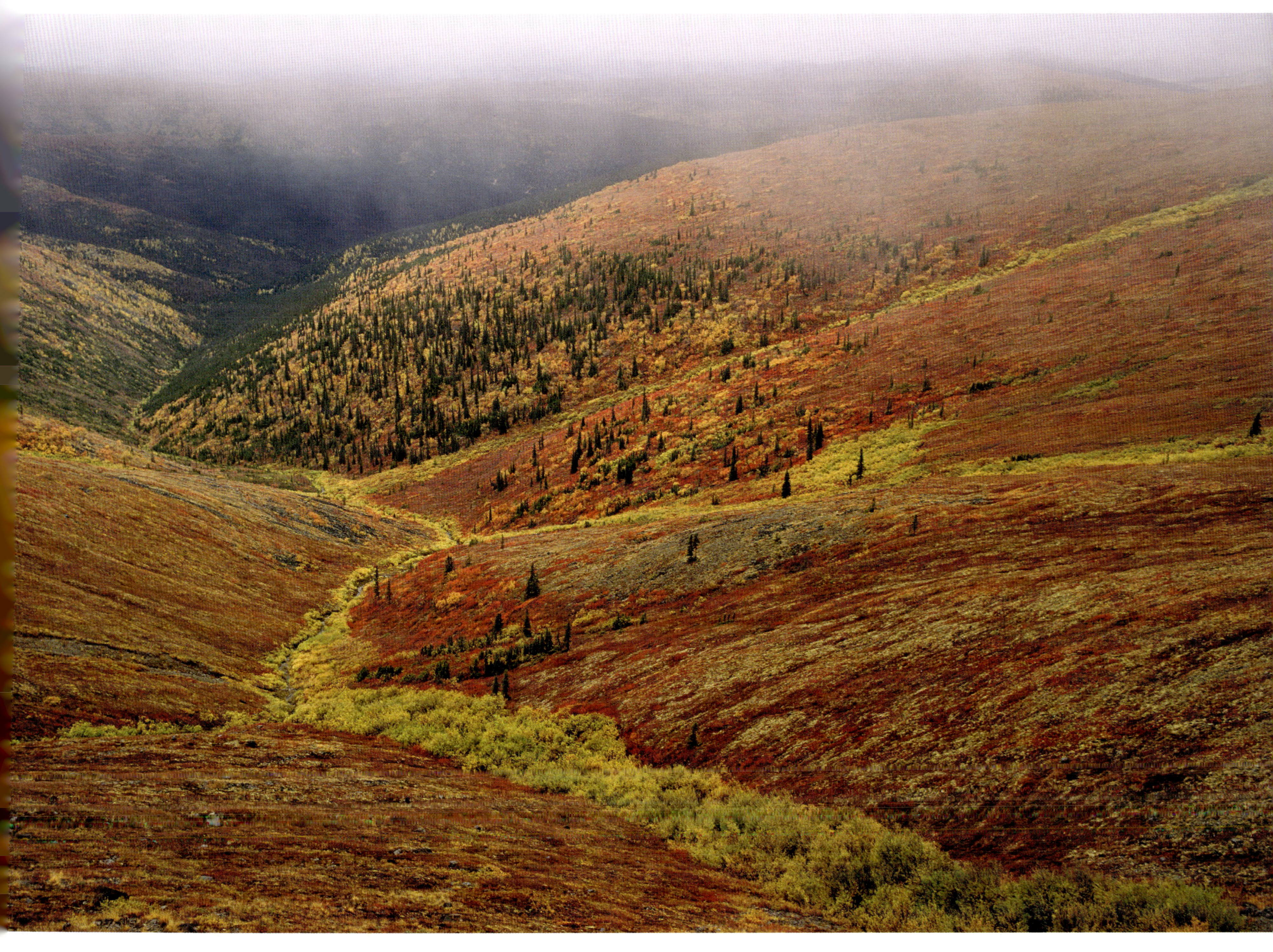

Northern Yukon is the only extensive region in Canada that
was not entombed during the last Ice Age because the climate
was too dry to allow the continuous accumulation of snow. An
aerial of the west slopes of the Richardson Mountains (left) and
a cloud-level view from the Top of the World Highway on the
Klondike Plateau show fluvial landscapes, the result of stream
erosion rather than glaciation.

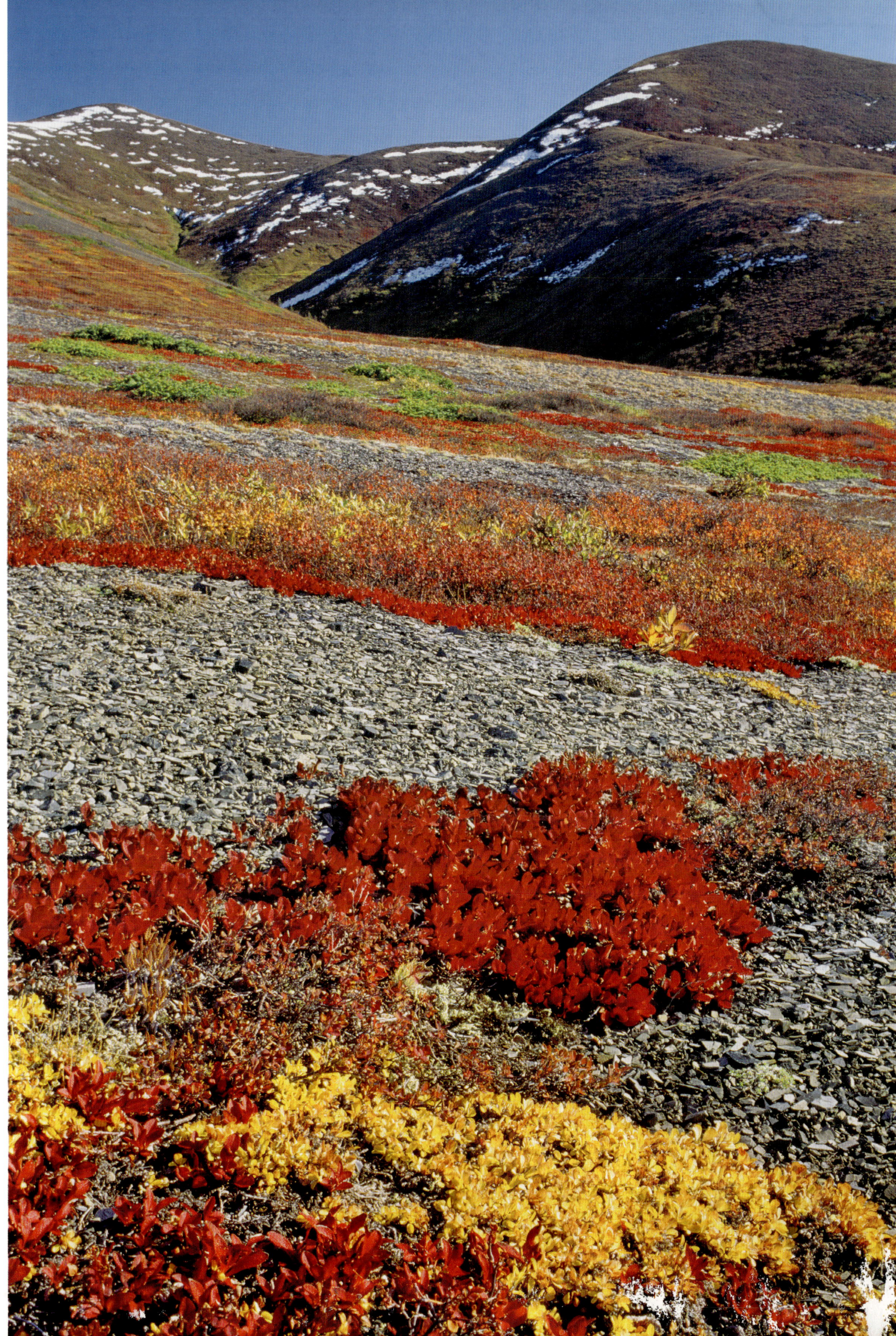

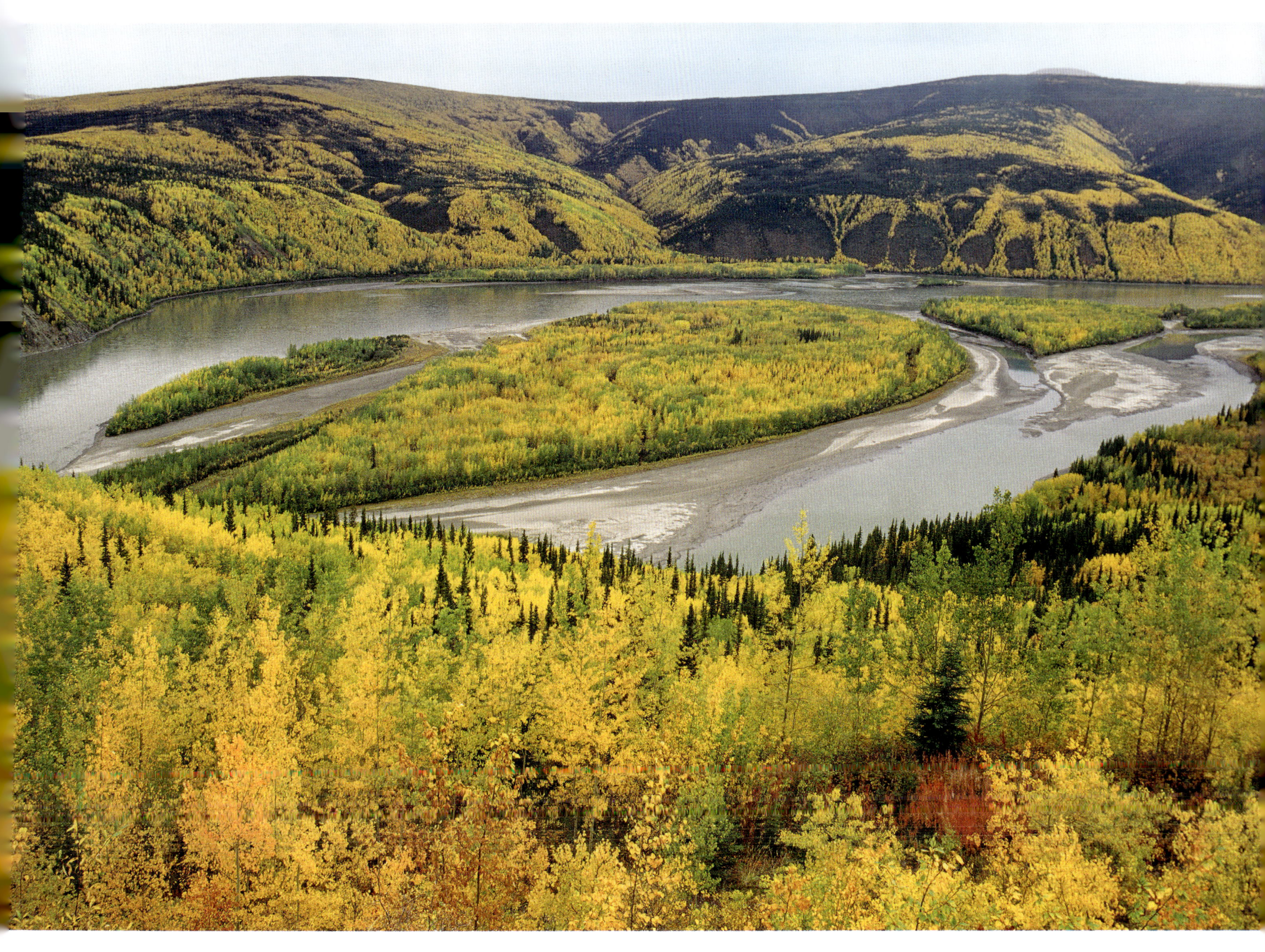

Late August brings autumn colour to the ground
cover of bearberry and willow in the Richardson
Mountains (left) while aspen turns gold across vast
tracts in Yukon, here on slopes and islands along
the Yukon River near Dawson City.

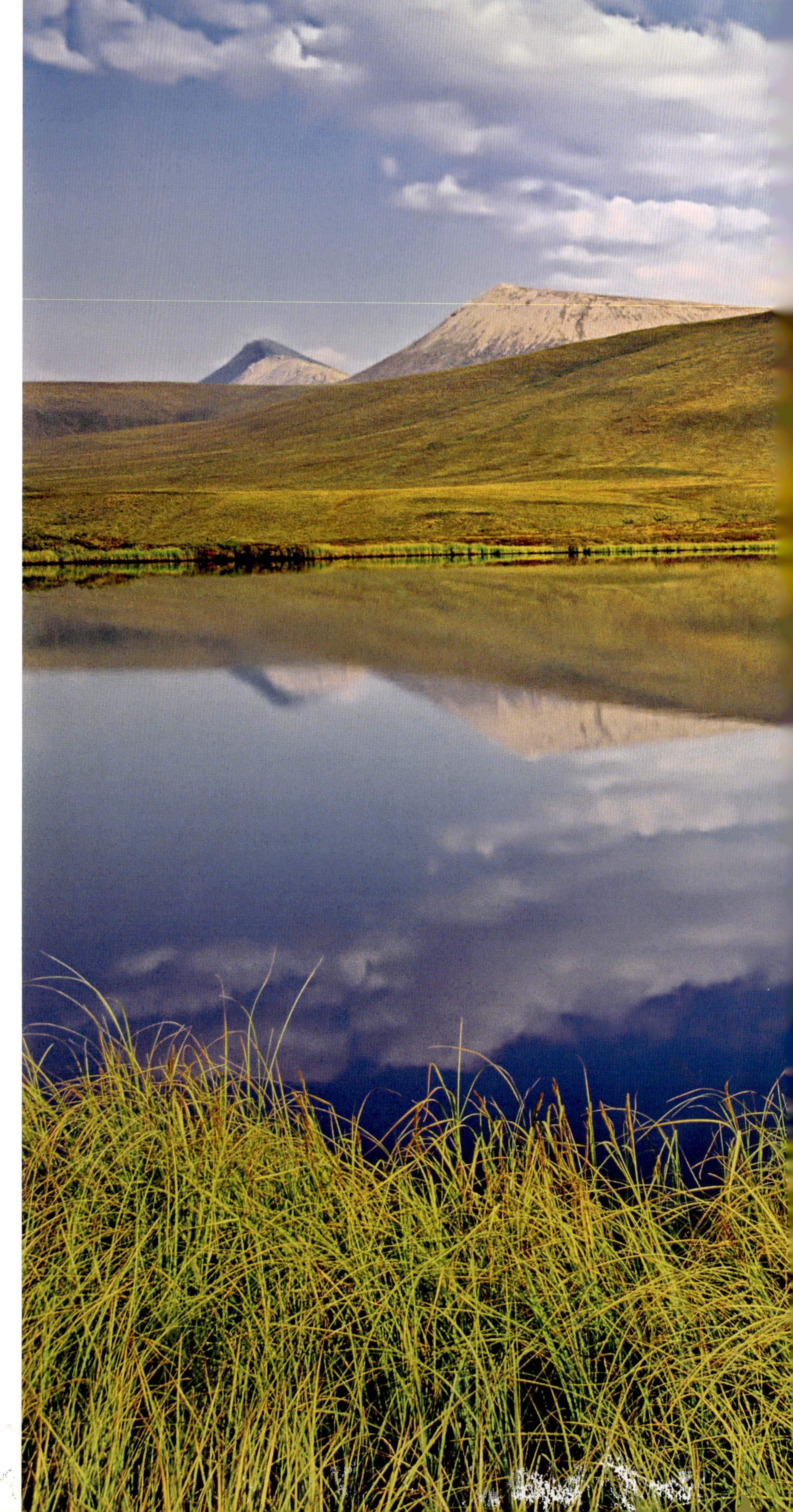

Ogilvie Mountains reflected in a pond beside the Dempster Highway in the treeless Blackstone Uplands, Yukon.

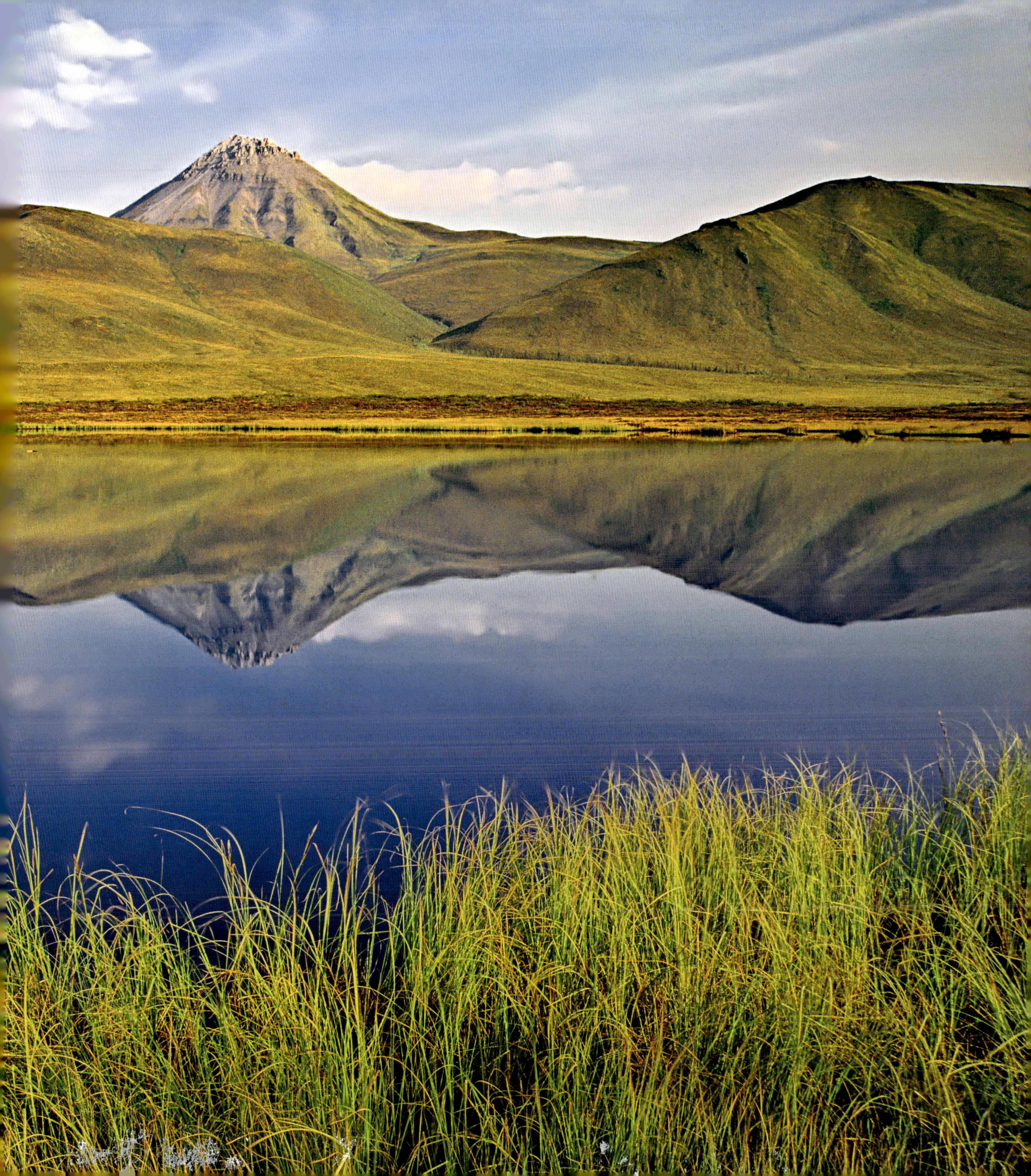

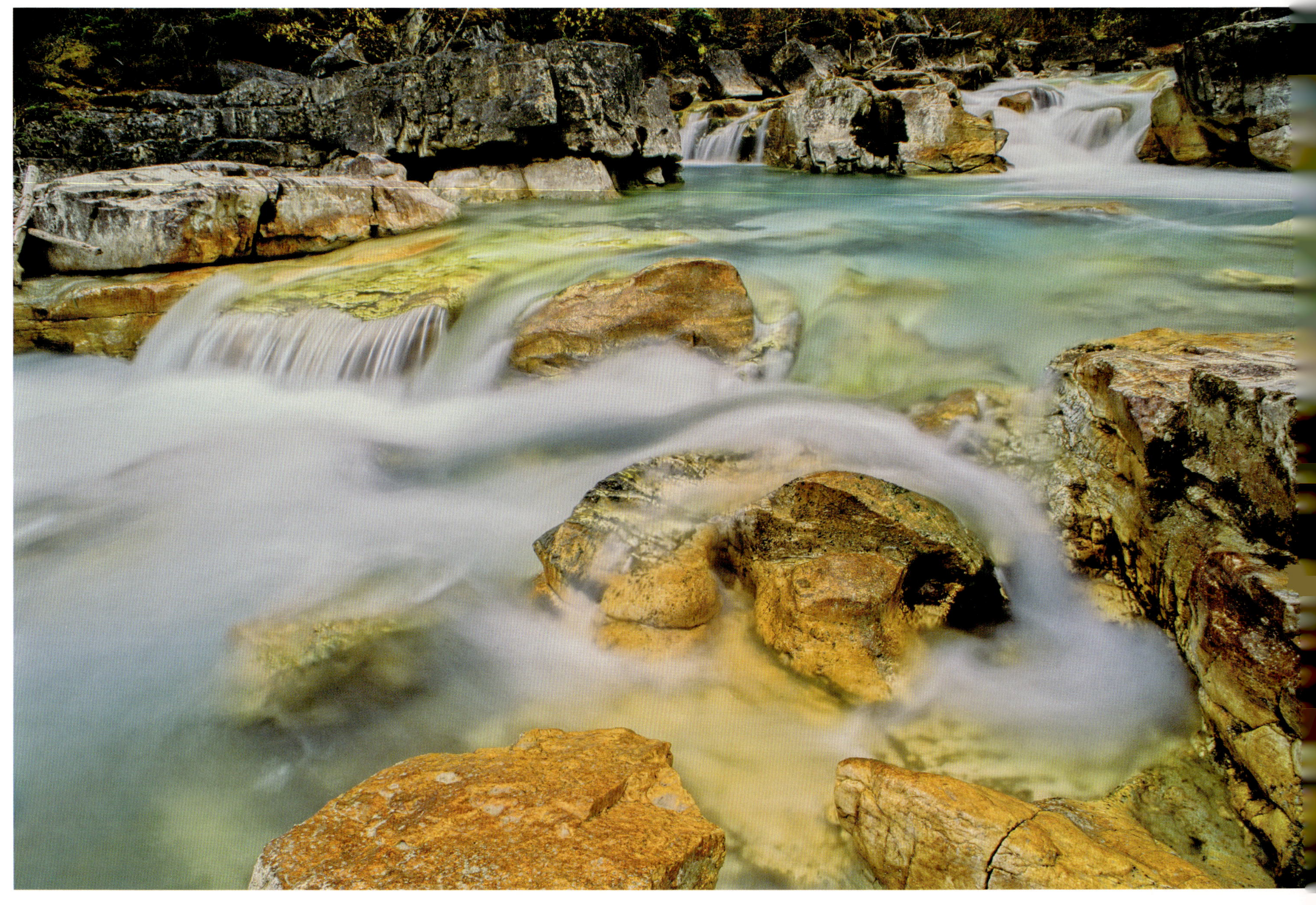

Tokumm Creek just before it drops into the deep
and narrow gorge of Marble Canyon, Kootenay
National Park, British Columbia.

# Index

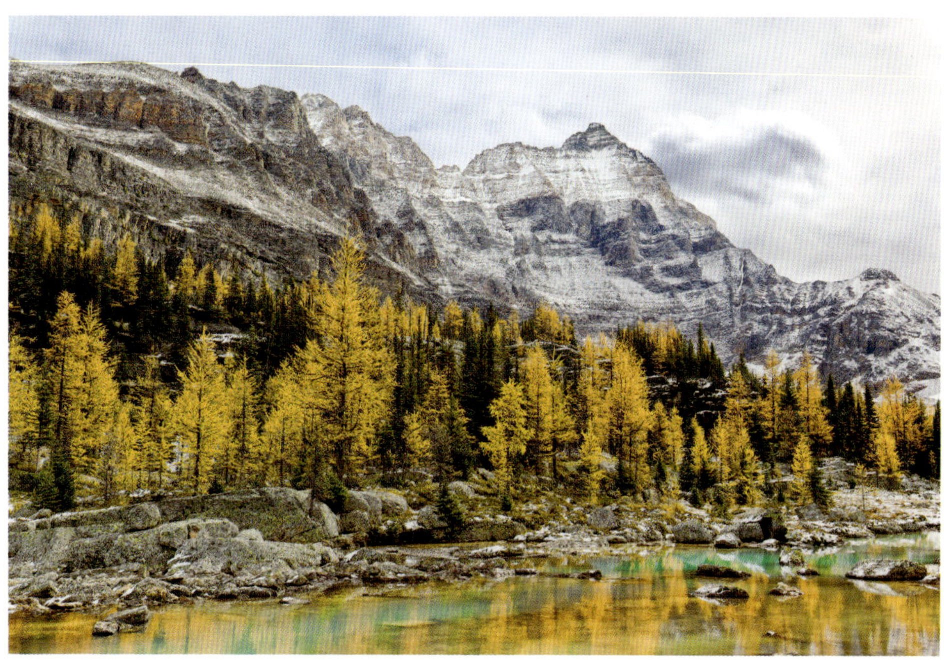

Alpine larch trees in autumn and Mounts Yukness, Ringrose and
Hungabee from Opabin Plateau, Yoho National Park, British Columbia.